S0-BZI-513

Space, Time, and Crime

Space, Time, and Crime

Third Edition

Kim Michelle Lersch

UNIVERSITY OF SOUTH FLORIDA POLYTECHNIC

Timothy C. Hart

UNIVERSITY OF NEVADA LAS VEGAS

CAROLINA ACADEMIC PRESS

Durham, North Carolina

Copyright © 2011
Kim Michelle Lersch
Timothy C. Hart
All Rights Reserved

Library of Congress Cataloging-in-Publication Data

Lersch, Kim Michelle.
Space, time, and crime / Kim Michelle Lersch, Timothy Hart. -- 3rd ed.
  p. cm.
Includes bibliographical references and index.
ISBN 978-1-59460-921-3 (alk. paper)
1. Criminology. 2. Crime--Sociological aspects. 3. Spatial behavior. 4.
Crime--United States. 5. Crime analysis--United States. 6. Crime prevention.
I. Hart, Timothy C. II. Title.

HV6150.L47 2011
364.01--dc23

2011022268

Carolina Academic Press
700 Kent Street
Durham, North Carolina 27701
Telephone (919) 489-7486
Fax (919) 493-5668
www.cap-press.com

Printed in the United States of America

Contents

Introduction

In the fall of 2002, residents of the Washington D.C. metropolitan area were absolutely terrified by a pair of serial snipers who had roamed the region, shooting 14 innocent people as they conducted the every-day business of their lives: shopping, pumping gas, dropping by the post office, running errands, or just going to school. There was no rhyme or reason to the selection of the victims. Men and women, old and young, and members of various racial and ethnic groups were slain at the hands of the well-trained shooter and his young stepson. In the days prior to their arrest, the gunmen had even issued a warning to parents that their children may be the next victims. No one was immune from this indiscriminate violence.

The most terrifying aspect of these incidents was the sheer randomness of their timing and the locations of their occurrence. There was no pattern in the shootings. Some of the victims were shot in the early morning hours, others at various times throughout the late morning and afternoon, while still others were gunned down in the late evening. A Florida tourist was wounded outside of a Ponderosa restaurant; a terror analyst for the Federal Bureau of Investigation was killed in a Home Depot parking lot. It seemed that no one was safe at any time or at any place in the region. Schools were closed and outdoor events such as high school football games were cancelled as the area was paralyzed by fear.

While the case of the Beltway snipers garnered international attention, it should be noted that this type of violence targeted against random victims is the exception, not the rule. In fact, one could argue that the lack of a pattern in the location, time, and victim selection is what made this horrible tragedy especially newsworthy. If these same madmen had been targeting drug dealers or prostitutes in poor urban neighborhoods, more than likely this book would have had a different introduction since few of us would have been able to recall any details from the media reports of the incident (if there had been any national coverage at all).

Our journey through space, time and crime begins with a basic statement of fact: Crime is not evenly distributed across locations, times, victims, or targets. In every city in America, there are "safe" areas where serious crimes are a relatively rare event. There are also not-so-safe areas where crimes—especially violent, predatory street crimes—are an everyday occurrence. Certain times of the day are safer than others, although this varies with the type of crime. While one is much less likely to become a victim of a violent assault during the daytime hours, one's home is at greater risk for an attack by a burglar during the same time frame. While some will (fortunately) live their entire lives free from serious incidents of crime, others, especially those who happen to be young, single, members of a minority group, and/or urban residents have a much higher likelihood of becoming a victim of crime. Far from being a random event that occurs without rhyme or reason, crime is concentrated in certain areas and at certain times.

The purpose of this book is to explore issues related to the spatial and temporal clustering of crimes. The book is divided into four sections. The first section, which includes Chapters 2 and 3, explores the issues of "why." Why are some neighborhoods overrun with crime, while others enjoy safety, peace, and harmony among the local residents? In the second section, Chapters 4 and 5 explore the issue of "what." Once a high crime location or time is identified, what can we do about it? How do the theories get translated into policy? The third section, which is comprised of Chapters 6 and 7, explores the issues of "how." How do we know where the crimes are located? How do police agencies, security managers, and others identify the areas that need more crime prevention services or special patrol operations? The book ends with a critical examination of the various theories, policies, and strategies that have been presented throughout the text.

In this third edition, the research and references have been updated throughout the text. More examples have been provided from practitioners in the field as we have tried to make the book relevant to both students and working professionals. The most notable update is that Dr. Timothy Hart has been added as a co-author. Dr. Hart is the founder and co-editor of *Crime Mapping: A Journal of Research and Practice*. Currently he is the Director of the Center for the Analysis of Crime Statistics at University of Nevada, Las Vegas. Prior to joining the faculty at UNLV, Dr. Hart worked as a Statistician for the Bureau of Justice Statistics, a Program Analyst for the Drug Enforcement Administration and a Research Analyst for the Hillsborough County (Florida) Sheriff's Office. Dr. Hart brings an added level of expertise to this third edition. We both hope that you enjoy this book.

Space, Time, and Crime

Chapter 1

The Basics of Space, Time, and Crime

Crime Places and Spaces in History

There has been a great deal of renewed interest in the study of space, time, and crime in the past 20 years. To some, this may seem like a hot "new" area in crime fighting. More and more police agencies are adopting technology that allows them to easily identify "hot spots" or clusters of criminal activity. Television programs regularly portray the use of crime mapping technology, displaying brightly colored maps of policing beats and zones. The highly publicized COMPSTAT system, made popular by the New York City Police Department, is based on a philosophy of geographic accountability in which a team of officers and supervisors are responsible for crime occurrences in specified areas. In the wake of the Beltway Sniper case, software programs designed to develop a geographic profile of the shooters received international media attention. While there is a great deal of excitement in the study of the geography of crime, it should be noted that interest in the examination of crime and space dates back to the early 1800s.

Adriano Balbi and Andre-Michel Guerry are usually credited as being the first creators of maps of crime (Weisburd & McEwen, 1998). The first national crime statistics were released in France in 1827, and Balbi and Guerry were intrigued. The pair combined the crime data with other demographic figures from the recent census, mapping areas based on the level of poverty, education, and crime. Their findings were of interest: the wealthy areas of France reported high levels of property crimes, while the areas with the lowest levels of education had the lowest rates of violent crimes (Vold, Bernard, & Snipes, 2002).

Another early pioneer in the area of crime and space was Adolphe Quetelet, a Belgian mathematician and astronomer. Quetelet was also interested in the newly released crime statistics from France and, with the use of his mathematical talents, was able to perform rather sophisticated statistical analyses with the data.

Working in the 1830s, Quetelet examined both the characteristics of those accused of criminal activity, as well as the locations in which the crimes occurred. He was able to determine that some individuals were more likely to commit crime than others, especially those who were young, poor, male, and unemployed. However, Quetelet also found that areas with high concentrations of poverty and unemployment actually had fewer reported crimes. Quetelet concluded that instead of victimizing other poor and unemployed persons close to home, crimes were more likely to be committed by poor and unemployed individuals against wealthy and educated persons. For Quetelet, inequality was an important factor in tempting individuals to commit crimes. The poor were drawn into areas of relative affluence in order to commit their crimes (Vold, Bernard, & Snipes, 2002).

While the work of Quetelet was influential, interest in the geography of crime decreased in the late 1800s for a variety of reasons. First, without the use of calculators or statistical programs, it was difficult to create maps and conduct meaningful spatial comparisons between the crime data and the census data. Furthermore, data availability was an issue, especially in the United States. While France had a great deal of relatively modern, national-level data readily available for analysis, in other counties (such as the United States) crime data and census data were not collected on such a wide-scale basis (Weisburd & McEwen, 1998).

In the United States, the study of crime and place sat dormant until the birth of the Chicago School of Criminology. In the early 1900s, a group of innovative sociologists found themselves working and writing in a rapidly changing urban environment. While the contributions of the Chicago School are explored at length in Chapter 2, one of the rather puzzling issues that intrigued researchers was why crimes were concentrated in certain areas of the city. Why did certain areas of the city seem to be troubled not only by crime, but also by other social problems? Why were other areas relatively safe and healthy spaces—neighborhoods where one would not hesitate to walk around at night, raise a family, or conduct the everyday business of life? One hundred years later, the same issues are being explored.

What Is "Space"?

Throughout this text, a number of different terms are used to refer to "space," such as location, place, address, neighborhood, census tracts, policing zones or crime reporting districts, or an entire city. While at times these terms may appear to be interchangeable, it is important to note that there are some subtle differences in the meanings of these words.

Most of the words describing an area or location listed above may be grouped into two general terms: place or space (Block & Block, 1995). A place might include a house, business, classroom, individual address, street corner, or other individual location. A place is a much smaller area than a space—it is an individual point in a space. A space may include such areas as neighborhoods, census tracts, or other larger territories.

The actual boundaries for spaces can be formed in a number of ways. For example, a police agency normally divides its area of responsibility into a number of small geographic areas. The specific term given to these smaller areas varies with the individual agencies, although names such as reporting districts, recording districts, or crime tracts seem to be the most common. These boundaries form the spaces as far as the police agency is concerned. These smaller crime tracts are then grouped into even larger spaces, sometimes called zones or districts. A municipal police department may have 50 different crime tracts that are grouped into three different districts.

Cities may also create space boundaries by posting signs at specific street boundaries such as "Welcome to the Kenwood Neighborhood Area" or "You are now entering the Seminole Heights Neighborhood." In one city where I (Kim) lived for a number of years, there was a great push by the local municipal government to build a sense of community among its residents. The city invested thousands of dollars in signs to alert people that they were passing from one community space into another. These officially recorded boundaries for community spaces had been established long before homes were built and neighborhoods were formed. These "official" boundaries often did not coincide with the informal boundaries that had historically developed among the local residents, as their own ways of dividing spaces often do not respect police or city boundaries. As illustrated later in this text, this can be somewhat problematic, especially when well-intentioned outsiders—like police agencies, social service agencies, and others—try to "force" official community boundaries in areas where local residents have defined their own spaces quite differently.

Space definition can also be made on a more personal, internal level. While driving or walking to work or school, certain areas along the way may be identified based on visual cues important to some individuals and not others. Spaces, then, may be defined based on a personal cognitive or internal mental map of a city, county, or region. An entertainment district, a cluster of apartments, or an area of single-family homes may all be defined as spaces.

Another interesting characteristic of spaces is that they tend to take on lives of their own. The spaces become more than just the sum of all of the individual places located within them. A stroll down Bourbon Street in New Orleans may present this sort of phenomenon. The individual bars, clubs, and restaurants become a blur as you are drawn into the overall feel of the larger space—the sights, smells, and sounds of the space are an experience beyond the individual places.

Of course, the distinction between places and spaces can get a bit blurred. For example, is a high school a place or a space? The answer depends on the person making the distinction between place and space. A school resource officer assigned to a high school would probably view the school as a space filled with many individual places—classrooms, hallways, auto shop area, cafeteria, etc. A resident of the local neighborhood might view the school as just another individual place located within the larger neighborhood space. This sort of confusion may arise when talking about large public housing projects—is it a space or a place?

What Is Time?
The Language of Temporal Analysis

Time is an important consideration in the study of crime. As seen in Table 1.1, just as there are dangerous high-risk places and spaces, there are also blocks of time in which victimization for certain types of crimes is more likely than in others. An individual is much more likely to become a victim of a homicide or aggravated assault during the evening hours on a weekend, especially Saturday nights (Miethe & McCorkle, 2001; 2006). As will be discussed in Chapter 3, many of these high-risk times can be traced to how we live our daily lives. Weekends are found to be especially dangerous times because people tend to venture out and involve themselves in social events that occur in public areas. They come into greater contact with problematic situations and problematic people. Throw in a good healthy dose of drugs and/or alcohol (remember the old advertisement slogan "Weekends were made for Michelob?") and you've got a good recipe for crime.

Temporal patterns of crime like those presented in Table 1.1 are also observed in different subsets of the overall population. For example, studies show that college students aged 18–24 experience most on-campus non-fatal violence during the day (i.e., between the hours of 6 a.m. to 6 p.m.) but most off-campus violence at night (i.e., between the hours of 6 p.m. and 6 a.m.) (Baum & Klaus, 2005; Hart 2003; 2007; Hart & Miethe, 2011). As research indicates, these temporal patterns of college-student victimization are best explained by opportunity and behavior. Most college students are on campus during the day, making the opportunity for victimization more likely. During the evening, however, students are more likely to engage in more "risky" behavior that may lead to increased risk of victimization.

Table 1.1 High Risk Places and Times

Type of Crime	High Risk Places	High Risk Times	High Risk Days/ Periods
Homicide	Street/Alley	Evening Hours (6 p.m.–6 a.m.)	Weekends
Aggravated Assault	Victim's home or street/parking lot	Evening Hours (6 p.m.–Midnight)	Weekends
Sexual Assault	At or in victim's home	Evening Hours (6 p.m.–Midnight)	Weekends, especially in Summer months
Robberies	Within 1 mile of victim's home	Personal—during day (6 a.m.–6 p.m.) Armed—at night (after 6 p.m.)	Late Summer, Fall, and Winter (esp. January)
Residential Burglaries	Victim's home	Daytime (Esp. 10:00–11:00 a.m.) and (1:00 p.m.–3:00 p.m.)	Weekdays
Motor Vehicle Theft	Near victim's home	Evening Hours	Summer months

Adapted from Miethe & McCorkle (2006).

In addition to time of day and day of the week, there are other important considerations with respect to time and its relationship to criminal victimization. Some of these factors include the week of the month, quarterly and yearly fluctuations, and seasonal trends. Some analysts even consider crime changes during full moon phases (Vellani & Nahoun, 2001). In general, the study of time in relation to the occurrence of crimes is often called **temporal analysis.**

Moments in Time

Understanding the concept of time can be a bit more elusive than the concept of space. This becomes especially problematic when one considers both time and space together. As discussed by Harries (1999, p. 11), there are a number of concepts to consider in the temporal and geographic analysis of crime. First, there is the issue of **moments.** A moment provides the time that a crime occurred in space—when and where the crime occurred. While pinpointing the exact time and location of a crime seems like a basic issue, it can be a bit complex for certain types of crimes.

With respect to identifying the moment of a crime occurrence, there are two important concepts that must be introduced: **exact time crimes** and **time span crimes** (Gottlieb, Arenberg, & Singh, 1998). An exact time crime is a crime in which the victim can identify the time that the crime occurred with relative accuracy. Violent personal crimes, such as robbery, rape, and assault, are more likely to be exact time crimes. Consider the following example: You are walking out of class today and are approached by a young man who demands your money. You hand over your wallet and immediately run into the nearest building to notify the campus police of the incident. Even if you were unable to check a clock on the wall, you could give the responding officer a good estimate of the exact time that the robbery took place. For example, "Gee, my class ends at 1:00, but we got out a few minutes early ... the crime occurred about 1:15 or so." Additionally, the campus police would have a record of your initial call for service, which would provide further information on the exact time of the crime. Crimes against persons are more likely to be exact time crimes.

Consider another scenario. You leave your apartment for school at 9:00 a.m. You attend your classes, and then go directly to work from the campus. You log in a few hours at work, and then you decide to drop by your friend's house to watch a game on television. After the game, you return to your apartment. When you arrive back at your apartment at 1:00 a.m., you find that your home has been burglarized. The police arrive and ask, "What time did this happen?" The only information that you can give is the time span—you left your home at 9:00 a.m. and returned at 1:00 a.m. The crime occurred somewhere between these two known time values—you know when you left and when you returned home. Property crimes, in particular burglary and auto theft, are more likely to be time span crimes.

Researchers and police agencies have a number of ways of dealing with time span crimes. For purposes of temporal analysis, a "best guess" single time is often much more useful than a large time span. Temporal analysts employ a number of techniques to assign a single "best guess" value to better identify the moment of a crime occurrence. One of the more basic techniques is called **midpoint analysis.** In midpoint analysis, the time value that is in the middle of the known range of times is reported as the "best guess." In the previous example, since you left your home at 9:00 a.m. and returned at 1:00 a.m. (a span of 16 hours) the midpoint for this range would be 5:00 p.m. The value of 5:00 p.m. would then be reported as a **split time** value to estimate the moment of the crime occurrence (for a more detailed discussion of the various estimation techniques for dealing with time span crimes, please see Gottlieb et al., 1998).

A second method for estimating the time that a crime occurred is known as the **weighted time span method.** This method is a bit more complicated but is usually viewed as more accurate than midpoint analysis. The weighted method provides a probability of risk for a crime occurrence for each unit of time across the known bounds. Let's say you leave your house at 9:00 a.m. and return at noon and discover your home has been broken into. You have a three-hour time window. To calculate the weighted risk, the number one is divided by three, or the number of hours in your window. In this case, there is a 33% chance that your house was broken into between 9:00 and 10:00, a 33% chance that the crime occurred between 10:00 and 11:00, etc. Where this method gets useful is when you have a serial burglar working—the same person is breaking into homes around your neighborhood. A risk score can be calculated for each hour of the day by adding the weighted risk for each hour for every known crime that this person has committed. These risk scores are then added up and the probability of occurrence by hour can be determined (for a more detailed discussion, please see Boba, 2009; Gottlieb et al., 1998; Helms, 2004).

Duration

According to Harries (1999), duration is defined as "how long an event or process continued in a specific space" (p. 11). Duration may refer to a specific criminal incident, such as how long it took to resolve a hostage situation. It may take on broader meanings: How long did the number of reported crimes remain above a specific level in a certain area? For how many days, weeks, months did a jurisdiction experience a high level of residential burglaries? How long was a "hot spot," or a specific place with a high level of criminal activity, active or "hot"? Duration may also refer to the length of time that a specific perpetrator was active. For example, what was the duration of the Beltway Snipers' activity?

Distance as Time

Have you ever asked anyone how far away a destination was and their response was, "Oh, about an hour?" Distance can be expressed as a time value. For some people, a time value can even be more informative than a mile value when expressing distance.

Things get even more interesting with respect to space, time, and crime when one considers issues related to travel time. For example, consider the case of a detective investigating reports of an individual who is exposing himself to women during the hours of noon to 1:00 p.m. The activities are limited to the downtown business district on weekdays only. The detective might begin to develop a theory that this perpetrator works downtown and is exposing himself during his lunch break. The locations of the reported events may be examined to visualize how far the perpetrator could travel in a rather limited period of time from his workplace location. Once a limited geographic area for the possible location of his workplace has been developed the information may be cross-checked against registered sex offenders to see if any of these known individuals work at businesses in the target area.

What Is Crime?

Though the discussions of the concepts of place and time thus far may seem surprisingly complex, answering the question "What is crime?" can actually take up an entire book. Part of the complexity is that crime is not absolute. What is considered "criminal" in one state may be acceptable behavior in another. What is considered a "normal" activity one year may violate a newly passed law the next. Laws that define what is and is not a crime are relative to both time and space.

A Note on Crime and Deviance

As many criminologists have degrees in sociology, it is easy to slip into sociological vocabulary when discussing issues related to crime. On the graduate level, sociologists do not study crime, but deviance. **Deviance** is a broad sociological term used to describe behavior that violates generally accepted expectations. These generally accepted expectations or rules for behavior are called **norms**. Criminals violate laws, while someone described as **deviant** violates a norm.

Similar to laws, norms are also not absolute and vary with time and space. The expectations for behavior in the classroom are much different than the norms governing behavior while attending a party on a Saturday night. If you walk into a local tavern, pull out your notebook and pen, and prepare to take notes on whatever pearls of wisdom the bartender shares, other people in the bar will look at you a bit strangely. Norms that define expected behavior in one location might be very different from norms in another time and place. Over time, some norms become more formalized into laws. Many norms, however, just stay norms. Though informal, they are powerful rules for controlling behavior.

It is important to consider norms and norm violations along with the discussions of laws and crimes. Oftentimes, norms can exert stronger influence over daily lives than criminal law and its accompanying threat of sanctions. Within the same city, the laws are the same regardless of the neighborhood in which one lives. However, the behaviors that are exhibited by the local residents with respect to themselves, their property, and their neighbors may be very different.

For example, in some neighborhoods there may be fairly rigid, shared expectations for behavior. People keep their yards well-mowed, with carefully maintain flowerbeds and other decorative landscaping. Garage doors are rarely left open, and homes are tastefully painted (in pre-approved colors only) and well cared for. Even though there may not be direct criminal sanctions for violating the "thou shalt mow once a week" commandment, few violate this norm. Children play outside under the watchful eyes of parents and other neighbors. If a child gets out of line, a neighbor may step in and correct the situation and/or inform the child's parents. Residents chat with each other over their fences and wave at passers-by.

In other neighborhoods, the norms may be quite different. People park cars on their front lawns, where one would be more likely to find empty beer cans than a decorative marigold or petunia. Grass mowing may be optional (if grass exists at all) and homes may sport broken windows, peeling paint, or gang-related graffiti. Unsupervised children play in the street and few adults are outside. A group of teenagers often loiters in front of a vacant house, throwing rocks at the windows and playing loud music. Neighbors do not recognize their neighbors and there is little conversation (if any) among the residents. Residents are generally suspicious and fearful of each other. While the laws governing these two neighborhoods are identical, the day-to-day lives of the residents and the level of social control may be very, very different.

Defining norms can be a bit difficult. For example, when first starting college, a good part of the adjustment period is trying to figure out how you are supposed to act. Of course, you are given a student code of conduct with the formal rules and regulations carefully laid out, but what about the all-important informal norms? How do you address your professor? Is it normal to raise your hand if you have a question, or should you go to office hours, or ask the teaching assistant? Do you have to set up an appointment for office hours, or do you just go? Are you going to be defined as a geek if you sit in the front of the classroom? What should you wear to class? Figuring out what the shared expectations for behavior are in a new setting can be a painful experience, especially since oftentimes it is not known that a norm exists until it is violated.

Defining Crimes

While defining norms can be a bit difficult, defining crimes is very easy. How does one know what is and is not considered a crime? In contemporary societies, one need look no further than the **penal code**, a highly organized, detailed record of all of the written criminal laws in a specified jurisdiction. Each state has its own set of written laws, as do different municipalities. There are also Federal level laws that can be found in the United States Code. The penal codes for all states can be found with a little digging on official state-sponsored websites.

The written criminal law is divided into two types: **procedural** and **substantive.** Substantive criminal law includes detailed definitions of what behaviors constitute a crime, as well as what punishments go along with violations of the law. For example, according to the New York State Penal Code Article 130—§ 130.25, the crime of rape in the third degree is defined in the following manner:

A person is guilty of rape in the third degree when:

1. He or she engages in sexual intercourse with another person who is incapable of consent by reason of some factor other than being less than seventeen years old;
2. Being twenty-one years old or more, he or she engages in sexual intercourse with another person less than seventeen years old; or
3. He or she engages in sexual intercourse with another person without such person's consent where such lack of consent is by reason of some factor other than incapacity to consent. Rape in the third degree is a class E felony.

There are a couple of things to note in the above definition. First, in the State of New York, the legal age of consent for sexual intercourse is seventeen. The legal age of consent may be higher or lower in other states. Second, in New York State the victim of rape may be male or female. In some jurisdictions, the crime of rape has not occurred if the victim is male. Finally, the classification of rape in the third degree as a class E felony means that the punishment for conviction of this crime in New York State is four years. In other states the punishment for a similar act may be more lenient or more punitive.

While the substantive criminal law applies to all members of a society, procedural law regulates the conduct of actors in the criminal justice system as they enforce elements of the substantive criminal law. Rules governing searches and seizures, rules of evidence, and trial proceedings fall under procedural law. This text does not concern violations of the procedural law. It does concentrate on allegations that someone has violated some element of the substantive criminal law.

Counting Crimes: Official Statistics

Penal Codes are sources for defining crimes. But how does one find how many crimes occur in a specific area? Law enforcement agencies are the most popular source of crime data. Federal, state, county, tribal, and local law enforcement agencies compile and report data from various sources regarding the number and types of crimes that have occurred in their jurisdiction. Many technologically advanced agencies make this data readily available to interested citizens on their websites. Data collected by law enforcement agencies are often called "official statistics" and include such things as calls for service, incident reports, and the Federal Bureau of Investigation's Uniform Crime Reports (UCR) and National Incident Based Reporting System (NIBRS). Depending on the source of data used, one can get a very different view of the level of criminal activity in an area (see Mosher, Miethe, & Hart, 2011).

Calls for Service

Calls for service are a rather crude measure of the level of criminal activity in an area. Police agencies have records of the number of citizen-initiated calls for assistance, based on their small geographic units (referred to here as recording districts). Each recording district reports the number of calls received (both 911 emergency and non-emergency calls), the preliminary nature of the call, the time that the call was received, and the location of the complaint. These data are often automatically compiled by computer-assisted dispatch (CAD) software systems. CAD systems allow vast amounts of data to be compiled over time, which can assist in identifying areas with high service demands (Swanson, Territo, & Taylor, 1998). Using calls for service data, one can get a basic picture of the crime problem in an area. Does the area seem to generate a higher than average number of calls? Has there been an increase or decrease in the number of calls over the past 5 years? Are the calls for relatively minor offenses, or are they primarily regarding serious felony allegations?

Unfortunately, one of the drawbacks of using calls for service as a primary measure of the level of crime in an area is that citizen reports of criminal activity are often not valid. One agency representative that I (Kim) worked with found the "gang problem" in his zone rather humorous. The area had a large elderly population especially fearful of teens and pre-teens. Whenever several young people gathered in the street to ride their skateboards, the police were immediately called to investigate allegations of gang activity in the neighborhood. When the police arrived, oftentimes the youths had already left the area or, upon investigation, found to be just harmless bored kids getting in a little exercise. Regardless of the reality of the situation, if one relied solely on the calls for service data in this example one would expect that a gang war was about to break out at any time.

Relying on calls for service data presents a second problem often described as the **dark figure of crime,** or crimes that go unreported to police. The crimes known to police are viewed as only the tip of the iceberg, with vast amounts of criminal activity never officially counted. People choose not to call the police to report a crime for a number of reasons. A citizen may fear reprisal by the offender if their identity as the complainant is somehow revealed. A citizen might assume that someone else has called the police to report the crime. The citizen may also feel that the police are not able to do anything about the crime or that the matter is not important enough to merit the attention of the police. If the relationship between the police and the local residents is strained, citizens are not likely to summon the police into their homes especially for relatively minor criminal incidents. Regardless of the justification, in reality, many legitimate crimes go unreported and hence, do not show up in any official crime reports.

Incident Data

As calls for service may not be the most accurate source of data, some researchers have turned to incident data. Incident data are based on reports written by a responding officer regarding the nature of the call. For example, a patrol officer may be dispatched to a citizen's home based on the complaint of a barking dog. Upon arriving at the address, the officer may find a very different situation. There may be evidence of forced entry into the home and, upon further investigation, the body of the unconscious homeowner may be found. Calls for service and actual incident reports can be very different.

Reliance upon incident data, however, is not without its problems. If there is no call for service, it would logically follow that there would be no incident report. The problem of measuring the dark figure of crime applies here as well. Beyond the underreporting issue, in many calls for service the responding police officer has the power to decide whether or not a crime has actually occurred. Patrol officers have a great deal of unchecked discretion in this area. One patrol officer shared an experience he had in responding to a disturbing the peace call. Upon arrival, the officer found a crying woman with a fresh bruise on her face. Her husband, who was still at home at the time of the officer's arrival, had struck her during an argument. There was clear evidence of battery. She begged the officer not to arrest her husband, as was required under the domestic violence laws of this state. According to the woman, her husband would lose his job and push the family into even greater financial and emotional distress. After careful deliberation, the officer classified the incident as "NR"— no report needed. Even though there was clear evidence that a crime had occurred and an arrest was mandated, no official report of the incident was ever made.

Federal Bureau of Investigation Uniform Crime Reports (FBI UCR)

The oldest and most widely recognized source for all crime related data are the FBI Uniform Crime Reports. At least once a year local papers will carry front-page headlines that herald the release of the latest FBI UCR statistics. Did crime go up? Did crime go down? Where is the new murder capital of the U.S.? How do we account for changes in the level of criminal activity? Since these numbers are so widely reported, it is useful to discuss this data source at some length.

The FBI UCR began in 1930 at the request of the International Association of Chiefs of Police (IACP). The IACP, which exists to this day, recognized the importance of having a standardized national database of criminal activity. The goal of the FBI UCR was to collect data from law enforcement agencies across the country on a limited number of crimes. To ensure standardized responses, the FBI provided very clear definitions as to what constituted each crime and under what circumstances the crimes should be reported. While all law enforcement agencies were encouraged to report all crimes that they were aware of being committed in their jurisdiction, reporting was and continues to be voluntary.

Today, the FBI (2009a) groups crimes into two general categories: Part I Offenses and Part II Offenses (see Table 1.2). As a whole, Part I Offenses are viewed as more serious offenses and usually garner much more publicity than the Part II Offenses. The FBI provides very clear definitions for Part I Offenses, which are as follows:

- **Criminal homicide**—a.) Murder and nonnegligent manslaughter: the willful (nonnegligent) killing of one human being by another. Deaths caused by negligence, attempts to kill, assaults to kill, suicides, and accidental deaths are excluded. The Program classifies justifiable homicides separately and limits the definition to: (1) the killing of a felon by a law enforcement officer in the line of duty; or (2) the killing of a felon, during the commission of a felony, by a private citizen. b.) Manslaughter by negligence: the killing of another person through gross negligence. Traffic fatalities are excluded.

- **Forcible rape**—The carnal knowledge of a female forcibly and against her will. Rapes by force and attempts or assaults to rape, regardless of the age of the victim, are included. Statutory offenses (no force used— victim under age of consent) are excluded.
- **Robbery**—The taking or attempted taking of anything of value from the care, custody, or control of a person or persons by force or threat of force or violence and/or by putting the victim in fear.
- **Aggravated assault**—An unlawful attack by one person upon another for the purpose of inflicting severe or aggravated bodily injury. This type of assault usually is accompanied by the use of a weapon or by means likely to produce death or great bodily harm. Simple assaults are excluded.
- **Burglary (breaking or entering)**—The unlawful entry of a structure to commit a felony or a theft. Attempted forcible entry is included.
- **Larceny-theft (except motor vehicle theft)**—The unlawful taking, carrying, leading, or riding away of property from the possession or constructive possession of another. Examples are thefts of bicycles or automobile accessories, shoplifting, pocket-picking, or the stealing of any property or article that is not taken by force and violence or by fraud. Attempted larcenies are included. Embezzlement, confidence games, forgery, worthless checks, etc., are excluded.
- **Motor vehicle theft**—The theft or attempted theft of a motor vehicle. A motor vehicle is self-propelled and runs on land surface and not on rails. Motorboats, construction equipment, airplanes, and farming equipment are specifically excluded from this category.
- **Arson**—Any willful or malicious burning or attempt to burn, with or without intent to defraud, a dwelling house, public building, motor vehicle or aircraft, personal property of another, etc.

Based on information provided by local law enforcement agencies, the FBI compiles the data and reports the total number of Part I Offenses based on various geographic areas such as cities, states, and national regions. In addition to the base incident counts and rates, arrest data are reported for both Part I and Part II Offenses. The arrest data are broken down both by the nature of the offense and by the characteristics of the arrestee, including age, gender, and race.

Table 1.2 FBI UCR Part II Offenses

Simple assault	Forgery and counterfeiting	Fraud
Embezzlement	Buying, receiving, possessing stolen property	Vandalism
Carrying/possessing a weapon	Prostitution and commercial vice	Drug abuse
Gambling	Offenses against the family/children	Liquor laws
Driving under the influence	Drunkenness	Disorderly conduct
Vagrancy	Suspicion	Curfew and loitering
Runaway (persons <18)	All other offenses	Sex Offenses (Except forcible rape, prostitution, and commercialized vice)

Source: Federal Bureau of Investigation (2009c). Crime in the United States, 2008 — Offense Definitions. Available on-line at http://www.fbi.gov/ucr/cius2008/about/offense_definitions.html.

Prior to June 2004, the FBI also reported the **Crime Index**, which was the total of all Part I Index Offenses excluding arson. Arson was not added as a Part I Offense until 1979 and was not included in the calculation of the Crime Index. The Crime Index was a very misleading figure for those who wished to get a good feel for the level of criminal activity in a geographic area. The problem really rests with the crime of larceny. While larceny is a Part I Offense, it is not exactly a heinous crime. The number of reported incidents of larceny greatly outnumbered all other crimes and inflated the Crime Index. As a result, the FBI now reports the total number of violent crimes, which is the total number of reported murders, aggravated assaults, forcible rapes, and robberies, and the total number of property crimes, which is the total of all reported burglaries, larceny-thefts, and motor vehicle thefts. The various crime totals, as well as the individual crime counts for the Part I Offenses for 2008 are reported in Table 1.3.

Like most measures of crime, the FBI UCR has some problems. First, since it is based on the crimes known to police, the accuracy or **validity** of the numbers is affected by under-reporting by citizens. The FBI UCR does not include the "dark figure" of crime. Second, since the state definitions and the FBI definitions of crime are often not consistent, individual agencies may not have

Table 1.3 Part I Index Offenses Crime (2008)

Offense	Number of Offenses	Rate per 100,000 Inhabitants
Murder & Manslaughter	16,272	5.4
Forcible Rape	89,000	29.3
Robbery	441,855	145.3
Aggravated Assault	834,885	274.6
Burglary	2,222,196	730.8
Larceny-theft	6,588,873	2,167.00
Motor Vehicle Theft	956,846	314.7
Total Violent Crimes	1,382,012	454.5
Total Property Crimes	9,767,915	3,212.50

Source: Federal Bureau of Investigation (2009b). Crime in the United States, 2008-Table 1. Available on-line at http://www.fbi.gov/ucr/cius2008/data/table_01.html.

the time or the resources to calculate separate crime reports for the FBI. Consider the crime of rape. According to the FBI definition, only women can be raped. Some states (like New York) have adopted gender-neutral language in their laws, which means that their internal crime statistics count forcible rapes of both men and women. Some agencies may separate their counts by victim gender and only report the forcible rapes as defined by the FBI to the UCR accounting office. Other agencies may report the same number of forcible rapes for both their internal purposes, as well as for the FBI UCR. Although state agencies responsible for submitting UCR data to the FBI are subject to a data quality review audit at least once every three years in order to assure compliance with national UCR guidelines, certain situations simply prohibit the UCR from including certain crime counts. For example, the following passage appears on the Data Declaration page, under Table 5, for the Crime in the United States, 2008 report (FBI, 2009c):

> The data collection methodology for the offense of forcible rape used by Illinois (with the exception of Rockford, Illinois) and Minnesota (with the exceptions of Minneapolis and St. Paul, Minnesota) do not comply with national UCR Program guidelines. Consequently, their figures for forcible rape were estimated for inclusion in this table.

Third, police agencies may intentionally manipulate their data. As an example, consider college and university police departments. These law enforcement agencies must report their Part I Offenses to the FBI. These reports are then published in national and international newspapers and magazines (*The Chronicle of Higher Education*, which is more than likely available in your university's library, regularly reports annual crime figures for a large number of colleges and universities). Imagine that a string of rapes has occurred in campus dorms. From a very cold business stance this sort of criminal incident is not good for the University's reputation and may impact potential enrollment. Part I Offenses (including forcible rape) are widely reported; Part II Offenses (which include simple assault) are not. Instead of reporting the incident as a forcible rape, the police agency may report the crime as a simple assault. This is often very true with attempted crimes. While the FBI requests counts for attempted violent crimes, once again it does not have control over the accuracy of the data it receives.

A fourth problem concerns the **hierarchy rule**. According to the FBI UCR guidelines, only the most serious crime should be reported. This seriously under-reports the occurrence of crimes. Imagine this example: Someone breaks into your house and you come home and surprise the burglar. The burglar demands your wallet, beats you to a pulp with a baseball bat, and then steals your television, stereo, and computer. While numerous Part I Offenses have been committed in this example, the FBI only wants the top charge reported, which in this example, would be the aggravated assault.

A fifth and final problem concerns what can be considered as a "the show must go on" issue. The FBI must have all of the requested data from local law enforcement agencies by a specific date. Sometimes agencies miss the due date. When this happens, "the show must go on," meaning the FBI publishes only the data that was received by the due date. Crimes that occurred in areas policed by agencies that were unable to meet the due date would then be excluded from any annual reports. I (Kim) witnessed this in the state of Florida, where a highly publicized decrease in the level of crime (as measured by the FBI UCR statistics) was reported by the local media. Politicians congratulated themselves for a job well done, taking credit for the decline as a direct result of their "get tough" policies. Interestingly, a few weeks later, an article buried on the back page of the metro section critiqued the accuracy of the UCR data. It seemed that a number of agencies had not reported their crime figures to the FBI. The highly publicized reduction in the number of crimes was due to the missing data and did not reflect an actual decline in the level of criminal activity. If all the agencies had reported their crime figures, an increase in the level of crime would have been reported for the state!

Despite its flaws, the FBI UCR remains one of the most widely cited sources of data on crime. This is especially true with respect to studies of the geography of crime. Over 90% of law enforcement agencies do report their crime figures to the FBI, so one can compare the number of homicides in Portland, Maine with the number of homicides in Honolulu, Hawaii. City, county, state, and regional totals of Part I Offenses are readily available for analysis. Additionally, because the FBI has collected data for over 70 years, one can readily monitor changes in the level and type of criminal activity over time. Even though the accuracy of the data may not be the best, it is generally recognized as one of the stronger sources of data. A criminology professor who was a mentor to both of your authors once summarized the FBI UCR data in the following manner: "It *is* bad, but at least it is *consistently* bad."

The National Incident-Based Reporting System: The New UCR?

We have reviewed a number of problems with the traditional FBI UCR figures. Because of the growing dissatisfaction with this data source, the law enforcement community called for a more comprehensive system for the reporting of crime data. In January 1986, the FBI's Technical Services Division was charged with the task of improving the UCR. The new system was developed through careful consultation with a number of shareholders including the International Association of Chiefs of Police, National Sheriffs' Association, National Alliance of State Drug Enforcement Agencies, and other federal, state and local criminal justice agencies (FBI, 2000). After a successful pilot project in South Carolina, where the system was refined and improved, the National Incident-Based Reporting System (NIBRS) was approved for wide-spread use by attendees at a national FBI UCR conference in March 1988. In a nutshell, the NIBRS system is designed to provide a much more accurate and detailed picture of criminal activity in a jurisdiction.

According to the FBI (2000; 2004), the NIBRS system differs from the traditional UCR in a number of ways. In the old system, law enforcement agencies report the total number of Part I Offenses and arrest data for Part I and Part II Offenses. These figures are then reported as aggregate totals to the FBI— with the exception of homicide, there are no detailed data that can easily be used for statistical analyses. For example, the date and time of an offense were not included in the data, nor could one retrieve any information on the victim of the crime (Faggiani & Hirschel, 2005). The FBI describes this system as a **summary reporting system.** In contrast, the NIBRS system requires much more detailed reporting on individual crime incidents and arrests. As opposed to a summary system, the NIBRS system involves **incident-based reporting.** As you will see, the NIBRS system provides much more information than the traditional UCR.

While the traditional system collected data on eight Part I Offenses, the NIBRS system collects information on 46 **Group A Offenses** and 11 **Group B Offenses.** These offenses are summarized in Table 1.4. For Group "A" crimes the

NIBRS system collects data on 53 different variables that describe various characteristics of the victims, the offenders, the individuals arrested, and the circumstances surrounding the criminal event (FBI, 2000). Group B Offenses are only reported when an arrest has been made. For Group B Offenses, data are collected on the characteristics of the arrestee (age, race, ethnicity, gender) and the circumstances of the arrest (such as whether the individual was armed). One very important point is that data are collected on all crimes that occur in a single incident regardless of their severity. In effect, the hierarchy rule no longer applies in the NIBRS system. Furthermore, because the data are not simply reported as summary figures, one can do meaningful comparisons between the characteristics of the victims, the offenders, and the specifics of the crimes.

The data collected by the NIBRS system can be quite extensive. Each incident report allows for up to ten different offenses, and each included offense then has a separate record. This record includes data on the victim(s), offender(s), and lost property. The victim data may contain a maximum of 999 separate victim records, which contain detailed information on each victim. The offense reports are similarly extensive, with each incident containing up to 99 offender reports. The data for the property loss are broken down by type of property taken, its value, and whether or not it was recovered (Faggiani & Hirschel, 2005).

The NIBRS system also adds an additional category of crime. The traditional summary system divided crimes into two general categories (violent and property). The NIBRS system adds a third: "Crimes against Society." This category includes liquor law violations, drug related offenses, weapons violations, driving under the influence, non-violent family offenses, pornography and obscene materials, gambling offenses, and prostitution related crimes. The justification for the addition of this third category was that these crimes neither involve an easily defined "victim," nor are they considered crimes against property.

One final, important distinction between the traditional summary reporting system and the NIBRS system concerns the reporting of attempted versus completed crimes. In the traditional UCR, one could not tell if a crime had been completed or simply attempted. Only a summary total for all crimes was reported with no distinction between these two very important characteristics. In the NIBRS system, each criminal offense carries the designation of attempted or completed.

While the use of NIBRS system would provide policymakers, law enforcement officials, and researchers with a much more useful and valid source of crime data, its very strength is also its greatest impediment to widespread use: The collection of highly detailed information is expensive, time consuming, and requires significant modification of current practices and records management systems. While almost 17,000 agencies send data to the FBI UCR, only a fraction of agencies participate in the NIBRS program. According to the FBI, as of

Table 1.4 NIBRS Offense Groups

Group "A" Offenses		
Arson	Assault Offenses (Aggravated Assault, Simple, Intimidation)	Bribery
Burglary/Breaking and Entering	Counterfeiting/Forgery	Destruction/Damage/Vandalism of Property
Drug/Narcotic Offenses (Includes Equipment Violations)	Embezzlement	Extortion/Blackmail
Fraud Offenses (Includes Credit Card/ATM Fraud, Welfare Fraud, etc.)	Gambling Offenses (Includes Betting, Equipment Violations, etc.)	Homicide Offenses (Murder; Negligent and Non-Negligent Manslaughter, Justifiable Homicide)
Kidnapping/Abduction	Larceny/Theft Offenses	Motor Vehicle Theft
Pornography/Obscene Material	Prostitution Offenses	Robbery
Sex Offenses, Forcible (Includes Rape, Sodomy, Assault with an Object, and Fondling)	Sex Offenses, Non-Forcible (Incest, Statutory Rape)	Stolen Property Offenses (Receiving, etc.)
Weapon Law Violations		
Group "B" Offenses		
Bad Checks	Curfew/Loitering/Vagrancy	Disorderly Conduct
Driving under the Influence	Drunkenness	Family Offenses, Non-Violent
Liquor Law Violations	Peeping Tom	Runaway
Trespass of Real Property	All Other Offenses	

Source: Federal Bureau of Investigation (2009d). National Incident Based Reporting System-Frequently Asked Questions. Retrieved on August 20, 2010, from http://www.fbi.gov/ucr/downloadables/nibrs_general_2008.pdf.

April 2009, 6,444 agencies contributed data to the NIBRS system, which represented only 25% of the crime statistics that were collected by the UCR program as a whole (FBI, 2009d). While more and more agencies are adopting this data collection system, agencies have generally been slow to embrace the new tool. Even though it has been more than 20 years since the system was launched, at this time, one cannot use the NIBRS system for the same level of geographic comparisons as one can use the traditional summary UCR data.

Counting Crimes: "Unofficial" Data

Because of shortcomings associated with UCR data and other "official data," some researchers have turned to other measures of crime, including surveys and qualitative research techniques. Results from these "unofficial" data sources can provide a much different (and in many cases, much more accurate) picture of the crime problem in an area.

Surveys: The Good, the Bad, and the Ugly

Surveys of local citizens can provide a great deal of information on the level and type of crimes that are occurring in a neighborhood. At one end of the extreme, surveys can be well funded, highly organized, and scientifically administered projects. At the other end, they can be loosely constructed, poorly administered, and yield questionable results. Regardless of the data source (whether official or unofficial), there are always problems with accuracy.

A substantial portion of courses in research methods is devoted to survey research and includes a number of important elements one must consider when designing and administering a "good survey." The following discussion will present a brief overview of a number of critical points.

In a survey to a group of local residents, one must first decide how one is going to administer the survey: in-person, mail, phone, or over the Internet? The mode of administration may be determined by cost. Phone surveys are cheaper than mail or in-person surveys, especially if only a local neighborhood or community is being contacted. However, the **response rate** of phone surveys is not great. The response rate is defined as the number of people who complete the survey based on the number of people contacted and eligible to complete the survey. Since people can easily hang up the phone when contacted for a survey, lower response rates can be expected. In-person surveys tend to have the highest response rate of the four methods, but usually take longer to complete and require a higher number of costly assistants to administer the survey. Finally, although many claim that Internet-based surveys can be conducted more quickly, effectively, cheaply, and/or easily than surveys conducted with more conventional modes, research shows that the actual cost and speed of this survey format do not always live up to the hype (Evans & Mathur, 2005; Fricker & Schonlau, 2002).

Second, who will be surveyed? This sounds like an easy question, but it is not. Even in a door-to-door survey with each resident, are questions posed to the entire household, the head of the household, or whoever answers the door? What if a teenager answers the door? Will the survey be administered to every resident of a community (called a **population**) or will a subset of the population (called a **sample**) be selected? If a sample of residents is used, there are a number of **sampling techniques** that are used to decide which members of a population will be selected into a sample. One can randomly select households from an accurate list of all possible households in the neighborhood, or set up a booth at a local grocery store and ask customers to fill out the survey as they walk by. The quality of the results of the survey will be determined by how accurately the sample represents the target population.

The actual wording of the survey can significantly impact the results. If a vocabulary that is above your target audience is used, the results will not be worth the paper they are printed on. In a survey I (Kim) once worked on, sixth graders were asked if they felt that police officers were prejudiced against minority persons. As the survey was administered, the children immediately began to overwhelm us with questions. This age group did not know what the words "prejudice" and "minority person" meant. Because we were in the classroom and were able to recognize their confusion, not much stock was put in their answers. Imagine if the surveys had been sent out by mail and we had no feedback from the students that they simply did not understand the wording. In addition to vocabulary, question order (earlier responses may affect later responses), poorly worded questions, or questions that direct the respondent to a preferred answer ("There's a lot of crime around here, isn't there?") may also influence a response.

While only a small part of survey construction and administration has been introduced, it should be clear that some surveys (and some results) are better than others. Bear in mind that some surveys may be very poorly constructed and administered. For example, it is not uncommon for a police chief to mandate that a survey of local residents be conducted. However, few police department employees have any formal training or education in survey construction. As explained later, many crime analysts, who are often given responsibility for completion of such tasks, only have a high school education.

National Crime Victimization Survey

While results from surveys conducted at the local level may elicit a bit of skepticism, there is one national survey that is held in high regard: the National Crime Victimization Survey (NCVS). The **National Crime Victimization Survey** is sponsored by the United States Department of Justice. Since its inception in 1973, the NCVS has grown into a widely respected source of data. According to the Bureau of Justice Statistics, nearly 50,000 household units are interviewed twice a year. Those individuals living in the selected households, age 12 and older, are asked about the frequency, characteristics, and consequences of crime victimizations. Only the following crimes are included in the survey: rape, sexual assault, robbery, assault, theft, household burglary, and motor vehicle theft. This limited range of crimes was selected in order to make comparisons with the FBI UCR findings (for a more extensive discussion of the differences between the UCR and the NCVS, please see Box 1.1).

The strongest aspect of the NCVS is that it provides an estimate of the dark figure of crime. Data are collected on crimes regardless of whether or not the police are notified. Based on data provided by the NCVS in 2000, 61% of the 25.4 million violent and property crimes went unreported to the police. It should be noted that there are differences in reporting patterns based on the type of criminal offense. While nearly half of the violent crimes were reported to the police, only about a third of property crimes (including burglary, auto theft, property theft, pocket pickings and purse snatchings) were reported (Hart & Rennison, 2003; Rand & Rennison, 2002). Clearly, the NCVS provides a needed complement to the FBI UCR statistics.

Additionally, the NCVS provides much more detailed descriptions of the crime, as well as the victim characteristics. For example, in the FBI UCR, if a robbery occurred, one would only be able to tell that the crime had taken place. With the exception of homicide, the FBI UCR does not include detailed data on crime and victim characteristics. Conversely, the NCVS asks respondents when and where the crime occurred, if a weapon was used, how the offender gained access to their property, if there were any injuries, the actions of the victim (did they resist, escape, etc.), and whether or not the police were notified of the crime. This more detailed information on victim characteristics and offender actions is very useful in developing explanations as to why certain victims and/or targets were selected by offenders. These issues will be discussed in much greater depth in Chapter 3.

As is the case with all data sources, there are limitations on the accuracy of the findings. One problem is called **sampling error**, a consideration in all surveys of samples. When a sample is surveyed, responses from this smaller group of people are used to estimate the responses of the whole group (the population). It would be surprising if the sample values were exactly equal to the population values. The values would be close, but not exact. For example, in a survey investigating the overall grade point average for all of the students enrolled in this course, students would write down their grade point averages and the class average would be calculated. This is the population value. If a sample was randomly selected from the class and the sample average was calculated, the sample value and the population value would be close, but not exactly the same. This difference between the sample value and the population value is known as the sampling error.

In addition to sampling error, there are other issues that may affect the accuracy of NCVS findings. Respondents are asked questions about criminal events that occurred over the past six months. Some victims may not be able to remember all of the crimes that occurred during this time frame, especially if they experience high levels of victimizations. **Series victimization** is defined as six or more similar but separate crimes in which the victim is unable to individually distinguish one crime from another. This can be a problem, as the NCVS interviewer will attempt to get as much detailed information on each incident as possible. In cases where detailed events cannot be recalled, one report is taken for the entire series of crimes. This policy for counting such multiple incidents can underestimate the actual number of crimes that have occurred (Rand & Rennison, 2002).

While the hope is that people readily report their victimizations to the NCVS interviewer, in reality, some individuals do not disclose all of their personal experiences. Incidents of domestic violence may go underreported, since victims may not wish to share the details of such personal crimes. The same may be said of the crime of rape. Even though it may be much less intimidating to disclose details to a NCVS interviewer than to a (oftentimes male) police officer or detective, a victim still has to reveal very personal, intimate details of their lives. Some may choose not to relive the details of such victimizations. For a more detailed discussion of the NCVS, especially as it compares to the FBI UCR, please see Box 1.1.

Box 1.1 Comparing the FBI UCR and the NCVS

The U.S. Department of Justice administers two statistical programs to measure the magnitude, nature, and impact of crime in the Nation: the Uniform Crime Reporting (UCR) Program and the National Crime Victimization Survey (NCVS). Each of these programs produces valuable information about aspects of the Nation's crime problem. Because the UCR and NCVS programs are conducted for different purposes, use different methods, and focus on somewhat different aspects of crime, the information they produce together provides a more comprehensive panorama of the Nation's crime problem than either could produce alone.

Comparing UCR and NCVS

Because the NCVS was designed to complement the UCR program, the two programs share many similarities. As much as their different collection methods permit, the two measure the same subset of serious crimes, defined alike. Both programs cover rape, robbery, aggravated assault, burglary, theft, and motor vehicle theft. Rape, robbery, theft, and motor vehicle theft are defined virtually identically by both the UCR and NCVS. (While rape is defined analogously, the UCR Crime Index measures the crime against women only, and the NCVS measures it against both sexes.) There are also significant differences between the two programs. First, the two programs were created to serve different purposes. The UCR Program's primary objective is to provide a reliable set of criminal justice statistics for law enforcement administration, operation, and management. The NCVS was established to provide previously unavailable information about crime (including crime not reported to police), victims, and offenders.

Second, the two programs measure an overlapping but non-identical set of crimes. The NCVS includes crimes both reported and not reported to law enforcement. The NCVS excludes, but the UCR includes, homicide, arson, commercial crimes, and crimes against children under age 12. The UCR captures crimes reported to law enforcement, but it excludes sexual assaults and simple assaults from the Crime Index.

Third, because of methodology, the NCVS and UCR definitions of some crimes differ. For example, the UCR defines burglary as the unlawful entry or attempted entry of a structure to commit a felony or theft. The NCVS, not wanting to ask victims to ascertain offender motives, defines burglary as the entry or attempted entry of a residence by a person who had no right to be there.

Fourth, for property crimes (burglary, theft and motor vehicle theft), the two programs calculate crime rates using different bases. The UCR rates for these crimes are per-capita (number of crimes per 100,000 persons), whereas the NCVS rates for these crimes are per-household (number of crimes per 1,000 households). Because the number of households may not grow at the same rate each year as the total population, trend data for rates of property crimes measured by the two programs may not be comparable.

In addition, some differences in the data from the two programs may result from sampling variation in the NCVS and from estimating for nonresponse in the UCR. The NCVS estimates are derived from interviewing a sample and are therefore subject to a margin of error. Rigorous statistical methods are used to calculate confidence intervals around all survey estimates. Trend data in NCVS reports are described as genuine only if there is at least a 90% certainty that the measured changes are not the result of sampling variation. The UCR data are based on the actual counts of offenses reported by law enforcement jurisdictions. In some circumstances, UCR data are estimated for nonparticipating jurisdictions or those reporting partial data.

Each program has unique strengths. The UCR provides a measure of the number of crimes reported to law enforcement agencies throughout the country. The UCR's Supplemental Homicide Reports provide the most reliable, timely data on the extent and nature of homicides in the Nation. The NCVS is the primary source of information on the characteristics of criminal victimization and on the number and types of crimes not reported to law enforcement authorities.

By understanding the strengths and limitations of each program, it is possible to use the UCR and NCVS to achieve a greater understanding of crime trends and the nature of crime in the United States. For example, changes in police procedures, shifting attitudes towards crime and police, and other societal changes can affect the extent to which people report and law enforcement agencies record crime. NCVS and UCR data can be used in concert to explore why trends in reported and police-recorded crime may differ.

Apparent discrepancies between statistics from the two programs can usually be accounted for by their definitional and procedural differences or resolved by comparing NCVS sampling variations (confidence intervals) of those crimes said to have been reported to police with UCR statistics.

For most types of crimes measured by both the UCR and NCVS, analysts familiar with the programs can exclude from analysis those aspects of crime not common to both. Resulting long-term trend-lines can be brought into close concordance. The impact of such adjustments is most striking for robbery, burglary, and motor vehicle theft, whose definitions most closely coincide.

With robbery, annual victimization rates based only on NCVS robberies reported to the police are possible. It is also possible to remove from analysis UCR robberies of commercial establishments such as gas stations, convenience stores, and banks. When the resulting NCVS police reported robbery rates are compared to UCR non-commercial robbery rates, the results reveal closely corresponding long-term trends.

Source: U.S. Department of Justice Office of Justice Programs, Bureau of Justice Statistics. The Nation's Two Crime Measures. Retrieved on August 20, 2010 from http://bjs.ojp. usdoj.gov/content/pub/html/ntcm.cfm.

Self Report Surveys

Self-report surveys are a common source of data for studies of criminal behavior. In this type of survey, respondents are asked about their personal involvement in a variety of criminal and deviant acts. Only the imagination and interests of the person who constructed the survey instrument limit the actual questions included in these surveys. People may be asked what crimes they have committed, why they committed them, and what happened to them as a result. Similar to the NCVS, self-report surveys allow a better estimate of the dark figure of crime.

Self-report surveys do have their own limitations. Because the surveys are individualized to meet the specific needs of each researcher and/or project, it is difficult to compare the results of one survey to the results of another. Further, because few people actually commit serious criminal offenses, oftentimes self-report surveys tend to focus on relatively minor crimes or acts of deviance. In order to conduct statistical analyses of the data, a good number of respondents who indicate that they did commit the crime in question is necessary. It is much easier to find a teenager who has skipped school, stayed out past curfew, or consumed alcoholic beverages than it is to find one who has committed a burglary, robbery, or aggravated assault.

The quality of the samples of respondents used in self-report surveys has also been scrutinized. For example, a researcher is interested in adolescent substance abuse and constructs a self-report survey to find out what kinds of drugs kids are taking, how often they are taking them, and why they feel the need to use drugs. What will be the sample? High school students would only represent teens that are still enrolled in school and are in attendance on that particular day. Dropouts, truants, and others who would be absent would not be included in the sample. What about the local juvenile detention center? This sample would only represent kids who have been picked up by the police on various charges of criminal activities.

It can be very difficult to identify a good representative sample of individuals. As a result, many self-report surveys are administered to **convenience samples**—large, but unrepresentative groups of people that may be quickly found in one location. If you have ever completed an attitude or behavioral survey in one of your larger social science classes, you were a part of a convenience sample. When you read the results of a self-report survey, in the back of your mind you might ask yourself who completed the survey? Are the respondents similar to all teens (adults, offenders—whatever)? Since the goal of many surveys is to generalize the results to the larger population, it is very important that the sample is a good representation of the population.

Qualitative Techniques

The last unofficial data source is qualitative techniques. While there are a variety of qualitative techniques out there, two will be discussed: in-depth interviews and participant observation studies.

For the skilled researcher, **in-depth interviews** may provide a wealth of information. The word "skilled" is stressed, since conducting a good interview requires much training and practice. The researcher needs to gain the trust of the respondent, know when to probe and push for more information, and know when to respectfully back off. In-depth interviews may be conducted in a variety of settings—homes, offices, street corners, wherever. Whenever possible, the researcher often records the responses with a tape recorder, in order to preserve the exact words of the respondent. Similar to a self-report survey, the questions posed during an in-depth interview are limited only by the imagination of the person conducting the exchange. Some in-depth interviews are highly structured with specific questions and probes (follow-up questions), while others are loosely constructed with few formal requirements.

The benefit of in-depth interviews is that the direction of the data collection may be modified during the course of the interview. The questions can go anywhere and are often driven by the responses of the person being questioned. In a pre-printed forced response survey, the survey instrument remains just as it was constructed. Hence, in-depth interviews are much more flexible than traditional surveys. In-depth interviews allow the respondent to elaborate, question, go off on (informative) tangents, and often provide answers to questions that the interviewer did not foresee being asked.

In-depth interviews may be conducted as part of a larger qualitative research effort called a **participant observation**. In this type of study, researchers climb down from their ivory towers and immerse themselves in the "real" world. It is one thing to study arrest statistics from the FBI UCR or examine results of self-report surveys on substance abuse, and quite another to spend the evening in a crack house, observing and talking with the houseguests. Participant observations can provide data from an insider's perspective. When properly conducted, the quality of this type of data are unparalleled by any of the other official or unofficial data sources we have discussed so far.

There are different types of participant observation studies that are based on the degree of participation and involvement of the researcher in the chosen site. In some studies, researchers essentially operate undercover. A researcher is simply an observer and individuals in the setting are unaware that the researcher is actually there to collect data. In other types of studies, a researcher makes his or her presence known to those in the site. A third type of participant observation is the case where the researcher is a complete participant—this type of study can be a bit problematic, especially when studying criminal activities!

Unfortunately, qualitative studies do not always get the respect that they deserve. Critics argue that the results are unrepresentative and heavily influenced by the personal perceptions of the researcher. For some, if a study does not feature the use of high-powered statistical tests as a central part of its data analysis, the quality of the study is severely undermined. Thankfully, there are still those who do value the unique perspective that qualitative research can provide.

Summary

A number of terms and concepts were examined that will assist with more in-depth discussions of space, time, and crime presented in later chapters. The basic vocabulary of spatial and temporal analysis has been introduced and the various methods by which criminal justice researchers measure crime and deviance have been explored. Comprehending these basic elements will assist in developing a better understanding of why certain locations seem to be more prone to crime than others, how these areas are identified, and what can be done to reduce the level of crime and deviance in such areas.

Chapter 2

Positivism, Social Ecology, and the Chicago School

Early in the 20th Century, a diverse group of sociologists found themselves at the University of Chicago. The ideas, method of study, and policy recommendations that grew from their work continue to influence the field of criminology today. While the pioneers of the Chicago School were not the first to study the relationship between crime and neighborhood characteristics, the names of a few of these early thinkers, such as Roger Park, Ernest Burgess, Clifford Shaw, and Henry McKay, have become synonymous with the sociological examination of crime and space. In this Chapter, the development of their ideas is traced, the major propositions are presented, some of the critiques of their work are examined, and the continued importance of their theories is discussed.

Setting the Stage: Chicago at the Turn of the 20th Century

In order to better understand the ideas of the early sociologists centered at the University of Chicago, one needs to have a grasp of the historical perspective of the times in which they wrote. The "heyday" of the Chicago School was from 1914–1934 (Martin, Mutchnick, & Austin, 1990), an era of great change, both in the city of Chicago and the United States. First, the history of the city of Chicago will be introduced. As described by Shaw and McKay (1969), the area that became the city of Chicago was originally plotted around 1830. At that time, Chicago was less than a square mile of area. By the time the town of Chicago was originally incorporated a few short years later, the territory of the town limits had grown to about 20 square miles and continued to increase as the population of the town grew. While the eastward growth of the city of Chicago was limited by Lake Michigan, by 1889 the city had grown to 170 square miles.

Table 2.1 Historical Growth of Chicago

| Year | Total Residents | Foreign Born | |
		Number	Percent
1870	298,977	144,557	48.4
1880	503,185	204,859	40.7
1890	1,099,850	450,666	41.0
1900	1,698,575	587,112	34.6
1910	2,185,283	783,428	35.9
1920	2,701,705	808,558	29.9
1930	3,376,438	859,409	25.5
1940	3,396,808	675,147	19.9

Source: Gibson and Lennon (1999).

In 1840, the population of Chicago was approximately 4,500 people. The number of people moving to Chicago to seek employment and a better life began to increase dramatically. In only 10 years, the number of residents grew to just over 25,000. By 1880, the population had multiplied to about 500,000. The growth had only begun. By 1900, Chicago boasted nearly 1.7 million residents. The population expansion of the city of Chicago, based on census data (Gibson & Lennon, 1999), is summarized in Table 2.1.

One of the more dramatic changes in the population composition of the United States as a whole, was caused by the large influx of immigrants around the late 19th and early 20th Century. From 1850–1930, the foreign-born population of the United States increased from 2.2 million to 14.2 million (Gibson & Lennon, 1999). Many of these immigrants settled in the growing northern cities, such as New York, Boston, Detroit, Philadelphia, and, of course, Chicago. There was a shortage of labor during this era and many industrialists actively recruited overseas for cheap labor to work in the factories (Feagin & Feagin, 1993). Table 2.1 summarizes the available data on the number of foreign-born residents in the city of Chicago. In 1870, nearly half of the residents of Chicago were born in other nations. While the proportion of foreign-born residents steadily declined after 1870, the immigrant population in Chicago remained significant, especially during the Chicago School era (1914–1934).

As the population of the city of Chicago grew by leaps and bounds, the city began absorbing a shifting demographic of new arrivals. Prior to 1880, most of the settlers hailed from England, northwestern European nations, and Scandinavia. After 1880, the immigrant population was largely from southern and eastern European nations. Large numbers of African Americans were leaving the Southern states looking for a better life and greater personal freedoms. In addition to the large number of foreign-born residents settling in the city of Chicago, the African American population of the city grew dramatically from 1880–1920 (Gold, 1987).

In the ethnic and racial mix, not all groups were viewed equally. Immigrants from southern and eastern Europe, such as Italians and Poles, were generally viewed as being inherently inferior to those from northern and western Europe (Gordon, 1964). African Americans experienced a great deal of discrimination and hostility, especially when the economy began to downturn (Feagin & Feagin, 1993). Competition between the various racial and ethnic groups was tight in the city of Chicago, not only for good paying jobs, but also for better housing and overall living conditions. Tensions in the city grew, culminating in a serious race riot that broke out in 1919 (Gold, 1987).

The attitude of many native-born Americans and older immigrant groups towards the swelling of the population, with more and more new arrivals from Europe, began to deteriorate. Immigrants, especially those labeled as "inferior," were no longer viewed as welcome additions to U.S. society. A great debate opened among scientists from various disciplines, including geneticists, anthropologists, sociologists, and psychologists as to whether or not certain groups of immigrants were of poor quality racial "stock" and should therefore be restricted from entering the United States (Gold, 1987).

Are Certain Groups Inherently Inferior? The "Feebleminded" Debate

There was a rather ugly era in United States Immigration Policy, and in American society in general, which culminated in the passage of the Immigration Act of 1924. A number of "scientists" were affirming the popular, but racist beliefs, that many social problems that existed in U.S. society, including crime and delinquency, were caused by the moral and intellectual inferiority of certain groups in society. If the growth of these groups were to be reduced, or even eliminated, then crime, delinquency, and other social problems would also be reduced.

Many of these ideas were not new, but seemed to resurface given the large influx of immigrants and the increased competition among the groups for scarce resources. Charles Darwin argued that in the natural evolution of the species, some were better adapted to their current environment than others. Certain individuals were born with "good" traits, while other weaker individuals were born with less desirable traits. Through the process of natural selection, the weaker individuals would eventually die out, and only the strong would survive.

Cesare Lombroso and The Criminal Man

The idea that certain individuals were born biologically and/or mentally inferior was picked up by a number of very popular thinkers in criminology, including Cesare Lombroso (1835–1919) and Henry Goddard (1866–1957). Cesare Lombroso has been described as the father of criminology and his work in the area of criminal anthropology remained very popular in the United States until about 1915 (Bohm, 1997). Lombroso was a physician in the Italian army. During this time, there was a general prejudice, held by many, that people from Southern Italy, including Sicily, were somehow inferior. During an autopsy on a thief who came from Southern Italy, Lombroso discovered what he felt was the key to the problem: The skull of the criminal resembled that of primitive human beings. In effect, the man was not as highly evolved as "normal" human beings (Vold, Bernard, & Snipes, 2002).

Lombroso then set out to develop a list identifiers, which he called stigmata, that could be used to determine whether a person was an evolutionary throwback. Lombroso's list contained several stigmata. Items on the list included ears that were either too big or too small, abnormal teeth, extra fingers or toes, too much hair or wrinkles, and long arms. If a man had 5 or more stigmata present, he was labeled as having a condition known as atavism. In effect, an atavistic man was more ape-like than human.

Lombroso first published his ideas in 1876 in *L'Uomo delinquente (The Criminal Man)*, and his work set off a heated debate, not only among academics, but also among members of the legal and penal communities (Gould, 1981). While many criticized his work, his central idea that the cause of crime was biological in nature remained influential for many years, and was still a very popular theory around the time that the Chicago School sociologists were developing their own ideas about the causes of crime and delinquency.

IQ, Heredity, and Crime: The Thoughts of Henry Goddard

Henry Goddard (1866–1957) focused on the idea that criminals were mentally inferior human beings. In *Feeblemindedness: Its Causes and Consequences* (1914), Goddard argued that criminals were "feebleminded" people who could be identified through the use of an IQ test. Goddard felt that feeblemindedness was genetically based and, through selective breeding, could be eliminated from society. Since all feebleminded people were potential criminals, due to their inferior mental capabilities, Goddard advocated either segregating the feebleminded in institutions and not allowing them to breed or forced sterilization.

Goddard was especially concerned with the arrival of immigrants to the United States, especially those from southern and eastern European countries. Goddard and his followers were able to institute the administration of an IQ test to newly arriving immigrants. This test, which was viewed by many as having the ability to measure innate intelligence, included such culturally-specific questions as the following:

Five hundred is played with:

a) rackets; b) pins; c) cards; or d) dice

Christe Matthewson is famous as a:

a) writer; b) artist; c) baseball player; d) comedian (quoted from Curran & Renzetti, 1994, p. 98)

Newly arriving immigrants who did not know that five hundred was played with cards or that Christe Matthewson was a famous baseball player would be identified as feebleminded, potential criminals, and innately inferior. Goddard advocated that individuals who did not score well on the IQ test should be barred from entry into the United States.

While in hindsight Goddard's ideas may appear to be almost comical, Goddard was able to "scientifically" validate what many Americans wanted to believe: Certain groups of individuals that would pollute the moral fiber of the country should not be allowed to enter. Goddard's recommendations factored heavily in the development of the Immigration Act of 1924. This Act established quotas limiting the number of people from certain regions from entering the United States. Groups that had arrived prior to 1880 and had demonstrated that they could become "good Americans," such as those from Great Britain, Germany, and Scandinavia, were given large quotas. Quotas for groups from southern and eastern European countries were very small in comparison (Gordon, 1964). For example, in 1929 the annual quota for Great Britain was 65,721 and for Germany it was 25,957. In comparison, the annual quota for Italians was only 5,802 (Feagin & Feagin, 1993).

Many criminologists ultimately dismissed Goddard's assertions that criminals were born feebleminded. However, his ideas remained popular until the 1930s (Bohm, 1997). It is important to recognize that the racist, genetically based theories, were quite influential among those who studied crime and delinquency at the turn of the 20th Century. The theories of the Chicago School represented a sharp break with the popular thinking of the time and added even more fuel to the fire in the debates concerning immigration in the United States (Gold, 1987). Instead of looking at the characteristics of the individual as the source of crime and other social problems, the Chicago School thinkers turned to external factors, such as neighborhood characteristics.

Enter the Chicago School

The first sociology program in the United States was established in 1892 at the University of Chicago (Curran & Renzetti, 2001). The early faculty members were most likely shocked by the hustle and bustle of a booming metropolis. Many of the early sociologists had led rather sheltered lives, growing up in small rural communities. Some of their fathers had been ministers, and others were actually ministers themselves (Greek, 1992). Imagine the excitement that these men must have felt as they walked the city streets of downtown Chicago. To say that these early thinkers were immersed in a diverse, rapidly changing society would be an understatement, given the demographics of the newly arriving residents and the overwhelming rate of growth in the city. The early faculty members were not tied to a single theoretical perspective or school of thought. Instead, they were willing to draw ideas from a number of different disciplines and theorists. Some of the ideas they incorporated related to human interaction, while others were based on the changing nature of plant and animal life. One of the early thinkers who had a great influence on the theoretical development of the Chicago School was Emile Durkheim, who is credited with being the father of modern sociology.

The Sociology of Emile Durkheim (1858–1917): Societal Growth and Anomie

Just as the theories developed by members of the Chicago School were affected by great changes in the city, the French Revolution of 1789 had an impact on Durkheim's ideas. Nineteenth century French society had undergone very rapid change, both politically and economically. The Industrial Revolution was transforming the way of life that had been in place for centuries. Society was becoming more and more complex. The norms, or shared expectations for behavior, that governed the way things had always been no longer applied in this new era, and new norms had yet to be developed.

Durkheim's ideas were centered on the development and evolution of societies. He used the term mechanical societies to refer to small, relatively isolated groups of people who are best described as homogeneous in nature. There is very little division of labor among the various members of the group. All share the same religion, values, and beliefs. Durkheim described the members of mechanical societies as sharing the same collective conscience, or in his words the "totality of social likenesses" (Durkheim 1965/1893, p. 80). By sharing the same collective conscience, the members have the same idea of what is "right" and what is "wrong." The collective conscience holds members of a society together and serves as a control on behavior. A violation of the norms or rules of a mechanical society is seen as a personal insult to the collective identity of the group. When a crime or act of deviance occurs, the punishments are very harsh.

On a continuum with mechanical societies at one end of the spectrum, **organic societies** would be at the other extreme. Organic societies are marked by an extreme division of labor—people do not share a common identity with their neighbors. Organic societies are generally large, modern, and technologically advanced. Instead of being tied together by a shared collective conscience, the glue that holds the society together is based on the extreme level of interdependence among the members of its society. Essentially, people come to depend on each other because of the diversity of the society. The law in organic societies is needed to regulate all of the various components of the society and enforce interactions or contracts among its members.

Durkheim was concerned with how societies move from mechanical to organic societies. As new members arrive to mechanical societies and the cluster of individuals becomes more diverse, the common identity of the group begins to erode. This can be very problematic, especially if the growth of the society is very rapid. The society may not be able to respond quickly enough to the changes in order to regulate the interactions of the members (Vold et al., 2002). Durkheim used the term **anomie** to describe this condition, where the behaviors of the members may not be adequately controlled. For Durkheim, anomie was the end result of rapid industrialization, urbanization, and growth of the population (Curran & Renzetti, 2001). He believed societies experiencing high levels of anomie may experience adverse conditions such as heightened levels of crime, disorder, suicide, and other social problems.

It is easy to see how Durkheim's analysis of how societies grow and change could be applied to the city of Chicago. Large numbers of diverse people from all over the United States, as well as European nations, were settling in the city on a daily basis. These individuals brought their own religion, customs, norms, and belief systems with them to their new world. Recently arriving immigrants would also bring their language. Under these conditions, a person would not share a common identity with his or her neighbor, and even carrying on a conversation was difficult. There would be no collective conscience or shared idea of right and wrong to control people's behavior.

The Invasion, Dominance, and Succession of Robert Ezra Park (1864–1944)

The Chicago School members drew heavily on the ideas of Durkheim, but also added an extra twist: the principles of **social ecology**. Social ecology examines how plant and animal life forms relate to each other in their natural habitat. The Chicago School member who is usually credited with initially integrating the ideas of social ecology, with the study of the city, is Robert Ezra Park.

Robert Park was a newspaper reporter for 25 years prior to beginning his career as a university professor. During his years as a journalist, Park focused on urban problems, especially issues related to housing. Park used the tools of a journalist—personal observations, in-depth interviews, and an immersion in the area being studied—to chronicle the conditions in the city (Taylor, Walton, & Young, 1973). For a while, Park lived in New York City. While working for the *New York Journal*, he was assigned as a police beat reporter. During this time, Park investigated many aspects of urban life and even managed to infiltrate opium dens (Martin et al., 1990). As a result of his experiences, Park brought a rather unique reality-based perspective to the discipline of sociology.

Today, there are two terms commonly used to describe Park's approach to the analysis of the city: positivism and functionalism. As a Positivist, Park's work is premised on a few assumptions. First, Positivists assume that human behavior is not a matter of free choice. Instead, a Positivist believes that our actions are, at least to some extent, determined by influences that are beyond our immediate control. Some Positivists adopt a "hard-core" stance on this assumption, maintaining that there is no free will at all—we have no choices and our behaviors are completely determined by these influences. Other Positivists lean toward what Robert Bohm (1997, p. 27) describes as "soft determinism." That is, human beings do have a restricted ability to make choices, but for some people, the number of choices may be quite limited.

The second assumption is related to the first. Using the scientific method, Positivists look for behavioral influences either within the constitutional make-up of the person (such as chemical imbalances in the brain or psychological problems) or external to the individual (such as the quality of the home life or other environmental influences). Therefore, a Positivist assumes that there are identifiable differences between criminals and non-criminals, and these differences cause some people to be criminals and others to be non-criminals. As a Positivist, Robert Park was looking for clearly identifiable factors that were the root causes of crime and other social problems.

As a Functionalist, Park viewed the city as a kind of social organism. When taken together, the various business districts and neighborhoods that make up

So what is a functionalist?

a city begin to take on the character of a living, breathing organism. Park began to integrate the principles of ecology, which focuses on the interrelationships and interdependencies of plants and animals in their natural environment, with his analysis of the city.

The Development of Natural Areas

If you will, picture a forest. Within this natural habitat, various plants and animals struggle to survive. Every organism is driven by the Darwinian, evolutionary goal to maximize reproduction of its own species. The plants and animals form symbiotic, cooperative relationships with each other in order to better their chances for life. Competition also exists in this system, as not all areas within the forest are equally beneficial to survival (Gold, 1987).

Park applied a forest model to competition and cooperation between various groups in the city. Within the city, Park was able to identify a number of "natural areas," or clusters that were somehow different or set off from the larger organism. These natural areas could be based on the race or ethnicity of those residing within the cluster. For example, in most major U.S. cities, there are areas that are dominated by a different culture, often called China Town, Greek Town, or Little Italy. Park would have described these neighborhoods as natural areas. Some clusters may form based on the income level of the residents, while other natural areas may be based on the concentration of factories or other businesses. Similar to how plants and animals compete in their natural environment, humans residing within these natural areas struggle to survive.

Just as areas of the forest are not all equally conducive to survival, some regions within the city are more desirable to live in than others. Less powerful groups within the racial and ethnic mix of the city are forced to make do with life in the less desirable areas, urban slums, and ghettos (Shaw & McKay, 1969). To better its chances for survival, a group of people "stuck" in a poorer area may seek out a better territory in which to live. To explain this phenomenon, Park applied the ecological concept of invasion, dominance, and succession. Irish people in one neighborhood may begin to invade another natural area dominated by Germans, for example. The Irish may come to dominate this natural area. In time, the Irish may lose control of the natural area as another group, such as the Italians, invades the area. If the Irish were able, then they would move on to invade another even more desirable neighborhood. If the Irish did not have the resources or the power to invade a better neighborhood, then they may be forced to live in a less desirable area. Business and industry, as well as groups of people, can be involved in the pattern of invasion, dominance, and succession as they try to expand and seek out a habitat that is better suited for survival.

Burgess's Contributions: Life in the Zones

Park had an office mate named Ernest Burgess. Park and Burgess worked very closely together on a number of projects, including the influential book *Introduction to the Science of Sociology* (1921) that was fondly dubbed the "Green Bible" by students at the University of Chicago (Martin et al., 1990). Burgess combined Park's ideas concerning invasion, dominance, and succession with a concentric model of city growth and change.

Burgess recognized that the city of Chicago appeared to expand and grow in a series of concentric circles that moved outward from the central business district. Each circle or Zone had distinct characteristics that set it off from the other zones (Burgess, 1925). Zone I, which was the innermost circle, was the central business district of the city (Figure 2.1). In Chicago, this area was (and still is) known as the Loop. Few people actually lived in Zone I, as factories and other businesses dominate the area.

Moving outward, Zone II was known as the Zone in Transition. Generally speaking, Zone II was the least desirable area to live in the city. Ever expanding businesses and factories attempted to invade and dominate Zone II from the Loop. Many real estate speculators had purchased housing units and other properties in the area, and as a result, most people living in the Zone in Transition were renters (Bursik & Grasmick, 1993). Landlords recognized that the value of their property was not in the housing or rental units that was on the property, but in the commercial value of the land itself (Vold et al., 2002). Factories and businesses had an eye toward buying the property, only to tear down the houses and apartment units in order to meet the needs of their expanding businesses. As a result, landlords did not invest a great deal of money into the care and maintenance of the housing units. Properties deteriorated to the point where they were no longer inhabitable. As a result, a family may have resided in a run-down apartment building surrounded by boarded up houses, dilapidated apartment buildings, vacant overgrown lots, and invading factories and businesses popping up around their home. Only the poorest, least powerful people resided in the Zone in Transition.

As one moved further out into Zone III, housing conditions generally improved. Burgess called this area the Zone of Workingmen's Homes. Second and third generation immigrants and other working class people who had the resources to move out of the Zone in Transition dominated the area. Living con-

Figure 2.1

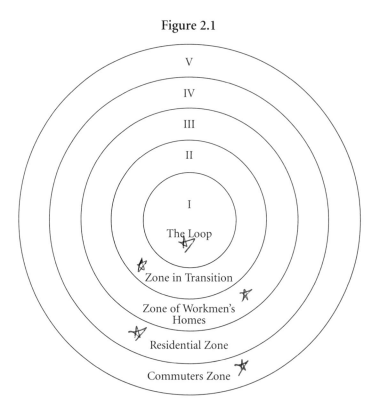

ditions were better still in Zone IV, or the Residential Zone. Single-family homes and better quality apartments marked this zone. Finally, Zone V, or the Commuter Zone, was made up of the suburban area and surrounding satellite cities, and was inhabited solidly by members of the middle and upper classes. Burgess noted that as the city continued to grow and expand in an outward manner, the inner zones would begin to invade, dominate, and succeed into the neighboring zone (Vold et al., 2002).

Clifford Shaw and Henry McKay: Delinquency and Place

The ideas of Robert Park and Ernest Burgess impacted a number of scholars studying and working at the University of Chicago. Few works, however, have had greater impact than the research efforts of Clifford Shaw and Henry McKay. Described as "one of the most fundamental sociological approaches to the study of crime and delinquency" (Sampson & Groves, 1989, p. 774),

Shaw and McKay's work represents a culmination of the foundations set by Park, Burgess, and other sociologists interested in the study of crime and place.

Beginning in 1924, a graduate student of Burgess's by the name of Clifford R. Shaw was interested in the geographic distribution of juvenile delinquency and other social problems. Shaw, a former probation officer, began to locate the residences of delinquent boys. A few years later, Henry D. McKay, who had just joined the Illinois Institute of Juvenile Research, worked with Shaw on this tedious, almost overwhelming task (Gold, 1987). Without the use of computers or sophisticated software, the researchers individually plotted the home addresses of male juvenile offenders who had been brought before the Juvenile Court in Cook County. Working with several different waves of data that had been collected over a period spanning four decades, Shaw and McKay manually located the home addresses of nearly 25,000 youths!

Shaw and McKay set out to answer a number of key questions in their influential book *Juvenile Delinquency in Urban Areas* (1942/1969). These questions included the following:

- How are the rates of delinquents in particular areas affected over a period of time by successive changes in the nativity and nationality composition of the population?
- To what extent are the observed differences in the rates of delinquents between children of foreign and native parentage due to a differential geographic distribution of these two groups in the city?
- Under what economic and social conditions does crime develop as a social tradition and become embodied in a system of criminal values? (Shaw & McKay, 1969, p. 4).

The questions that Shaw and McKay set out to answer were a sharp break from the popular thinking of the times. Recall that there was a great deal of political and scientific debate concerning whether or not many of the newly arriving immigrants were of inferior stock and ultimately potential criminals. Shaw and McKay did not focus on genetic causes of crime, delinquency, and other social problems, but instead looked at social and environmental influences on human behavior. Essentially, Shaw and McKay viewed juvenile delinquents not as evolutionary throwbacks or inherently inferior beings, but as "normal" kids whose behavior was somehow tied to the environment in which they lived.

The Data: Official Delinquency Reports

In order to answer their research questions, the homes of the juvenile delinquents had to be identified. For the purposes of their study, Shaw and McKay defined a "juvenile delinquent" as a youth under the age of 17 who was brought before the Cook County Juvenile Court—or other courts having jurisdiction over the case—on a petition of delinquency or whose case was dealt with by an officer of the law without the need of a court appearance. Shaw and McKay noted that a better term for this group would be "alleged delinquents," as in many cases the charges against the youth were not sustained. It should be noted that Shaw and McKay studied only male juvenile delinquents. Shaw and McKay looked at the geographic distribution of three different waves of data from the Juvenile Court: 8,056 juveniles from 1900–1906; 8,141 juveniles from 1917–1923; and 8,411 juveniles from 1927–1933.

In addition to the juvenile court referral data, Shaw and McKay also included two other sources of information in their analysis: the home addresses of juvenile delinquents who had been committed to correctional institutions by the Juvenile Court of Cook County and the home addresses of alleged delinquent boys who had been dealt with by a police probation officer. The time span for the data concerning the number of residential commitments mirrored the 3 waves for the Juvenile Court referrals. With respect to the allegedly delinquent boys who had been dealt with by a juvenile probation officer, only 3 years of data were used: 1926, 1927, and 1931. While this may not sound like a great deal of information when compared to the other data sources Shaw and McKay used, in each of the 3 years the police probation officers saw nearly 10,000 boys. In the city of Chicago, any youth who was arrested, or somehow came to the attention of the police, was automatically referred to a juvenile probation officer for screening. Based on the evaluation made by the probation officer, the vast majority of the cases (85%) were disposed of without any further referral to the juvenile court.

Spot, Rate, and Zone Map Construction

Shaw and McKay then set out to create a number of maps based on their various data sources. A **spot map** was based on the place of residence for the alleged juvenile delinquents. In a spot map, the homes of the alleged juvenile delinquents were identified using a dot. The information in these spot maps was then converted into rate maps. In order to create the **rate maps**, Shaw and McKay broke the city of Chicago down into 140 different areas, approximately one square mile in size. Using census data, Shaw and McKay calculated the number of alleged delinquents, based on the number of 10–16 year old males in the square mile area, so that a rate of x number of delinquents (for example, 5.8) per 100 boys residing in the area was reported. Finally, Shaw and McKay plotted a series of **zone maps** based on their various data sources. In a

Table 2.2 Zone Rates for Court Referrals, Juvenile Commitments, and Police Contacts Data Source

Data Source	Zone I	Zone II	Zone III	Zone IV	Zone V
Court Referrals					
1900–1906	16.3	9.1	6.2	4.4	5.6
1917–1923	10.3	7.3	4.4	3.3	3
1927–1933	9.8	6.7	4.5	2.5	1.8
Committed Youths					
1900–1906	7	3.6	2.4	1.6	2.1
1917–1923	3.5	2.5	1.4	0.9	0.9
1927–1933	3.4	2.2	1.4	0.6	0.4
Police Contacts					
1926 series	10.9	8.2	5	2	2.2
1927 series	9.9	7.8	4.3	2.4	2.2
1931 series	9.6	7.8	5.3	3.9	3.2

Adapted from Shaw and McKay (1969).

zone map, the number of alleged male juvenile delinquents was converted to a rate based on the juvenile population residing in each of Burgess's five zones. Separate spot, rate, and zone maps were created for each of the various types of data (police contacts, juvenile court referrals, and commitments) and for each time period of data.

The Distribution of Delinquency and Other Social Conditions by Zones

An analysis of the various map types revealed that juvenile delinquency was not evenly distributed throughout the city of Chicago. Shaw and McKay found a regular decrease in the level of juvenile delinquency as one moved outward from the center of the city. This pattern was consistent for all types of data examined — the number of court referrals, number of juvenile commitments, or police contacts — or even the time period in which the data was collected. A compilation of the zone rates reported by Shaw and McKay is presented in Table 2.2.

As can be seen, the zones with the highest rates of delinquency were Zone I, or the Loop, and Zone II, the Zone in Transition. In some cases, the difference between the rates for the inner zones and the outer zones was quite dramatic. For example, in 1926, the zone rate for police contacts in the Loop was 10.9. This means that for every 100 male youths aged 10–16, nearly 11 juveniles had a police contact. In the Residential Zone (Zone IV) or the Commuter Zone (Zone V), the rate of juvenile-police contacts dropped to around two contacts per 100 youths.

Shaw and McKay set out to explain this pattern. Shaw and McKay viewed juvenile delinquency as indicative of some degree of pathology or "sickness" within a neighborhood. Of course, juvenile delinquency and crime are not the only problematic conditions a neighborhood may experience. Neighborhoods with high levels of unemployment, sickness, death, and poverty would be considered by most to possess less desirable living conditions. Shaw and McKay examined relationships (or correlations) between the distributions of juvenile delinquency and other social problems, including infant mortality, tuberculosis, and mental disorders within each of the five zones.

Additionally, Shaw and McKay examined other neighborhood characteristics that existed in the various zones, such as the economic conditions, community stability, and racial or ethnic composition. Economic conditions were measured by the percentage of families receiving welfare enhancements and the median rent paid per month. The level of neighborhood stability was measured by the percentage of homeowners living in a particular zone and the population increase or decrease from 1920–1930. Also, Shaw and McKay included a number of measures of the racial or ethnic composition in a zone, including the percentage of foreign-born and African American heads of household. The neighborhood characteristics by zone, as well as the delinquency measures for comparable time periods, are presented in Table 2.3.

As can be seen in Table 2.3, living conditions generally improved as one moved outward from the center of the city of Chicago. The infant mortality rate, which was based on the number of infant deaths per 1,000 live births, was over twice as high in the Zone I Loop as compared to the Zone V Commuter Zone. The tuberculosis rate was calculated based on the average number of cases reported annually from 1931–1937. There was a dramatic decrease in the rate as one moved from the inner city zones to the suburban areas. A similar pattern was found with respect to the mental disorder rate, as fewer individuals in the outer zones were admitted to state and private hospitals for insanity and other mental disorders.

Economic Conditions and Population Shifts

The general economic conditions in the outer zones were much better than those found in the inner city areas. If one compared the living conditions in Zone II to Zone V, there were nearly four times as many families receiving welfare in the inner city than in the outer zone. Further, the median rental amount

Table 2.3 Neighborhood Characteristics by
Zone Neighborhood Characteristic

Neighborhood Characteristic	Zone I	Zone II	Zone III	Zone IV	Zone V
Infant Mortality Rate (1928–1933)	86.7	67.5	54.7	45.9	41.3
Tuberculosis Rate (1931–1937)	33.5	25	18.4	12.5	9.2
Mental Disorder Rate (1922–1934)	32	18.8	13.2	10.1	8.4
Percentage of Families on Welfare Relief (1934)	27.9	24	14.8	8.6	5.9
Median Monthly Rent (1930)	$38.08	$36.51	$53.08	$65.38	$73.51
Percentage of Home Owners (1930)	12.8	21.8	26.2	32.8	47.2
Percentage of Foreign-Born and African American Family Heads (1934)	62.3	64.9	55.9	40.4	39.4
Percent Population Increase or Decrease (1920–1930)	-21.3	-9.3	12.3	42.9	140.8
Delinquency Measures Court Referrals (1927–1933)	9.8	6.7	4.5	2.5	1.8
Committed Youths (1927–1933)	3.4	2.2	1.4	0.6	0.4

Adapted from Shaw and McKay (1969).

was much lower in the inner zones. It would cost a family nearly half as much to live in the Zone in Transition than it would to live in the Commuter Zone.

With respect to neighborhood stability, homeownership was much higher in the outer zones than in the inner city zones. It should not be inferred that people who rent are the cause of criminal activity. Most people will rent a home or apartment at some point in their lives. However, if a person is renting their home, their living arrangement is by definition temporary in nature. Generally speaking, renters do not share the same stake in the community as homeowners do. Renters come and go at the end of their lease, while homeowners tend to reside in neighborhoods for a longer period of time and therefore, tend to identify with their community to a greater extent. Homeowners are more likely to get involved in their local community institutions, such as churches, schools, and various local clubs and organizations, than are renters.

Neighborhoods with high numbers of rental units tend to be less stable and so-cially organized than areas with fewer rental units.

Shaw and McKay also found that the population in the inner city zones was decreasing. In Zone I, there was a 21% decrease while the Zone in Transition experienced a 9% population decline. In contrast, the outer zones were grow-ing, in some cases dramatically so. Shaw and McKay noted that business and industry were engaging in the pattern of invasion, dominance and succession in the innermost zones. Not only were the numbers of available housing units reduced by the expanding businesses, but also as commercial development ex-panded into these inner zones the number of condemned buildings increased. The invasion of business and industry into these residential areas contributed to the instability and lack of social cohesion in the inner most zones.

Finally, Shaw and McKay found that the percentage of African American and foreign-born heads of households was much higher in the inner zones than in the outer zones. As can be seen in Table 2.3, the inner zones were also associated with the highest rates of alleged juvenile delinquency. Given the era in which Shaw and McKay were writing, it would have been very easy for them to use this finding to support the popular racist ideas of their times. Shaw and McKay could have argued that the higher rate of delinquency in the inner zones was due to the fact that these areas were populated by inherently inferior be-ings. However, Shaw and McKay broke with the thinking of the times, instead focusing on the characteristics of the neighborhoods and not the groups that inhabited them.

Arguably, the most important finding reported by Shaw and McKay was re-lated to the fact that even though the types of immigrant groups residing in the inner city areas had changed dramatically over the years, the delinquency rate remained high. The ethnicity within the inner zones had experienced almost a complete turnover as different groups went through the pattern of invasion, dominance, and succession. It did not matter which racial or ethnic groups resided in the inner zones—delinquency and other social problems remained high. Recall that the popular thinking of the times held that certain groups, such as the Italians, were morally inferior and should be barred from entering the country. What Shaw and McKay were able to demonstrate was that a boy's in-volvement in delinquency did not depend on *who* the boy was (or which racial or ethnic group he belonged to) but *where* he lived in the city. In effect, no group was found to be inherently more criminogenic than another.

Among the Italians and Poles, for example, Shaw and McKay reported a wide range of delinquency rates that was similar to the range found among native whites. Among Italians, Shaw and McKay found that the rate of juve-nile court referrals ranged from 0.89 to 11.76 while the rate for native whites was 0.48 to 14.94. The delinquency rate among Italians youths residing in the outer zones was low. If, in fact, the Italian youths were more likely to become juvenile delinquents than their native white peers due to some sort of in-born deficiency, one would not have found such a pattern. Instead of focusing on biology, Shaw and McKay looked to the characteristics of the community as a contributing factor to the delinquency rate of boys. As stated by Shaw and McKay (1969):

> While it is apparent from these data that the foreign born and the Negroes are concentrated in the areas of high rates of delinquents, the meaning of this association is not easily determined … Clearly, one must beware of attaching causal significance to race or nativity. For, in the present social and economic system, it is the Negroes and the foreign born, or at least the newest immigrants, who have the least access to the necessities of life and who are therefore least prepared for the competitive struggle. It is they who are forced to live in the worst slum areas and who are least able to organize against the effects of such living (p. 154–155).

So, What Is Happening in the Inner Zones?

Once Shaw and McKay had determined that juvenile delinquency and other social problems were related more to geography than to biology, they tried to determine how life was different for people living in the inner zones as compared to those residing in the outer zones. Why had delinquency become a popular lifestyle for many of the boys living within these inner zones? To answer this question, Shaw and McKay again demonstrated their willingness to draw on a divergent set of theoretical perspectives.

Shaw and McKay theorized that in the outer zones, residents had adopted a uniform set of conventional norms and values, especially with respect to how children were raised and the importance of respecting the rule of law. In Durkheim's terms, people in the outer zones shared a sort of collective conscience. In the outer zones, a common sense of what is acceptable behavior and what is not is consistently presented to children. Adults serve as role models for law-abiding behavior and the children are immersed in conventional activities (such as school and church programs) where this same message is provided. This is not to say, however, that criminals do not live within the outer zones. While crime and delinquency do exist, children are not constantly bombarded with peers or adult role models that support a competing set of values. Living according to the conventional, collective conscience is seen as the dominant, desirable way of life by children being raised in the outer zones.

Shaw and McKay felt that life in the innermost zones was quite different. Instead of being presented with consistent messages supporting a conventional moral order, children were instead immersed in a society marked by extreme diversity. While some children were presented with messages that were consistent with the dominant values of society, other children were exposed to messages that stood in stark contrast to what are commonly referred to as "middle class values." Instead of being raised to think that success was achieved through hard work, honesty, and delayed gratification, children in the inner zones may have grown up to believe that lying, stealing, and seeking pathways to easy money was the only way of getting ahead.

As such, the inner zones also had higher concentrations of adult criminals. Children growing up in the inner zones learned to emulate the behaviors and values of the adult criminals. Shaw and McKay noted that these deviant role models existed not only in the neighborhood, but also within the immediate families of some of the children. In such areas, criminal and/or delinquent subcultures could develop and thrive. Gangs of juvenile delinquents were found to be common within the inner zones, each with their own distinct and often deviant expectations for behavior.

Social Disorganization and Juvenile Delinquency

Oftentimes, the term social disorganization is used in conjunction with the work of Shaw and McKay and the other Chicago School theorists. According to Sampson and Groves (1989, p. 777), social disorganization may be defined as the "inability of a community structure to realize the common values of its residents and maintain effective social controls." The inner zones were marked by a high level of social disorganization. There was little residential stability in the inner city zones. Renters came and went within the neighborhoods. New immigrant groups and Southern blacks arrived on a daily basis and, since they tended to be poor and relatively powerless, ultimately settled in the cheaper inner zones. As new people came into the neighborhood, the stabilizing ties that had been established prior to their arrival were destroyed. Children did not identify with a single over-arching conventional order. Instead, the high degree of neighborhood diversity and heterogeneity led to the growth and development of competing moral orders. The high level of population turnover and community heterogeneity hindered the ability of the family and other primary groups to control the behavior of the children and local residents (Bursik & Grasmick, 1993). As argued by Sampson (1995), one of the major problems associated with socially disorganized areas is the inability to control the behavior of teenage peer groups, especially gangs.

In this type of socially disorganized environment, norms and values that support criminal and delinquent behaviors develop. Left unchecked, these alternative norms and values may come to support a subculture of delinquency. As the local residents came and went, the subcultural values remained in the neighborhoods and were passed along to the new residents in a process called cultural transmission (Eistadter & Henry, 1995; Kornhauser, 1978). Whatever social organization existed in these areas had the tendency to be supportive of delinquent and criminal norms and values (Gold, 1987).

Critiques of Social Disorganization Theory

A number of critiques have been raised against Shaw and McKay's work. Arguably, the most serious charge has been leveled against the data sources that were used to build their theory. Data based on court referrals, police contacts, and juvenile commitments to residential institutions are often called official records. In order for a boy to make his way into the spot maps of Shaw and McKay, his alleged misconduct had to be "officially" identified by the police or other agent of the criminal justice system. A popular theory in criminology called labeling theory argues that less powerful people in society, such as the poor and members of racial and ethnic minority groups, are more likely to be apprehended by the police and subsequently processed through the criminal justice system (Becker, 1963). Because of the seriousness of this particular critique (as well as the continued reliance upon official records as a source of data both in research and in practical law enforcement applications) more time will be spent discussing this assessment in the following example.

The Saints and the Roughnecks: A Lesson in Labeling

Noted critical sociologist William Chambliss used labeling theory in his classic study of the Saints and the Roughnecks, two groups of delinquent boys who attended the same high school. The Saints were a popular group of white, upper-middle-class youths. All were active in school activities and all but one of the seven boys eventually went on to college. In contrast, the Roughnecks were a group of lower class white boys who were not as well polished as the Saints. Their clothes were not as nice as the Saints' apparel, and their mannerisms were not as polite and deferential. Despite the fact that the Saints committed more acts of delinquency than the Roughnecks, not one of the Saints was ever arrested or taken to the precinct house during the two years that Chambliss observed them. While the delinquent acts of the upper middle class Saints were viewed as "good kids just sowing some wild oats," the delinquency of the Roughnecks was perceived as much more serious. The Roughnecks were viewed as bad kids headed for nothing but trouble. The police targeted the Roughnecks for sporadic harassment and arrested the boys if given any hint that they had been involved in a delinquent act. As a result, each of the members was arrested at least once during the period that Chambliss was studying the boys, and a few of them accumulated a number of arrests. Several had spent a night or two in jail and two of the six Roughnecks were sentenced to a residential commitment in a boys' home for their deviant acts.

If one relied solely upon the use of official data, such as the number of arrests, police contacts, or juvenile commitments, one would conclude that the Roughnecks were much more delinquent than the Saints. This was simply not the case. Chambliss discussed the impact of the social class structure on the behavior and bias of the police and the community. More powerful individuals in our society hold control of our legal institutions. When an upper class boy was delinquent, his parents would be more likely to dismiss the act as a momentary lapse in judgment and berate the police for arresting their son. In effect, upper class parents would not accept the law's definition of their son's behavior as delinquent or problematic. As a result, officers would be less likely to arrest or officially process a youth from an upper socioeconomic class home.

In contrast, when a lower class boy was arrested, an officer would be met with either a cooperative parent or a parent who was indifferent to the actions of the police. The authority of the police would not be challenged in such incidents, and the officers would then be more likely to make arrests in the future. As phrased by Chambliss (1996):

> Selective perception and labeling—finding, processing and punishing some kinds of criminality and not others—means that visible, poor, non-mobile, out-spoken, undiplomatic "tough" kids will be noticed, whether their actions are seriously delinquent or not. Other kids, who have established a reputation for being bright (even though underachieving), disciplined and involved in respectable activities, who are mobile and monied, will be invisible when they deviate from sanctioned activities. They'll sow their wild oats—perhaps even wider and thicker than their lower-class cohorts—but they won't be noticed (p. 54).

Essentially, what Chambliss and others found is that lower class youths are more likely to be arrested and officially processed through the criminal justice system than youths from middle and upper class homes. This means that as Shaw and McKay were looking at their spot maps of where the alleged juvenile delinquents lived, they pondered why so many boys from poorer areas were more likely to be delinquent than boys who lived in the more affluent outer zones. Critics have argued that their entire theory was based on a biased data set. Boys in the outer zone may have been committing just as many delinquent acts, but their actions never showed up in the official statistics used by Shaw and McKay.

As described in Chapter 1, there are alternative means of gathering data on the level of crime, including self-report surveys. It has been argued that official data are more reflective of the behavior of the police and the criminal justice system than the behavior of the person apprehended. Self-reports were designed to gather information concerning the behavior of the individual actor and not the behavior of the police. In using self-report data, some researchers have argued that there are no differences in the delinquent involvement of lower and middle and upper class youths (see, for example, Tittle, Villemez, & Smith, 1978) while others would disagree (Elliott & Huizinga, 1983).

A thorough discussion of the debate centering on the accuracy of self-report versus official data is beyond the scope of this text. However, it should be mentioned that there is some debate over whether or not the use of official records provides a "true" measure of the level of criminal activity in a community. This is especially important in light of the fact that the vast majority of research studies exploring the social ecology of crime continue to use official data, such as police reports and the Uniform Crime Reports put out by the FBI, in their analyses (Byrne & Sampson, 1986). Certainly, Shaw and McKay are not the only theorists who are "guilty" of using official data sources.

Other Critiques of Social Disorganization

A second critique of social disorganization theory that has commonly been raised concerns the **ecological fallacy**. Maxfield and Babbie (2011) define the ecological fallacy as "erroneously drawing conclusions about individuals based solely on the observation of groups" (p. 449). In their analysis, Shaw and McKay noted that delinquency was highest in the inner zones of the city. Based on that observation, one cannot assume that an individual young boy growing up in Zone II would then be a delinquent. Just because a higher level of delinquency was found in Zone II does not automatically imply that an individual growing up in this area would be delinquent. One cannot make individual predictions based on group level data. Because of the lack of ability to predict the behavior of individuals, it has been argued that the social disorganization theory is relatively weak and its usefulness has been questioned (Bohm, 1997; Einstadter & Henry, 1995).

A third critique that has been raised asserts that the theory is **tautological** in nature. If a theory is tautological, it suffers from circular reasoning. As noted by Akers and Sellers (2009), this problem has arisen when researchers have tested social disorganization theory in other settings. In order to test Shaw and McKay's theory, the researchers must identify an area as socially disorganized. Oftentimes, an area is defined as "socially disorganized" because of its high level of crime and delinquency. Why is crime high in this area? Crime is high because the area is socially disorganized. For a more complete discussion of some of the problems associated with social disorganization theory, see Bursik (1988).

The Legacy of The Chicago School

Despite the critiques of their ideas, the legacy of Shaw, McKay, and the Chicago School continues on. Described by Vold et al. (2002) as a "gold mine that continues to enrich criminology today" (p. 133), the ecological approach has experienced a great resurgence in interest and influence. The popularity and influence of social ecology is not confined to academic debates concerning the effectiveness of the theory. As presented in Chapter 4, a number of practical policy suggestions and programs have developed based on the theories of the Chicago School.

Crime and Community-Level Factors

Before leaving our discussion of social ecology, we will briefly examine some of the contemporary applications and empirical tests of the Chicago School's principles. Most notable in the advancement of social ecology has been Robert J. Sampson and his colleagues (see, for example, Byrne & Sampson, 1986; Sampson, 1995; Sampson & Groves, 1989; Sampson, Morenoff, & Gannon-Rowley, 2002; Sampson, Morenoff, & Raudensush, 2005; Sampson & Raudenbush, 1999; 2004; Sampson, Raudenbush, & Earls, 1997). As noted by Sampson, et al. (2002), over the past 20 years or so there has been a virtual explosion of interest in neighborhood-based research, with nearly 100 papers per year published on the topic.

In the essay "The Community," Sampson (1995) summarized the research that has explored variations in crime rates across communities. Shaw and McKay noted three factors that ultimately led to the deterioration of social organization in a community: low economic status, ethnic heterogeneity, and residential instability. Juvenile delinquency was found to be highest in the poorest areas that also had higher levels of ethnic and racial diversity and residential turnover. As noted by Sampson, contemporary researchers have explored these issues in depth, and a number of other community factors, such as family structure and the level of housing and population density, have been added to the mix.

Crime and Poverty

Many applications of social disorganization theory have focused on the use of one variable: economic status (Byrne & Sampson, 1986). While there has been some debate on the issue, a consistent finding has been that communities with the highest levels of crime also have the highest rates of poverty (Kornhauser, 1978; Lee, Maume, & Ousey, 2003; McGahey, 1986). Furthermore, other social problems such as infant mortality and low birth weight, suicide rates, dropping out of high school, social and physical disorder, the maltreatment and neglect of children, and teenage pregnancies seem to closely coincide with poverty levels and community disadvantage (Brooks-Gunn, Duncan, & Aber, 1997; Sampson & Raudenbush, 2001; 2004).

Some have argued that it is not poverty in and of itself that causes crime and other social ills, but inequality (Rosenfeld, 1986). As phrased by Michalowski (1985), "Poverty is the condition of having little. Inequality is the condition of having less than others, and it is this condition more than poverty itself that serves to stimulate crime" (p. 407). Inequality can lead to heightened levels of social disorganization by highlighting the differences between various racial and ethnic groups, as well as further delineating social class lines (Blau & Blau, 1982). This inequality can be especially intense when wealthy neighborhoods are located in close proximity to poor ones, leading to feelings of **relative deprivation**. Poorer individuals may experience feelings of anger and injustice, which may ultimately lead to criminal behavior (Morenoff, Sampson, & Raudenbush, 2001; Stiles, Liu, & Kaplan, 2000).

Sampson (1995) further elaborated on the nature of the relationship between poverty and crime, adding the concept of mobility. Citing the work of Smith and Jarjoura (1988), Sampson concluded that poverty alone does not cause crime— areas with high levels of population turnover, combined with poverty, have higher levels of violent crime than high poverty areas with stable residential patterns.

Crime and Ethnic/Racial Heterogeneity

As noted by Sampson, a great deal of research has focused on the relationship between community racial composition and violent crime. A consistent finding of these studies has been that areas with higher numbers of African American residents tend to have higher levels of violent crime. For example, Moore and Tonry (1998), in a discussion of the growing number of violent incidents involving American youths, noted that the epidemic of youth violence has been concentrated among inner city minority males. Why? Is race the sole cause? Few, if any, would answer this question with yes. The relationship between race and crime is highly complex. Part of the problem is that it is very difficult to completely isolate the sole contributing effects of race. In our society, race is closely tied to other important factors, such as income, unemployment rates, educational attainment, school quality, divorce, and number of single-parent homes. Some have argued that the effect of race on crime, delinquency and other social problems is declining in its significance (Wilson, 1980; 1987). While community racial composition continues to be examined by those interested in social ecology theories, Sampson argues that it is debatable whether or not race adds anything new and distinct to the explanation of crime and delinquency, especially if poverty, mobility, and other related factors are already included in the discussion.

Crime and Population Density

In his review of the literature, Sampson also discussed the influence of housing density on crime. Citing the work of Roncek (1981), Sampson argued that the most dangerous places to live were those areas with large numbers of people living in apartment housing or multi-unit structures. As more and more people share the same living space, interactions become less frequent and more impersonal. Neighbors do not recognize each other, nor do they watch out for each other. This effect may be intensified in densely populated public housing units, where high concentrations of poor oftentimes minority residents reside. Regoeczi (2003) found that increased density can lead to an increase in aggressive and withdrawn behavior, an issue that was further complicated by the fact that an individual may not only live in a densely populated neighborhood, but the household itself may be densely populated.

William J. Wilson (1987) discussed life in Robert Taylor Homes, which was the largest public housing project in the city of Chicago in the early 1980s. The complex was comprised of 28 sixteen-story buildings that covered a landmass of 92 acres. While the official population neared 20,000 residents, it was expected that up to 27,000 residents actually lived in the complex. In 1980, less than 1% of the city's population lived in Robert Taylor Homes. However, 11% of the city's murders, 9% of the rapes, and 10% of the aggravated assaults occurred within the complex.

Crime and Instability

Contemporary social ecologists have expanded the definition of community instability beyond a simple analysis of residential turnover. Recall that

Shaw and McKay (1969) noted that social disorganization was closely linked to the concept of invasion, dominance, and succession. Groups of people or businesses displaced previous residents in an area, and these invading forces competed for scarce resources. Ultimately, the shared sense of community that had existed prior to the residential turnover would be lost, resulting in social disorganization. Social ecologists have continued to examine the issue of residential mobility and have expanded the examination of changes in a city's residential turnover to include the rapid growth of suburban areas (Bursik, 1986).

While community instability is an important factor in the discussion of crime and delinquency, instability within the family has also been explored. Sampson (1985; 1986) has investigated the impact of family structure on crime and delinquency, noting that there is a strong relationship between family disruption and rates of violent crime. There are a number of reasons that such a relationship exists. Neighborhoods with higher rates of divorced, separated, and female-headed families have lower levels of formal and informal social control. Formal social control is derived from participation in community institutions and local affairs, such as clubs and committees that may be promoted through local churches, volunteer organizations, schools, or sporting events. Involvement in formal community institutions has several advantages. Participants may have a higher degree of integration and identification with their local community, thereby reducing the feelings of social isolation. Communities whose members have high levels of participation in formal organizations are better able to take charge of the destiny of their own neighborhoods. For example, residents may pursue what Bursik and Grasmick (1993) call extralocal resources, such as block grants and other additional municipal services to better their own living conditions and increase the level of crime control. The involvement of local residents in these organized efforts is related to family structure, as divorced, separated, and unmarried people are less likely to participate in formal community institutions than married-couple families.

Informal social control is derived from neighbors watching out for the well being of each other. Sampson (1986) provides the following examples of informal social control: "neighbors taking note of and/or questioning strangers, watching over each other's property, assuming responsibility for supervision of general youth activities, and intervening in local disturbances" (p. 27). In order for these informal control mechanisms to exist, neighbors must know each other and feel comfortable taking action when a potential problem occurs, such as a group of neighborhood youths hanging around on a street corner drinking beer and vandalizing buildings. Adults assume responsibility not only for the behavior of their own children, but also for the behavior of their neighbors' children. Sampson maintains that areas with higher numbers of intact families will also have higher levels of informal social control.

Sampson's Concept of Collective Efficacy and Crime

Most recently, Sampson and his coauthors have explored the effects of **collective efficacy** on the level of crime and disorder in a community. Collective efficacy has been defined as "social cohesion among neighbors combined with their willingness to intervene on behalf of the common good" (Sampson et al., 1997, p. 918). In order for communities to have a high level of collective efficacy, there must be a high level of mutual trust among the neighbors. High levels of trust can only result when people know their neighbors and can anticipate their reactions. In addition to fostering trust, social cohesion in neighborhoods leads to the development of shared expectations for behavior. People know what the rules are and respect them. Because of the mutual trust and knowledge and appreciation of the neighborhood rules, if an adult observed a violation of the neighborhood norms then he or she would feel comfortable stepping in to correct the situation.

It is important to note that both strong social ties and the expectation of intervention if/when something goes wrong in a neighborhood must be in place for true collective efficacy to thrive. Just because a neighborhood has a strong social network does not automatically guarantee that collective efficacy will exist. A community may have a strong gang or subcultural social network that may serve to hinder informal social control mechanisms and the development of collective efficacy (Browning, Feinberg, & Dietz, 2004; Sampson & Raudenbush, 2004). In a study of a lower middle class African American neighborhood, Patillo (1998) found that members of gangs and other criminal networks were woven into the social fabric of the community. Since these individuals were still able to contribute to the neighborhood in some positive ways (such as providing financial support), there was some tolerance for the existence of these law violators and for their actions. So, even though there was a strong social network in this community, it had limited impact on the reduction of crime. Other researchers have found that the strength of collective efficacy in a neighborhood may be impacted by a number of factors, including population change and residential mobility, the concentration of lower-income residents, racial segregation, and the number of female-headed households. For example, Rountree and Warner (1999) found that the impact of women's social networks on violent crime is weakened in neighborhoods with larger numbers of households headed by women. The women simply may not be able to exercise control over the questionable behavior of neighborhood youth, especially young males.

In effect, collective efficacy may be thought of as the opposite of social disorganization (Vold et al., 2002). According to Sampson, collective efficacy is the key to understanding the level of crime and other social ills in a community. Sampson and his coauthors have found support for the effects of collective efficacy on crime and disorder using a number of methods, including videotaping and categorizing more than 23,000 street segments within the city of Chicago (Sampson & Raudenbush, 1999). Other researchers have found support for the notion of collective efficacy as well. Morenoff and Raudenbush (2001) found that as the level of collective efficacy in neighborhoods increased, the number of incident and victim-based homicides decreased, even when controlling for a number of other factors including the prior homicide rates. Reisig and Cancino (2004) reported that residents living in areas with higher levels of collective efficacy reported much fewer problems related to physical decay and social disorder in their neighborhoods. And Browning et al. (2008) identified a link between collective efficacy and risky sexual behavior among urban teens: Youths living in neighborhoods with greater levels of collective efficacy had fewer sexual partners than those living in neighborhoods with less collective efficacy.

Summary

The work of the Chicago School continues to be an influential area of criminological thought. Prior to the development of their theories of social ecology, the popular thinking of the time focused attention on various characteristics of the individual as the root cause of human behavior. The Chicago School theorists argued that individual characteristics, such as race or IQ, were not of great importance in the study of crime and delinquency. Instead, they focused on the characteristics of the neighborhoods in which a person lived as an influential factor in whether or not a person became involved in crime and delinquency. Crime, delinquency, and other social problems tended to be concentrated in socially disorganized areas marked by low economic status, ethnic heterogeneity, and residential instability. Contemporary social ecologists have also added the influences of family structure, formal and informal social control, and community cohesion. Together, these various influences impact the socialization of youths as they grow up and learn to function as members of society.

In the Chicago School Tradition …

We will close this chapter with an excerpt from a participant observation study conducted by Elijah Anderson, a prominent sociologist. While the theories of the Chicago School continue to be highly influential, others would argue that the greatest contribution to criminology was their use of participant observation as a research technique. As you read the first Spotlight on Research, we hope you can appreciate the richness of this type of data. Participant observation provides a much different picture of the everyday life of the local residents than could ever be provided by an examination by more traditional "official statistics," such as the FBI UCR. While Professor Anderson's study was conducted on the streets of Philadelphia, many of the same sights, sounds, and neighborhood transitions could easily be seen in any older large urban area.

SPOTLIGHT ON RESEARCH I

From "The Social Ecology of Youth Violence"
Elijah Anderson, Ph.D.*

This spotlight on research features an excerpt from one of the many outstanding works of Elijah Anderson, professor of sociology in the Department of Sociology at the University of Pennsylvania. In this essay, Professor Anderson takes us for a walk down Germantown Avenue, richly describing the sights and sounds we encounter along the way. As you read this passage, pay careful attention to the various perceptual cues that signal that the neighborhood is changing as one moves down the avenue. Can you visualize the various zones? How would life be different for a child growing up in the various neighborhoods along the Avenue? Why have the neighborhoods changed? What, if anything, can be done to improve the quality of life for the residents living in the impoverished areas? These are the types of issues we will be exploring in this text. So, sit back, relax, and enjoy your stroll down Germantown Avenue with our host Elijah Anderson.

---

* Reprinted with permission from Anderson, E. (1998). The social ecology of youth violence. In M. Tonry & M. Moore (Eds.) *Youth Violence* (pp. 68–79). Chicago, IL: University of Chicago Press. Copyright University of Chicago Press.

Zone 5

Down Germantown Avenue

Germantown Avenue is a major Philadelphia artery that goes back to colonial days. Eight and a half miles long, it links the northwest suburbs with the heart of inner-city Philadelphia. It traverses a varied social terrain as well. Germantown Avenue provides an excellent cross-section of the social ecology of a major American city. Along this artery live the well-to-do, the middle classes, the working poor, and the very poor. The story of Germantown Avenue with its wide social and class variations can serve in many respects as a metaphor for the whole city. This essay about the "code of the street" begins with an introduction to the world of the streets, by way of a tour down Germantown Avenue.

One of the most salient features of urban life, in the minds of many people today, is the relative prevalence of violence. Our tour down Germantown Avenue will focus on the role of violence in the social organization of the communities through which the avenue passes, and on how violence is revealed in the interactions of people up and down the street. The avenue, we will see, is a natural continuum characterized by a code of civility at one end and a code of conduct regulated by the threat of violence—the code of the street—at the other. But the people living along this continuum make their own claims on civility and the streets as well.

Zone 5

We begin at the top of the hill that gives Chestnut Hill its name. Chestnut Hill is the first neighborhood within the city of Philadelphia as you come into town from the northwest. Often called the "suburb in the city," it is a predominantly residential community of mostly white, affluent, educated people, which is becoming increasingly racially and ethnically mixed. The houses are mostly large single buildings, surrounded by lawns and trees. The business and shopping district along Germantown Avenue draws shoppers from all over the city. At the very top of the hill is a large Borders Bookstore. Across the street is the regional rail train station, with the local library in close proximity. Moving southeast down the avenue, you pass a variety of mostly small, upscale businesses: gourmet food shops, a camera shop, an optician's, a sporting goods store, a bank, jewelry stores, clothing boutiques. Many of the buildings are old or built to look old and are made of fieldstone with slanted slate roofs, giving the area a quaint appearance. You see many different kinds of people—old and young, black and white, affluent, middle- and working-class, women (some of them black) pushing babies who are white. Couples stroll hand in hand. Everyone is polite and seems relaxed. When people pass one another on the sidewalk, they may make eye contact. People stand about nonchalantly on the sidewalk, sometimes with their backs to the street. You do not get the feeling that there is any hostility or that people are on guard against being compromised or insulted or robbed. There is a pleasant ambience—an air of civility.

One of the things you see at this end of Germantown Avenue is that relations in public appear racially integrated, perhaps self-consciously so. There are integrated play groups among small children on the playgrounds. At the bank, there is relaxed interaction between a black teller and a white client. There are biracial friendship groups. At the Boston Market restaurant blacks and whites sit and eat together or simply share the restaurant. A black man drives by in a Range Rover; two well-dressed black women pull up in a black Lexus. In their clothing and cars, the black middle class choose styles and colors that stand out and are noticed as expensive; they are quite expressive in laying claim to middle-class status.

In the upscale stores here, there is not usually a great concern for security. During the day the plate-glass windows have appealing displays; some shops even have unguarded merchandise out on the sidewalk.

Once in a while, however, a violent incident does occur. There was a holdup at the bank in the middle of the day not long ago, ending in a shootout on the sidewalk. The perpetrators were black. Such incidents give the residents here the overly simplistic yet persistent view that blacks commit crime and white people do not. That does not mean that the white people here think that the black people they ordinarily see on the streets are bound to rob them: many of these people are too sophisticated to believe that all blacks are inclined to criminality. But the fact that black people robbed the bank does give a peculiar edge to race relations, and the racial reality of street crime speaks to the relations between blacks and whites. Because everybody knows that the simplistic view does exist, even middle-class blacks, as well as whites, have to work against that stereotype. Both groups know that the reality is that crime is likely to be perpetrated by young black males. While both black and whites behave as though they deny it, this background knowledge threatens the civility of the neighborhood. The cleavages of wealth, and the fact that black people are generally disenfranchised and white people are not, operate in the back of the minds of people here.

Once can see this as a black male walking into the stores, especially the jewelry store. The sales personnel pay particular attention to people until they feel they have passed inspection, and black males almost always are given extra scrutiny. Most blacks in Chestnut Hill are middle-class or even wealthy, although some come into the neighborhood as day workers, and many are disturbed by the inability of some whites to make distinctions between middle-and lower-class blacks or between people who are out to commit crime and those who are not.

The knowledge that there are poor blacks further down the avenue also results in people "here" being on guard against people from "there." Security guards may follow young black males around stores, looking for the emblems and signs that they are from there and not from here. And at night the stores do have interior security devices, although they are outwardly decorative. These elements can, but most often do not, compromise civility between the races in Chestnut Hill; in fact, people generally "get along."

Down the hill, beyond the Boston Market, is Cresheim Valley Road, a neighborhood boundary. On the other side, we are in Mount Airy, a different social milieu. Here there are more black homeowners, interspersed among white ones, and there is more black street traffic on Germantown Avenue. Mount Airy is a much more integrated neighborhood than Chestnut Hill, and the black people who live here are mostly middle class. But Germantown Avenue in Mount Airy and the shops and stores along it are disproportionately used by blacks rather than whites and by poorer blacks rather than middle-class blacks. Whites and middle-class black adults tend to use the stores in Chestnut Hill, finding them more consistent with their tastes. As a result, the shops here are blacker, even though they may be middle class.

A sign that we are in a different social milieu is that exterior bars begin to appear on the store windows and riot gates on the doors, at first on businesses such as the liquor store. Pizza parlors, karate shops, take-out stores that sell beer, and storefront organizations such as neighborhood health care centers appear—establishments that are not present in Chestnut Hill. There are discount stores of various sorts, black barbershops, and other businesses that cater to the black middle class but also to employed working-class and poorer blacks. Many of the black middle-class youths use the streets as a place to gather and talk with their friends, and they adopt the clothing styles of the poorer people further down the avenue. So people who are not familiar with social types sometimes cannot distinguish between who is middle class and who is not. This confusion appears to be a standing problem for store owners and managers, and may lead to a sense of defensiveness among middle-class people who do not want to be violated or robbed. But it is a confusion that the youth tend not to mind.

Continuing down the avenue, we pass the Mount Airy playground with its basketball court, which is always buzzing. Evenings and weekends it is full of young black men playing pick-up games. There is a real social mix here, with kids from middle-class, working-class, and poor black families all coming together in this spot, creating a staging area. The urban uniform of sneakers and baggy jeans is much in evidence, which gives pause to other people, particularly whites (many of whom avoid the area). In many ways, however, the atmosphere is easy-going. The place is not crime-ridden or necessarily feared by most blacks, but there is a certain edge to it compared with similar but less racially complex settings further up the avenue. Here it is prudent to be wary—not everyone on the street here recognizes and respects the rule of law, the law that is encoded in the criminal statutes and enforced by the police.

Yet next to the playground is a branch of the Free Library, one of the best in the city, which caters mainly to literate people of Mount Airy, both black and white. Indeed, the social and racial mix of the community is sometimes more visible in the library than on the street itself.

There are many beautiful old buildings in Mount Airy. But the piano re-pair shops, sandwich stores, and plumbing-supply companies tend to have exterior bars and riot gates, which militates against the notion of civility as the dominant theme of the place. A competing notion crystallizes, and that is the prevalence of crime, the perpetrators of which are more often concerned not with legality but with feasibility. Ten years ago there were fewer bars on the windows and the buildings were better maintained. Today more relatively poor people are occupying the public space. There are still whites among the storekeepers and managers of various establishments, but whites have been displaced in the outdoor public spaces by poorer blacks. Moreover, the further down the avenue we go, the less well maintained the buildings are. Even when they are painted, for example, the painting tends to be done haphazardly, without great regard for architectural detail.

In this section, a billboard warns that those who commit insurance fraud go to jail. (No such signs appear in Chestnut Hill). There is graffiti—or signs that it has recently been removed. More dilapidated buildings appear, looking as though they receive no maintenance. Yet among them are historic buildings, some of which are cared for for just that reason. One of them is the house where the Battle of Germantown was fought during the Revolutionary War. Another was a stop on the underground railroad.

As Mount Airy gives way to Germantown, check-cashing agencies and beeper stores appear, as well as more small take-out stores selling beer, cheese steaks, and other snack food. More of the windows are boarded up, and riot gates and exterior bars become the norm, evoking in the user of the street a certain wariness.

Germantown appears to be a more solidly black working-class neighborhood. Whites, including middle-class whites, do live here, but they either tend to avoid the business district or the stores simply do not attract them. On Germantown Avenue, discount stores of all sorts appear—supermarkets, furniture stores, and clothing stores. Of the people you pass, many more are part of the street element. Here people watch their backs, and more care is given to one's presentation of self. It is not that you are worried every moment that somebody might violate you, but people are more aware of others who are sharing the space with them, some of whom may be looking for an easy target to rob or just intimidate.

Germantown High School, once a model of racially integrated high-quality education, is almost all black, a shadow of its former academic self. Resources have declined and many of the students are now impoverished and associated with the street element, and most of those who are not still have a need to show themselves as being capable of dealing with the street. In fact, the hallways of the school are in some ways an extension of the streets. Across the street from the high school is a store selling beer. Continuing down the avenue, we pass blocks of small businesses: taverns, Chinese take-out places, barbershops and hair salons, laundromats, storefront churches, pawnshops. Groups of young people loiter on street corners. We also begin to see boarded-up buildings, some of them obviously quite grand at one time, and empty lots. A charred McDonald's sign rises above a weed-covered lot. A police car is parked at the corner, its occupants keeping a watchful eye on the street activity. After a time, they begin to drive slowly down the street.

Just before Chelten Avenue, a major artery that intersects Germantown Avenue, is Vernon Park. The park has a caretaker who is trying to keep it maintained despite the carelessness and even vandalism of the people who like to gather there. A mural has been painted on the side of an adjacent building. Flowers have been planted. On warm days, couples "making time" sit about on the benches, on the steps of statues, and on the hoods of cars parked along the park's edge. But even during the day you can see men drinking alcohol out of paper sacks, and at night the park is a dangerous place where drug dealing and other shadowy business is conducted. This is what I call a major "staging area," because the activity that occurs here sets the stage for other activity, which may either be played out on the spot, in front of an audience of people who have congregated here, or in less conspicuous locations. An altercation in Vernon Park may be settled with a fight, with or without gunplay, down a side street. People come here to see and be seen, to "profile" and "represent," presenting the image of themselves by which they would like to be known— who they are and how they stand in relation to whom. The streets are buzzing with activity, both legal and illegal. In fact, a certain flagrant disregard for the law is visible. We see a teenage boy walk by with an open bottle of beer in his hand, taking a swig when he wants to.

A young man in his twenties crosses the street after taking care of some sort of business with another young man, gets into his brand-new black BMW Sidekick, and slides up next to his girlfriend who has been waiting there for him.

He is dressed in a crisp white T-shirt with Hilfiger emblazoned across the back, black satin shorts with bright red stripes on the sides, and expensive white sneakers. He makes a striking figure as he slides into his vehicle, and others take note. He moves with aplomb, well aware that he is where he wants to be and, for that moment at least, where some others want to be as well. His presentation of self announces that he can take care of himself should someone choose to tangle with him.

Here in Germantown, especially in some pockets, there is less respect for the code of civility, and that fact necessitates a whole way of moving, of acting, of getting up and down the streets, which suggests that violence is just below the surface. The people of Germantown are overwhelmingly decent and committed to civility, yet there is something about the avenue, especially at night, that attracts the street element. When that element is present in numbers, there is a sense that you are on your own, that what protects you from being violated is your own body, your own ability to behave the right way, to look as though you can handle yourself, and even to be able to defend yourself. While it is not always necessary to throw down the gauntlet, so to speak, and be ready to punch someone out, it is important, as people here say, to "know what time it is." It is this form of regulation of social interaction in public that I call the "code of the street" in contrast to the "code of civility," based on trust and the rule of law, that strongly prevails up the avenue. You are not always tested, but you have to be ready for the test if you are. Mr. Don Moses, an old head of the black community, described the code this way: "Keep your eyes and ears open at all times. Walk two steps forward and look back. Watch your back. Prepare yourself verbally and physically. Even if you have a cane, carry something. The older people do carry something, guns in sheaths. The can't physically fight no more so they carry a gun." People here feel they must watch their backs, because everything happens here. And if the police are called, they may not arrive in time. People get killed here, they get stabbed, but they also relax and have a good time. In general, there is an edge to public life that you do not find in Chestnut Hill.

Chelten Avenue is lined with discount stores and fast-food restaurants. Yet just around the corner and two blocks down is a middle-class residential area. Most people here are black, but there are representatives of the wider society here, as well, including the police, the welfare office, the fast-food and clothing store chains. On Tuesday mornings, food-stamp lines snake around Greene Street at Chelten. There are also little people running small, sometimes fly-by-night businesses. Hustlers and small-time money men canvas the food stamp line with wads of cash—ready to buy discounted food stamps. It is this lack of resources that encourages a dog-eat-dog mentality that is concentrated at Chelten Avenue. Yet there is a great deal of other activity too. Especially during the summer, there is sometimes a carnival atmosphere. And the fact that the general area is diverse both racially and socially works to offset the feeling of social isolation that the poor black residents of Germantown have.

Occasionally, residents of Chestnut Hill drive this far down Germantown Avenue, and seeing what this neighborhood looks like has an impact on their consciousness. But they do not see below the surface. Mainly, they take in the noise and the seeming disorder, the poverty, and the incivility and when raving about urban violence they associate it with places like this, when in fact this neighborhood may not be as violent as they assume. To be sure, welfare mothers, prostitutes, and drug dealers are in evidence, but they coexist with—and are in fact outnumbered by—working people in legitimate jobs who are trying to avoid trouble.

As you move on past Chelten Avenue, you pass through quieter stretches colored by the residential nature of the surrounding streets, alternating with concentrated business strips. Many of the businesses are skin, hair, and nail salons. A common aspiration of the poorer girls in these neighborhoods is to go to beauty school and become cosmetologists.

We pass by the old town square of Germantown, which is surrounded by old, "historically certified" houses. Such houses appear sporadically for a long way down the avenue. Unfortunately, some are badly in need of maintenance. Just beyond the square is Germantown Friends School, a private school founded 150 years ago on what was then the outskirts of town but is now surrounded by the city.

Further down Germantown Avenue, thrift shops and discount stores predominate. Most are equipped with window bars and riot gates. Both the bars and the residents' understanding proclaim that this is a tough place. Some people can be counted on to behave according to the laws of force, not those of civility. Many people have to be forced to behave in a law-abiding way. The code has violence, or the possibility of violence, to back it up, and the bars on the windows signify the same thing—a lack of trust, a feeling that without the bars the establishment would be vulnerable. The code of the street has emerged.

The further we go down the avenue, the more boarded-up buildings there are, and more and more empty lots. In fact, certain areas give the impression of no-man's-lands, with empty overgrown or dirt lots, a few isolated buildings here and there, few cars on the street, and almost no people on the sidewalks. We pass billboards advertising "forties" (forty-ounce malt liquor) and other kinds of liquor. Churches are a prominent feature of the cityscape as a whole. Along this part of Germantown Avenue some of them are very large and well known, with a rich history, and are architecturally like those in Chest-

nut Hill and Mount Airy, but others are storefront churches that sometimes come
and go with the founding pastor.

People move up and down the street. Even in the middle of the morning,
groups of young men can be seen standing on corners, eyeing the street traffic. Yet the morning is the safest time of day. As evening approaches, the possibility of violence increases, and after nightfall the rule of the code of the street
is being enforced all along the lower section of the avenue. Under that rule,
the toughest, the biggest, the boldest prevail. We pass a school at recess. Kids
are crowding into a makeshift store where someone is barbecuing hot dogs
and ribs. Even at play, they hone their physical skills, punching each other
lightly but seriously, sizing each other up. This sort of play-fighting, playing
with the code, is commonplace.

Continuing, we pass collision shops—former gas stations surrounded by many
cars in various states of disrepair—music stores, and nightclubs. We arrive at
Broad Street, Philadelphia's major north-south artery, where Germantown Avenue also intersects Erie Avenue, forming a large triangle that is one of the
centers of the ghetto of North Philadelphia. It is a staging area that is racially
diverse, drawing all kinds of people from adjacent areas that are extremely
poor. In Germantown there are a fair number of working people. In North
Philly there is extensive concentrated poverty. North Philly is in the depths of
the inner city—the so-called hyperghetto—and people here are more isolated
from others who are unlike themselves in terms of both class and race (Massey
and Denton 1993).

Just beyond Broad Street is a business strip with the same sort of establishments we saw further up the avenue—clothing stores, sneaker stores, furniture stores, electronics stores. Many offer layaway plans. In addition, there are
businesses that cater mostly to the criminal class, such as pawnshops and beeper
stores. Pawnshops are in a sense banks for thieves; they are places where stolen
goods can be traded for cash, few questions asked. Check-cashing exchanges,
which continue to be a common sight, also ask few questions, but they charge
exorbitant fees for cashing a check. As in Chestnut Hill, merchandise is displayed
on the sidewalk, but here it is under the watchful eye of unsmiling security
guards. The noise level here is also much louder. Cars drive by with their stereo
systems blaring. A young man wearing headphones saunters down the street.
On the adjacent streets, open-air drug deals occur, prostitutes ply their trade,
and boys shoot craps, while small children play in trash-strewn abandoned
lots. This is the face of persistent urban poverty.

This is another staging area. People profile and represent here, standing
around, "looking things over," concerned with who is where, but also aware
of others "checking them out." Here, phrases like "watch your back," or as

friends reassure their friends, "I got your back," takes on meaning, for some people are looking for opportunities to violate others, or simply to get away with something. A man opens his car door despite approaching traffic, seeming to dare someone to hit him. Further down the block a woman simply stops her car in the middle of the street, waiting for her husband or boyfriend to emerge from a barbershop. She waits for about ten minutes, holding up traffic. No one complains, no one honks his horn; they simply go around her, for they know that to complain is to risk an altercation, or at least heated words. They prefer not to incur this woman's wrath, which could escalate to warfare. In Chestnut Hill, where civility and "limited" warfare are generally the orders of the day, people might call others on such behavior, but here the general level of violence can keep irritation in check. In this way, the code of the street provides social organization and actually lessens the probability of random violence. When the woman's man arrives, he simply steps around to the passenger side and, without showing any concern for others, gets into the car. The pair drive off, apparently believing it to be their right to do what they just did.

At Tioga Street and Temple University Hospital, whose emergency room sees gunshot and stabbing victims just about every night, the code of the street is much in evidence. In the morning and early afternoon, the surrounding neighborhood is peaceful enough, but in the evening the danger level rises. Tensions spill over, drug deals go bad, fights materialize seemingly out of nowhere, and the emergency room becomes a hub of activity. Sometimes the victim bypasses the hospital: by the time he is found, there is no place to take him but the morgue. Nearby there is a liquor store and a place selling cold beer. People buy liquor there and drink it on the street, adding to the volatility of the street scene.

More and more gaps in the rows of houses appear, where buildings have burned down, been torn down, or simply collapsed. Others are shells, their windows and large parts of their walls gone, leaving beams exposed. Still others are boarded up, perhaps eventually to collapse, perhaps to be rebuilt. Indeed there are signs of regeneration among those of destruction. Here and there a house is well-maintained, even freshly painted. Some of the exposed outer walls of standing structures have colorful, upbeat murals painted on them, often with religious themes. We pass a large building a car repair shop, gaily decorated with graffiti art. Further down we pass a hotel that rents rooms by the hour.

There continue to be signs of the avenue's past life—large churches built by European immigrants at the turn of the century, an old cemetery, an occasional historic building. The many open areas—empty lots, little overgrown parks—underline the winding character of this old highway as it cuts through the grid pattern of streets formally laid out well after this became an established thoroughfare.

We drive through another business district with the usual stores catering to the very poor. Two policemen pass by on foot patrol. This is another staging area. The concentration of people drawn by the businesses increases the chance of violence breaking out. A lot of people are out, not just women and children but a conspicuous number of young men as well, even though it is still morning. Practically all of them are black, with just an occasional Asian and even rarer white face among them.

We enter an area where there seem to be more empty lots and houses you can see right through than solidly standing buildings. Some of the lots are a heap of rubble. Others are overgrown with weeds or littered with abandoned cars. This is a spot where the idea of a war zone comes to mind. Indeed, gunshot marks are visible on some of the buildings. The black ghetto here gives way to the Hispanic ghetto. The faces are different but the behavior is similar.

Yet in the midst of this desolation there is a newly built gated community in the Spanish style. Just beyond it, we reach Norris Street; at this intersection three of the four corners are large empty lots. But we also pass an open area that has been transformed into a community garden. Now, in late spring, vegetables in the early stages of growth are visible.

We are now just north of Philadelphia's center city area. This used to be a bustling commercial area, with factories producing everything from beer to lace and huge warehouses in which the goods were stored before being shipped out either by rail, traces of which are still visible, or through a nearby port on the Delaware River. Here and there some of the behemoths are still standing, although one by one they are falling victim to arson.

And so we reach the other end of Germantown Avenue, in the midst of a leveled area about a block from the river and overshadowed by the elevated interstate highway that now allows motorists to drive over North Philadelphia rather than through it, thereby ignoring its street life, its inhabitants, and its problems.

References

Massey, D. S., & Denton, N. A. (1993). *American apartheid: Segregation and the making of the underclass.* Cambridge, MA: Harvard University Press.

Chapter 3

Choosing Crime

Theories based on the Positivists' perspective, described in Chapter 2, are not the only methods used to explain a person's involvement in crime and deviance. In this Chapter, theories that are based on the idea of crime as a matter of *choice* are explored. According to proponents of choice-based theories, people are involved in crime because they have carefully weighed the pros and cons of criminal activity and have made a rational decision to get involved in criminal activity. This Chapter begins with a discussion of the historical roots of this alternative perspective, a school of thought commonly known as **Classical criminology**.

Prostitutes
Temptation)

The Evolution of the Classical School of Criminology

The ideas, assumptions, and policy recommendations of Classical criminologists were a sharp break with the popular thinking of the times. For over a thousand years in Europe, spiritual explanations of crime were the driving force behind the criminal justice system. These spiritual explanations, sometimes called **demonology**, were based on the assumption that crime and deviance were the result of possession by demons or temptation at the hands of the Devil (Einstadter & Henry, 1995). Demonologists assumed that human beings were essentially good people. This natural tendency to do "good" was constantly under attack by demons and the forces of evil. It was only through strong faith in God that one could resist the temptation of Satan.

Because of the strong influence of the church, these theologically-based theories of crime did not include a distinction between "crime" and "sin." The writings of St. Thomas Aquinas (1225–1274) were very influential in this era. Aquinas argued that crime violated the natural law, which was derived from the law of God himself. If a person committed a crime, then he or she also committed a sin. Violations of the law were taken very seriously, since the criminal had broken not just the law of humans, but also the law of God. As a result, punishments for criminal acts were horrific (Vold et al., 2002). The state had a divine right to exercise moral authority and inflict painful punishments on the accused. Consider, for example, the fate of Damiens, who was convicted of stabbing King Louis XV of France:

> On 2 March 1757, Damiens the regicide was condemned 'to make the *amende honorable* before the main door of the Church of Paris', where he was to be 'taken and conveyed in a car, wearing nothing but a shirt, holding a torch of burning wax weighing two pounds'; then, 'in the said cart, to the Place de Greve, where on a scaffold that will be erected there, the flesh will be torn from his breasts, arms, thighs and calves with red-hot pincers, his right hand, holding the knife with which he committed the said parricide, burnt with sulphur, and, on those places where the flesh will be torn away, poured molten lead, boiling oil, burning resin, wax and sulphur melted together and then his body drawn and quartered by four horses and his limbs and body consumed by fire, reduced to ashes and his ashes thrown to the winds' (Foucault, 1977, p. 3). *Whoa...*

In addition to the use of brutal public punishments, the criminal justice system also regularly made use of trials by ordeal and torture to elicit confessions for alleged crimes (Hibbert, 1966). For example, if you were accused of being a witch, you might be tied up and thrown into a lake. If the water would not accept you and you floated, this would indicate that you were indeed a witch and you would then face punishment (torture, burning at the stake, etc.) for this crime. If the water accepted you, then this was seen as an indication that you were pure and therefore innocent of the charges. Of course, you would also be dead.

Many times, these "trials" resulted in convictions of the weak. Physically strong individuals who were able to endure the rack and other forms of torture had a better chance of being found innocent of the charges, regardless of whether or not they had actually committed the crime for which they were accused. As stated by Beccaria (1764/1963):

> Of two men, equally innocent or equally guilty, the strong and courageous will be acquitted, and weak and timid condemned, by virtue of this rigorous rational argument: "I, the judge, was supposed to find you guilty of such and such a crime; you the strong, have been able to resist the pain, and I therefore absolve you; you the weak, have yielded, and I therefore condemn you. I am aware that a confession wrenched forth by torments ought to be of no weight whatsoever, but

I'll torment you again if you don't confirm what you have confessed." (pp. 32–33).

In this system of justice, judges had unlimited discretion to make laws, decide guilt or innocence, and impose whatever punishment was felt to be appropriate. Oftentimes, the harshness of the punishment was determined not by the severity of the crime, but by the status, power, and influence of the convicted person (Monachesi, 1955). The end result was that the laws, convictions, and punishments were completely arbitrary.

There was a wave of growing dissatisfaction with the criminal justice system of the time, and many philosophers and critical thinkers began to search for a system that would be more effective. These social theorists were part of a larger movement called the Enlightenment, which sharply disagreed with the authority and dominance of the church in all aspects of life. It was out of this revolutionary philosophy that Cesare Bonesana, Marquis of Beccaria wrote a highly influential essay, _On Crimes and Punishments_ (1764/1963). Beccaria's reforms greatly impacted the development of the criminal justice system in the United States and other western societies (Curran & Renzetti, 2001). Even in contemporary times, his ideas continue to have a significant influence on the way we view crimes and punishments.

Cesare Beccaria on Crimes and Punishments (1764)

The name Cesare Beccaria is often synonymous with the school of Classical criminology. Beccaria built on the ideas of several philosophers, including Hobbes (1588–1678), Locke (1632–1704), and Rousseau (1712–1778). The general philosophy of these thinkers was that crime was not a result of satanic influence or demonic possession, but rather an issue of rationality.

You might recall that the theologically-based theorists assumed human beings were essentially "good" people who were under an attack of sorts by the forces of evil. Beccaria and other Classical theorists assumed the opposite. At their very core, people were seen as hedonistic, self-serving, and interested only in the pursuit of their own selfish pleasures, without any regard for the feelings of other people. If left to their own devices, humans always revert back to this selfish tendency.

While Beccaria and other Classical theorists assumed that humans were hedonistic by nature, they also argued that humans were rational beings. If everyone did what he or she wanted to do, whenever they wanted to do it, the result would be total chaos. Society could not function under such circumstances. To avoid what Hobbes called a "war of each against all," Classical theorists proposed that we enter into a **social contract** with each other. All members of a society come together and form an understanding that certain types of behavior are acceptable, while other actions are not. Since this social contract limits personal freedoms, people do not really want to enter into this contract. However, they recognize the need for it.

Punishments are necessary to enforce the social contract. If there were no penalties associated with violations of the social contract, all would revert back to their selfish nature. Beccaria assumed that human beings exercise free will in deciding on a course of action. Before engaging in a criminal act, humans carefully weigh the consequences and rewards associated with their behavior. Because humans are rational beings, punishments need only be harsh enough to convince a person that more harm than good would come from violating the law.

The Keys to Deterrence: Certain, Swift, and Proportionate Punishments

Reacting against the popular use of horrific punishments, as well as the arbitrary nature of their application, Beccaria made a number of assertions regarding the effective use of punishment to deter crime. In order for punishments to reduce crime, Beccaria argued that punishments should be **certain, swift, and proportionate** to the severity of the crime.

Certainty refers to the inescapable application of the punishment. In the case of a bank robber, Beccaria would assume that prior to the commission of the robbery, the robber would carefully weigh out the pros and cons of such an action. How much money would be gained? How much prison time would be mandated for this crime? Beccaria would argue that it is not so much the number of years of prison time but the fact that the prison term could not be avoided that would influence the decision. In the criminal's rational deliberations, it would not be a question of "What will I get *if* I get caught" but "What will I get *when* I get caught."

The punishment must also fit the severity of the crime. The punishment should be punitive enough to make a person think twice about committing a crime. Punishments that are too severe for a specific offense may actually lead to the commission of more serious criminal acts. For example, for a moment assume that the punishment associated with conviction for armed robbery is the death penalty. If an individual has made up her mind that she is going to rob the local 7-11, she might ask, "Why not shoot everyone in the store while I am at it? There would be no witnesses who could identify me, and since the punishment is the same for both, why not?" In this example, the application of the death penalty for the armed robbery would be too severe a punishment, since the would-be robber would not be deterred from committing the more serious offense of mass murder.

The application of the punishment must be closely linked in time to the commission of the crime. Being rational human beings, we would not associate the pain of conviction and punishment with the commission of the crime if there were a long period of time between the criminal act and the consequences. This is especially true given that in many cases the rewards of criminal activity are immediate. If a man robs the convenience store, he would not have to wait to get the money—when he walked out of the store, he would have his reward. If he were to be identified as a suspect, the process of investigation, arrest, trial, and sentencing (if he was actually convicted) could take months, and even years.

In addition to his revolutionary ideas concerning the application of punishments, Beccaria also called for judicial reform. Beccaria wanted to limit the role of judges in the criminal justice system. In his opinion, it should be the job of the legislatures, not the judges, to define what actions constituted a crime and then to define the appropriate punishments for such an action (Beccaria, 1764/1963). Judges should only be concerned with determining whether or not a person was guilty of an offense. Once guilt had been determined, the judge would have no alternative but to assign the pre-determined sanction for the act. Since all people were equal under the law, regardless of their power and influence, there would be no mitigating circumstances or other excuses for criminal behavior. Everyone was responsible for his or her behavior and there were no allowances for individual differences between those convicted of crimes.

From Classical to Neoclassical and Beyond

While Beccaria's ideas were extremely influential in modifying the criminal justice system, in practice there was some difficulty in implementing his model, especially with respect to the equal application of punishments, regardless of the characteristics of the offender (Taylor, et al., 1973). If one adopted a pure classical philosophy, all individuals convicted of a similar offense, such as murder, would be given the same punishment. It would not matter if the convicted person was a juvenile, mentally ill, or if the offense was considered a crime of passion. Under a pure classical interpretation, all individuals have roughly the same capacity to make a rational choice regarding whether or not to engage in a criminal activity.

The recognition that certain individuals were incapable of making rational decisions and exercising full freedom of choice led to the development of **Neoclassical criminology**. In this school of thought, free choice and individual accountability are still important elements. However, Neoclassicists began to adopt a "softer" approach when presented with certain types of offenders. Children, the elderly, mentally ill, or those suffering from conditions like Down's Syndrome or other challenging conditions did not seem to fit well within the basic assumptions upon which Classical criminology was built. Neoclassical criminologists began to recognize that there were individual differences between criminals and that these differences may have an impact on the type of reaction that would be appropriate. As phrased by Taylor et al. (1973):

> The criminal had to be punished in an environment conducive to his making the correct moral decisions. Choice was (and still is) seen to be a characteristic of the individual actor—but there is now a recognition that certain structures are more conducive to free choice than others (emphasis in the original) (p. 9).

In effect, Neoclassicists began to recognize that the ability of many offenders to exercise free will was constrained by factors that were beyond their immediate control. Because of their inability to make a rational choice, convicted offenders who fell into one of these classifications should receive special treatment at the hands of the criminal justice system. Instead of a "one-size-fits-all" punishment, sentences for criminal behavior should be tailored to meet the needs of the individual offender.

Some may not see a great deal of difference between the Neoclassical school and Positivism, discussed in Chapter 2. Imagining a continuum with Classical criminology on one extreme end and Positivism on the other may help. Classical criminology assumes that crime is a matter of free choice. After carefully weighing the punishments and rewards, people freely choose crime as a rational means to a desired end. There are no excuses or justifications for criminal behavior. Poverty, peer influence, biology, psychiatric disorders, or neighborhood characteristics should not be considered. Crime is a matter of individual choice.

At the other end of the spectrum is Positivism. In its most extreme form, a hard core Positivist would argue that there is no free choice at all. Our behavior is determined by factors beyond our immediate control. Even those adopting a softer approach would hold that our behavior is strongly influenced by various societal structures and individual differences.

Between these two extremes lies the Neoclassical school. Proponents of this tradition began to open up the door to the notion that perhaps, for some people, their ability to make a rational decision is somehow affected by their individual life circumstances. Choice is still recognized as a powerful element of the Neoclassical school, as most criminals have the ability to exercise their free will in choosing crime.

So What Works?
The Never Ending Debate

Understanding the underlying assumptions of various schools of thought is important, since the perspective that an individual subscribes to, with respect to the root cause of crime, has an impact on what he or she feels is the best response to criminal activity. If one adopts the Classical criminology perspective, then the policy recommendations for curbing crime would include the use of certain, swift, and proportionate punishments. Criminals freely choose crime knowing full well that the act is wrong. In order to keep a person on the straight and narrow path, the perceived pain associated with commission of a criminal act must outweigh the perceived benefits.

A Positivist, on the other hand, would argue that the use of punishment as a deterrent to criminal behavior would have little if any impact on the behavior of the offender. Crime is not a matter of choice. A person engages in criminal activity for a variety of reasons—inadequate socialization, poor role models, neighborhood influences, psychological imbalances, etc. Law violators need treatment for their condition, not punishment. Proponents of a Positivistic orientation would advocate the use of various reformation and rehabilitation programs, including education, vocational training, and behavior modification therapy.

Consider, for a moment, the case of Lindsay Lohan, a celebrity who has had a highly publicized struggle with alcohol and drug use since 2006. Lohan has been in and out of various treatment centers for drug and alcohol problems, and her continued substance abuse problems have led to several arrests. According to People.com (2010), Lohan's entanglements with the law begin in May 2007, when she was arrested for driving under the influence of alcohol. In July of the same year, she was again arrested for DUI, possession of cocaine, driving on a suspended license, and other charges. This arrest came just a few days after Lohan had completed a 45-day rehabilitation program and had just been formally booked on charges from the May incident. There was public outrage that Lohan's behavior was not impacted by the experience of the rehabilitation program or having to go through the booking process. Those calling for a punishment model were not happy when Lohan served a total of 84 minutes in jail for both DUI arrests, but those advocating treatment would argue that a lengthy jail term would have had no impact on her behavior.

Closely monitored probation combined with treatment would provide the best possible chance for a positive outcome.

Unfortunately, in 2010 Lohan's problems continued. She accumulated several violations of the terms of her probation guidelines, including testing positive for cocaine in random drug tests, missing required classes, consuming alcohol, and failing to appear for mandatory court appearances. Because of her violation of the terms of her probation, the judge ordered Lohan to spend 90 days in jail and 90 days in a secured drug rehabilitation facility (Winton & Blankstein, 2010). This sentence was much more severe than that sought by the prosecution team. In the court of public opinion, there were some who certainly agreed with the judge's decision. To those individuals, Lohan had demonstrated a complete lack of respect for the judge, the law, and the criminal justice system as a whole. How is Lohan ever going to learn if she simply receives another slap on the wrist for her actions? Since Lohan is making choices here—choices not to attend the required classes, choices to drink, choices to use cocaine—then a lengthy jail term should be the only appropriate reaction to her criminal behavior. Punishment will make her think twice about the decisions that she is making. Others have argued that Lohan's behavior is a result of an illness. Far from being a free choice, her actions are symptoms of a disease. Jail time will not cure her illness; treatment is the best option to modify her behavior.

As of this writing, Lohan continues to go in and out of jail and rehabilitation programs as she fights her addiction to drugs and alcohol (People.com, 2010). As for the impact of the 90-day jail sentence, due to security concerns at the jail and overcrowding issues, Lohan served only 13 days of the 90-day sentence.

The debate between Positivists and Classical criminologists regarding the appropriate response to criminal behavior has been going on throughout the history of crimes and punishments. The pendulum swings back and forth between punishment and treatment as the appropriate response to criminal behavior. The most recent philosophical shift began in the late 1940s. Prior to World War II, America's correctional system was punitive in nature. Large maximum-security institutions were popular and administrators were too fearful of escapes to incorporate rehabilitation treatments into their institutions (Barnes & Teeters, 1959). After World War II, a Positivistic philosophy took hold, as rehabilitation and reintegration were the driving principles. Individual and group therapy sessions were commonplace in prisons as psychologists and other professionals attempted to identify and correct problems within the individual offender.

Beginning in the 1970s, a growing wave of dissatisfaction with the rehabilitation and treatment ideal began to take hold. The country was in the midst of a dramatic increase in the crime rate, and rehabilitation programs began to be viewed as part of the problem. Public skepticism was validated in a report released by Robert Martinson in 1974. Martinson reviewed 231 research studies that had been conducted to evaluate the effectiveness of rehabilitation programs. Martinson limited his review to studies that had a sound evaluation research design, with treatment and control groups, and valid outcome measures that could be directly linked to the rehabilitation program. What Martinson found was devastating: No one program had any appreciable effect on the recidivism rate. This report, coupled with a number of studies that reported high recidivism rates for repeat offenders, effectively ended the treatment and rehabilitation era. The pendulum began to shift from a more liberal Positivistic philosophy back to a more conservative stance based on Classical criminology.

Contemporary Applications of Classical Criminology

The resurgence in popularity of the Classical criminology perspective in the 1970s spawned the growth of a number of related theories and crime prevention strategies. These contemporary applications of Classical criminology have been developed across a number of disciplines, including: economics, sociology, psychology, victimology, and geography. While a number of theories may be included under this umbrella, rational choice theory, routine activities theory, and crime pattern theory are among the most noteworthy and deserving of further discussion.

Rational Choice

The names most closely associated with the development of rational choice theory are Derek Cornish and Ronald Clarke (see, generally, Clarke & Cornish, 1985; Clarke & Felson, 1993; Cornish & Clarke, 1986; 1987). In the 1960s and 1970s, Cornish and Clarke worked on a research project that involved an examination of the effects of institutional treatments on juvenile delinquents. Cornish and Clarke began to question whether or not the treatments had any long-term impact on the behavior of the juveniles. Furthermore, when they compared the rates of running away and other forms of misconduct that occurred at the various treatment centers, Cornish and Clarke found that even though the centers serviced the same types of delinquents, some of the treatment centers had more problems than others. Cornish and Clarke began to develop the idea that something about the specific environmental characteristics in some of the treatment centers provided greater opportunities for misconduct than in centers with fewer problematic incidents. In effect, some situations provided greater opportunities for deviant behavior than others (Cornish & Clarke, 1986).

Cornish and Clarke's model rests on the assumption of a rational offender making decisions about whether or not to commit a crime. Would-be criminals process available information from their physical and social environment. Prior to the commission of a crime, an individual assesses his or her personal needs and wants; evaluates the risk of apprehension, the severity of the expected punishments, and the expected gain; and reacts selectively to the specific situational factors, such as whether or not a target is well guarded. Criminals make rational decisions about when and where to commit their crimes, carefully selecting targets that offer the highest probability for pleasure with the lowest probability for pain (Clarke & Cornish, 1985; Cornish & Clarke, 1986; Lab, 2000).

Cornish and Clarke's Decision Models

Rational choice theorists differentiate between several different types of criminal decisions, not all of which are directly related to the crime itself. Cornish and Clarke (1985; 1986; 1987) have developed a rather complex model to explain the decision-making process a potential offender goes through in deciding whether or not to commit a specific type of crime, in this case burglary in a middle-class residential suburb. The first phase of this model is described as the initial involvement model. According to Cornish and Clarke (1986), "Criminal involvement refers to the processes through which individuals choose to become initially involved in particular forms of crime, to continue, and to desist" (p. 2). These involvement decisions are affected by a number of factors, outlined below.

1. Background Factors: This includes the individual characteristics of the would-be offender, including their gender, temperament, intelligence, and cognitive decision-making style as well as the characteristics of their family life, available role models, social class, and educational level.
2. Previous Experience and Learning: Potential offenders evaluate their direct and indirect experiences with crime and the police and assess their conscience and moral attitudes towards criminal activity.
3. Assessment of Generalized Needs: The needs of the individual may center on money and the attainment of material goods, or may be driven by sex, enhanced status within the peer group, or simply excitement.

4. Solutions Evaluated: This involves the weighing of perceived risks and punishment versus potential gains. Would-be offenders also consider the degree of effort required in the commission of the crime as well as the moral costs of their actions.

5. Perceived Solutions: Would-be offenders must consider their options. "Should I pursue a legitimate job in order to get what I want, or should I commit a crime? If crime is the answer, what type of criminal behavior should I engage in? Would burglary meet my needs (and suit my personal strengths), or is robbery a better personal choice?"

6. Chance Event: As the would-be offender goes through their daily life, he or she eventually will encounter an event that will force them to make a decision. This chance event may involve being presented with an easy opportunity to commit a crime, peer pressure, or an urgent need for money.

7. Readiness: This is described as the first decision point. At this stage, the individual makes a conscious decision, recognizing that he or she is ready to commit a specific type of crime.

8. Decision: This is the second decision point. When confronted with a chance event, the offender makes a decision to commit the crime.

Event Decisions

While involvement decisions may be made over an extended period of time, event decisions are made quickly using information based on the characteristics of the specific situation. Once the decision has been made to commit a residential burglary, the offender must select a specific target. A neighborhood must be selected that offers the lowest level of risk, and within this neighborhood the burglar must choose which home will be attacked. These choices will be based on the burglar's assessment of opportunity, required effort, and risk. For example, neighborhoods that have organized crime watches or large numbers of stay-at-home mothers may be avoided due to the heightened perception of risk of detection. Once a neighborhood has been selected, homes with obvious displays of wealth, overgrown shrubs, or high privacy fences may be more attractive targets than homes with large dogs or visible alarm systems.

Persistence and Desistence

Once an individual has made the choice to become involved in crime, the decision-making process is not over. The offender constantly re-evaluates the decision of whether or not to continue his or her involvement not only in crime, but also in this particular form of crime. Cornish and Clarke argue that with continued success, a burglar will increase the frequency of offending until he or she attains a level that is personally judged to be the most favorable. Decisions to persist in this chosen area of crime will be enhanced by a number of factors, including increased professionalism, changes in life style and values, and changes in the peer group. Increased professionalism is marked by better skills in the planning and selection of targets, larger gains from criminal activities, better skills in talking with the police and dealing with the court system, and heightened levels of pride taken in one's work. Changes in lifestyle and values include choosing legitimate occupations to enhance burglary opportunities, such as working for a delivery service in order to gain a better view of the insides of people's homes; placing greater value on illegitimate enterprises and less importance on legitimate avenues for success; and enjoying "life in the fast lane." Changes in the peer group that facilitate criminal involvement include losing contact with non-criminal friends and disagreeing with "straight" family members.

Finally, there are also decisions that must be made in order for a criminal to choose to stop committing crimes. In the case of a residential burglar, events may occur during the commission of a burglary that may cause the individual to reassess their level of readiness to commit further burglaries, such as getting apprehended by the police, being surprised by a homeowner, getting bitten by the family's dog, or reduced profit from the burglary. Other life events may also occur, such as getting married or having a child, having friends or co-offenders get arrested for their criminal involvement, being offered suitable legitimate employment, or running out of available targets in the neighborhood. These events present the burglar with decision-making opportunities to persist with the chosen criminal path, desist and choose legitimate employment, or perhaps even choose other forms of criminal activity that may be more attractive, such as commercial burglary, becoming a fence for stolen goods, or perhaps burglarizing a different type of residence.

As you can see, the process developed by Cornish and Clarke is highly complex. The would-be offender, as well as the active offender, constantly evaluate and re-assess their level of readiness, personal abilities, individual needs, and the target attractiveness based on the information available to them. This is a rational process in which offenders try to benefit themselves by choosing the best course of action, be it to get involved in crime, persist in criminal activities, or instead to engage in legitimate pathways to success.

Summary: Rational Choice Theory

Rational choice theory is based on the assumption of a rational offender carefully weighing out the risks, perceived punishments, and perceived gains in a decision-making process. This decision-making process needs to be assessed with respect to both the individual offense (for instance, why a burglary has been committed of a middle class residence versus a low-income public housing unit) as well as the individual offender, as he or she assesses his or her own motivations, skills, and prior learning experiences.

Proponents of this perspective do not focus on trying to identify individual differences between criminals and non-criminals the way Positivists do. Rational choice theorists argue that this practice of dividing the world into two groups—criminals versus non-criminals—lumps all criminals together in a homogenous group and makes the assumption that all criminal behaviors and all motives to commit crimes are essentially the same. Rational choice theorists argue that what is really needed is a closer examination of specific types of crimes, as well as the motives for that particular crime and the methods used. In order to reduce crime, the focus needs to be on the criminal event itself and the situational factors that contribute to the commission of the crime.

Routine Activities

Routine activities theory was initially proposed by Lawrence Cohen and Marcus Felson (1979). Proponents of routine activities theory hold many of the assumptions held by supporters of rational choice theory. In fact, many times the theories are presented as complimentary perspectives, offering both a macro- and micro-level analysis. Routine activities theory is said to be oriented at the macro-level. Macro level theories focus on broad changes across societies or populations. Conversely, the decision models implicit within rational choice theory are at a more individual, micro level (Clarke & Felson, 1993). Taken together, these theories examine how work, recreation, spending patterns, and our every day involvement in "routine activities" can contribute to the likelihood of converging in time, space, and place with a rational motivated offender, thereby increasing the opportunity for a crime to occur.

When Cohen and Felson initially developed routine activities theory, a number of rather interesting changes had been occurring in American society. First, as previously noted, the crime rate had experienced a rather dramatic upsurge. Citing the most recently available FBI Uniform Crime Reports, Cohen and Felson pointed out that from 1960–1975 the robbery rate had increased 263%, the forcible rape rate had increased 174%, and the homicide rate had gone up 188%. Similar increases were also found with respect to property crimes, with the burglary rate experiencing an increase of 200% (FBI, 1975).

What was somewhat perplexing was that the crime wave had occurred in spite of the fact that other pathological social conditions that are often tied to crime rates, such as poverty and unemployment, had actually been on the decline. One would expect that when the general social conditions in metropolitan areas experience improvement then the crime rate in these areas would decrease. This was not the case—in fact, just the opposite had happened. The crime rate had experienced a dramatic increase despite substantial improvement in the educational levels, median incomes, and employment rates in our cities and surrounding metropolitan areas.

Cohen and Felson set out to explain these seemingly incompatible trends by focusing on structural changes in the way Americans lived their lives. In a nutshell, changes in the routine activities of everyday life increased the opportunity for crimes to occur. Cohen and Felson focused on illegal activities (termed **direct contact predatory violations**) in which a perpetrator intentionally takes or otherwise harms a target. In their definition, at least one criminal must come into direct physical contact with at least one target, which could include people or their property. Cohen and Felson argued that changes in life patterns had occurred after World War II that had contributed to the increase in direct contact predatory violations. People were spending less time at home with family members and more time outside of the home with non-family members—either at work, school, recreation, or other activities.

According to Cohen and Felson, in order for a direct contact predatory violation to occur, three "almost always" elements must converge in space and time: **motivated offenders, suitable targets,** and the **absence of capable guardians.** Recently "often important" elements of a crime have been added to the "almost always" elements that were part of Cohen and Felson's original theoretical framework. The "often-important" elements of a crime include (1) **props** that aid in the facilitation or prevention of a crime, such as weapons or tools; (2) **camouflage** that aid an offender in avoiding being noticed; and (3) an **audience** that a potential offender desires to impress or intimidate (Felson, 2002; Felson & Boba, 2010). At the heart of the theory—in its original form—was the notion that the shift in routine activities that occurred after World War II increased the likelihood that a motivated offender would come together in time and space with a suitable target in the absence of a capable guardian. Today, this is commonly depicted in what is referred to as the "crime triangle".

The Crime Triangle

The three elements essential for the occurrence of a crime—motivated offenders, suitable targets, and the absence of capable guardians—are sometimes referred to as "the crime triangle." In Cohen and Felson's original model, motivated offenders were a given—in their theory, it was not really relevant to explore whether an individual person or group was more or less criminally inclined than another. What was important was to examine the circumstances that provide the opportunity for criminally motivated people to translate their inclinations into action.

At the time, the availability of suitable targets had also increased since World War II. Cohen and Felson noted marked increases in consumer spending patterns from 1960–1970. Americans were accumulating more and more possessions, which translated into more property available for theft. Along with the change in quantity of potential targets, Cohen and Felson also noticed a change in the size and weight of many products. For example, in 1960 the lightest television listed in the Sears catalog weighed in at 38 pounds. By 1970, the lightest television available weighed only 15 pounds. Similar reductions in size and weight were also noted in radios, record players, toasters, and other small electrical products. Smaller, lighter items make better targets for illegal removal, since they are easier to conceal and carry off. Of course, this trend of smaller, more expensive, lightweight gadgets did not stop in 1970. Think of all of the items that have become commonplace in the past decade—laptops, Blackberries, iPads, Kindels, MP3 players, USB flash drives, etc.—that make very suitable targets for a motivated offender.

When you hear the phrase "absence of capable guardians," you might think of the police (or lack thereof). The police are only one type of capable guardian, and some would argue that their level of effectiveness in crime prevention is questionable. In what has become a classic study on the effectiveness of random patrol activities on crime, data from the Kansas City Preventive Patrol Experiment indicated that substantial increases in the normal level of patrol had no significant effect on the level of criminal activity reported in the area (Kelling, Pate, Dieckman, & Brown, 1974). This study will be discussed in greater detail in Chapter 4.

This point should not be taken as an attack on the effectiveness of the police. The police are simply outnumbered and over-extended. For example, a popular measure of the level of police protection is the police-population ratio, which is defined as the number of sworn officers per 1,000 residents of a particular jurisdiction. According to information released by the Bureau of Justice Statistics, in 2004, the police-population ratio for the entire U.S. was 2.5 sworn officers per 1,000 residents (Reaves, 2007). It should also be pointed out that not all of these sworn officers were assigned to full time patrol activities. Some of the sworn officers included in the ratio were administrators, while others may have been assigned to special units such as school resource officers, traffic duty, detectives, or desk duties. This means that the ratio of *patrol officers* per 1,000 residents is actually much lower.

Further, as discussed by Felson (1998a), the actual time that a patrol officer can devote to guarding your home against crime is minimal. Few patrol officers are assigned to large geographic areas with many suitable targets that must be protected over a 24-hour period. Felson estimated that an individual home would lack the capable guardianship of the police 99.98% of the time. Even if a patrol officer happens to be driving by a home, the likelihood is very low that a particular patrol officer would be familiar enough with the residents and routine activities of the home to recognize that the person carrying a brand new color television out of the front door is not authorized to do so. Felson (1998a) estimates that less than 1% of criminal offenders are "caught in the act" by a patrol officer who happens to be driving through a neighborhood at the right place and the right time.

For Cohen and Felson, the more effective capable guardians were ordinary citizens, moving through the routine activities of their daily lives, all the while keeping an eye out for the safety of others and their property. The availability of capable guardians also changed after World War II. For example, consider the crime of residential burglary. Since the 1960s, the proportion of residential burglaries that have occurred during the day has increased dramatically (Miethe & McCorkle, 2001; 2006). Why?

Consider an episode of *Happy Days*, a television series based on the life of the Cunningham family in the 1950s. Both parents resided in their home, and Mrs. Cunningham was a stay-at-home mom who took care of their two children. In Cohen and Felson's terminology, Mrs. Cunningham was a capable guardian. Her presence in the home was a strong deterrent to a would-be rational offender assessing the suitability of her home and the homes of her neighbors as potential targets. Compare life at the Cunningham's home to the type of life most experience today. More than likely, kids come home to an empty house after school. Even if living in a two-parent household (which is becoming more and more of a rare event), it is likely that a mother works outside of the home. Many of these neighborhood children return to empty homes as well. Structural changes in our society—such as the increase of women entering the workplace and the decrease in two parent homes—alter our routine activities and decrease the availability of capable guardians, thereby increasing the likelihood for crime to occur.

Cohen and Felson maintained that the lack of any one of the three elements—motivated offenders, suitable targets, or absence of capable guardians—was enough to prevent the successful completion of a direct contact predatory crime. Furthermore, Cohen and Felson made the argument that even if the number of motivated offenders or suitable targets were to remain the same in a community, changes in the routine activities of residents could lead to greater opportunities for criminal acts to occur.

The Problem Analysis Triangle: The Addition of Controllers

Figure 3.1 displays a modified version of Cohen and Felson's crime triangle. As you can see, the inner triangle contains the original components of offender, victim or target, and place. In the updated version, an outer triangle has been added which addresses the issue of "controllers." **Controllers** are those individuals who have a responsibility—either formal or informal—to monitor each aspect of the original crime triangle. With respect to the offender, he or she may be monitored by a **handler, defined as someone who is close to the offender and can exercise** some level of control over his or her actions. While the role of handlers will be described in greater detail in the next section, informal handlers may be parents, teachers, spouses, or siblings. When these informal systems fail, formal handlers may include probation and parole officers.

The controller for a specific location is known as the "**manager.**" The manager is an individual who has some responsibility for monitoring the behavior in a place. Examples of managers include landlords, business owners, classroom teachers, and restaurant or bar managers. All have some level of accountability to ensure the safety of a specific area. Finally, the controller for the target or victim is known as a capable guardian, which is a carry-over from the original language of Cohen and Felson. Formal guardians may include the police and private security guards, while an informal guardian may simply be

Figure 3.1

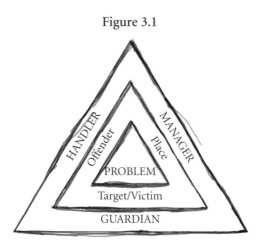

you keeping an eye on your classroom neighbor's backpack while she uses the restroom.

The addition of the controllers to the crime triangle is important because it forces those who are thinking about crime to carefully consider all elements of opportunity as intervention and/or prevention strategies are developed to curb crime. Controllers may be called upon to shore up the surveillance and control of an individual or place, thereby reducing the likelihood that a crime will occur (Clarke & Eck, 2005). More recently, the concept of "super controllers" has been introduced. A super controller exerts some form of control over a controller. Sampson, Eck, and Dunham (2010) provided the example of the State alcohol beverage control bureau as one form of a super controller. This bureau does not have any direct control over making changes to the direct safety of a place, but instead the bureau influences the behavior of the bar or restaurant owner by regulating the sale of alcohol. This may be done by limiting the hours of sale, restricting the sale of alcohol to minors, etc. These regulations influence the behavior of the place manager, and these changes may then influence the overall safety of the bar or restaurant. Other examples of super controllers include the media, insurance companies and other financial institutions, government agencies, and even the market. If a place is not safe, potential customers may choose not to go to a particular business.

Regardless of the role of an individual, the crime triangle also illustrates that each uses "tools" to help accomplish their criminal or crime control objective. For example, a place manager may use security gates, electronic key swipes, or close circuit television systems to regulate conduct and behavior. Likewise, a guardian may install a LoJack car security system, padlock a bicycle to a light pole, or use engraving devises to mark property in order to reduce the risk of property victimization. Similarly, tools that offenders, such as gang members, use may include spray paint cans, guns, and cars.

Advances in Routine Activities Theory: The Addition of Social Control

In his later writings, Felson (1986; 1998a; 1998b; 2002; Felson & Boba, 2010; Felson & Clarke, 1995) began to incorporate the ideas of social control theorist Travis Hirschi with routine activities theory. According to Hirschi (1969), an individual's involvement in crime and delinquency was dependent upon his or her bond to society. If an individual had a strong bond with society, then he or she would be more likely to lead a life of conformity. If, however, the bond to society had been weakened, then an individual would choose crime as a reasonable alternative.

For Hirschi, the social bond is made up of four components: attachment, commitment, involvement, and belief. Attachment refers to a person's ties with others, specifically whether or not the person cares about the opinions of other people. Consider the unfortunate situation of living with a roommate from hell. Does one care to wash the dishes, take phone messages, vacuum, or otherwise follow the rules of the house? Probably not. Without attachment, a person does not feel bound by the norms of society (or the apartment). A person with strong attachment to others has internalized the norms of society and developed a strong sense of conscience (Curran & Renzetti, 2001).

Hirschi described commitment as the rational element of his theory. For example, by simply reading this book a strong commitment to conformity is indicated. You are enrolled in college and are actually taking the time to read your assigned materials. You have made an investment in your future and have much to lose if you do not play by the rules. When the weekend comes up and your friends encourage you to go out for a wild night of drinking on the town, chances are you will weigh your commitment to conventional society. If you go out and get stupid-drunk and get arrested, what will happen? Will you lose everything you worked for? According to Hirschi, because of the investment of time and effort in the pursuit of conventional activities, the rules of society will be followed.

Involvement refers to the amount of time a person spends engaged in conventional activities. If a teenager plays on sports teams, has an after school job, takes trumpet lessons, attends church activities, and spends a great deal of time doing homework there simply are not enough hours in the day to get into trouble. Opportunities for criminal involvement are limited because of the person's involvement in conventional activities. Finally, belief has to do with whether a person believes that the rules of society are "good," necessary, and should be followed. If a person does not believe that the rules of society apply to him or her, then he or she will not feel any pressure to follow them.

In tying Hirschi's ideas with routine activities theory, Felson compares the elements of the social bond to handles on a suitcase. According to Felson (1998a):

> Social bonds are like the handles on a suitcase: The more handles, the easier it is to carry. The more bonds you have to society, the easier it is for society to carry you along. This does not mean you have no free will; it only means you will *choose* to go along with the rules because the price you pay for not doing so is too high. This is why control theory has a strong 'rational' component and is consistent with the offender decision-making perspective … (emphasis in original) (p. 44).

Felson argues that almost everyone has a handle, and the handle is necessary in order for informal social control to occur. If a child does not care about what other people think, does not feel that the rules apply to him, is not in-volved in any conventional activities, and has no stake in conformity, then the child does not have a "handle" by which society can grab onto and keep the child's behavior controlled by informal means.

Felson uses the term "intimate handler" to describe parents or other adults who are both physically and emotionally close to the child. Everyone's handle is a bit different, so if an adult is going to effectively control the behavior of a child, then the adult must know the child well enough to grab onto his or her unique handle. What works to shame and control one child may be completely ineffective with another—it takes intimate knowledge of the child to know what words or actions will get the child back on track.

Due to their closeness with the child, intimate handlers are also able to rec-ognize if items that are entering the home are of questionable origin—for ex-ample, if a child is caught wearing a new pair of expensive pants that the parent did not purchase for the child. An intimate handler will be able to recognize that the pants were probably stolen and be able to grab onto the appropriate handle to correct the behavior, such as making the child return the stolen pants and apologize to the store manager.

Even the best parent cannot monitor the actions of the child 24 hours a day, 7 days a week. This is where informants become an important element of in-formal social control. If you grew up in a tightly knit community, where every-one knew everyone, then you may have experienced this form of informal social control. A neighbor may have seen you doing something wrong, like skipping school, and reported your actions to your parents. While this may seem like a "normal" thing for the neighbor to do, in contemporary societies this type of informal social control is on the wane. This type of intervention requires that the neighbor have intimate knowledge of you and your family. The neighbor must 1) recognize you; 2) be familiar enough with the routine activities of your life to know that on Tuesdays at 11:00 a.m. you should be in school; 3) know who your parents are; 4) and feel comfortable enough calling your parents to let them know what you had been up to.

Felson argues that changes in contemporary society have reduced our ability to exert informal social control. These changes include: the increase in the number of working mothers, the movement towards larger schools, greater distances between one's home and place of work, lower fertility rates, greater geographic mobility, higher rates of divorce, blended families, and even widespread use of the automobile. These changes reduce the likeli-hood that an individual child engaging in a criminal act will be detected, recognized, and either handled appropriately or reported to the proper in-timate handler.

This advancement in routine activities theory is quite similar to many of the ideas discussed in Chapter 2, with respect to social disorganization, collective efficacy, and the importance of informal social control. Communities with high levels of social disorganization (in the words of Shaw and McKay) will tend to have higher numbers of children with weak bonds to society whose behavior is monitored by few intimate handlers and informants. Strengthening the bonds that both children and adults have with their neighbors may ultimately reduce crime. In Chapter 4, a number of policy recommendations based on re-building communities and enhancing informal social control will be discussed.

Summary: Routine Activities

Like rational choice theory, routine activities theory is premised on the basic assumption of a rational offender carefully weighing the costs and benefits of his or her actions. While rational choice theory is focused on the individual offender, routine activities theory takes more of a macro level approach, incorporating broad changes in contemporary society and the way these changes have impacted how we live our every day lives. In order for crime to occur, three elements need to converge in space and time: motivated offenders, suitable targets, and the absence of capable guardians. Changes in American society have increased the likelihood that a motivated offender will come together in time and space with a suitable target in the absence of a capable guardian.

Since its inception, routine activities theory has had a great impact on crime prevention strategies. Practical applications of Cohen and Felson's ideas will be covered in the next unit. For now, the last choice-based theory, crime pattern theory, will be introduced.

Crime Pattern Theory

Crime pattern theory may be viewed as a combination platter of rational choice, routine activities, and environmental principles (Rossmo, 2000). Crime pattern theory begins with the assumption of a rational offender. During the course of everyday movements through time and space, suitable targets may be brought to the attention of a motivated offender. So far, this is nothing new. The added twist of crime pattern theory is that the level and the type of criminal activity can be predicted through an analysis of a city's geographic environment, such as land use patterns, street networks, and transportation systems. Proponents of crime pattern theory hold that crimes do not occur randomly in time or space, but are influenced greatly by the physical movements of offenders and victims.

The criminologists most closely associated with the development of crime pattern theory are Paul and Patricia Brantingham. Their theoretical orientation is a marriage (in more ways than one) between traditional criminology (Paul) and training in urban planning and mathematics (Patricia). The pair has written extensively in the area of environmental criminology, of which crime pattern theory is a principle component (see, for example, Brantingham & Brantingham, 1981; 1991; 1998; 1999; 2008). According to the Brantinghams (1991), environmental criminology is the study of the spatio-temporal or locational dimension of crime. Environmental criminologists are concerned with answering questions such as where and when will crimes occur; what are the movements that bring the offender and the target together at the location of the crime; what is involved in the thought processes that lead to the selection of the crime location; and how are targets and offenders distributed spatially in urban, suburban, and rural settings?

The Language of Crime Pattern Theory: Nodes, Paths, and Edges

Crime pattern theory introduces us to a number of new vocabulary terms. First is the idea of **action space**. As potential offenders live their daily lives, they travel throughout their city conducting both legitimate and illegitimate activities. These activities may include going to the mall or shopping district, to work, to attend classes, and down to the entertainment district on the weekends. These areas—shopping, work, school, or entertainment areas—are referred to as **nodes,** or the areas that people travel to and from. The movements between these various nodes form an **awareness space, or the parts of the city that an individual has at least some information about**. Since the awareness space requires only minimal knowledge, the awareness space is larger than (and completely contains) the action space (Rossmo, 2000).

Chances are, most people are not intimately familiar with their entire city. In fact, in a large city, there are more than likely areas that they have never been to and, in some respects, do not really even exist to them. However, most are intimately familiar with the travel **paths** that they take between their personal activity nodes—the path from home to work to school and so forth. A path can follow any form of transportation: highways, streets, sidewalks, mass transit lines, or even a footpath from a dorm to classroom buildings.

Based on the movements along the paths between personal activity nodes a **cognitive map** or mental image of the environment is formed. In addition to personal activity nodes and highly familiar paths, a cognitive map may also include various special locations within the environment, like tourist attractions or necessary places of business (like the county courthouse). Cognitive

maps may be different depending upon the time of day or day of the week—
a mental image of the entertainment district node and the path to it may be
very different on Friday nights at 11:00 p.m. than on Sunday mornings.

As long as people remain in the areas defined by their cognitive map, they feel
safe. When they travel off of the beaten path, so to speak, they may feel some
anxiety. Landmarks are no longer recognized and strangers are all around. It is
difficult to tell who belongs and who does not. Furthermore, people tend to be
creatures of habit. The routine activities of daily life rarely require ventures into
unchartered territory. As a result, people may rarely leave their awareness space.

Moving along the paths between various personal activity nodes introduces
edges. According to the Brantinghams (1998), an edge is a "sharp visual break
between different types of land use, between different socioeconomic and demographic residential and commercial areas. Edges are clearly apparent along
major parks, next to single-family areas, and surrounding high-activity shopping centers" (p. 33) An edge may be a major street that separates one neighborhood or land use area from another (Felson, 2006).

Edges can be quite striking. I (Kim) recall driving into Detroit with some
friends from high school to go to a Tigers baseball game. We got off at the
wrong interstate exit and ended up right next to a large university campus.
The sharp visual break was quite dramatic: On one side of the street was a
beautiful well groomed urban campus, while on the other side of the street
was a string of dilapidated vacant homes with broken windows and overgrown,
littered lawns. College students walked the street beside homeless people, local
residents, merchants, and of course, a motivated offender or two. While some
edges are quite visible, in other areas edges are not that dramatic. One neighborhood may gradually transition into another without a sharp break between
the two communities (Felson, 2006).

Edges can be high crime areas. Within a node, people have a sense of who
belongs and who does not. This is not the case with an edge where strangers
come and go, moving with relative anonymity. Felson (2006) made the distinction between "discrete" and "connected" edges. An example of a discrete edge
would be a convenience store, parking lot, or park that divides two different
neighborhoods. This edge draws both victims and motivated offenders to the
same rather anonymous area. As noted by Felson, it is easier for an offender
to steal a vehicle that is between two different neighborhoods—no one really
knows whose car it is.

If the various edges are connected by a motorized transport system (streets, subway or bus lines, etc.) the risk for victimization is even higher. These connected
edges allow offenders to easily move from one edge to another. This increased
mobility results in the spread of crime in a much larger area (Felson, 2006).

Crimes and Cognitive Maps

Just as college students have a cognitive map based on their awareness space, so do criminals. At the heart of crime pattern theory is the assumption that crimes will occur in the areas where suitable targets intersect an offender's awareness space. A burglar will tend to search out suitable targets during the course of his or her routine movements through time and space. Since both criminals and non-criminals rarely venture away from their regular awareness space, most offenses will occur close to the home, workplace, shopping centers, or entertainment areas frequented by the offender or along the paths between these activity nodes. Offenders search for suitable targets, outward from the nodes and paths, following what has been called a **distance decay function**: The further offenders move away from the comfort zone of their cognitive maps, the less likely they will be to search for targets in the area.

In studies of offender mobility, a number of interesting trends have been noted. In general, the distance between an offender's home and the location of the crime tends to be relatively short, with a sharp drop off in the number of crimes as one moves further and further from the offender's home (Eck & Weisburd, 1995; Rengert, Piquero, & Jones, 1999). However, the distance decay function may vary based on the type of offense, whether expressive or instrumental in nature.

Expressive crimes (or affective crimes) are more spontaneous, emotional, and impulsive crimes that are done in anger. These include domestic violence, some forms of rape, and assaults. Instrumental crimes are crimes committed in order to achieve a goal, such as money, status, or other personal gain (Miethe & McCorkle, 2006). Examples of instrumental crimes include burglary and robbery. In general, expressive crimes are committed closer to home than instrumental crimes (Eck & Weisburd, 1995; Phillips, 1980; Rossmo, 2000). For predatory instrumental crimes, there appears to be a sort of "buffer zone" located around the home of the offender. In this buffer zone, targets may be viewed as being too risky, because of the likelihood of being recognized and ultimately arrested. Because expressive crimes by definition are more emotional (and hence less rational) in nature, the buffer zone does not seem to be as important in the selection of an appropriate target (Brantingham & Brantingham, 1981; Rossmo, 2000).

Cognitive Maps and Urban Development

As noted previously, one added component of crime pattern theory is the study of the relationship between a city's geographic environment and the level and type of criminal activity. As argued by the Brantinghams (1991), the awareness spaces and cognitive maps for both offenders and non-offenders will vary based on the actual structure of the city and its transportation system. For example, in a major city that has a thriving mass transit system, awareness spaces are more nodal in nature—most are very familiar with their end location (shopping node, entertainment node, etc.) but not so familiar with the actual paths to get between the nodes. Criminals living in this type of city have the same cognitive maps. Therefore, criminal activity is expected to be higher in and near the major nodes along the transportation network than along the paths (which may not cognitively exist).

In newer cities or cities without mass transit, the prediction of high crime areas is different. For example, in newer cities with sprawling strip malls for shopping, dispersed entertainment centers, and separate residential and commercial areas, crime is expected to be more spread out than in older, more densely concentrated cities. This has to do with the size of the awareness spaces and cognitive maps of potential offenders. Because the nodes are so spread out, extensive travel is necessary in order to conduct the routine activities of life. More travel translates into larger search areas for potential targets. Since the targets are not concentrated, it follows that the level of criminal activity is not concentrated either.

The relationship between urban design, traffic patterns, and criminal activity has important considerations for real estate developers and city planners (for a more in-depth discussion of these issues, see generally Felson, 1998b). For example, in the development of a new suburban housing development, a number of residential streets may be designated as major traffic routes for the subdivision. Since the volume of traffic is expected to be higher along these paths, houses along these arteries will be exposed to a greater number of motivated offenders who will incorporate the road into their awareness space. Planners and developers should take steps to reduce the likelihood that one of these homes would become a target for criminal activity, such as incorporating landscaping or architectural designs to enhance visibility and guardianship of the homes along this major path.

Additionally, the physical layout of the streets in a neighborhood can also have an impact on the level of criminal activity. Brantingham and Brantingham (1991; 1998) have noted that neighborhoods with highly predictable street grid networks will more than likely have higher crime rates than areas with more "organic" street layouts. In a city based on a grid system, it is very easy to get around. For a number of years, we (both authors) lived in St. Petersburg, Florida, which is based on a grid system. In St. Pete, all streets run north and south and all avenues run east and west, in a highly predictable manner. Kim used to own a pizza shop that was located at 5570 4th Street North. Based solely on the address a person even remotely familiar with the city would know exactly where the business was located: on 4th Street North about midway between 55th and 56th Avenues.

The problem with this type of layout is that people feel very comfortable venturing into unknown parts of the city. Cognitive maps become very large because the city is so predictable. If a person needed to go to 9810 66th Street South, the journey would not be difficult. This place could easily be located within a cognitive map even if an individual had never been in the area. For criminals, larger cognitive maps and larger awareness spaces translate into larger search areas for potential targets. Therefore, to design a neighborhood for safety, a number of winding roads, dead-end streets, or cul-de-sacs that lend a bit of uncertainty to those unfamiliar with the neighborhood should be included. A number of crime prevention strategies based on rational choice, routine activities, and crime pattern theories will be explored in the next unit.

Target Selection and the Rational Offender

It is important to stress the basic assumption upon which crime pattern theory is based: a rational motivated offender searching for suitable targets within his or her awareness space. Brantingham and Brantingham (1991) have proposed the following outline that describes the process of crime site selection:

1. Individuals exist who are motivated to commit specific offenses.
   a. The sources of motivation are diverse. Different etiological models or theories may appropriately be invoked to explain the motivation of different individuals or groups.
   b. The strength of such motivation varies.
   c. The character of such motivation varies from affective to instrumental.
2. Given the motivation of an individual to commit an offense, the actual commission of an offense is the end result of a multistage decision process, which seeks out and identifies, within the general environment, a target or victim positioned in time and space.
   a. In the case of high affect motivation, the decision process will probably involve a minimal number of stages.
   b. In the case of high instrumental motivation, the decision process locating a target or victim may include many stages and much careful searching.
3. The environment emits many signals, or cues, about its physical, spatial, cultural, legal, and psychological characteristics.
   a. These cues can vary from generalized to detailed.
4. An individual who is motivated to commit a crime uses cues (either learned through experience or learned through social transmission) from the environment to locate and identify targets or victims.

5. As experiential knowledge grows, an individual who is motivated to
    commit a crime learns which individual cues, clusters of cues, and se-
    quences of cues are associated with "good" victims or targets. These
    cues, cue clusters, and cue sequences can be considered a template,
    which is used in victim or target selection. Potential victims or targets
    are compared to the template and either rejected or accepted depend-
    ing on the congruence.
    a. The process of template construction and the search process may
        be consciously conducted, or these processes may occur in an un-
        conscious, cybernetic fashion so that the individual cannot articu-
        late how they are done.
6. Once the template is established, it becomes relatively fixed and influ-
    ences future search behavior, thereby becoming self-reinforcing.
7. Because of the multiplicity of targets and victims, many potential crime
    selection templates could be constructed. But because the spatial and
    temporal distribution of offenders, targets, and victims is not regular,
    but clustered or patterned, and because human environmental per-
    ception has some universal properties, individual templates have sim-
    ilarities, which can be identified (p. 28).

For purposes of this discussion, the point made in (2) is most relevant: Given
the fact that he or she is motivated, the offender carefully and rationally searches
out an appropriate target or victim. For certain types of crimes, this decision-
making process can be quite involved. For other types of crimes, the process can
be much shorter. The important point is that there is a decision-making process
by which crime victims are rationally selected by offenders, as both the hunted
(targets) and hunters (offenders) move through time and space.

Also of interest in this decision-making model is the idea of a **template**, or
a mental image of a "good" target. Information used to build this template
comes from a variety of sources and the offender may not even consciously be
aware of some of the criteria. For example, in a large university, with a diverse
number of course offerings, students may hunt for a "good" course. Based on
their own experiences and discussions with peers, they have a mental image or
template of what the perfect course would be. During drop-add week, they
may shop various sections comparing the instructor, course content, and requirements laid out in the syllabus to their template. When comparing potential courses to the template, some rejections are easy to articulate (no 8:00
a.m. classes!), while other reasons for not taking a course are a bit "fuzzy," such
as a "bad" feeling from the instructor on the first day. The general argument
here is that criminals select "good" targets in the same manner that students

choose a "good" course—through a rational decision-making process based on a variety of data available. Students might also have different templates constructed for courses in their major versus elective courses, day classes versus night, etc., much the same way that a criminal will have different templates for different potential targets. Rational decision-making processes follow the same general path, whether a person is choosing a suitable course or a suitable target.

Summary: Crime Pattern Theory

Crime pattern theory incorporates elements of both rational choice and routine activities theory. Through the course of the routine activities of daily life, rational motivated offenders are exposed geographically and temporally with rather limited portions of a city. It is along the pathways, edges, and within the nodes of their awareness space that offenders select appropriate targets or victims through a multistage decision-making process. The actual occurrence of crimes in a city will be affected by the geographic structure of the city's land use patterns, transportation system, and street networks.

The Bottom Line: Is Crime Rational?

It appears now that we have come full circle. We began this Chapter with a discussion of Classical criminology, which was based on the assumption of a rational, hedonistic offender whose behavior can only be kept in check through the careful application of certain, swift, and proportionate punishments. We then learned of rational choice theory, which explored the decision-making processes through which would-be offenders try to benefit themselves by carefully choosing the best course of action, whether it be to get involved in crime, persist in criminal activities, or to, instead, desist and engage in legitimate pathways to success. Routine activities theory presented us with the notion of motivated offenders, suitable targets, and the lack of capable guardians converging in time and place as we conduct the business of our everyday lives. Finally, crime pattern theory incorporated the notion of a rational, motivated offender with an analysis of a city's geographic environment in order to predict the level and type of criminal activities that would be most likely to occur. If you can pick up on a common thread in this various theories, it would be the idea of a rational offender. So, the question remains: Is crime rational?

If you are looking for a simple yes or no answer to this question, then you will be sadly disappointed. I've (Kim) taught Theories of Criminal Behavior courses more times than I care to admit and one of the most consistent complaints that I hear from students is that you never get a definite answer. Half of the empirical research studies seem to support a theory, while an equal number of studies refute the propositions. Research studies testing choice theories are no different. While a number of studies have found support for the idea of a rational offender, carefully assessing the potential gains against perceived certainty and severity of punishment (see, generally, Cornish & Clarke, 1986; Cromwell, Olson, & Avery, 1991; Katz, 1988; Tunnell, 1992), others have not (see, for example, Paternoster, 1987). The issue is even more complicated when one considers the type of crime (either expressive or instrumental, white collar crime versus street crimes), as well as various offender characteristics (like adults versus juveniles).

For example, consider the crime of auto theft. As noted by Miethe and Mc-Corkle (2001; 2006), there are two very different images of a typical car thief. On one extreme, there are professional car thieves who carefully seek out targets that will provide the greatest profit. Clarke and Harris (1992) found that certain types of cars are targeted for stripping for their parts, like Volkswagens or Saabs. Professional auto thieves engage in more elaborate decision-making processes, from learning which cars have the most marketable parts, to acquiring more sophisticated equipment to increase the likelihood of success in their thefts.

At the other end of the spectrum is the image of juvenile joy riders that happen to stumble across opportunities (like a motorist leaving the keys in the ignition) with no planning or foresight, stealing the car simply for the fun of it. While it may appear that juvenile auto thieves are less rational in their criminal involvement, Fleming (1999) found that juvenile auto thieves voiced a number of motivations for committing their crimes. Some of the most active juvenile offenders described motivations that were instrumental (for profit) in nature, while others were categorized as irrational and immature in their thinking. However, even among the joy riders and thrill-seekers, there may have been some level of rationality on the part of the offenders. Fleming argued that for teens and pre-teens, thrill and excitement might be as rational a goal as money and economic gain for older offenders.

Part of the issue in trying to assess whether or not an offender behaved rationally is trying to tease out the meaning of "rationality." In a study of active residential burglars, Cromwell, et al. (1991) found evidence that the offenders did engage in a rather simple decision-making process in which they assessed the risk of apprehension based on a number of environmental cues. In effect, the burglars exercised a sort of "limited rationality," where long term costs, risks, or gains were not heavily weighted in the decision-making process. The concept of limited rationality recognizes that most people are unwilling or unable to completely assess every minute detail prior to making a decision. Instead, offenders develop what Cook (1980) called a "standing decision" to commit crimes if a certain type of opportunity presents itself. The idea is that given a certain set of environmental cues, a burglar may decide to select a particular target. This target may not be the *best* (or most rational) choice, but it may be a satisfactory choice.

Decisions do not have to be completely rational in order to fit in with the assumptions of choice theories. The theories only require that a minimal degree of planning and deliberation has occurred prior to the commission of a crime (Cromwell, Parker, & Mobley, 1999; Hirschi, 1986). This concept of limited rationality should also be considered in light of the fact that many offenders are under the influence of drugs or alcohol at the time the decision was made to commit their crimes. According to information released by the Bureau of Justice Statistics, in 2004, nearly one-third of State prisoners and one-quarter of Federal prisoners committed their offense while under the influence of drugs (Mumola & Karberg, 2007). The ingestion of certain types of drugs and/or alcohol may lower inhibitions, reduce fear and perception of risk, and increase aggression (Akers, 1992). Under these circumstances, the concept of limited rationality may become even more limited.

Gottfredson and Hirschi (1990) have incorporated the concept of rational decision-making—or lack thereof—in their General Theory of Crime, which has become a very popular explanation for a variety of criminal and deviant activities. According to Gottredson and Hirschi (1990), all criminal behavior can be explained by an individual's level of self-control. People with low levels of self-control "will tend to be impulsive, insensitive, physical (as opposed to mental), risk-taking, short sighted, and nonverbal" (p. 90). Basically, individuals who commit crimes are not able to really understand the long-term impact that their actions have on themselves or on others. Because they are selfish and insensitive, individuals with low self-control do not accurately determine the costs and the benefits of engaging in an activity that provides immediate gratification; immediate gratification becomes much more important than any long-term consequences of their behavior. In effect, they are unwilling or unable to make a truly rational choice. According to Gottfredson and Hirschi (1990):

> The dimensions of self-control are, in our view, factors affecting calculation of the consequences of one's acts. The impulsive or short-

sighted person fails to consider the negative or painful consequences of his act; the insensitive person has fewer negative consequences to consider; the less intelligent person has fewer negative consequences to consider (has less to lose) (p. 95).

Gottfredson and Hirschi have argued that increased punishments will not impact the level of crime in society. The threat of lengthy prison terms will not deter an individual with low self-control because the individual cannot accurately weigh the pros and cons of their actions. Instead, Gottfredson and Hirschi emphasize the need for improved parenting and childrearing skills, as they argue that self-control is developed through early childhood socialization in the family (Akers & Sellers, 2009). If children are raised to have higher levels of self-control, then they will have the ability to make rational decisions.

Summary

The resurgence in interest in Classical criminology has brought about a number of interesting changes in the way we think about crime, criminals, and what to do about the crime problem. While all begin with the concept of a rational offender, the choice theories that we have explored in this unit—rational choice, routine activities, and crime pattern theory—each add their own unique contributions to or understanding of crime. In Chapter 5, some of the practical applications of choice theories in crime prevention and crime reduction strategies are examined.

Decision Process: To Rob or Not to Rob

We close our discussion of choice-based theories with a reprint of an article by Bruce Jacobs and Richard Wright. This study was conducted using semi-structured interviews with active armed robbers, which is no small feat. As you read this piece, ask yourself if these robbers fit the image of a calculating, rational individual carefully weighing out the pros and cons of their actions.

Spotlight on Research II

"Stick-Up, Street Culture, and Offender Motivation"
Bruce A. Jacobs and Richard Wright*

Abstract

Motivation is the central, yet arguably the most assumed, causal variable in the etiology of criminal behavior. Criminology's incomplete and imprecise understanding of this construct can be traced to the discipline's strong emphasis on background risk factors, often to the exclusion of subjective foreground conditions. In this article, we attempt to remedy this by exploring the decision-making processes of active armed robbers in real-life settings and circumstances. Our aim is to understand how and why these offenders move from an unmotivated state to one in which they are determined to commit robbery. Drawing from semistructured interviews with 86 active armed robbers, we argue that while the decision to commit robbery stems most directly from a perceived need for fast cash, this decision is activated, mediated, and shaped by participation in street culture. Street culture, and its constituent conduct norms, represents an essential intervening variable linking criminal motivation to background risk factors and subjective foreground conditions.

Motivation is the central, yet arguably the most assumed, causal variable in the etiology of criminal behavior. Obviously, persons commit crimes because they are motivated to do so, and virtually no offense can occur in the absence of motivation. Though the concept inheres implicitly or explicitly in every influential theory of crime, this is far from saying that its treatment has been comprehensive, exhaustive, or precise (but see Tittle, 1995). In many ways, motivation is criminology's dirty little secret—manifest yet murky, presupposed but elusive, everywhere and nowhere. If there is a bogeyman lurking in our discipline's theoretical shadows, motivation may well be it.

Much of the reason for this can be located in the time-honored, positivistic tradition of finding the one factor, or set of factors, that accounts for it. Causality has been called criminology's "Holy Grail" (Groves and Lynch, 1990:360), the quest for which makes other disciplinary pursuits seem tangential, sometimes inconsequential. The search typically revolves around identification of background risk factors (Katz, 1988)—behavioral correlates—that establish nonspurious relationships with criminal behavior (Groves and Lynch, 1990:358). A panoply of such factors have been implicated over many

---

* Reprinted with permission. *Criminology, 37*(1), 149–173.

decades of research—spanning multiple levels, as well as units, of analyses. They include, among other things, anomie, blocked opportunities, deviant self-identity, status frustration, weak social bonds, low self-control, social disorganization, structural oppression, unemployment, age, gender, class, race, deviant peer relations, marital status, body type, IQ, and personality (see e.g., Akers, 1985; Becker, 1963; Chambliss and Seidman, 1971; Cloward and Ohlin, 1960; Cohen, 1955; Cornish and Clarke, 1986; Felson, 1987; Hirschi, 1969; Merton, 1938; Miller, 1958; Quinney, 1970; Sampson and Laub, 1992; Shaw and McKay, 1942; Sutherland, 1947).

Common to all such factors, however, is their independent status from the "foreground" of criminal decision making—the immediate phenomenological context in which decisions to offend are activated (see also Groves and Lynch, 1990; Katz, 1988). Though background factors may predispose persons to crime, they fail to explain why two individuals with identical risk factor profiles do not offend equally (see e.g., Colvin and Pauly, 1983), why persons with particular risk factors go long periods of time without offending, why individuals without the implicated risk factors offend, why persons offend but not in the particular way a theory directs them to, or why persons who are not determined to commit a crime one moment become determined to do so the next (see Katz, 1988:3–4; see also Tittle, 1995, on "theoretical precision"). Decisions to offend, like all social action, do not take place in a vacuum. Rather, they are bathed in an "ongoing process of human existence" (Bottoms and Wiles, 1992:19) and mediated by prevailing situational and subcultural conditions.

In this article we attend to these important foreground dynamics, exploring the decision-making processes of active armed robbers in real life settings and circumstances. Our aim is to understand how and why these offenders move from an unmotivated state to one in which they are determined to commit robbery. We argue that while the decision to commit robbery stems most directly from a perceived need for fast cash, this decision is activated, mediated, and channeled by participation in street culture. Street culture, and its constituent conduct norms, represents an essential intervening variable linking criminal motivation to background risk factors and subjective foreground conditions.

Methods

The study is based on in-depth interviews with a sample of 86 currently active robbers recruited from the streets of St. Louis, Missouri. Respondents ranged in age from 16 to 51. All but 3 were African-American; 14 were female. All respondents had taken part in armed robberies, but many also had committed strong-arm attacks. Respondents did not offend at equal rates, but all

(1) had committed a robbery within the recent past (typically within the past month), (2) defined themselves as currently active, and (3) were regarded as active by other offenders. Sixty-one of the offenders admitted to having committed 10 or more lifetime robberies. Included in this group were 31 offenders who estimated having done at least 50 robberies. Seventy-three of the offenders said that they typically robbed individuals on the street or in other public settings, 10 reported that they usually targeted commercial establishments, and 3 claimed that they committed street and commercial robberies in roughly equal proportions.

Though "total" institutions afford the chance to obtain data from armed robbers without the risk of harm associated with "street" interviews (Agar, 1973), collecting valid and reliable data may not be possible there because incarcerated offenders "do not behave naturally" (Wright and Decker, 1994:5; see also Polsky, 1967:123; Sutherland and Cressey, 1970:68). Studies of incarcerated robbers also are susceptible to the charge of being based on "unsuccessful criminals, on the supposition that successful criminals are not apprehended or are at least able to avoid incarceration" (McCall, 1978:27). Traditional methods, such as household surveys, likely would not be able to identify such persons in the first place because they "cannot produce reliable samples," they are inefficient, and because most hidden populations (such as active armed robbers) are "rare" (Heckathorn, 1997:174).

Respondents were located using a snowball sampling strategy. Probably the most difficult aspect of researching active offenders using this technique is making the initial contacts. The first study participants were recruited by a specially trained "street ethnographer" (Weppner, 1977). This person, an ex-offender who had retired from crime after being shot and paralyzed in a gangland-style execution attempt, earlier had supported himself for many years as a highly skilled thief. He had been arrested just a few times and was never convicted. As a thief, he had acquired a solid reputation among his fellow criminals for both toughness and integrity. Trading on his reputation, he initiated the recruitment process by approaching former criminal associates. Some of these contacts still were committing crimes; others either had retired or remained involved only peripherally. After explaining the project to them, and stressing that the police were not involved, he asked them to provide referrals of active robbers. Informants were paid $10 for each successful referral.

In an attempt to construct a more representative sample, we recruited respondents through a variety of contacts, thereby reducing the chances of tapping into only one or two networks of criminals. Respondents also were questioned extensively about their knowledge of other offenders to guard against having a sample of highly atypical robbers. Such measures are not foolproof, and offenders outside of the penetrated networks inevitably will remain unknown. This is to say nothing of the fact that the representativeness of a sample of active offenders can never be determined conclusively because the parameters of the population are impossible to estimate (Glassner and Carpenter, 1985). The most that we can reasonably claim is that the sample appears to be broadly representative of the population of active offenders known to the interviewees.

The interviews were semistructured and conducted in an informal manner. They revolved around a basic set of questions that focused on the offenders' thoughts and actions before, during, and after their crimes. As with all such research, other promising areas of inquiry presented themselves throughout the study period. Every attempt was made to follow up on these areas in subsequent interviews, even though this meant that only a subsample of offenders would have an opportunity to comment. The nature of open-ended qualitative interviewing is such that not all topics can be anticipated and all offenders asked the same questions about issues that emerge later, often serendipitously, during the research process (Henslin, 1972:52). The fact that responses became repetitious indicated sufficient topical covering, though this could have been an artifact of the sampling design. The sample's purposive design prevents us from claiming to have achieved theoretical saturation.

Interviews typically lasted between one and two hours, were taperecorded, and transcribed verbatim. Considerable time was devoted to explaining questions and probing answers. The truthfulness of what the offenders said was monitored by questioning vague or inconsistent responses. Some of the interviewees went to great lengths to back up their claims with hard evidence—for example, by bringing parole papers or newspaper clippings with them to the interview or by revealing recently acquired bullet wounds. Though skeptical at first, most interviewees relaxed and opened up soon after the interview began. A number of offenders seemed to enjoy speaking with someone "straight" about their criminal experiences, as it may have provided some sort of outlet for them to disseminate their expertise and teach "squares" a thing or two about street life. The secrecy of criminal work "means that offenders have few opportunities to discuss their activities with anyone besides associates, a matter which many find frustrating"(Wright and Decker, 1994:26). Active offenders have certain skills and knowledge that researchers lack (Berk and Adams, 1970:107), and this asymmetry may empower them to open up or open up sooner than they otherwise would. The fact that respondents may see something in the research that benefits them, or an opportunity to correct faulty impressions of what it is they actually do (Polsky, 1967), only facilitates openness (for a comprehensive discussion of the interview process, see Wright and Decker, 1997).

The internal validity of our data warrants comment. Here, we were intruding into the lives of individuals engaged in felonies for which they could receive hard time. How could we know they were giving us the "straight story"? How could it have been in their best interest to give incisive, accurate comments about their lives, when divulging such details might ultimately undermine their success as criminals? As others have noted, "interviewees are people with a considerable potential for sabotaging the attempt to research them" (Oakley, 1981:56) since "every researcher could be a cop" (Yablonsky, 1966:vii). Though street criminals have a stereotypical image of lying or avoiding the truth to a greater extent than others, there is little evidence to support this claim (Maher, 1997:223). The validity and reliability of self-report data have been carefully assessed by a number of researchers, all of whom conclude that selfreports are among the best, if not the best, source of information about serious criminality (Ball, 1967; Chaiken and Chaiken, 1982; Hindelang et al., 1981). Indeed, the most accurate self-report designs are said to be those that ask questions about serious offenses and those that involve face-to-face data collection, our technique, rather than surveys administered impersonally (see Huizinga and Elliott, 1986). This is not to say that offenders' reports are immune from "exaggerations, intentional distortions, lies, self-serving rationalizations, or drug-induced forgetfulness" (Fleisher, 1995:80). Rather, it is to suggest that they appear to be less susceptible to inaccuracy than some might think.

Money, Motivation, and Street Culture Fast Cash

With few exceptions, the decision to commit a robbery arises in the face of what offenders perceive to be a pressing need for fast cash (see also Conklin, 1972; Feeney, 1986; Gabor et al., 1987; Tunnell, 1992). Eighty of 81 offenders who spoke directly to the issue of motivation said that they did robberies simply because they needed money. Many lurched from one financial crisis to the next, the frequency with which they committed robbery being governed largely by the amount of money—or lack of it—in their pockets:

> [The idea of committing a robbery] comes into your mind when your pockets are low; it speaks very loudly when you need things and you are not able to get what you need. It's not a want, it's things that you need, ... things that if you don't have the money, you have the artillery to go and get it. That's the first thing on my mind; concentrate on how I can get some more money.
> I don't think there is any one factor that precipitates the commission of a crime, ... I think it's just the conditions. I think the primary fac-

tor is being without. Rent is coming up. A few months ago, the land-
lord was gonna put us out, rent due, you know. Can't get no money
no way else; ask family and friends, you might try a few other ways of
getting the money and, as a last resort, I can go get some money [by
committing a robbery].

Many offenders appeared to give little thought to the offense until they found
themselves unable to meet current expenses.

[I commit a robbery] about every few months. There's no set pattern,
but I guess it's really based on the need. If there is a period of time
where there is no need of money…, then it's not necessary to go out
and rob. It's not like I do [robberies] for fun.

The above claims conjure up an image of reluctant criminals doing the best
they can to survive in circumstances not of their own making. In one sense, this
image is not so far off the mark. Of the 59 offenders who specified a particular use for the proceeds of their crimes, 19 claimed that they needed the cash
for basic necessities, such as food or shelter. For them, robbery allegedly was
a matter of day-to-day survival. At the same time, the notion that these offenders were driven by conditions entirely beyond their control strains credulity.
Reports of "opportunistic" robberies confirm this, that is, offenses motivated
by serendipity rather than basic human need:

If I had $5,000, I wouldn't do [a robbery] like tomorrow. But [i]f I
got $5,000 today and I seen you walkin' down the street and you look
like you got some money in your pocket, I'm gonna take a chance and
see. It's just natural…. If you see an opportunity, you take that opportunity…. It doesn't matter if I have $5,000 in my pocket, if I see
you walkin' and no one else around and it look like you done went in
the store and bought somethin' and pulled some money out of your
pocket and me or one of my partners has peeped this, we gonna approach you. That's just the way it goes.

Need and opportunity, however, cannot be considered outside the openended
quest for excitement and sensory stimulation that shaped much of the offenders' daily activities. Perhaps the most central of pursuits in street culture,
"life as party" revolves around "the enjoyment of 'good times' with minimal
concern for obligations and commitments that are external to the … immediate
social setting" (Shover and Honaker, 1992:283). Gambling, hard drug use, and
heavy drinking were the behaviors of choice:

> I [have] a gambling problem and I … lose so much so I [have] to do something to [get the cash to] win my money back. So I go out and rob somebody. That be the main reason I rob someone. I like to mix and I like to get high. You can't get high broke. You really can't get high just standing there, you got to move. And in order to move, you got to have some money … Got to have some money, want to get high.

While the offenders often referred to such activities as partying, there is a danger in accepting their comments at face value. Many gambled, used drugs, and drank alcohol as if there were no tomorrow; they pursued these activities with an intensity and grim determination that suggested something far more serious was at stake. Illicit street action is no party, at least not in the conventional sense of the term. Offenders typically demonstrate little or no inclination to exercise personal restraint. Why should they? Instant gratification and hedonistic sensation seeking are quite functional for those seeking pleasure in what may objectively be viewed as a largely pleasureless world.

The offenders are easily seduced by life as party, at least in part because they view their future prospects as bleak and see little point in long-range planning. As such, there is no mileage to be gained by deferred gratification:

> I really don't dwell on [the future]. One day I might not wake up. I don't even think about what's important to me. What's important to me is getting mine [now].

The offenders' general lack of social stability and absence of conventional sources of support only fueled such a mindset. The majority called the streets home for extended periods of time; a significant number of offenders claimed to seldom sleep at the same address for more than a few nights in a row (see also Fleisher, 1995). Moving from place to place as the mood struck them, these offenders essentially were urban nomads in a perpetual search for good times. The volatile streets and alleyways that criss-crossed St. Louis's crime-ridden central city neighborhoods provided their conduit (see also Stein and McCall, 1994):

> I guess I'm just a street person, a roamer. I like to be out in the street … Now I'm staying with a cousin … That's where I live, but I'm very rarely there. I'm usually in the street. If somebody say they got something up … I go and we do whatever. I might spend the night at their house or I got a couple of girls I know [and] I might spend the night at their house. I'm home about two weeks out of a month.

Keeping Up Appearances

The open-ended pursuit of sensory stimulation was but one way these offenders enacted the imperatives of street culture. No less important was the fetishized consumption of personal, nonessential, status-enhancing items. Shover and Honaker (1992:283) have argued that the unchecked pursuit of such items—like anomic participation in illicit street action emerges directly from conduct norms of street culture. The code of the streets (Anderson, 1990) calls for the bold display of the latest status symbol clothing and accessories, a look that loudly proclaims the wearer to be someone who has overcome, if only temporarily, the financial difficulties faced by others on the street corner (see e.g., Katz, 1988). To be seen as "with it," one must flaunt the material trappings of success. The quest is both symbolic and real; such purchases serve as self-enclosed and highly efficient referent systems that assert one's essential character (Shover, 1996) in no uncertain terms.

> You ever notice that some people want to be like other people … ? They might want to dress like this person, like dope dealers and stuff like that. They go out there [on the street corner] in diamond jewelry and stuff. "Man, I wish I was like him!" You got to make some kind of money [to look like that], so you want to make a quick hustle.

The functionality of offenders' purchases was tangential, perhaps irrelevant. The overriding goal was to project an image of "cool transcendence," (Katz, 1988) that, in the minds of offenders, knighted them members of a mythic street aristocracy. As Anderson (1990:103–104) notes, the search for self-aggrandizement takes on a powerful logic of its own and, in the end, becomes all-consuming. Given the day-to-day desperation that dominates most of these offenders' lives, it is easy to appreciate why they are anxious to show off whenever the opportunity presents itself (particularly after making a lucrative score). Of course, it would be misleading to suggest that our respondents differed markedly from their law-abiding neighbors in wanting to wear flashy clothes or expensive accessory items. Nor were all of the offenders' purchases ostentatious. On occasion, some offenders would use funds for haircuts, manicures, and other mundane purchases. What set these offenders apart from "normal citizens" was their willingness to spend large amounts of cash on luxury items to the detriment of more pressing financial concerns.

Obviously, the relentless pursuit of high living quickly becomes expensive. Offenders seldom had enough cash in their pockets to sustain this lifestyle for long. Even when they did make the occasional "big score," their disdain for long-range planning and desire to live for the moment encouraged spending with reckless abandon. That money earned illegally holds "less intrinsic value" than cash secured through legitimate work only fueled their spend-thrift ways (Walters, 1990:147). The way money is obtained, after all, is a "powerful determinant of how it is defined, husbanded, and spent" (Shover, 1996:104). Some researchers have gone so far as to suggest that through care-free spending, persistent criminals seek to establish the very conditions that drive them back to crime (Katz, 1988). Whether offenders spend money in a deliberate attempt to create these conditions is open to question; the re-spondents in our sample gave no indication of doing so. No matter, offend-ers were under almost constant pressure to generate funds. To the extent that robbery alleviated this stress, it nurtured a tendency for them to view the of-fense as a reliable method for dealing with similar pressures in the future. A self-enclosed cycle of reinforcing behavior was thereby triggered (see also Lemert, 1953).

Why Robbery?

The decision to commit robbery, then, is motivated by a perceived need for cash. Why does this need express itself as robbery? Presumably the offenders have other means of obtaining money. Why do they choose robbery over legal work? Why do they decide to commit robbery rather than borrow money from friends or relatives? Most important, why do they select robbery to the exclu-sion of other income-generating crimes?

Legal Work

That the decision to commit robbery typically emerges in the course of illicit street action suggests that legitimate employment is not a realistic solution. Typically, the offenders' need for cash is so pressing and immediate that legal work, as a viable money-making strategy, is untenable: Payment and effort are separated in space and time and these offenders will not, or cannot, wait. Moreover, the jobs realistically available to them almost all of whom were un-skilled and poorly educated—pay wages that fall far short of the funds re-quired to support a cash-intensive lifestyle:

> Education-wise, I fell late on the education. I just think it's too late for that. They say it's never too late, but I'm too far gone for that … I've thought about [getting a job], but I'm too far gone I guess … I done seen more money come out of [doing stick-ups] than I see working.

Legitimate employment also was perceived to be overly restrictive. Working a normal job requires one to take orders, conform to a schedule, minimize informal peer interaction, show up sober and alert, and limit one's freedom of movement for a given period of time. For many in our sample, this was un-fathomable; it cramped the hedonistic, street-focused lifestyle they chose to live:

> I'm a firm believer, man, God didn't put me down on this earth to suffer for no reason. I'm just a firm believer in that. I believe I can have a good time every day, each and every day of my life, and that's what I'm trying to do. I never held a job. The longest job I ever had was about nine months … at St. Louis Car; that's probably the longest job I ever had, outside of working in the joint. But I mean on the streets, man, I just don't believe in [work]. There is enough shit on this earth right here for everybody, nobody should have to be suffering. You shouldn't have to suffer and work like no dog for it, I'm just a firm believer in that. I'll go out there and try to take what I believe I got comin' [because] ain't nobody gonna walk up … and give it to me. [I commit robberies] because I'm broke and need money; it's just what I'm gonna do. I'm not going to work! That's out! I'm through [with work]. I done had 25 or 30 jobs in my little lifetime [and] that's out. I can't do it! I'm not going to!

The "conspicuous display of independence" is a bedrock value on which street-corner culture rests (Shover and Honaker, 1992:284): To be seen as cool one must do as one pleases. This ethos clearly conflicts with the demands of legit-imate employment. Indeed, robbery appealed to a number of offenders pre-cisely because it allowed them to flaunt their independence and escape from the rigors of legal work.

This is not to say that every offender summarily dismissed the prospect of gainful employment. Twenty-five of the 75 unemployed respondents claimed they would stop robbing if someone gave them a "good job"—the emphasis being on good:

> My desire is to be gainfully employed in the right kind of job … If I had a union job making $16 or $17 [an hour], something that I could really take care of my family with, I think that I could become cool with that. Years ago I worked at one of the [local] car factories; I really wanted to be in there. It was the kind of job I'd been looking for. Un-fortunately, as soon as I got in there they had a big layoff.

Others alleged that, while a job may not eliminate their offending altogether, it might well slow them down:

[If a job were to stop me from committing robberies], it would have to be a straight up good paying job. I ain't talkin' about no $6 an hour … I'm talkin' like $10 to $11 an hour, something like that. But as far as $5 or $6 an hour, no! I would have to get like $10 or $11 an hour, full-time. Now something like that, I would probably quit doing it [robbery]. I would be working, making money, I don't think I would do it [robbery] no more … I don't think I would quit [offending] altogether. It would probably slow down and then eventually I'll stop. I think [my offending] would slow down.

While such claims may or may not be sincere, it is unlikely they will ever be challenged. Attractive employment opportunities are limited for all inner-city residents and particularly for individuals like those in our sample. Drastic changes in the post World War II economy—deindustrialization and the loss of manufacturing jobs, the increased demand for advanced education and high skills, rapid suburbanization and out-migration of middle class residents (Sampson et al., 1997)—have left them behind, twisting in the wind. The lack of legal income options speaks to larger societal patterns in which major changes in the U.S. economy have reduced the number of available good-paying jobs and created an economic underclass with unprecedented levels of unemployment and few options—beyond income-generating crime—to exercise (Wilson, 1987). Governmental directives, such as changes in requirements and reductions in public transfer payments, decidedly reduce the income of already marginalized persons in inner-city communities (Johnson and Dunlap, 1997)—those at highest risk for predatory crime. This only intensifies their economic and social isolation (Sampson et al., 1997), makes their overall plight worse, and their predisposition to criminality stronger.

Most offenders realized this and, with varying degrees of bitterness, resigned themselves to being out of work:

I fill out [job] applications daily. Somebody [always] says, "This is bad that you got tattoos all over looking for a job." In a way, that's discrimination. How do they know I can't do the job? I could probably do your job just as well as you, but I got [these jailhouse] tattoos on me. That's discriminating. Am I right? That's why most people rob and steal because, say another black male came in like me [for a job], same haircut, same everything. I'm dressed like this, tennis shoes, shorts and tank top. He has on [a] Stacy Adams pair of slacks and a button-up shirt with a tie. He will get the job before I will. That's being racist in a way. I can do the job just as well as he can. He just dresses a little bit better than me.

Clearly, these offenders were not poster children for the local chamber of commerce or small business association. By and large, they were crudely mannered and poorly schooled in the arts of impression management and customer relations. Most lacked the cultural capital (Bourdieu, 1977) necessary for the conduct of legitimate business. They were not "nice" in the conventional sense of the term; to be nice is to signal weakness in a world where only the strong survive.

Even if the offenders were able to land a high-paying job, it is doubtful they would keep it for long. The relentless pursuit of street action—especially hard drug use—has a powerful tendency to undermine any commitment to conventional activities (Shover and Honaker, 1992). Life as party ensnares street-culture participants, enticing them to neglect the demands of legitimate employment in favor of enjoying the moment. Though functional in lightening the burdensome present, gambling, drinking, and drugging—for those on the street—become the proverbial "padlock on the exit door" (Davis, 1995) and fertilize the foreground in which the decision to rob becomes rooted.

Borrowing

In theory, the offenders could have borrowed cash from a friend or relative rather than resorting to crime. In practice, this was not feasible. Unemployed, unskilled, and uneducated persons caught in the throes of chronically self-defeating behavior cannot, and often do not, expect to solve their fiscal troubles by borrowing. Borrowing is a short-term solution, and loans granted must be repaid. This in itself could trigger robberies. As one offender explained, "I have people that will loan me money, [but] they will loan me money because of the work [robbery] that I do; they know they gonna get their money [back] one way or another." Asking for money also was perceived by a number of offenders to be emasculating. Given their belief that men should be self-sufficient, the mere prospect of borrowing was repugnant:

> I don't like always asking my girl for nothing because I want to let her keep her own money ... I'm gonna go out here and get some money.

The possibility of borrowing may be moot for the vast majority of offenders anyway. Most had long ago exhausted the patience and goodwill of helpful others; not even their closest friends or family members were willing to proffer additional cash:

> I can't borrow the money. Who gonna loan me some money? Ain't nobody gonna loan me no money. Shit, [I use] drugs and they know [that] and I rob and everything else. Ain't nobody gonna loan me no

money. If they give you some money, they just give it to you; they
know you ain't giving it back.

When confronted with an immediate need for money, then, the offenders perceived
themselves as having little hope of securing cash quickly and legally. But this does
not explain why the respondents decided to do robbery rather than some other
crime. Most of them had committed a wide range of income-generating offenses
in the past, and some continued to be quite versatile. Why, then, robbery?

For many, this question was irrelevant; robbery was their "main line" and
alternative crimes were not considered when the pressing need for cash arose:

> I have never been able to steal, even when I was little and they would
> tell me just to be the watch-out man ... Shit, I watch out, everybody
> gets busted. I can't steal, but give me a pistol and I'll go get some
> money.... [Robbery is] just something I just got attached to.

When these offenders did commit another form of income-generating crime,
it typically was prompted by the chance discovery of an especially vulnerable
target rather than being part of their typical modus operandi:

> I do [commit other sorts of offenses] but that ain't, I might do a bur-
> glary, but I'm jumping out of my field. See, I'm scared when I do a bur-
> glary [or] something like that. I feel comfortable robbing..., but I see
> something they call "real sweet," like a burglary where the door is open
> and ain't nobody there or something like that, well ...

Many of the offenders who expressed a strong preference for robbery had come
to the offense through burglary, drug selling, or both. They claimed that robbery had several advantages over these other crimes. Robbery took much less
time than breaking into buildings or dealing drugs. Not only could the offense
be committed more quickly, it also typically netted cash rather than goods.
Unlike burglary, there was no need for the booty "to be cut, melted down, re-
cast or sold," nor for obligatory dealings with "treacherous middlemen, insurance adjustors, and wiseguy fences" (Pileggi, 1985:203). Why not bypass all
such hassles and simply steal cash (Shover, 1996:63).

> Robbery is the quickest money. Robbery is the most money you gonna
> get fast ... Burglary, you gonna have to sell the merchandise and get
> the money. Drugs, you gonna have to deal with too many people, [a]
> bunch of people. You gonna sell a $50 or $100 bag to him, a $50 or
> $100 bag to him, it takes too long. But if you find where the cash
> money is and just go take it, you get it all in one wad. No problem.
> I've tried burglary, I've tried drug selling ... the money is too slow.

Some of the offenders who favored robbery over other crimes maintained that it was safer than burglary or dope dealing:

> I feel more safer doing a robbery because doing a burglary, I got a fear of breaking into somebody's house not knowing who might be up in there. I got that fear about house burglary ... On robbery I can select my victims, I can select my place of business. I can watch and see who all work in there or I can rob a person and pull them around in the alley or push them up in a doorway and rob them. You don't got [that] fear of who ... in that bedroom or somewhere in another part of the house. [I]f I'm out there selling dope somebody gonna come and, I'm not the only one out there robbing you know, so somebody like me, they'll come and rob me ... I'm robbin' cause the dope dealers is the ones getting robbed and killed you know.

A couple of offenders reported steering clear of dope selling because their strong craving for drugs made it too difficult for them to resist their own merchandise. Being one's own best customer is a sure formula for disaster (Waldorf, 1993), something the following respondent seemed to understand well:

> A dope fiend can't be selling dope because he be his best customer. I couldn't sell dope [nowadays]. I could sell a little weed or something cause I don't smoke too much of it. But selling rock [cocaine] or heroin, I couldn't do that cause I mess around and smoke it myself. [I would] smoke it all up!

Others claimed that robbery was more attractive than other offenses because it presented less of a potential threat to their freedom:

> If you sell drugs, it's easy to get locked up selling drugs; plus, you can get killed selling drugs. You get killed more faster doing that. Robbery you got a better chance of surviving and getting away than doing other crimes ... You go break in a house, [the police] get the fingerprints, you might lose a shoe, you know how they got all that technology stuff. So I don't break in houses ... I leave that to some other guy.

Without doubt, some of the offenders were prepared to commit crimes other than robbery; in dire straits one cannot afford to be choosy. More often than not, robbery emerged as the "most proximate and performable" (Lofland, 1969:61) offense available. The universe of money-making crimes from which these offenders realistically could pick was limited. By and large, they did not hold jobs that would allow them to violate even a low-level position of financial trust. Nor did they possess the technical know-how to commit lucrative commercial break-ins, or the interpersonal skills needed to perpetrate successful frauds. Even street-corner dope dealing was unavailable to many; most lacked the financial wherewithal to purchase baseline inventories—inventories many offenders would undoubtedly have smoked up.

The bottom line is that the offenders, when faced with a pressing need for cash, tend to resort to robbery because they know of no other course of action, legal or illegal, that offers as quick and easy a way out of their financial difficulties. As Lofland (1969:50) notes, most people under pressure have a tendency to become fixated on removing the perceived cause of that pressure "as quickly as possible." Desperate to sustain a cash intensive lifestyle, these offenders were loathe to consider unfamiliar, complicated, or long-term solutions (Lofland, 1969:50–54). With minimal calculation and "high" hopes, they turned to robbery, a trusted companion they could count on when the pressure was on. For those who can stomach the potential violence, robbery seems so much more attractive than other forms of income-generating crime. Contemplating alternative offenses becomes increasingly difficult to do. This is the insight that separates persistent robbers from their street-corner peers:

> [Robbery] is just easy. I ain't got to sell no dope or nothing, I can just take the money. Just take it, I don't need to sell no dope or work ... I don't want to sell dope, I don't want to work. I don't feel like I need to work for nothing. If I want something, I'm gonna get it and take it. I'm gonna take what I want ... If I don't have money, I like to go and get it. I ain't got time [for other offenses]; the way I get mine is by the gun. I don't have time to be waiting on people to come up to me buying dope all day ... I don't have time for that so I just go and get my money.

Discussion

The overall picture that emerges from our research is that of offenders caught up in a cycle of expensive, self-indulgent habits (e.g., gambling, drug use, and heavy drinking) that feed on themselves and constantly call for more of the same (Lemert, 1953). It would be a mistake to conclude that these offenders are being driven to crime by genuine financial hardship; few of them are doing robberies to buy the proverbial loaf of bread to feed their children. Yet, most of their crimes are economically motivated. The offenders perceive themselves as needing money and robbery is a response to that perception.

Though background risk factors, such as pressing financial need, predispose persons to criminality, they fail to provide comprehensive, precise, and deep explanations of the situational pushes, urges, and impulses that energize

actual criminal conduct (Tittle, 1995). Nor do such factors identify the "necessary and sufficient" conditions for criminal motivation to eventuate in criminal behavior. Focusing on the foreground attends to these problems. A
foreground analytic approach identifies the immediate, situational factors that
catalyze criminal motivation and transforms offenders from an indifferent state
to one in which they are determined to commit crime.

Though the theoretical priority of the criminological foreground is unrivaled,
one would scarcely know this from its extant treatment (but see e.g., Gibbons,
1971; Hagan and McCarthy, 1997; Katz, 1988). The dearth of attention is em-
blematic of criminology's positivistic bent, which holds paramount the study
of "background and developmental variables" (Hagan and McCarthy, 1997:81)
to the virtual exclusion of precipitating foreground influences. Sutherland
(1947:77) may have set the precedent for this in his seminal, persuasive, and
widely disseminated statement in which he insisted that background risk factors
determine the way in which persons define situations and act on them through
deviance. Briar and Piliavin (1965) and Gottfredson and Hirschi (1990) echoed
the same sentiment years later. Indeed, the most popular, prominent, and influential paradigms of our discipline attest to the extent to which Sutherland's
lead has been followed by scholars who shun the foreground in favor of more par-
simonious, though less precise, explanations of criminal motivation (but see
Tittle, 1995).

To be sure, strain, anomie, subcultural, labeling, radical, and conflict theories specify some motivating forces but not the majority, nor even the most
important ones (see Empey and Stafford, 1991; Tittle, 1995). Such approaches
also drip with determinism by assuming that criminal behavior is preordained
by developmental background factors that accumulate over time (see Hagan and
McCarthy, 1997:81). Social learning/reinforcement theories are contingent
upon assumptions of positively reinforced, crime favorable messages being internalized as deviant propensities, as well as "preexisting distributions of potentially reinforcing elements" (see Tittle, 1995:47)—distributions that are not
explained well within the theory. Rational choice and routine activities theories assume rather than account for motivation, and they fail to recognize contingencies and reciprocal relationships that moderate, mediate, or mitigate
predicted outcomes (see Tittle, 1995). Biological and psychological theories
are notoriously tautological, a consequence of their inability to discuss or measure deviant motivation independently of deviant behavior (see Gottfredson
and Hirschi, 1990). Transcendence theory (Katz, 1988) places justifiable emphasis on the foreground of offender decision making, but it locates deviant
motivation in the seductiveness of crime to the exclusion of other, equally ger-
mane explanations (especially material concerns—see McCarthy, 1995). Con-

trol theory is arguably the only "honest" paradigm with regard to deviant motivation by dismissing it altogether: Criminal/deviant motivation (i.e., propen-
sity) inheres in all of us to varying degrees; only those with weak social bonds
become offenders (Gottfredson and Hirschi, 1990; Hirschi, 1969; Kornhauser,
1978).

Although the streets were a prime focus of much early criminological work,
the strong influence of street culture on offender motivation has largely been
overlooked since (but see Baron and Hartnagel, 1997; Fleisher, 1995; Hagan and
McCarthy, 1992, 1997). Below, we attempt a conceptual refocusing by exploring the criminogenic influence of street culture and its constituent conduct norms
on offender decision making (see also Hagan and McCarthy, 1997). In doing so,
we do not wish to make a Katzian attempt to "outgun positivism" with a sensu-
ally deterministic portrait of crime (see Groves and Lynch, 1990:366). Our goal
rather is to highlight the explanatory power and conceptual efficiency of street
culture participation as a mediating foreground factor in the etiology of armed
robbery.

Street culture subsumes a number of powerful conduct norms, including but
not limited to, the hedonistic pursuit of sensory stimulation, disdain for conventional living, lack of future orientation, and persistent eschewal of responsibility (see Fleisher 1995:213–214). Street culture puts tremendous
emphasis on virtues of spontaneity; it dismisses "rationality and long range
planning ... in favor of enjoying the moment" (Shover and Honaker, 1992:283).
Offenders typically live life as if there is no tomorrow, confident that tomorrow will somehow take care of itself. On the streets, "every night is a Saturday
night" (Hodgson, 1997), and the self-indulgent pursuit of trendy consumerism
and open-ended street action becomes a means to this end.

The pursuit of fast living is more than symbolic or dramaturgical, it cuts to
the very core of offenders' perceptions of self-identity. To be cool, hip, and
"in," one must constantly prove it through conspicuous outlays of cash. The
fetishized world of street-corner capitalism dictates that fiscal responsibility
be jettisoned and money burned on material objects and illicit action that assert in no uncertain terms one's place in the street hierarchy. Carefree spending creates the "impression of affluence" (Wright and Decker, 1994:44) by
which offenders are judged; it serves to demonstrate that they have indeed
"made it"—at least for the time. On the streets, the image one projects is not
everything, it is the only thing (see Anderson, 1990). To not buy into such an
approach is to abandon a source of recognition offenders can get nowhere else
(see Liebow, 1967) or, worse, to stare failure full in the face. It is not hard to
fathom why many offenders in our sample regarded a lack of funds as an immediate threat to their social standing.

The problem becomes one of sustenance; the reputational advantages of cash-intensive living can be appreciated and enjoyed to their fullest "only if participants moderate their involvement in it" (Shover and Honaker, 1992:286). This requires intermittent and disciplined spending, an anomalous and ultimately untenable proposition. Offenders effectively become ensnared by their own self-indulgent habits—habits that feed on themselves and constantly call for more of the same (Lemert, 1953; Shover, 1996). These habits are expensive and create a pressing and pervasive need for cash—a need remedied through robbery but only temporarily, since the proceeds of any given robbery merely "enable" more action (Shover, 1996). The seductive attractions of street life appear to take on a powerful logic of their own (Hagan and McCarthy, 1997); offenders burn money only to create (albeit inadvertently) the conditions that spark their next decision to rob. This self-enclosed cycle of reinforcing behavior (see also Lemert, 1953) is depicted schematically in Figure 1. Predisposing background risk factors also are represented (see Hagan and McCarthy, 1997, for a comprehensive discussion of these factors as they relate to street-culture participation).

As much as these offenders sought liberation through the hedonistic, open-ended pursuit of sensory stimulation, such a quest ultimately is both self-defeating and subordinating. Those hooked on street action may never see it this way, but objective assessments of reality are difficult to render when rationality is as severely bounded (Walsh, 1986) as it is here. Suffice it to say that, for those in our sample, the "choice" to rob occurs in a context in which rationality not only is sharply bounded, it barely exists. If one takes the influence of context seriously, most offenders "decide" to commit robbery in a social and psychological terrain bereft of realistic alternatives (Shover, 1996). Street-culture participation effectively obliterates, or at least severely circumscribes, the range of objectively available options, so much so as to be almost deterministic. Offenders typically are overwhelmed by their own predicament—emotional, financial, pharmacological, and otherwise—and see robbery as the only way out. Chronic isolation from conventional others and lifestyles only reinforces their insularity (Baron and Hartnagel, 1997:413–414), driving them deeper and deeper into a "downward life trajectory" of ever-increasing criminal embeddedness (see Hagan and McCarthy, 1997; see also Ekland-Olson et al., 1984, on "role engulfment").

That our respondents typically perceived themselves to be in a situation of pressing need at the time of actually contemplating their offenses has a number of powerful implications for rational choice theory. It suggests a mind-set in which offenders are seeking less to maximize their gains than to deal with a present crisis. It also indicates an element of emotional desperation that undoubtedly weakens the influence of threatened sanctions. Glazed by the anomic pursuit of street action, threats of legal sanctions become "remote and improbable contingencies" (Shover, 1996:102). Offenders are increasingly likely to "dispense with [care] and proceed quickly at high risk" (Letkemann, 1973:143). This is to say nothing of the fact that thoughts about getting caught are typically dismissed anyway during the course of many crimes (Bennett and Wright, 1984; Feeney, 1986; Tunnell, 1992; Wright and Decker, 1994)—a function of perceptions of invincibility, superoptimism (Walters, 1990:145), or beliefs that since the risk of offending is quick, the threat of detection is over "in a flash" and thus not something over which to fret (Felson, 1987). Even if offenders are caught, periodic bouts of prison time are regarded by many as a welcome respite from the "dog-eat-dog" world of the streets (see Fleisher, 1995, on jails as "sanctuaries"; Tunnell, 1992). Finally, the experiential effects (Minor and Harry, 1982) on which offenders can draw (as a result of being caught) and iatrogenic influences (Klein, 1992) accrued from prison life result in increasingly refined techniques for avoiding detection and capture in the future (see Shover, 1996: Ch. 6). Taken together, all of these factors systematically undermine the deterrent power of legal sanctions and seemingly enhance rather than inhibit criminal behavior.

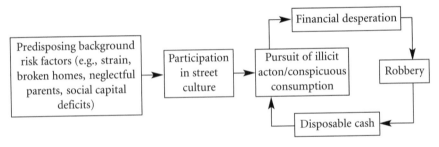

Being a street robber is more than a series of offenses that allow one to meet some arbitrarily specified inclusion criteria; it is a way of behaving, a way of thinking, an approach to life (see e.g., Fleisher, 1995:253). Stopping such criminals exogenously—in the absence of lengthy incapacitation—is not likely to be successful. Getting offenders to "go straight" is analogous to telling a lawful citizen to "relinquish his history, companions thoughts, feelings, and fears, and replace them with [something] else" (Fleisher, 1995:240). Self-directed going-straight talk on the part of offenders more often than not is insincere—akin to young children talking about what they're going to be when they grow up: "Young story tellers and ... criminals ... don't care about the [reality]; the pleasure comes in saying the words, the verbal ritual itself brings pleasure" (Fleisher, 1995:259). Gifting offenders money, in the hopes they will reduce or stop their offending (Farrington, 1993), is similarly misguided. It is but twisted enabling and only likely to set off another round of illicit action that plunges offenders deeper into the abyss of desperation that drives them back to their next crime.

References

Agar, Michael. 1973. Ripping and Running: A Formal Ethnography of Urban Heroin Addicts. New York: Seminar Press.

Akers, Ronald L. 1985. Deviant Behavior: A Social Learning Approach. 3rd ed. Belmont, Calif.: Wadsworth.

Anderson, Elijah. 1990. Streetwise. Chicago: University of Chicago Press.

Ball, John C. 1967. The reliability and validity of interview data obtained from 59 narcotic drug addicts. American Journal of Sociology 72:650–654.

Baron, Stephen and Timothy Hartnagel. 1997. Attributions, affect, and crime: Street youths' reactions to unemployment. Criminology 35:409–434.

Bennett, Trevor and Richard Wright. 1984. Burglars on Burglary: Prevention and the Offender. Aldershot: Gower.

Berk, Richard A. and Joseph M. Adams. 1970. Establishing rapport with deviant groups. Social Problems 18:102–117.

Bottoms, Anthony and Paul Wiles. 1992. Explanations of crime and place. In David Evans, Nigel Fyfe, and Derek Herbert (eds.), Policing and Place: Essays in Environmental Criminology. London: Routledge.

Bourdieu, Pierre. 1977. Outline of a Theory of Practice. Cambridge: Cambridge University Press.

Braithwaite John. 1989. Crime, Shame, and Reintegration. Cambridge: Cambridge University Press.

Briar, Scott and Irving Piliavin. 1965. Delinquency, situational inducements, and commitment to conformity Social Problems 13:3545.

Chaiken, Jan M. and Marcia R. Chaiken. 1982. Varieties of Criminal Behavior. Santa Monica, Calif.: Rand Corporation.

Chambliss, William J. and Robert Seidman. 1971. Law, Order, and Power. Reading, Mass.: Addison-Wesley.

Cloward, Richard A. and Lloyd E. Ohlin. 1960. Delinquency and Opportunity. New York: Free Press.

Cohen, Albert K. 1955. Delinquent Boys. New York: Free Press.

Colvin, Mark and John Pauly. 1983. A critique of criminology: Toward an integrated structural-Marxist theory of delinquent production. American Journal of Sociology 89:513–551.

Conklin, John. 1972. Robbery. Philadelphia: JB Lippincott.

Cornish, Derek B. and Ronald V. Clarke (eds.). 1986. The Reasoning Criminal: Rational Choice Perspectives on Offending. New York: Springer-Verlag.

Davis, Peter. 1995. Interview, "If You Came This Way." All Things Considered, National Public Radio, October 12.

Ekland-Olson, Sheldon, John Lieb, and Louis Zurcher. 1984. The paradoxical impact of criminal sanctions: Some microstructural findings. Law & Society Review 18:159–178.

Elliott, Delbert S., David Huizinga, and Suzanne S. Ageton. 1985. Explaining Delinquency and Drug Use. Beverly Hills, Calif.: Sage.

Empey, LaMar T. and Mark C. Stafford. 1991. American Delinquency. 3d ed. Belmont, Calif.: Wadsworth.

Farrington, David P. 1993. Motivations for conduct disorder and delinquency. Development and Psychopathology 5:225–241.

Feeney, Floyd. 1986. Robbers as decision-makers. In Derek B. Cornish and Ronald V. Clarke (eds.), The Reasoning Criminal: Rational Choice Perspectives on Offending. New York: Springer-Verlag.

Felson, Marcus. 1987. Routine activities in the developing metropolis. Criminology 25:911–931

Fleisher, Mark S. 1995. Beggars and Thieves: Lives of Urban Street Criminals. Madison: University of Wisconsin Press.

Gabor, Thomas, Micheline Baril, Maurice Cusson, Daniel Elie, Marc LeBlanc, and Andre Normandeau. 1987. Armed Robbery: Cops, Robbers, and Victims. Springfield, Ill.: Charles C Thomas.

Gibbons, Donald L. 1971. Observations on the study of crime causation. American Journal of Sociology 77:262–278.

Glassner, Barry and Cheryl Carpenter. 1985. The feasibility of an ethnographic study of adult property offenders. Unpublished report prepared for the National Institute of Justice.

Gottfredson, Michael and Travis Hirschi. 1990. A General Theory of Crime. Stanford, Calif.: Stanford University Press.

Groves, W. Byron and Michael J. Lynch. 1990. Reconciling structural and subjective approaches to the study of crime. Journal of Research in Crime and Delinquency 27:348–375.

Hagan, John and Bill McCarthy. 1992. Streetlife and delinquency. British Journal of Sociology 43:533–561. 1997 Mean Streets: Youth Crime and Homelessness. Cambridge: Cambridge University Press.

Heckathorn, Douglas D. 1997. Respondent-driven sampling: A new approach to the study of hidden populations. Social Problems 44:174–199.

Henslin, James M. 1972. Studying deviance in four settings: Research experiences with cabbies, suicides, drug users, and abortionees. In Jack Douglas (ed.), Research on Deviance. New York: Random House.

Hindelang, Michael J., Travis Hirschi, and Joseph Weis. 1981. Measuring Delinquency. Beverly Hills, Calif.: Sage.

Hirschi, Travis. 1969. Causes of Delinquency. Berkeley: University of California Press.

Hodgson, James F. 1997. Games Pimps Play. Toronto: Canadian Scholars' Press.

Huizinga, David and Delbert S. Elliott. 1986. Reassessing the reliability and validity of self-report delinquency measures. Journal of Quantitative Criminology 2:293–327.

Johnson, Bruce D. and Eloise Dunlap. 1997. Crack Selling in New York City. Paper presented at the 49th Annual Meeting of the American Society of Criminology, San Diego.

Katz, Jack. 1988. Seductions of Crime: Moral and Sensual Attractions in Doing Evil. New York: Basic Books.

Klein, Malcolm W. 1992. Personal communication, University of Southern California, Los Angeles.

Kornhauser, Ruth R. 1978. Social Sources of Delinquency. Chicago: University of Chicago Press.

Lemert, Edwin. 1953. An isolation and closure theory of naive check forgery. Journal of Criminal Law, Criminology, and Police Science 44:296–307.

Letkemann, Peter. 1973. Crime as Work. Englewood Cliffs, N.J.: Prentice Hall.

Liebow, Eliot. 1967. Tally's Corner. Boston: Little, Brown.

Lofland, John. 1969. Deviance and Identity. Englewood Cliffs, N.J.: Prentice-Hall.

Maher, Lisa. 1997. Sexed Work. Oxford: Clarendon Press

McCall, George. 1978. Observing the Law. New York: Free Press.

McCarthy, Bill. 1995. Not just for the thrill of it: An instrumentalist elaboration of Katz's explanation of sneaky thrill property crimes. Criminology 33:519–538.

Merton, Robert K. 1938. Social structure and anomie. American Sociological Review 3:672–682.

Miller, Jody. 1998. Up it up: gender and the accomplishment of street robbery. Criminology 36:37–66.

Miller, Walter B. 1958. Lower class culture as a generating milieu of gang delinquency. Journal of Social Issues 14:5–19.

Minor, W. William and Joseph Harry. 1982. Deterrent and experiential effects in perceptual deterrence research: A replication and extension. Journal of Research in Crime and Delinquency 19:190–203.

Oakley, Annie. 1981. Interviewing women: A contradiction in terms. In Helen Roberts (ed.), Doing Feminist Research. London: Routledge & Kegan Paul.

Pileggi, Nicholas. 1985. Wiseguy. New York: Simon & Schuster.

Polsky, Ned. 1967. Hustlers, Beats, and Others. Chicago: Aldine.

Quinney, Richard. 1970. The Social Reality of Crime. Boston: Little, Brown.

Sampson, Robert J. and John H. Laub. 1992. Crime and deviance in the life course. Annual Review of Sociology 24:509–525.

Sampson, Robert J., Stephen W. Raudenbush, and Felton Earls. 1997. Neighborhoods and violent crime: A multilevel study of collective efficacy. Science 277:918–924.

Shaw, Clifford R. and Henry D. McKay. 1942. Juvenile Delinquency and Urban Areas. Chicago: University of Chicago Press.

Shover, Neal. 1991. Burglary. In Michael Tonry (ed.), Crime and Justice: A Review of Research. Chicago: University of Chicago Press.

———. 1996. Great Pretenders: Pursuits and Careers of Persistent Thieves. Boulder, Colo.: Westview.

Shover, Neal and David Honaker. 1992. The socially-bounded decision making of persistent property offenders. Howard Journal of Criminal Justice 31:276–293.

Stein, Michael and George McCall. 1994. Home ranges and daily rounds: Uncovering community among urban nomads. Research in Community Sociology 1:77–94.

Sutherland, Edwin. 1947. Principles of Criminology. 4th ed. Philadelphia: JB Lippincott.

Sutherland, Edwin and Donald Cressey. 1970. Criminology. 8th ed. Philadelphia: JB Lippincott.

Tittle, Charles R. 1995. Control Balance: Toward a General Theory of Deviance. Boulder, Colo.: Westview.

Tunnell, Kenneth D. 1992. Choosing Crime: The Criminal Calculus of Property Offenders. Chicago: Nelson-Hall.

Waldorf, Dan. 1993. Don't be your own best customer: Drug use of San Francisco gang drug sellers. Crime, Law, and Social Change 19:1–15.

Walsh, Dermot. 1986. Victim selection procedures among economic criminals: The rational choice perspective. In Derek B. Cornish and Ronald V. Clarke (eds.), The Reasoning Criminal: Rational Choice Perspectives on Offending. New York: Springer-Verlag.

Walters, Glenn. 1990. The Criminal Lifestyle. Newbury Park, Calif.: Sage.

Weppner, Robert. 1977. Street Ethnography. Beverly Hills, Calif.: Sage.

Wilson, William J. 1987. The Truly Disadvantaged. Chicago: University of Chicago Press.

Wright, Richard T. and Scott H. Decker. 1994. Burglars on the Job. Boston: Northeastern University Press.

———. 1997. Armed Robbers in Action. Boston: Northeastern University Press.

Yablonsky, Lewis. 1966. The Violent Gang. New York: Macmillan.

Author Affiliation

Bruce Jacobs is an Assistant Professor of Criminology and Criminal Justice at the University of Missouri-St. Louis. His research focuses on the dynamics and processes relevant to street-level drug markets. He is author of the forthcoming book, Dealing Crack: The Social World of Streetcorner Selling (Boston: Northeastern University Press, 1999).

Richard Wright is a Professor in the Department of Criminology and Criminal Justice, University of Missouri-St. Louis and a Fellow in the National Consortium on Violence Research. Currently, he is co-principal investigator (with Bruce Jacobs) of a field based study of active drug robbers.

Chapter 4

Theory into Practice I: Building Communities

In the previous two Chapters, a number of theories that have examined issues related to space, time, and crime were explored. Chapter 2 introduced the ideas of the Chicago School theorists, as they tried to explain crime and other social problems based on neighborhood characteristics. In Chapter 3, a number of choice theories were presented that examined how a motivated rational offender finds and selects suitable targets. The next two chapters move beyond the sometimes-abstract theoretical principles and into practical applications. As discussed in the following Chapters, a number of programs stem from the thoughts of Shaw and McKay, Cornish and Clarke, Cohen and Felson, Patricia and Paul Brantingham, and others who have studied the relationship between crime and place. For ease of presentation, the various programs are divided into three general categories: 1) programs designed to build communities; 2) programs designed to prevent crime through target hardening; and 3) programs designed to enhance law enforcement tactics (which will be presented in the third unit on crime analysis and crime mapping). In this Chapter, programs designed to build communities are presented.

Building Communities

As detailed in Chapter 2, Shaw and McKay tried to explain why juvenile delinquency and other social problems seemed to be concentrated in certain areas within the city of Chicago. Higher levels of infant mortality, tuberculosis, mental disorders, poverty, and residential turnover were just a few of the conditions facing residents living in the inner city zones. The term social disorganization was used to describe a condition in which neighbors did not know their neighbors, and lacked a common set of norms and values. Shaw and McKay's theory had very obvious practical implications. In order to reduce crime and improve social conditions in areas marked by social disorganization, programs designed to build community ties and enhance social cohesion were needed. If local residents had a real sense of community, then the mechanisms of informal social control could be used to keep peoples' behavior in check, especially with respect to the monitoring of juveniles growing up in the area.

The Chicago Area Project (CAP)

In 1932, Clifford Shaw took his theoretical ideas to the streets of the city of Chicago in the form of the Chicago Area Project (CAP). The goal of Shaw and CAP was (and continues to be) a noble one: "To work toward the prevention and eradication of juvenile delinquency through the development and support of affiliated local community self-help efforts, in communities where the need is greatest" (http://www.chicagoareaproject.org). From its humble roots as an experimental program in three low-income areas, the CAP has grown to serve as an umbrella organization with over 40 affiliated social service agencies and various special programs aimed at curbing juvenile delinquency and other social problems through community organization (See Box 4.1 for a further discussion of CAP).

Box 4.1 The Chicago Area Project: The Legacy Lives On

The Chicago Area Project is the longest running community based delinquency prevention program in the United States. The goal of CAP is to develop and oversee special projects and encourage the growth of locally-controlled organizations that seek to improve the quality of life for residents of the city of Chicago and surrounding Cook County. The CAP model is based on the premise that a child has the best opportunity for a successful, productive life when all residents of a community work in a positive, cooperative manner to care for and watch over the children growing up within that community. To achieve the goal of building cooperation among community residents, the CAP has a number of affiliated community organizations, programs, and special projects that fall under its organizational structure. The following is a description of a few of the components of the modern-day CAP:

African American Male Rites of Passage (ROP). This Afrocentrically-based program is designed to assist African American males, ages 14 to 21, in the development of life skills necessary to lead an independent life. Many of the participating youths reside in group homes or foster care. Youths are provided instruction in a number of topical areas, including African and African/American history, financial management and budgeting, problem solving skills, interpersonal relations, conflict resolution, taking responsibility for their actions, and pre-employment training. Participants also attend a two-day retreat and, upon successful completion of the program, attend a graduation ceremony where they are welcomed by members of their community and praised for their commitment to live their life based on the principles taught

---

through the ROP. After graduation, the youths are eligible to receive other CAP services, such as vocational training, job placement, and assistance with housing.

Women in Transition (WIT). Established in 1997, this program is designed to provide career counseling and placement, pre-employment skills, and assistance to families in the transition from welfare to the workforce. The Welfare Reform Act of 1996 mandated time limits for individuals on welfare to receive benefits and to find employment. Little assistance was provided to individuals as they moved from welfare to work. This program targets individuals who have been classified as 'hardcore' and unemployable. This classification may be due to a number of factors including lack of basic literacy skills, little or no previous work experience, substance abuse issues, or other similar challenges. To date, the WIT program has successfully placed about one-third of its clients in gainful employment.

Youth as Resources (YAR). YAR is a program for young people ages 5 to 21. The goal of YAR is to get youths involved in the identification of problems within their own communities and develop solutions. Instead of adults telling the youths what to do, the program asks the youths to take on the responsibility of shaping their own roles in their communities. The underlying philosophy is that if youths know that they can contribute to the improvement of their own neighborhoods, they will be more likely to get involved.YAR includes three components: community service, in which youths identify and implement projects to improve the quality of life in their own communities; service learning, which is a school based component that ties the community projects to academic learning; and violence prevention. Since its inception in 1968, YAR has funded over a hundred different projects that have impacted the lives of thousands of young people in the Chicago area. YAR programs have worked successfully in a variety of environments, including public housing communities such as Robert Taylor Homes, juvenile correctional facilities, and schools. Additionally, YAR works with juvenile female offenders, assisting them with their transition back into the community to ultimately lead productive lives as full participating members of their neighborhoods.

For more information on these and other programs, please see the website for the Chicago Area Project at http://chicagoareaproject.org.

From its inception, CAP has been focused on the neighborhood. Once a neighborhood was identified for intervention, Shaw and his colleagues set out to identify and draw upon pre-existing community resources: the most influential residents and the most powerful institutions within that particular community (like a church, community center, local businesses, or other central point for local community activities). The overarching philosophy was to bring together community leaders and local resources to achieve three goals: to bring positive adult role models into contact with local juveniles, to provide local residents with resources to assist with child rearing and juvenile delinquency prevention, and to encourage communication between local residents and various institutional representatives who could provide needed benefits and resources to the community (Bursik & Grasmick, 1993). Through these conscious efforts to organize the local residents, Shaw believed that the natural ability of the community to develop and enforce norms of social control would be enhanced (Vold, et al., 2002).

One of CAPs more innovative (and controversial) approaches was to recruit local community leaders to serve as "indigenous workers." It was the job of the indigenous worker to organize local residents to achieve the goals of CAP. The utilization of indigenous workers offered a number of benefits. As a local resident, the indigenous worker would already have intimate knowledge of the neighborhood. The indigenous worker would be able to identify the local hangouts for juveniles, as well as the kids who were headed for trouble. Additionally, the indigenous worker would be accepted by the local residents, and would not generate the same level of scrutiny, suspicion, and resentment that an outsider would (Kobrin, 1959).

While the idea to use local residents to staff the centers seemed like a good idea, there were some problems. Professional social workers felt that the use of untrained workers was unwise and potentially harmful to the youths (Bennett, 1981; Kobrin, 1959). What made this issue particularly sticky was that the character of some of the indigenous workers was called into question. In some instances, individuals with serious criminal records were placed into positions of authority within the community organizations. The public did not favor such appointments, nor did the professional social workers who felt that their positions were being taken away by ex-convicts with no education or professional experience (Bursik & Grasmick, 1993; Sorrentino & Whittaker, 1994).

Nevertheless, the CAP initiated a number of positive experiences for youths, including sports and recreational programs, summer camps, scouting activities, arts and crafts workshops and other opportunities to engage in legitimate activities. Local youths were encouraged to interact with community adults who would supervise their activities and serve as positive role models for behavior. Detached workers were recruited to work closely with neighborhood kids, especially targeting youths known to be gang members. Much like the indigenous workers, detached workers were often local residents who had little or no formal training in working with juveniles. Detached workers were expected to work with gang members during after school and evening hours, providing "curbside counseling," supervision, and to serve as stable, positive role models for conventional behavior (Bursik & Grasmick, 1993; Schlossman & Sedlak, 1983).

The CAP was truly a noble effort to reduce juvenile delinquency in the city of Chicago's socially disorganized areas. Unfortunately, the effectiveness of the CAP to reduce the level of juvenile crime has been described as negligible at best (Hope, 1995; Lundman, 1993). Schlossman, Zellman, and Shavelson (1984) noted that as time passed Shaw himself relied less and less on official statistical reports of juvenile delinquency to demonstrate the overall effectiveness of the CAP's efforts. However, in analyses of the overall impact of programs similar to the CAP that were launched in other major cities, evaluators reported a number of positive results. Youths in the similar programs were provided with opportunities to interact with positive adult role models, had structured vocational and recreational activities available to them, and were given the opportunity to learn various problem-solving techniques (Curran & Renzetti, 1994; 2001; Miller, 1962).

Despite its shortcomings, the CAP was and continues to be an important community crime prevention strategy. Many of the strategies employed by Shaw, while controversial at the time, have become commonplace in a variety of community outreach programs (Bursik & Grasmick, 1993).

Empowerment Zones, Enterprise Communities, and Renewal Communities

The general guiding principle of reorganizing and rebuilding communities towards the goal of self-help can be found in many contemporary crime prevention efforts. For example, recent federal programs designed to assist economically disadvantaged communities designated as Empowerment Zones, Enterprise Communities, or Renewal Communities have been developed. These community-building efforts are large-scale programs funded through the Department of Housing and Urban Development (HUD) of the United States federal government. While the emphasis of many of these programs is on economic development, others focus on promoting social services and overall community improvement (Howell & Hawkins, 1998). This is a relatively new strategy in which tax incentives are offered to businesses willing in invest in geographically small, economically depressed areas (Sherman, Gottfredson, MacKenzi, Eck, Reuter, & Bushway, 1997).

In 1982, then President Reagan proposed the Urban Jobs and Enterprise Zone Act, which was designed to lay the groundwork for private, free enterprise to grow and develop in economically depressed areas. The hope was that by providing hefty tax credits, for-profit small businesses would move to a relatively small area and set up shop. The initial emphasis of the program was to assist small businesses. "Mom and Pop" shops are the life-blood of many cities, providing about half of all jobs in an urban area (Butler, 1980). Despite their importance to the economic well-being of a region, small businesses face a number of unique challenges that make them much more likely to fail. For example, small businesses tend to suffer more from various government regulations, such as minimum wage legislation or various (expensive) health and safety regulations (Walton, 1982). On the positive side, because of the nature of their business, many small business owners tend to employ younger workers with minimal education or training. Therefore, the Urban Jobs and Enterprise Zone Act was designed to maximize the ability of entrepreneurs to succeed. Small business owners not only provide opportunities for less skilled residents, but they also become a stakeholder in local community life (Butler, 1980; Walton, 1982).

The program began somewhat slowly and was initially limited to the identification of 10–25 communities, as pilot sites. Each year the program would add additional opportunities for other communities to apply for assistance (Walton, 1982). The program has continued to grow. In December 1994, 105 communities were designated as Empowerment Zones or Enterprise Communities. Five years later, another 40 distressed communities were added to the list. The Community Renewal Tax Relief Act of 2000 provided funding for nearly 50 additional areas to receive funding either as a Renewal Community (RC) or an Empowerment Zone. More recently, the designations of some of the original RC/EZ/EC locations have begun to expire. For example, the rural EZ/EC program expired on December 31, 2009 per P.L. 111-20. This meant that all *rural* EZ/ECs designations no longer exist. In addition, some of the Round I urban and rural Enterprise Communities that HUD and USDA designated in 1994 are no longer classified as such. Nevertheless, there are currently 100 RC/EZ/ECs still active across the country.

The process of designating a region as an RC/EZ/EC is dependent upon a number of factors, including: unemployment rates, poverty rates, median incomes, number of individuals receiving welfare or other government assistance, level of property abandonment, and level of population decline (Sherman et al., 1997). For example, the San Diego Renewal Community project has breathed new life into an old community when it recently received a $113,700 Community Redevelopment Development (CRD) grant. (see Box 4.2 for a detailed description of this project; for more information on the EZ/EC program, please visit http://www.hud.gov/offices/cpd/economic development/programs/rc).

Box 4.2 San Diego, California Renewal Community

"It's a huge success in our community," said Karen Whitehead of Golden Hill when asked about a building in her community that was gutted and restored with the help of CRD allocations. The building now houses Krakatoa, a trendy neighborhood coffee house. She continued by saying, "The Krakatoa Coffee House is the latest example of property owners making investments in their properties here in Golden Hill to make the area more attractive and to create a more family feeling in the neighborhood." The owner-developer of the property applied for and received a $113,700 CRD allocation for the coffeehouse, which helped create six jobs, three of which are held by RC residents.

In January 2002 HUD granted an RC designation to an area of San Diego that had been suffering from high poverty, unemployment, crime, and other problems. Businesses in the San Diego RC are eligible to apply for a share of $12 million in CRD allocations each year through 2009.

The RC status has helped spur investment. The renovation of the Pepitone building is a good example. This historically significant building in the downtown Gaslamp Quarter was dilapidated and in need of extensive renovation in order to be used again. A $4.9 million CRD allocation resulted in a beautifully rehabilitated structure in older downtown San Diego that will create 100 jobs, about 50 of which will go to RC residents. "This rehabilitation not only substantially restores a historic building, it also adds critical housing, restaurant, and office spaces to a revitalizing downtown arena," said Jim Schneider, spokesman for the project.

Another Gaslamp Quarter project got underway with the help of a sizeable CRD allocation. Borders Books and Music Store constructed a large store on a long-vacant corner in the Gaslamp Quarter. The company invested $7.8 million in the project, which created 350 full-time and part-time jobs, about 280 of which are for RC residents. "I used to work in a fast food restaurant without benefits. Now I work at Borders, make more than minimum wage and have health benefits for me and my family," said Betty Washington, a Borders Books and Music Store employee. (Source: http://www.hud.gov/offices/cpd/economicdevelopment/programs/rc/tour/ca/sandiego/gs1.cfm.)

As noted previously, businesses operating within the designated areas are eligible for a number of federally funded incentives. For example, if I (Tim) decided to open up a business within the limits of a designated EZ in Deming, New Mexico (for example), I could receive an annual tax credit of up to $3,000 for *each* employee who lives and works for me; and I could take an increase in deduction up to $35,000 of the cost of eligible equipment purchases. I could also qualify for low-cost loans to improve or expand my operation, receive some relief on capital gains if certain assets were sold, as well as a variety of other incentives. Furthermore, some requirements of federal regulatory agencies may be suspended if a local or state government requests special waivers within the designed zone. The goal of these incentives is to encourage business owners to open new businesses, expand their operations, and hire local residents. Businesses are carefully monitored to ensure that they are operating within the spirit of the EZ redevelopment plan; employers must verify that the employees do reside within the limits of the geographic bounds of the EZ in order to qualify for incentives. Collectively, the incentives to businesses operating in areas designated as Empowerment Zones or Renewal Communities are worth over $10 billion dollars.

Once designated as an EZ/EC/RC area, the local community is eligible to receive a variety of state and federal dollars designed to improve the quality of life in the area. For example, the Youth Out of the Education Mainstream Program provides special assistance to schools located in EZ/EC areas. Training for students and staff is provided in the areas of truancy, school discipline, on-campus violence, and overall school safety. Other programs have provided employment training for public housing residents, youth leadership and development programs, and anti-crime and anti-drug use programs for youths living in EZ/EC designed areas (Coordinating Council and Juvenile Justice Delinquency Prevention, 1996).

As noted by Sherman et al. (1997), EZ/EC programs are designed to assist local residents and their neighborhoods. By stimulating the local economy, local residents have a variety of legitimate employment opportunities available to them, thereby reducing the pressure to resort to criminal activities in order to earn a living. These new jobs offer hope to the youths growing up in economically depressed areas, and enhance their motivation to learn the skills and training required to perform such jobs. Ultimately, the improved economic conditions lead to increased interactions among local residents and strengthen neighborhood resources, including churches, schools, and other local businesses. Since many business owners avoid high crime areas, the reduction in crime in successful EZ/EC program areas brings new businesses to the community. In the spirit of the CAP, the economic development results in the natural growth of informal social control.

How effective are these programs at building local communities? Sherman et al. (1997) reviewed the evaluations of a number of such initiatives. Since the EZ/EC programs are relatively new, few evaluations of their effectiveness exist. In the eleven studies that were examined, the results were generally positive. Employment opportunities and commercial investments increased in the targeted zones, sometimes dramatically so. Papke (1994) found a long-term decline of 19% in the unemployment rates in a number of Indiana cities that had Enterprise Zones. In contrast, Boarnet and Bogart (1996) found no change in the level of unemployment or property values in areas designated as Enterprise Zones in the state of New Jersey.

But what about the impact on crime and delinquency? Sherman et al. (1997) concluded that EZ/EC programs are promising as a crime prevention program, if the program is designed with that specific goal in mind. The idea behind EZ/EC programs—to rebuild economically depressed areas—may provide a necessary ingredient in the overall plan to reduce crime and improve the overall quality of life in these areas.

In addition to the EZ/EC/RC programs, a number of federal and state agencies have funds set aside specifically for the development and empowerment of local neighborhoods. The Office of Juvenile Justice and Delinquency Prevention (1995) lists over 50 different community based initiatives funded through a variety of federal agencies, including the Department of Justice, the Department of Health and Human Services, the Department of Education, the Department of Labor, the Department of the Interior, as well as a number of private funding agencies.

Building Communities and the Role of Law Enforcement Agencies

In this section, the efforts of the Department of Justice to build communities through partnerships with local law enforcement agencies will be explored. Over the past 30 years or so, a revolution of sorts has been taking place in the delivery of services by the American law enforcement industry. The phrase "community policing" is now a common element of the language of policing. One cannot discuss contemporary issues in policing without devoting a good deal of time to the topic. But just what does the phrase "community policing" mean? How does community policing fit in with rebuilding communities and reducing levels of social disorganization? Because organizational issues associated with the adoption of a community policing philosophy will come up again and again in this text (especially with respect to geographic accountability and the role of crime analysis), a good deal of attention is devoted to the topic.

The Rise of Contemporary Community Policing

Since its origination in the late 1970s and early 1980s, community policing has become a commonplace practice in both rural and urban police departments. Walker (1999) argued that community policing and problem-oriented policing (a closely related philosophy) emerged in response to a number of crises in the American policing industry. First and foremost, the turbulent era of the 1960s was a public relations nightmare for law enforcement agencies, especially in minority communities. Riots rocked many major cities, and many of the triggering events for the violent uprisings could be traced to an unpleasant exchange between a police officer and a citizen. A number of federal inquiries were conducted into the practices of the police, including the President's Crime Commission (1967), the Kerner Commission (National Advisory Commission on Civil Disorders, 1968), and the National Advisory Commission on Criminal Justice Standards and Goals (1973). These evaluations of the police suggested that a change from the more traditional "professional model" of law enforcement was needed to overcome the feelings of mistrust and animosity that many citizens harbored towards the police.

The **professional model of policing** was popularized by August Vollmer, who was the chief of police of the Berkley, California police department in the early 1900s. Vollmer was quite a visionary in the science of policing and a pioneer in the area of crime analysis. Prior to the professionalism era, the police had been involved in a number of social service functions, such as feeding the hungry and housing the less fortunate. Vollmer felt that the enforcement of the law should be the primary responsibility of the police, not social work. Vollmer's vision of the ideal police officer was a college-educated, crime-fighting professional that would interact with citizens in an impartial, neutral manner. Discretion would be highly regulated in an organizational environment based on a paramilitary model (Bartollas & Hahn, 1999; Schafer, 2002).

In theory, Vollmer's ideal professional police officer did not sound bad at all. An educated, highly trained professional would apply the law without regard to race, creed, gender, or other extra-legal factors. There would be no room for "alternative courses of action" or the use of discretion. Today, an officer confronted by a number of juveniles drinking beer in an abandoned house may tell the kids to pour out the beer and go home. The law requires that the officer take a certain course of action, namely to take the juveniles into custody and charge them with a number of offenses: possession of alcohol, trespassing, perhaps a curfew violation. Under the professional model, the officer would have been provided little or no individual decision-making in the application of the law. A law violation is a law violation, and the law must be enforced.

Additionally, in order for officers to maintain a professional distance from the citizenry, Vollmer advocated that patrol officers should be rotated from district to district. Since the primary responsibility of the patrol officer was impartial enforcement of the law, close personal relationships with the citizens in a beat or zone would make this task difficult. The end result of this philosophy was that officers did not know residents of the local community, nor were they encouraged to get to know them. Officers were often perceived as aloof and distant from the citizens they were assigned to protect and to serve.

In addition to the crisis of police-community relations, Walker (1999) also attributed the growth of community policing to a number of studies and reports that called the effectiveness of traditional police patrol practices into question. Throughout the 1960s and 1970s, the nation had experienced a rather dramatic increase in the level of crime, especially violent crime (Cohen & Felson, 1979). This crime wave placed even greater demands on the police to "do something" to reduce crime. The usual response to citizen demands to "do something" about crime normally results in an increase in the level of patrol activity in high crime areas.

In the mid-1970s, the results of one of the most influential pieces of police research were released which seriously questioned the effectiveness of routine police patrol activities. The results of the Kansas City Preventive Patrol Experiment (Kelling, et al., 1974) suggested that even dramatic increases in the level of routine patrol activity had little or no impact on crime. Even more interesting was the fact that the public did not perceive increases (or decreases) in the level of patrol in their local communities. Citizens did not feel any more or less safe in their neighborhood based on changes in police presence. As we shall see, fear of crime can have a crippling effect on neighborhood cohesion and the overall quality of life in communities. If increases in the level of patrol do not significantly reduce crime or levels of fear, then something else must be done. Because of the significance of the Kansas City Preventive Patrol experiment, a detailed description of this study may be found in Box 4.3.

Box 4.3 The Kansas City Preventive Patrol Experiment

"This study is a bunch of horse-pucky."

—Former Chief of Police in a mid-sized Southern police agency.

Even introductory courses in criminology include something about the Kansas City Preventive Patrol Experiment. This research study can only be described as a classic in the study of policing. Whenever crime rates increased, the standing cry from sheriffs and police chiefs was (and continues to be) to request more funds for more patrol officers on the street. Prior to the Preventive Patrol Experiment, the blind assumption by police professionals and the general public was that routine police patrols had a significant impact on the level of crime in an area. If you've got a crime problem in a neighborhood or district, simply send more officers to the area. Well, the results of the Preventive Patrol Experiment seriously called this assumption into question.

In 1971, a task force of patrol officers and supervisors within the Kansas City Police Department was faced with a number of serious crime problems, especially in its South Patrol Division. The task force members felt that if attention was focused on a few pressing issues in the South Division, then the resources available for routine patrol activities within the Division would suffer. It was during these discussions that some of the task force members began to question what impact, if any, routine patrol activities had on criminal activity in an area. The Kansas City Police Department requested and was awarded funds from the Police Foundation in order to conduct an experiment on the true impact of patrol. In addition to the effects of patrol on criminal activity, the task force and research team were also interested in measuring the effects of patrol on a number of other variables, including citizen fear, citizen behavior as a result of fear, and citizen perception of police services.

Without getting too technical, there are a number of ways of testing whether or not a change in the level of patrol activities has any impact on the level of crime, feelings of citizen security, or other variables of interest. Some of these research designs can produce results that are "better" than others. One of the reasons that this study has become such a classic is the type of research design that was selected: a **strong, quasi-experimental design**. Given the research situation, this was the strongest, "best" design that the research team could have selected.

The South Patrol division was divided into 24 beats. The research team sat down and took a look at the demographics of these 24 areas and determined that nine of the beats were unrepresentative of the rest of the city. The remaining 15 beats were then divided up into five groups containing three beats. In order to be assigned as part of one of the five groups, the three beats were matched up with each other based on a number of characteristics including crime data, number of calls for service, ethnic and racial diversity, median income, and residential stability.

The research team had three different patrol levels in mind: reactive patrol, proactive patrol, and a "control" condition which maintained the usual level of patrol activity. Within each of the five groups of three beats, one beat was assigned to the reactive condition, one to the proactive condition, and one to the control condition. This matching process, while seemingly cumbersome, was one of the strongest aspects of the study. If the research team had not assigned matched beats to the different conditions, they might have ended up with all high crime areas experiencing the reactive condition or the poorest areas receiving the proactive patrol. By matching the beats, the research team tried their best to remove any influence that pre-existing neighborhood characteristics could have had on the results.

The research team ended up with three experimental conditions with five beats assigned to each. In the reactive condition, there was no preventive patrol as is traditionally thought of. Officers did not randomly drive around in the beats, looking for suspicious activity. The only time that a patrol vehicle went into these beats was to answer a call for service, handle the call, and then leave the beat. During the times that the officer was not answering a call for service he or she was told to patrol the boundary of the reactive beat or to go to the beats assigned to the proactive condition.

In the five beats assigned to the proactive patrol condition, the level of police presence was two to three times the normal level. Additional patrol vehicles had been assigned here, and officers from the adjacent reactive beats were instructed to patrol the area as well. Finally, in the five beats assigned to the control condition, the normal level of patrol was maintained.

In order to explore the effects of patrol level on crime and citizen perceptions, the research team used a variety of techniques, including surveys, interviews, observations, and official departmental statistics. To many police practitioners and researchers, the results of the study were almost unbelievable. With a few rare exceptions, changes in the level of patrol had no impact on the level of reported crime (as measured by both official departmental statistics and interviews with citizens), arrest patterns, fear of crime, protective behaviors by citizens in response to their fear of crime, and citizen satisfaction with the police. Even response time was unaffected by changes in the level of routine preventive patrol.

In sum, the results of the Kansas City Preventive Patrol Experiment concluded that simply increasing the level of routine preventive patrol in an area had little or no impact on the level of crime, citizen attitudes, or their behavior. The dramatic findings fueled the fire for police agencies to question their underlying philosophies and re-think how police services could be more effective. This study not only increased the interest in community policing, but also enhanced interest in crime analysis and other "smart" policing tools.

Of course, it should be noted that not all police practitioners "buy into" the findings of this study. As the quote at the beginning of this section indicates, despite contrary evidence some police administrators maintain the traditional belief that the only way to win the war on crime is to send in more troops. Community policing, crime analysis, and crime mapping are nothing more than fads that have no real impact on crime. The police chief's quote was repeated to me by students enrolled in a Policy Analysis class that I (Kim) was teaching. During my lecture, I had spent several hours presenting the Kansas City Preventive Patrol Experiment, discussing the strengths of the design, the findings, and its impact on the future of policing. I noticed that several of the students were laughing. When questioned, the students reported that a local police chief had covered the experiment in their Police Administration class the night before, and had summarized the results in just seven words: "This study is a bunch of horse-pucky."

Study description and results adapted from Kelling, F., Pate, T., Dieckman, D., & Brown, C. (1974). The Kansas City preventive patrol experiment: A summary report. Washington, DC: Police Foundation.

"Broken Windows" and Broken Communities

A few years after the results of the Kansas City Preventive Patrol Experiment were released, a second influential thought-piece on police practices was published. To this day, James Q. Wilson and George Kelling's "Broken Windows: The Police and Neighborhood Safety" essay continues to impact many police practices. The focus of their essay was how police services have changed over the years from a personal, hands-on delivery of order-maintenance to a more impersonal crime-control orientation.

Wilson and Kelling (1982) argued that foot patrols, which had almost disappeared from use with the arrival of the automobile, provided a better means of delivering police services. Based on observations and interviews with Newark, New Jersey officers assigned to foot patrol, officers who walked their beats had greater opportunity to interact informally with members of a neighborhood than officers who drove around in a patrol vehicle. These one-on-one interactions allowed the officers to identify who belonged in a neighborhood and who did not. "Strangers" were watched closely, and the "decent folk" who were neighborhood regulars were able to work with their beat officer to develop acceptable rules for conduct. Different neighborhoods may have had very different rules for behavior, and it was up to the officer to work with the local residents to find out what rules worked best in that particular area.

The goal of the foot patrol officer was to increase the level of public order in the neighborhood that they were assigned to. Wilson and Kelling argued that crime and disorder are closely tied to each other, hence the "broken windows" analogy. If someone breaks a window and that window is left unrepaired, then, in a short time, all of the other windows will soon be broken. An unrepaired broken window sends the signal that "no one cares." Ultimately, this leads to the breakdown of informal community control. Wilson and Kelling (1982) describe the community deterioration that may result from a broken window or other physical signs of disorder:

> A stable neighborhood of families who care for their homes, mind each other's children, and confidently frown on unwanted intruders can change, in a few years or even a few months, to an inhospitable and frightening jungle. A piece of property is abandoned, weeds grow up, a window is smashed. Adults stop scolding rowdy children; the children, emboldened, become more rowdy. Families move out, unattached adults move in. Teenagers gather in front of the corner store. The merchant asks them to move; they refuse. Fights occur. Litter accumulates. People start drinking in front of the grocery; in time, an inebriate slumps to the sidewalk and is allowed to sleep it off. Pedestrians are approached by panhandlers. At this point it is not inevitable that serious crime will flourish or violent attacks on strangers will occur. But many residents will think that crime, especially violent crime, is on the rise, and they will modify their behavior accordingly. They will use the streets less often, and when on the streets will stay apart from their fellows moving with averted eyes, silent lips, and hurried steps. "Don't get involved." For some residents, this growing atomization will matter little, because the neighborhood is not their "home" but "the place where they live" (p. 31).

To assist in better understanding their assertions, the eight core ideas of Wilson and Kelling's broken windows concepts have been later summarized as follows (Wagers, Sousa, & Kelling, 2008):

1. Disorder and fear of crime are strongly linked.
2. Police (in the examples given, foot patrol officers) negotiate rules of the street. 'Street people' are involved in the negotiation of those rules.
3. Different neighborhoods have different rules.
4. Untended disorder leads to the breakdown of community controls.
5. Areas where community controls break down are vulnerable to criminal invasion.
6. The essence of the police role in maintaining order is to reinforce the informal control mechanisms of the community itself.

7. Problems arise not so much from individual disorderly persons as it does from the congregation of large numbers of disorderly persons.
8. Different neighborhoods have different capacities to manage disorder (p. 253).

Once urban decay begins, it is very difficult in contemporary times to turn things around. Wilson and Kelling noted that in previous centuries, neighborhood level increases in crime and disorder had a sort of built-in correction mechanism. People could rarely leave their neighborhoods, so the residents would be forced to reclaim their turf. Now, if a neighborhood deteriorates, anyone who has the ability to leave the area will move, leaving behind the elderly, the very poor, or those whose ability to move are blocked by prejudice.

Disorder, Fear of Crime, and the Role of the Police

Disorder, crime, fear of crime, neighborhood deterioration, and social disorganization all go hand in hand. Skogan (1986; 1990) described both human forms of disorder and physical forms of disorder. Human forms of disorder may include: groups of teenagers hanging out on street corners, street prostitution, panhandling, public drinking, open gambling, and open drug use and sales. Physical disorder includes: vandalism, graffiti, junk and trash in vacant lots, boarded up deserted homes and commercial buildings, and stripped or abandoned cars. Regardless of its form, visible signs of disorder are signals of social disorganization and a lack of a sense of social control—both informal and formal. As argued by Taylor and Hale (1986), "social and physical incivilities are fear-inspiring not only because they indicate a lack of concern for public order, but also because their continued presence points at the inability of officials to cope with these problems" (p. 154). Visible signs of disorder make people feel more susceptible to crime and leave them with the fear that the police and other officials can do little to protect them from victimization (Roh & Oliver, 2005).

Signs of disorder in a community also contribute to feelings of insecurity and fear of crime, even if there has been no real change in the level of criminal activity in an area. Fear of crime has serious negative consequences on the quality of community life. As Skogan (1986) argued, people who are experiencing heightened levels of fear withdraw from their neighborhoods. They no longer feel comfortable walking the streets after dark, nor do they get involved when they see behavior that violates the informal social controls of the neighborhood. Fearful individuals no longer feel close personal ties to their neighborhoods and they do not participate in community life. It is as if the problems in their neighborhoods become larger than life, and local grass roots efforts will do nothing to solve them.

Additionally, the level of fear of crime also has an impact on what Skogan called spatial radius. A person who is comfortable and confident in his or her neighborhood has a large territory (spatial radius) in which they feel some sense of responsibility to defend the space from suspicious activities and unsavory persons. Fear of crime reduces the spatial radius, which leaves areas without caring guardians. These untended areas then become prime targets for criminal activity and disorder.

So, what is to be done in neighborhoods that have experienced a spiral of deterioration? How can the community be turned back to the "decent folk" who live there? Herein enters the "new" responsibility of local law enforcement. At the first sign of physical or human disorder, the police need to intervene and assist local residents in shoring up their informal social control mechanisms (Wilson & Kelling, 1982). Instead of relying upon traditional crime fighting strategies, a new philosophy of policing needs to be adopted. In this new form of policing, local residents will be viewed as partners with local law enforcement in the process of identifying problems and developing solutions. This new form of policing has become known as "community policing."

Community Policing

The term "community policing" has become a buzzword used to describe a variety of programs and organizational philosophies. Trojanowiez and Bocqueroux (1990) defined the philosophy of community policing in the following manner:

> Community Policing is a new philosophy of policing, based on the concept that police officers and private citizens working together in creative ways can help solve contemporary community problems related to crime, fear of crime, social and physical disorder, and neighborhood decay. The philosophy is predicated on the belief that achieving these goals requires that police departments develop a new relationship with the law-abiding people in the community, allowing them a greater voice in setting local police priorities and involving them in efforts to improve the overall quality of life in their neighborhoods. It shifts the focus of police work from handling random calls to solving community problems (p. 5).

Others have translated the philosophy of community policing into practical applications. Permanent assignment by both beat and shift is an essential element of community policing (Bracey, 1992; Goldstein, 1993). In order for the police to establish community partnerships with local citizens, the officers must be provided with the opportunity to develop close personal relationships with residents. One common measure of the success of community policing is whether or not local residents know their locally assigned community police officer by name (Goldstein, 1987).

In addition to enhancing police-community relationships, permanent assignment also leads to the establishment of geographic responsibility and accountability (Weisel & Eck, 1994). If an officer has been assigned to a specific beat, then that officer should know what is going on in their area and be held responsible for the conditions in that area. If a rash of graffiti suddenly appears or a group of teenagers is hanging out at the local convenience store late at night, it is the duty of the locally assigned police officer to recognize that these conditions have surfaced and to work in conjunction with local residents and business owners to do something about it. Officers assigned to different areas may not have the opportunity to recognize subtle "broken windows" changes.

In order to enhance geographic responsibility, many agencies have also adopted a decentralized approach to the delivery of services. Instead of having one large, sometimes ominous, centralized command post for all police services, many police departments have turned to smaller district offices. These smaller offices may be located in strip malls, shopping malls, or freestanding buildings. Regardless of their physical design, the decentralized system provides service centers that are viewed as less intimidating and more convenient for local residents to visit. Residents can stop by the station and meet one-on-one with their locally assigned regular officer, hopefully a familiar face to them.

Another essential element of community policing is the notion that the police must become more proactive in the prevention of crime and disorder (Goldstein, 1993). Instead of just responding from call to call, police (with the assistance of the community) should attempt to identify root causes of problems in the area. Crimes are viewed as symptoms of other underlying problems in the community (Lab, 2000). An arrest may take care of a specific incident, but will do nothing to solve the larger problem. The emphasis on solving community problems has been described as "the most important element of community policing" (p. 164). This approach, often called problem-oriented policing (POP), oftentimes goes hand in hand with community policing.

Herman Goldstein, a prominent policing scholar, popularized the idea of problem-oriented policing in an essay on the improvement of police practices. Goldstein (1979) argued that police agencies had become more concerned with improving organizational aspects of policing than with the end product of their efforts, a condition he described as the "means over ends" syndrome.

Staffing issues and other internal management concerns had become paramount, while community safety and quality of life issues had taken a back seat. Additionally, police agencies had become preoccupied with arrests and enforcement of the law, which Goldstein felt was simply another indication of the continued emphasis on the "means" as opposed to the "ends." Goldstein felt that the end product of policing should be re-elevated to its place of primary importance. Further, Goldstein defined the end product as dealing with community problems. In his view, community problems were the very soul of police work and the true reason for having a police force.

While Goldstein's vision of problem-oriented policing received a great deal of attention, his ideas began to have a profound impact on policing when millions of dollars were offered in incentives to agencies that adopted community policing principles (see Box 4.4 for more information).

Box 4.4 Office of Community Oriented Policing Services COPS Office

In his State of the Union Address in January 1994, former President Bill Clinton vowed to put 100,000 new police officers on the streets of America. These officers would be specially trained in the principles of community and problem-oriented policing. As part of this initiative, the Violent Crime Control and Law Enforcement Act of 1994 provided nearly $9 billion for a number of projects related to the development of community policing. In addition to the hiring of the new officers, part of this funding was designated for the creation of the Office of Community Oriented Policing Services, which is commonly called the COPS office. It was the responsibility of the COPS office to act as a clearing-house, of sorts, for agencies wishing to take advantage of the federal funds.

Since 1994, the COPS Office has awarded more than $12 billion to add community policing officers to the nation's streets, enhance crime fighting technology, support crime prevention initiatives, and provide training and technical assistance to help advance community policing. Nearly 500,000 law enforcement personnel, community members, and government leaders have been trained through COPS Office-funded training organizations. The COPS Office provides training and technical assistance to law enforcement agencies and other organizations throughout the country through its many training partners, including a number of Regional Community Policing Institutes. As of 2009, the COPS Office has distributed more than 2 million topic-specific publications, training curricula, white papers, and resource CDs. COPS distributes these documents at a variety of law enforcement and public safety conferences throughout the nation, through the COPS Office Response Center, and website, www.cops.usdoj.gov.

Regional Community Policing Institutes (RCPIs). There are 28 RCPIs located throughout the United States. These Institutes provide training and technical assistance to law enforcement officers as well as community partners. Since 1997, more than 130,000 officers and community members have received training through their local RCPI. Training is provided in a number of areas, including school violence, cultural diversity, domestic violence, citizen complaint intake, the use of volunteers in policing, and partnership building.

Center for Problem-Oriented Policing. This is a non-profit group that brings together practitioners, researchers, and universities (including the University of Wisconsin Madison, Rutgers, and the University at Albany) to advance the practice of problem-oriented policing. The Center has an extensive library and offers various training resources, including interactive exercises to assist crime analysts in identifying the steps to solve crime problems.

For more information on the Office of Community Oriented Policing Services and Regional Community Policing Institutes, see the COPS website at http://www.cops. usdoj.gov.

Community/Police Problem Solving in Action

According to the Community Policing Consortium, community policing problem solving is best defined by its parts:

- The identification of crime, disorder, fear and other neighborhood problems;
- The development of an understanding of the underlying causes that result in neighborhood problems;
- The development and implementation of long-term, innovative solutions uniquely designed to address the neighborhood-specific problems; and
- The assessment of the solution's results on the neighborhood problems.

This four-step process is commonly known in policing circles as the SARA model: Scanning, Analysis, Response, and Assessment. The SARA model will be covered in much more depth in Chapter 6 when crime analysis is discussed. Suffice it to say that prior to developing solutions, problem-oriented policing involves careful analytical examination into the problems of concern. In order for the police and the community to work together to develop a solution to a problem, community residents and the police must have a clear idea of what, exactly, the problem actually is. For an example of Goldstein's principles in practice, see Box 4.5 for a description of a community policing problem solving effort in Roger's County, Oklahoma.

Box 4.5 Rogers County Hauls Down Trailer Theft

A 1997 Problem-Solving Partnership grant helped Oklahoma's Rogers County Sheriff's Office reduce trailer thefts. Theft of general livestock, horse, utility, and flatbed trailers increased significantly in Rogers County during the mid-1990s. This problem adversely impacted the livelihood and recreation of area residents and businesses. Rogers County Sheriff's Office field deputies began to monitor the problem when they noticed unusually high numbers of trailer theft calls for service. Thieves claimed more than 37 trailers during the first eight months of 1996 and only three were ever recovered. These thefts resulted in average losses of $2,500, but losses were as high as $35,000.

Approach/Methods

The COPS Problem-Solving Partnerships grant allowed Rogers County deputies to review crime reports, conduct site visits to theft locations, speak with victims, and conduct a community survey. Theft reports from 1996 and 1997 indicated that thefts of privately-owned equipment usually occurred between 8 a.m. and 3 p.m., while thefts of commercially-owned equipment usually occurred during the early morning hours—between midnight and 4 a.m. In 95% of the cases, the theft locations were remote but easily accessible to one of the county's four major highways.

Deputies discovered during site visits to theft locations and interviews with victims that most trailers were stolen from open areas not visible from residential dwellings. These locations proved to be tempting to thieves: they offered no means to secure a trailer, and little opportunity for natural surveillance. Stolen trailers had usually been chained and padlocked to the ground or a tree, which could be overcome with a common bolt-cutter. A random community survey of 200 Rogers County residents indicated that while most citizens had not been victims of trailer theft, they were interested in protecting their property and recovering it in the event of a theft.

While trailers might not seem concealable, it is extremely difficult to determine legitimate ownership by their appearance. Stolen trailers are very difficult to find at a private sale or auction in large part due to lack of legislated licensing or registration requirements. The small number of trailers recovered led deputies to believe that they were being repainted and sold at regional auctions. Rogers County implemented a four-pronged response strategy in March 1998.

Educating the Community: Sheriff's deputies attended meetings with residents and members of organizations such as the Cattleman's Association to make the community aware of the increase in trailer theft, identify at-risk locations, and discuss how new tracking and monitoring equipment could help prevent thefts.

Harnessing New Technologies: The Rogers County Sheriff 's Office offers the installation of tracking and monitoring microchips into at-risk property for a low fee. Deputies install rice-grain-sized microchip tracking devices into trailers at public clinics for only $35 per vehicle. Once installed in a trailer, these microchip devices permanently identify the owner's name and a description of the property, which is then entered in a police database.

Visually Archiving At-Risk Properties: Deputies also take photographs of microchip-equipped trailers and equipment. This allows deputies to visually confirm the identification of trailers registered in the database and immediately place pictures of stolen property onto the Internet when they are stolen. It also allows deputies to dispatch information quickly to neighboring law enforcement agencies, auction organizers, and community members.

Publicizing the Project to Potential Offenders: The Sheriff 's Office also warned trailer thieves and potential buyers of stolen goods through an extended media campaign. One press release stated, "if a trailer is found in the possession of a person other than the owner without the owner's permission, that person will be going to jail." This almost immediately detracted from the value of a potentially stolen trailer. The Rogers County Sheriff's Office worked closely during this project with members of the Cattleman's Association, Professional Rodeo Cowboy Association, Quarter Horse Association, and the Farm Bureau, which serves as an insurance underwriter in many rural areas, to learn more about the financial and emotional costs of trailer theft. Sheriff's deputies also worked with the members of these organizations to spread the word of the Office's response to the problem and to seek their participation in the microchip program. National Microchip Horse Registry technicians installed the microchips in the trailers, and the mass media helped publicize the program throughout the state of Oklahoma.

Results

Trailer theft dropped 69% during the first year of the response program. Trailer theft was virtually eliminated in Rogers County shortly thereafter. Only one trailer was stolen in 2000 and 2001, and the owner of the stolen trailer had not participated in the Rogers County theft reduction program. The program has saved residents and the insurance companies serving Rogers County an estimated $300,000 since 1998.

Community participation in the program is strong—there is currently a list of over 100 trailers waiting to be registered and tagged. The success of the trailer program has led the Rogers County Sheriff's Office to expand the installation of microchips to include tractors, recreational vehicles, and all-terrain vehicles. Demand for the program is so high that the Sheriff's Office is working to purchase a mobile microchip installation unit so that owners will no longer need to transport their equipment to central locations for tagging. This mobile installation unit will greatly increase the number of participants in the program and the types of property it can protect.

Collaborative partnerships and problem-solving projects are two core elements of community policing. The Rogers County Sheriff's Office proved once again how effective community policing strategies can be—Rogers County deputies essentially eliminated the targeted crime problem in a single year. COPS is pleased to support agencies like the Rogers County Sheriff's Office as they work to keep their communities safer through community policing.

Reprinted from COPS Innovations: Promising Strategies from the Field. Spotlight on Sheriffs. *U.S. Department of Justice, Office of Community Oriented Policing Services. March, 2003: 13–17.*

The Current State of Community Policing

Community policing continues to be a popular law enforcement strategy. Since 1994, the Office of Community Oriented Policing Services has awarded more than $11.4 billion in grant funds to over 13,000 agencies across the country. This funding has been used for specialized training in community policing/problem solving policing practices, the hiring of additional police officers trained in community policing principles, and for special projects aimed at specific problems in local communities. The budget for fiscal year 2006 totals nearly a quarter of a billion dollars, with funds designated for training and various technology enhancements. The funds are clearly available for agencies wishing to make a change, but just how widespread is community policing?

There have been several surveys of law enforcement agencies to assess how widely used community policing strategies have become. For example, in 1992, the Police Foundation received a grant from the U.S. National Institute of Justice (NIJ) to conduct a nationwide survey of 2,337 agencies. Agency representatives were asked whether their organization had adopted community policing and the types of programs and practices they had implemented. A follow-up survey was conducted in 1997 with about 71% of the original group of agencies responding. In 2002, the Police Executive Research Forum (PERF) conducted a third survey. This survey included a sub-set of 282 agencies that had responded to both the 1992 and 1997 surveys and that had indicated in the prior surveys that the agency had adopted community policing. Finally, in 1999, 2000, 2003, and 2007 the Bureau of Justice Statistics (BJS) included questions about community policing in its broader Law Enforcement Management and Administrative Statistics (LEMAS) survey, which is sent to all U.S. law enforcement agencies employing 100 or more full-time sworn officers (i.e., "large" law enforcement agencies).

Collectively, results from all of these surveys paint a somewhat mixed picture. In the 1990s, agencies indicated that the community policing philosophy was an attractive strategy. For example, in the 1992 Police Foundation survey 20% of agencies indicated that they had adopted community policing and an additional 31% stated that they were in the initial stages of adopting the new strategy. By 1997, the number of agencies had increased quite dramatically, with 58% indicating that they had already adopted community policing and another 27% reported that their agency was in the planning stages. The report also concluded that community policing was much more likely to be implemented in larger agencies than in smaller ones. Furthermore, municipal police agencies were more likely to report community-policing activities than were sheriffs' departments (Fridell, 2004).

Based on the results of the 2002 PERF survey, a number of community policing activities were found to be quite popular. As noted by Cordner (2004), the following 16 strategies were reported by at least 75% of the responding agencies:

1. Citizens attend police-community meetings
2. Citizens participate in neighborhood watch
3. Citizens help police identify and resolve problems

4. Citizens serve as volunteers within the police agency
5. Citizens attend citizen police-academies
6. Police hold regularly scheduled meetings with community groups
7. Police have interagency involvement in problem solving
8. Police have youth programs
9. Police have victim assistance programs
10. Police use regulatory codes in problem solving
11. Police work with building code enforcement
12. Agencies used fixed assignments to specific beats or areas
13. Agencies give special recognition for good community policing work by employees
14. Agencies classify and prioritize calls
15. Agencies do geographically based crime analysis
16. Agencies use permanent neighborhood-based offices or stations

Agency respondents were very positive about their experiences with community policing strategies. Many noted improved community relations, reduced fear of crime, reduced levels of criminal activity, and enhanced job satisfaction among the officers involved in community policing projects (Cordner, 2004). However, as pointed out by Cordner, most agencies adopted a relatively modest form of community policing and excluded or limited the participation of citizens in a variety of activities, such as the evaluation of officer performance, the review of citizen complaints, or any voice in the selection or promotion process of law enforcement personnel. There is still a limit to the level of community participation that agencies will welcome.

Finally, recent findings from the 2007 LEMAS survey suggest the popularity of community policing might be waning. For example, only 15% of responding agencies indicated that they maintained or created a formal, written community policing plan, only 14% said that they maintained a community policing unit with full-time personnel, and only 20% said they actively encouraged patrol officers to engage in SARA-type problem solving projects on their beats, (B. Reaves, personal communication, January 24, 2011). In light of the earlier results from the Police Foundation and PERF surveys, results of the most recent LEMAS survey indicated agencies might be losing interest (or may no longer be able to afford—see the upcoming section, *Community Policing: Post September 11th*) in the community policing approach.

It is important to note that just because an agency has adopted (or, more importantly, *claims* to have adopted) an over-arching strategy of community policing does not automatically guarantee that these strategies will result in a change in every-day behaviors (Skogan, 2004). Further, the actual implementation of these bold initiatives may not resemble what the planners initially had in mind. In an analysis of the implementation of problem-solving strategies, Roth, Roehl, and Johnson (2004) noted an "astonishing variety" in how local agencies had implemented the practice. In their on-site visits with thirty different agencies, only one had a model that fit the prototype originally developed by Goldstein. Roth et al. stated that in some agencies, the working definition of problem solving had evolved into a local one that did not align with any of the more commonly known definitions. For one agency, the problem-solving strategy to combat a community burglary problem was to simply drive around and keep an eye out for the suspect's car. In other agencies, the incorporation of problem solving was "all but invisible." Sometimes, a single agency incorporated several different models for problem solving that varied between (and sometimes within) the site visits. The authors concluded that despite claims to the contrary, the process of formal problem solving was, at best, minimal in most of the agencies they visited.

Community Policing: Post September 11th

A few years back in my (Kim) academic department, the COPS funding was flowing freely. Many faculty members were working on various community policing projects, as evaluators or consultants. A number of our graduate students were funded as research assistants on these projects. If you asked your instructor for this course (assuming he or she has been around for a while), I would venture a bet that they worked on a COPS grant in some capacity. As you might imagine, assessments on the impact of this funding have found that the availability of COPS dollars had a significant positive impact on the adoption of community policing initiatives (He, Zhao, & Lovrich, 2005). The money was flowing so freely that on one particular project I (Kim) worked on, the agency tried to give the money back, but was unsuccessful. The agency had applied for the funds to establish a truancy program. The grant funds took almost a year to be awarded and in the interim the agency had gone ahead and set up the program without the benefit of federal funds. The chief had retired and no one really wanted that project anymore. The agency representative contacted the COPS office and let them know that the agency no longer wanted or needed the funds. The agency was told that they would create more problems if they returned the money and were encouraged to find another use for it. As long as the project kept in the spirit of community policing, the COPS office was okay with it. Well, the funding situation has changed dramatically since the 9-11 terrorist attacks, and these changes will have implications for the future of community policing.

The challenges for community policing will increase in our post-September 11th reality. While there is still funding available for community policing, the level has dropped dramatically, as priorities have shifted to Homeland Security. As noted by Myers (2004), there has been talk of the elimination of the COPS program because of a lack of funding. At the local level, law enforcement personnel are being reassigned from community policing duties to assignments associated with basic security functions. Resources that would have been used to support problem-solving initiatives are now being funneled into programs and technologies to assist first responders. Local police agencies have also been particularly hard hit by the activation of National Guard and members of the military Reserves, which has left vacancies that cannot be filled (Hanson, 2004; Myers, 2004). In some agencies, police officers are much more heavily armed and have adopted a more aggressive style of policing, a style inconsistent with the community policing philosophy.

While it is still very early to judge whether community policing can continue to exist in this new era, there are some positives to note. First and foremost, after the September 11th tragedy, the general public has a much stronger respect for our public servants and the potential sacrifices they are asked to make. We all have images of the firefighters and police officers rushing into the World Trade Center Twin Towers prior to their collapse. This unselfish action has brought people closer to the police (Myers, 2004). Second, because of the threat of terrorism on American soil, citizens may be much more likely to monitor and report suspicious activities to the police (Flynn, 1998; Myers, 2004). Furthermore, because of the essential need for citizen cooperation in reporting terrorist activities, community policing becomes much more important as an organizational philosophy. A citizen may literally be risking their life if they report suspected terrorist activities to their local police. If there is no trust in the local police, then the likelihood of information being reported is virtually zero. Of course, this applies not only to reports of terrorism, but to other forms of serious criminal behavior such as murder, drug dealing, or gang activities (Flynn, 1998).

Zero Tolerance Policing

Before the end of the discussion on community policing, it should also be noted that in addition to the comparatively "warm and fuzzy" community policing approach to curb crime and disorder, another policing philosophy has also been adopted by some agencies in an attempt to address the broken windows phenomenon: zero tolerance policing. This form of aggressive law enforcement has been popularized by the New York City Police Department. Under zero tolerance policing, officers focus on minor criminal offenses: pubic urination, vandalism of public property, jumping the turnstiles at the subway to avoid paying the fare, and various forms of panhandling (Walker, 1999). When an officer confronts a citizen committing a minor violation the officer is expected to take care of the problem, normally by making an arrest or issuing a citation. This punitive system is in stark contrast to the methods of community policing.

Under the philosophy of community policing, an officer should use his or her arrest powers as the last resort to a problem. The idea is that while making an arrest may take care of an immediate concern, an arrest does nothing to address the underlying problem that caused the situation to arise in the first place. Furthermore, issuing citations and making arrests for minor offenses may ultimately erode the confidence and trust needed to make police-community partnerships effective.

Conversely, zero tolerance policing advocates the full use of the formal criminal justice process for any and all minor law violations. Arrests for even trivial offenses send the message that acts of disorder will not be tolerated under any circumstances. By tightening the formal control mechanisms, ultimately the "decent folk" may regain control of their neighborhoods, feel more comfortable walking the streets at night, and institute their own informal forms of social control. While the goals of zero tolerance policing and community policing are the same (fear reduction, reduction of physical and human forms of disorder, reduced levels of crime), the means by which to achieve these goals are very different.

Zero tolerance policing in practice will be explored in much greater detail in later chapters when the COMPSTAT model of the New York City Police Department is examined. For now, suffice it to say that while some strongly endorse this aggressive form of law enforcement, others have leveled strong criticisms (Chambliss, 1996; Greene, 1999; Sampson & Raudenbush, 1999). Some have argued that this type of policing disproportionately targets the economically disadvantaged and minority citizens. The idea behind zero tolerance policing is that if a person has many arrests and convictions for minor offenses, if and when the person commits a serious offense, he or she will be subject to harsher punishment since the serious offense will not have been the first blemish on their record. Ultimately, this practice of arresting people again and again for even trivial offenses undermines any hope for a normal family life and may destroy communities, especially in minority neighborhoods (Chambliss, 1996).

Problems with Community Building Efforts

Theoretical Summary

So far, a number of related theories and ideas have been examined that stress the importance of community in controlling crime. Shaw and McKay noted that social disorganization was the root cause of many social ills in the city of Chicago. People did not share the same set of rules and expectations for behavior, and children were not socialized to respect and abide by a uniform set of conventional norms and values. Sampson added the concept of collective efficacy, which he defined as "social cohesion among neighbors combined with their willingness to intervene on behalf of the common good" (Sampson, et al., 1997, p. 918). Felson and Hirschi added the ideas of social bonding that might occur within communities, where children choose to follow the rules of society because the price they pay for breaking the rules is too high.

All of these support the idea that in neighborhoods that have a strong sense of community identity, people will step in and exercise informal social control if they see something wrong. Concerned adults will monitor the activities of neighborhood children and all members of the community will address visible signs of disorder. Fear of crime will be low in these areas, and residents will have a large territory or spatial radius where they exercise guardianship against crime and suspicious activities. Broken windows will be tended to, and all will be right with the world.

In this Chapter, the programs examined were all designed to build communities. Regardless of the specific plans associated with the individual programs, all have common goals:

- Improve neighborhood cohesion
- Enhance informal social control
- Renew a sense of order by reducing visible signs of human and physical disorder
- Reduce fear of crime
- Improve the quality of life for neighborhood residents

The question is, can forces from outside the community succeed in building a sense of neighborhood identity? Can externally imposed programs enhance informal social control? Problems with programs designed to build communities tend to fall into two general categories. First, the success or failure of these programs rests in large part on the pre-existing strength of the neighborhood. Second, many of these programs fail to address the underlying conditions that caused the community integrity to diminish.

Can a Community Be Built Where No Community Exists?

According to Flynn (1998), a community is much more than just a matter of geography. Just because people live near each other does not automatically guarantee that they will feel a sense of community with their neighbors. In order to be a true community, local residents must also share an identity (such as ethnicity, age, religious beliefs, or similar socio-economic status) and they must have similar concerns or problems. In some neighborhoods, the sense of community may be quite strong. In others, there is no such sense of belonging. This is where the problem lies. Can community-building programs be successful when they must start from scratch?

Arguably, the most serious problem facing programs designed to build communities is that the programs are least successful in the neighborhoods that need them the most (Bursik & Grasmick, 1993; Peak & Glensor, 2002). In lower income areas plagued by high levels of crime, high residential turnover, and racial heterogeneity, community programs have had the lowest levels of success. Conversely, community programs in middle class, relatively homogeneous neighborhoods, where a "core" of a community already exists tend to report higher levels of success (Skogan, 1990). If there is no pre-existing sense of community or a base of local resources to initially draw upon (such as influential community leaders, churches, neighborhood alliances, or other active community centers) then any community-building effort is starting out with two strikes already against it.

Part of the problem has to do with participation in community events. Some segments of the population are more likely to get involved in their community than are others. For example, Bursik and Grasmick (1993) noted that involvement in various crime prevention and community programs is dependent upon social class, marital status, residential stability, and age. The most typical participants are middle aged, higher educated, upper to middle class, residentially stable homeowners who are married with children. Therefore, in areas with high numbers of elderly residents and/or poor, single parents renting their homes, participation is expected to be low. As many of these same characteristics go hand in hand with socially disorganized neighborhoods, the lack of success in economically challenged, residentially unstable neighborhoods should not come as a surprise.

For example, in an analysis of participation at community policing meetings in Chicago, Skogan (2004) noted that certain segments of the community were much more likely to attend than others. While renters occupied about 60% of the beat dwellings, on average 75% of the meeting participants were homeowners. Latinos were seriously under-represented, but older residents and those with higher levels of education were regular attendees. Long-time residents were the norm; individuals who attended the meetings lived in their homes nine years longer than the typical area resident. Only about 25% of the attendees were male. Skogan also noted that individuals who attended the meetings were much more concerned about neighborhood problems than were their non-attending neighbors.

With respect to the relationship between levels of community participation and citizen race, there have been some interesting findings. Bursik and Grasmick cited the work of Skogan (1988) who found that African American residents were more likely to participate in community crime prevention programs than were whites. Skogan argued that this was due to the limited ability of minority residents to leave their communities. While white residents had a number of options (they could choose to participate in the program, not participate, or move from the deteriorating area), African Americans were more likely to be stuck in their neighborhoods. African Americans were then left with only two choices: ignore the problem, or get involved in a program to try to do something about it.

However, participation by African Americans and other minorities may be dependent upon which organizations are backing the program. In some minority communities, programs that have a number of trusted partners may have a higher probability for success than those developed solely by a local law enforcement agency. In areas with strained police-community relations, any attempt by the police to intervene in the local neighborhood may be viewed with suspicion and hostility, no matter how well intentioned the police may be. The police have not had a proud past with respect to their relations with minority citizens, and recent events involving Rodney King, Amadou Diallo, Abner Louima, the CRASH unit of the Los Angeles Police Department, and the shooting of Oscar Grant by Bay Area Rapid Transit police officer Johannes Mehserle have not helped to improve the image of the police in minority communities (see, generally Feagin & Feagin, 1993; Kappeler, Sluder, & Alpert, 1994). Skogan (2004) has argued that the major reason that many cities adopt community policing strategies is to remedy their community-relations crisis and try to establish some level of peace and harmony among alienated residents.

While a detailed discussion of police-community relations in minority communities is beyond the scope of this text, the image of "Officer Friendly" is a tough sell in African American and other minority communities that have been plagued by decades of discriminatory, sometimes brutal actions of locally assigned officers. If you add an aura of resentment, suspicion, and mistrust of the police to other challenging neighborhood demographics, such as high levels of crime, high residential turnover, and high levels of poverty, you may very well end up with community policing efforts that are doomed for failure.

Do Community Building Efforts Ignore the "Real" Problems?

A second problem facing community-building programs is related to the first: Do these programs address the real problems facing local residents? Is the lack of success of many of these programs due to the fact that the efforts only treat the symptoms of the true underlying problems, while the real issues are overlooked or ignored? This is a question that has haunted many community programs, including the granddaddy of them all, the Chicago Area Project.

As noted earlier in this Chapter, the overall impact of the Chicago Area Project in the reduction of crime and delinquency in socially disorganized areas was negligible at best. The initial programs developed by Shaw focused on social and recreational activities. While these programs did provide legitimate recreational opportunities for juveniles in the troubled areas, it has been argued that the programs did nothing to address the real problems facing residents of the inner zones. Jon Snodgrass (1976) has stated that wealthy outsiders who were using the inner city neighborhoods for their own greedy self-interests caused the social problems that existed in the inner zones. Landowners allowed their properties to deteriorate, while business owners and speculating capitalists bought up the cheaper properties and expanded their commercial enterprises into residential areas with no regard for the communities that they were destroying in the process. The poor inner city residents did not have the organizational power, political influence, or monetary resources to combat the invasion of their neighborhoods.

If Shaw and the Chicago Area Project organizers wished to address the real problems that existed in the area, then something needed to be done about the wealthy industrialists who had caused the problems in the first place. Unfortunately, Shaw was caught in a difficult predicament. The CAP was dependent upon the local businesses and wealthy speculators for donations and other acts of philanthropy. If Shaw had adopted more of a confrontational stance with the local business and landowners, then he would have jeopardized the funding and survival of the CAP.

So what were the true causes of crime, disorder, and other social problems? What caused crime and disorder to flourish in some neighborhoods but not others? Sampson and Raudenbush (1999; 2001) linked both crime and disorder to a number of structural characteristics that were specific to certain areas. The single most important factor related to the prevalence of both crime and disorder was poverty. Mixed land use, where commercial and residential areas were combined, was also found to be a strong predictor of crime and disorder. Residential instability was also noted as an important factor. If community programs do not address these real issues, then the long-term success of the program may be in jeopardy.

Sampson and his colleagues (see, for example Byrne & Sampson, 1986; Sampson, 1995; Sampson & Groves, 1989; Sampson & Raudenbush, 1999; Sampson, et al., 1997) have been quick to point out that all is not lost in the most challenged areas. Collective efficacy has been described as a key element in the reduction of both crime and disorder. Earlier, collective efficacy was defined as cohesion, trust, and informal control mechanisms that may exist in some communities. To reduce crime and disorder in even the most impoverished communities, Sampson and his colleagues have advocated a number of policies designed to empower residents to take control of their neighborhoods. Included among their recommendations are (1) enacting policies that allow low-income residents to buy their homes or take over the management of their apartment buildings to reduce residential turnover; (2) the use of housing vouchers and other programs designed to scatter public housing residents throughout cities as opposed to concentrating the poor in centralized locations; and (3) increasing the level of services available to urban residents (Vold et al., 2002). The goal of the programs should be to increase collective efficacy, which will ultimately improve the quality of life in many urban areas.

Sampson and his colleagues have maintained that although these types of community building programs may have achieved limited success in some neighborhoods, community programs should not be completely abandoned. Even small improvements in the quality of community life may go a long way towards long-term change in urban areas.

Summary

Many practical policy recommendations have been derived from theories that focus on the role of the community in reducing crime, disorder, and other social problems. Regardless of the specifics of the program, the goal is the same: increase the level of informal social control. By enabling local residents to control the destiny of their own neighborhoods, the overall quality of life for local residents should improve. Locals will feel safe outside of their homes, neighbors will recognize outsiders, and children will be monitored and socialized by intimate handlers and other guardians who do not feel intimidated intervening when misdeeds occur. While there have been some problems with the success of these programs in the most challenging neighborhoods, programs designed to rebuild communities do show some promise in the improvement of the overall quality of life for many residents.

Chapter 5

Theory into Practice II: Altering the Physical Environment

Previously, a number of practical policies derived from Shaw and McKay's concept of social disorganization and Sampson's ideas about collective efficacy were examined. These theoretical models argue that in order to reduce crime and fear of crime, the sense of community and level of informal social control must be enhanced. Neighborhoods with high levels of informal social control will have lower crime rates, fewer signs of physical and social disorder, and more adults willing to step in when something is wrong.

In this Chapter, a second set of policy recommendations, primarily derived from the choice-based theories presented in Chapter 3, is discussed. Regardless of the specifics, all of the policies examined are based on the same basic assumption: a rational offender searches out a suitable target that will net the greatest reward with minimal risk of detection and apprehension. The ultimate goal of this set of policy recommendations is to somehow alter the situation to make a target less attractive for attack by a motivated, rational criminal. Some of these recommendations are rather minor, such as adding more streetlights or keeping hedges trimmed so that homeowners can see clearly out of their windows and onto the streets. Other policy suggestions are on a larger scale and involve planning models for buildings, communities, and entire cities under the driving principle of improving guardianship and reducing opportunities for criminal activities.

These choice-based policies tend to fall into three related groups: defensible space, crime prevention through environmental design, and situational crime prevention. Here they are examined in detail, beginning with a look at a few of the "classic" writings in the study of physical environment and crime.

The Beginnings:
The Works of Jane Jacobs and Oscar Newman

In 1961, Jane Jacobs's classic book *The Death and Life of Great American Cities* was published. Jacobs's work was written as a strong critique of the manner in which cities were being planned and rebuilt. In her words, "To build city districts that are custom made for easy crime is idiotic. Yet that is what we do" (1961, p. 31).

Jacobs derived her arguments from observations of a number of major cities, including the Greenwich Village area of New York City where she lived. The underlying assumption upon which she built her work sounded very similar to the arguments made by Shaw and McKay in their observations of the Chicago area: Certain areas were not more susceptible to high rates of crime because a "criminal class" of people resided there. In fact, Jacobs found strong communities with high levels of informal social control in areas where the predominant residents were poor and/or were members of racial or ethnic minorities living in lower-income housing. As she observed, "Some of the safest sidewalks in New York City, for example, at any time of the day or night, are those along which poor people or minority groups live. And some of the most dangerous are in the streets occupied by the same kinds of people" (1961, p. 31). The problem was not with who lived there, but the characteristics of the places themselves. According to Jacobs, some areas were more crime-ridden than others because of their poor design and planning (Crowe & Zahm, 1994; DeLeon-Granados, 1999; Jacobs, 1961).

Based on her observations, Jacobs offered a number of practical suggestions to urban planners that could reduce the level of crime and disorder and improve the overall quality of life for urban residents. For example, Jacobs discussed the importance of a well-designed sidewalk system in urban areas. To be a "successful" sidewalk, first the pathway should provide a clear boundary between what is public space where one would expect to see strangers and what is private space where strangers should be noticed and monitored. Second, buildings along the sidewalk should be oriented in such a manner as to encourage the "natural proprietors" of the area to keep their "eyes upon the street." Third, the sidewalk should have a good level of continuous use. More people using the sidewalk at various hours of the day and night lead to greater surveillance of the area. Further, the greater level of activity on the sidewalks encourages people to look out of their window and observe the passers-by. As an added benefit, a well-used sidewalk can enhance what Jacobs called the "normal, casual manpower for child rearing." Any adult—strangers, residents, the owner

of the corner store and other natural proprietors—who happens to be walking by can easily monitor and correct inappropriate behavior of children playing on the safe, exciting city street.

Jacobs felt that the physical design of an urban area would have an impact
on the behavior of local residents—whether they interacted with each other,
whether they were able to recognize who belonged and who did not, and
whether they intervened to maintain the peace and serenity of their neighborhood. Furthermore, the cohesive behavior of the local residents would in
turn have an impact on the behavior of potential offenders. If a rational offender
perceived a strong sense of community, apprehension and detection would be
more likely since local residents would be more likely to notice their presence
and step in if they attempted to commit a crime (Taylor & Gottfredson, 1986).

While Jacobs's work was influential, a book released a few years later by
Oscar Newman had worldwide impact. Newman built on the notion that given
the proper environmental design, residents would alter their behavior to defend their homes and neighborhoods from the intrusion of criminals (Murray,
1995; Newman, 1972). While Jacobs focused on broader city planning and
urban design issues, Newman was an architect and tended to be more nar-
rowly focused on the design of buildings.

Oscar Newman's Defensible Space

Newman's book was released in 1972 during an era of rapidly increasing
levels of crime. The crime wave was a very serious concern for police practitioners, academics, and the general public. Additionally, after the turbulent
decade of the 1960s, there were questions raised about the effectiveness of the
police to control crime and criminals, especially in our nation's inner cities.
Newman stressed the important role of informal community control in the
task of crime reduction. In Newman's (1972) words:

> Within the present atmosphere of pervasive crime and ineffectual authority,
> the only effective measure for assuring a safe living environment is com-
> munity control. We are advocating a program for the restructuring of
> residential developments in our cities to facilitate their control by the
> people who inhabit them. We see this as the only long-term measure of
> consequence in the battle for the maintenance of a sane urban society.
> Short-term measures involving flights to suburbia or additional police
> manpower and equipment are only palliatives (p. 204).

Newman's theory was based on the idea that many buildings (especially high
rise public housing buildings) had been poorly designed. Many of these build-

ings were enormous and impersonal, making it difficult for residents to recognize who belonged and who did not. In addition to their sheer size, the buildings had too many unsupervised entry doors that made it very easy for a motivated offender to access the living space of the residents and escape unrecognized (Clarke, 1995). Newman felt that the design of the physical environment needed to be changed in order to engender feelings of ownership and encourage the level of guardianship by the legitimate users. In order to encourage the local residents to take ownership of their neighborhood and defend it, his **defensible space** theory had four elements: territoriality, natural surveillance, image, and milieu.

Newman (1972) defined the concept of **territoriality** as "The capacity of the physical environment to create perceived zones of territorial influence" (p. 50). His idea was based on the fact that human beings are territorial animals who will defend an area they define as their own. Places need to be designed to enhance the perception of territoriality and ownership not only for the homeowner or apartment dweller, but also for the motivated offender. If a rational offender feels a strong sense of proprietary ownership, then they may select a less guarded target.

Newman provided a number of practical design suggestions that he felt would increase this sense of territoriality. A properly designed environment needed to provide visual cues or boundaries that would indicate where a personal territory began and ended. These boundaries between public and private space could be real or symbolic. "Real" barriers included such things as high walls and fences or locked gates and doors. "Symbolic" barriers would include such things as an open gateway, changes in the lighting or in the texture of the walkway, a short distance of steps, or the use of shrubs or other plants. According to Newman (1972), both real and symbolic barriers served the same purpose: "To inform that one is passing from a space which is public where one's presence is not questioned through a barrier to a space which is private and where one's presence requires justification" (p. 63).

Newman felt that **natural surveillance** was essential. A building or housing project with good surveillance opportunities will reduce feelings of fear and uneasiness for the residents. The entire building will project a sense of safety to both residents and potential offenders. Because their movements may be easily seen and detected by the local residents, motivated offenders may seek out a less guarded target.

In order to enhance natural surveillance, Newman argued that buildings should be oriented in such a manner that the residents could easily see the outside street. Lobby areas should be designed so that activities occurring inside the building may easily be seen from the street. As an example, Newman described a poorly designed lobby area at the entrance of a Bronx, New York housing project. In order to get to the elevators, residents had to make two turns. This design forced the residents to enter the building with no idea what (or who) was waiting at the end of the second turn. Additionally, once a resident made it to the elevators, if a problem did occur, their location was out of sight and sound of people passing by on the street as well as the residents who were inside of their apartments. Newman argued that fire escapes, windows, floor plans, and roof landings could all be altered to enhance the ability of residents to monitor the activities of both friends and strangers and thereby reduce the opportunities for crimes to occur.

Image refers to the "message" that the building sends out about itself. Newman felt that in the United States, high-rise, publicly supported housing projects had been designed to be very visually distinctive from the urban landscape. Newman argued that if you stood on the street looking at two housing buildings, one a low income housing building and the other an upper middle income housing building, you could easily distinguish which was the low income housing project because of the use of cheaper finishes on the facades, the lack of outdoor balconies, and other cues sending out a stigmatizing message about the project and its residents. Newman felt that the design of lower income housing projects emitted a negative image that made the residents easy targets for crime. To reduce crime, lower income housing projects should be designed in such a manner that they better fit in with the surrounding buildings.

Milieu refers to the placement of housing projects in areas that are considered to be safe places. In the spirit of Jacobs, Newman felt that housing projects built in commercial and industrial areas with large numbers of people coming and going were generally viewed as being safe due to the large number of "eyes on the streets." However, Newman added that one must be careful to evaluate the nature of the commercial activity, the hours of operation, the intended users of the businesses, and whether or not the users of the business identified with the local residents. Not all commercial enterprises would automatically enhance the safety of local residents. While pool halls, schools, or hangouts for bored teens may increase foot traffic in an area, these commercial establishments may also increase the level of criminal activity in the neighboring homes.

Will Defensible Space Be Defended?

Within just a few years, Newman's defensible space theory enjoyed worldwide excitement, especially in Great Britain (Poyner, 1983). In the United States, interest was fueled by a multi-million dollar project funded through the Law Enforcement Assistance Administration to implement design modifications suggested by defensible space theory (Murray, 1995). The Department of Housing and Urban Development (HUD) similarly provided funding to renovate public housing projects (Merry, 1981). All around the globe, urban planners, architects, and law enforcement agencies turned to defensible space as the answer to the growing crime problem. While the implementation of Newman's concepts of territoriality, natural surveillance, image and milieu may seem like common-sense approaches to fight the war on crime, the question remains: Does it work? The answer depends on whom you ask.

While some studies that have tested the effectiveness of defensible space applications have enjoyed positive results with respect to the reduction of fear of crime and actual crime levels, other studies have reported either short-term reductions or a negligible impact at best. For example, Newman and Franck (1980) reported that residents who lived in buildings with defensible space features such as limited access, better surveillance opportunities, and not as many floors were more likely to report lower levels of victimization and reduced levels of fear. Other studies have found some evidence to support greater social interaction among the residents, but little or no consistent reduction in the level of crime (Fowler & Mangione, 1982).

When practical aspects of defensible space theory were implemented, in many cases the more important element of Newman's theory was lost in the translation. It is relatively easy to add shrubs to demarcate private space, add lighting to enhance natural surveillance, or repaint a building to reduce its stigmatizing appearance. However, if these simple physical alterations are the only steps taken, then the effectiveness of defensible space theory may be questionable at best. What is lost is an understanding of the underlying social processes at work in buildings or communities where defensible space theory is applied (Merry, 1981). The pre-existing social fiber (or lack thereof) can ultimately "make or break" any changes in the physical environment.

Recall that Newman's central thesis was that the physical design of buildings has an effect on the behavior of its residents. If a building was properly designed with defensible space in mind, the physical environment would enhance social cohesion and increase the level of informal social control. This heightened level of informal social control would then reduce crime (Murray, 1995; Newman, 1972). Unfortunately, when defensible space concepts have been implemented, this very important intermediate step between changes in the physical environment and its effect on crime rates has been skipped.

In what has become somewhat of a "classic" critique, Sally Merry tested the effectiveness of defensible space theory in a small, inner city, low-income housing project she called Dover Square. In terms of physical design, Dover Square followed many of the suggestions of defensible space. The buildings were small in size. The placement of the windows made it easy for the residents to survey their territory, and access to private space was limited with appropriate real and symbolic barriers. Despite the "good" design that was found in most of the areas of the housing project, crime was high and the residents were fearful. Defensible spaces were not being defended like they were supposed to be. Merry set out to find out why.

Merry found that modifications in the physical environment were not enough to reduce crime. The fragmented social organization of the residents of Dover Square seemed to override the strengths of defensible space theory. Even though turnover was relatively low in the project (which would seem to lead to strong social cohesion), the residents were sharply divided along racial and ethnic lines. This lack of community seemed to undermine the positive impact of the design of the project. In her words:

> Spaces may be defensible but not defended if the social apparatus for effective defense is lacking. Residents will not look out well-positioned windows if there is nothing to see. Even if buildings are low, entrances and public spaces clearly linked to particular apartments, residents will not respond to crimes if they feel that the space belongs to another ethnic group, if they believe that the police will come too late or they will incur retribution for calling them, or if they are unable to distinguish a potential criminal from the neighbor's dinner guest (Merry, 1981, p. 419).

As a result of Merry's critique, a second generation of defensible space theory began to evolve (Taylor, Gottfredson, & Brower, 1980; Taylor & Harrell, 1996). In this new and improved model, greater emphasis was placed on the pre-existing social and cultural setting in which the design modifications were made. Researchers needed to carefully consider how the physical alterations to the environment would encourage social interaction and greater use of communal space. These neighborly interactions would lead to heightened levels of resident-based informal social control. It is important to bear in mind that if all sense of community has collapsed, changes in the physical environment may have little or no impact on the level of crime or resident fear (Merry, 1981; Murray, 1995).

Despite the limited success of defensible space modifications in some settings, Newman's ideas continue to have great impact. While Newman's primary focus was on the design of buildings, others have applied his ideas to a variety of settings including schools, commercial strip centers, and entire residential communities (Clarke, 1992; Poyner, 1983).

Crime Prevention through Environmental Design

Newman's basic ideas were used in the development of **crime prevention through environmental design** (CPTED), a popular prevention technique that is praised by many law enforcement agencies and city planners. The first use of this phrase is usually credited to C. Ray Jeffrey who used it as the title for a book (1971). In this work, Jeffrey argued that the current crime control policies being used were ineffective. According to Jeffrey, the predominant method of crime control involved what he called "indirect measures" that were used after a crime had occurred. These indirect measures included: various forms of rehabilitation and vocational training, arrest, court proceedings, prison sentences, probation, and parole. Instead of the current practice of addressing criminal acts "after the fact," Jeffrey felt that the best way to reduce crime was to initiate direct controls over environmental conditions prior to the commission of an offense. According to Jeffrey, "Placing a man on probation or giving him remedial education will not prevent him from breaking the window and stealing jewelry; placing a steel bar over a window will prevent the theft of jewelry from that window" (1971, p. 20). Jeffrey argued that through the use of environmental engineering, the number of crimes could be reduced.

Jeffrey's concept of CPTED was usually viewed as incorporating a more diverse set of techniques than were advocated by Newman's defensible space theory. This was especially true with respect to places where territoriality may seem less natural than the protection of one's personal residence, such as the workplace or school (Clarke, 1992). The strategies used by CPTED closely dovetail with the ideas developed by Newman.

The Strategies of CPTED

According to Crowe (2000), there are three interrelated strategies associated with CPTED: access control, surveillance, and territorial reinforcement. **Access control** refers to limiting the opportunities for a motivated offender to come into contact with a potential target. If a potential target is perceived as being hard to get to, then an offender may feel that any attempts to gain access to the target would involve greater risk of detection and apprehension. Since the offender is assumed to be rational, the offender may move on to a different target that is viewed as an easier hit. Access control strategies are sometimes referred to as **target hardening** (Lab, 2000).

Access control strategies usually fall into one of three categories: organized, mechanical, and natural. An example of organized access control includes guards posted at the entrances to gated communities. Mechanical access control is best defined by the use of devices designed to limit entry to only legitimate users, such as locks, key-pad entry systems, or swiping identification cards prior to access. Natural access control refers to what Crowe calls "spatial definition." This is a rather broad category that would include the relationships between space type—such as whether a space is public, semi-public, or private; commercial or residential—and traffic or pedestrian flow patterns in and around the space. In a well-designed space with good natural access control, it should be unnatural for people to easily wander into areas where they do not belong. Limiting the number of entrances or exits may enhance natural access in buildings. In communities, natural access may involve using fewer through streets as access routes and, instead, relying on more cul-de-sacs and dead end streets to limit traffic flow.

Closely related to access control is **surveillance**. Space should be designed in such a manner that potential offenders may be easily observed. It is assumed that a rational offender would not select targets that are easily monitored by residents, business owners, or other legitimate users of the space. Surveillance is also broken down into the same three categories: organized (including such things as routine patrols by police or private security officers), mechanical (strategic placement of street lights or surveillance cameras), and natural (windows and lobbies that enhance the monitoring of the outside streets; carefully placed park benches; landscaping that is designed with surveillance in mind, such as low hedges or well trimmed trees).

Territorial reinforcement has to do with how the physical environment impacts feelings of ownership of a space. A well-designed space enhances feelings of proprietary ownership by the legitimate users while at the same time sending out a message to potential offenders that the space they are entering is off limits to outsiders. According to Crowe, territorial reinforcement is closely linked to natural access control and natural surveillance. Traditionally, CPTED projects primarily used mechanical and organized strategies to reduce opportunities for crime. It is relatively easy (though expensive) to add more locks, alarm systems, lights, or a security guard or two. However, primary reliance upon mechanical and organized strategies does not encourage territorial reinforcement. In order to build feelings of ownership, the natural elements of the environment must be considered. When natural access control and natural surveillance are taken into account, legitimate users will be more likely to get involved in the protection of their turf. Strangers will be monitored and suspicious behaviors will be reported to the police. The effectiveness of even the best security systems will not operate to its greatest potential if the primary users do not share a real sense of ownership and truly care about their residence, workplace, or community.

CPTED in Practice

CPTED strategies have been applied in a variety of settings, including schools, parking garages, parks and recreation areas, and entire residential and commercial developments as well as individual homes and businesses. The physical changes implemented as part of an overall crime prevention strategy are limited only by the imagination of the police agency, planning office, business owner, or resident. Some changes may be relatively minor, such as moving the desk of a receptionist to a more centralized location where he or she may better monitor the lobby area, or planting prickly bushes to cut off pathways for escape used by burglars. Other modifications may be more extensive in nature and involve planning and design considerations for entire cities (see, for example, Wekerle & Whitzman, 1995). In some areas, such as Tempe, Arizona; Sarasota, Florida; or Alexandria, Virginia, police officers carefully trained in CPTED techniques regularly review blueprints of all newly proposed structures and building renovation plans to ensure that crime prevention strategies have not been overlooked. In the case of Tempe, Arizona, planners are required by city ordinance to have blueprints approved by the police prior to the issuance of a building permit (Bureau of Justice Assistance, 1997; Davis, 1998; Plaster & Carter, 1993). As the popularity of CPTED grows, more and more police agencies are becoming involved in urban planning issues (Deleon-Gradanos, 1999).

Many CPTED projects have been initiated in conjunction with community policing efforts. According to the National Institute of Justice (2000), CPTED projects and community policing complement each other. Both community policing and CPTED begin with a careful analysis of problems that occur in a specific geographic location. Based on the specifics of that particular location, various crime prevention strategies may be adopted. Because each CPTED solution is tailor-made to fit a specific location, no two CPTED projects are exactly the same (Crowe, 2000; National Institute of Justice, 2000). Regardless of the CPTED project, however, success hinges in large part on **stakeholder** involvement. According to Zahm (2007), stakeholders can be individuals, departments, organizations, or agencies that could be impacted by the problem that the CPTED project is designed to resolve:

- **Neighborhood**
  - homeowners
  - non-resident property owners tenants
- **Community association representatives**
  - from the study neighborhood
  - from adjacent neighborhoods
  - from adjacent localities
- **Business community**
  - business owners and managers
  - employees
  - business association representatives
- **Institutions**
  - schools (public and private)
  - places of worship
  - clubs
  - cultural facilities (theatre, art gallery, museum)
- **Nonprofit organizations**
  - community development corporations
  - social services providers
- **Government**
  - elected officials
  - administration and management
  - police
  - community/neighborhood planning and, depending on the issue, traffic and transportation, transit, parks and recreation, housing and redevelopment, economic development, etc.

The following section highlights some successful CPTED projects that were conducted in collaboration with community policing efforts.

SPOTLIGHT ON PRACTICE I

Rebuilding Genesis Park, Charlotte, North Carolina

Encompassing a relatively small area of only eight square blocks, an inner-city neighborhood known as Genesis Park had become one of the worst areas in the city of Charlotte, North Carolina some time ago. Violent crime and open-air drug markets, especially heroin sales, were common occurrences in this area. Yards were overgrown and the homes that had not been vacated were in need of repairs.

In order to improve the quality of life for the urban residents, the Charlotte-Mecklenburg Housing Partnership (CMP) and the Charlotte Police Department initiated a number of environmental changes. First, the poor neighborhood conditions were addressed. Vacant homes being used as centers for drug sales were closed down. Dilapidated, rental duplexes were converted into single-family residences, and low-income families were provided special financing opportunities to purchase these newly renovated properties.

Second, in order to gain better control of the area, traffic barriers were put in place to restrict free vehicle movement. As a result, a more complex street pattern was created. No longer could potential drug customers easily come and go in the targeted area. To add even more confusion to outsiders entering the area, street names were officially changed. After one year of implementing these and other changes (including a greater emphasis on community policing), crime rates dropped dramatically in the Genesis Park area (Feins, Epstein, & Widom, 1997).

Fresno, California's Child Custody Program

The city of Fresno, California Police Department was experiencing a number of problems related to the transfer of custody of minor children, from one parent to another, for their scheduled visitation outings. In a single 12-month period, the department responded to over 2,000 calls for service related to child custody violations and requests for assistance with child custody transfers. To make the matter even more frustrating for the officers, very few cases were ultimately prosecuted by the State Attorney's Office.

As part of their response to this problem, a centralized facility for child custody transfers was designed using CPTED principles. The Child Custody Program (CCP), which is housed in this carefully designed facility, fosters a safe environment for peaceful custody exchanges. In order to reduce the opportunities for unpleasant and potentially violent confrontations between parents or other child guardians, each parent is assigned a separate building entrance for the transfer. At no time do the parents come into contact with each other. Additionally, private security guards are on hand to assist in surveillance of the facility. By implementing simple and common sense CPTED design techniques, the CCP boasts that the police have never been summoned to the facility to resolve a child custody transfer issue (National Institute of Justice, 2000).

Taking Back an Intersection

A single intersection in Vancouver, Canada's Grandview Woodland community was identified as being especially problematic for the Vancouver Police

Department. The agency's 911 system was bombarded with complaints related to "quality of life issues," such as aggressive panhandling, public intoxication, graffiti, litter, and frequent attacks by "squeegee people"—individuals who wash car windows at traffic lights, often uninvited, for a fee.

As part of a larger community policing project, criminology students from Simon Fraser University, under the direction of Patricia Brantingham, attempted to identify and implement CPTED strategies that could ultimately improve the poor conditions that existed at the intersection. First, the students observed that a bench located on the northeast corner of the intersection was a common location for disputes between intoxicated people. Behind the bench were a number of newspaper vending boxes that provided a convenient hiding spot for liquor bottles and squeegees. The bench and the newspaper boxes were located adjacent to an automatic teller machine (ATM), and fearful legitimate users frequently called out the police to the location. Once the bench was removed and the newspaper boxes relocated nearer to the curb, 911 calls for service dropped dramatically.

Local businesses got involved as well. A branch of the Royal Bank was located on the southwest corner of the intersection. Alcoves, built into the structure of the buildings, had become a popular place for panhandlers to rest and squeegee people to hide the tools of their trade. The Bank made a number of design modifications to the alcoves to make them less attractive to unwanted users. A slanted structure was installed in the alcoves that made it impossible for the panhandlers to sit down. A glass window was installed near the entrance of the bank, which effectively eliminated a convenient hiding place for squeegee storage. Landscaping was also modified to enhance surveillance and reduce cover. Additionally, the Vancity Credit Union, which was located on the northwest corner of the intersection, took steps to eliminate a hiding space for squeegee people awaiting the next red light. By adding a gate to an alcove that housed an ATM, access to this hiding area and makeshift shelter was reduced. These relatively easy design modifications resulted in fewer calls for service to the area and greater feelings of safety by the legitimate users of the area (National Institute of Justice, 2000).

The Bottom Line: Does CPTED Work?

As is the case with many "bottom line" questions, the answer depends on whom you ask. If you posed this question to Timothy Crowe, former director of the National Crime Prevention Institute and author of many articles and several books on the topic, you would get a resounding "yes." Crowe, who provides training workshops to law enforcement agencies and serves as a consultant for CPTED techniques, has noted rather dramatic success stories in a variety of settings, including the following (Crowe, 2000 p. 9–10):

- Convenience stores have used CPTED to increase sales and reduce losses from theft of up to 50% and from robberies of 65%.
- Malls in Sacramento and Knoxville have reduced incidents by 24% and noncrime calls to police by another 14% using CPTED parking management concepts; the largest mall in the world located in West Edmonton, Alberta, Canada, has used CPTED concepts with well documented success.
- Neighborhoods in Ft. Lauderdale, Tallahassee, Bridgeport, Knoxville, Jacksonville, Dayton, North Miami Beach, Calgary, Toronto, and many others have produced dramatic reduction in drug sales, burglaries and general crime by 15–100%.
- Schools using CPTED throughout the world are reducing construction costs, lowering conduct and crime violations, and improving achievement and matriculation levels.
- Design research on office environments has determined that the lack of territorial identity in the office space contributes to lower morale, less productivity, and greater tolerance of dishonesty among fellow workers.

Other researchers have been less enthusiastic about the impact of CPTED techniques (Clarke, 1992; Lab, 2000; Taylor & Harrell, 1996). For every study that has reported reduced levels of crime and lower levels of fear after CPTED techniques were introduced, one may uncover another study reporting little or no impact. Without getting too in-depth on the subtle nuances of policy evaluation techniques, the problem has to do with how CPTED techniques are implemented and their effectiveness measured.

For example, Kim's father owned a pizza shop for many years. After being robbed several times, he installed a number of CPTED design modifications, which included: adding more lighting both inside and out, raising the front counter height by several feet (to prevent potential robbers from jumping over the counter), removing posters and decals from the front windows to enhance surveillance of the parking area, and adding various access control devices, such as automatic locking doors and a buzzer system for limiting entrance into the business. After implementing these various CPTED techniques, he did not have another robbery occur at the business. So, what worked? Was it the lighting, the counter height, the locks, the improved surveillance ability, or some combination? Or was something else responsible for the reduction in robberies? It is impossible to tell for sure.

Oftentimes, when CPTED techniques are employed, it is not just a single modification that is made. This makes it difficult to isolate the impact of each modification alone. When multiple techniques are used, it is impossible to zero in on which technique had an impact. Also, one cannot be sure whether it was the CPTED techniques that were responsible for the reduction in robberies or other factors at work. It is always possible that the police had increased patrols in the area or the local economy had improved and more jobs were available.

Additionally, it should also be noted that CPTED techniques are more than just adding a lock and measuring whether or not this physical change had an impact on the number of burglaries. The effectiveness of the design change rests on territorial reinforcement—have the modifications caused the proprietary owners to take control of the area? As noted by Lab (2000), if the changes to the physical environment do not bring out the desired changes in the behaviors of the residents, storeowners, and other legitimate users of the space, then the design change may appear to be a failure.

Situational Crime Prevention

The third and final group of techniques designed to reduce criminal opportunities is referred to as **situational crime prevention**. These strategies may involve various techniques to reduce the opportunity for crimes to occur, including physical changes to the environment and/or target hardening techniques. Situational crime prevention may also involve the use of broader strategies than those used in defensible space or CPTED. For example, consider the crime of motorcycle theft. By enacting laws requiring the use of helmets, motorcycle thefts may be reduced since it would be difficult for a potential thief to drive off unnoticed (Mayhew, Clarke, & Elliot, 1989). When was the last time you received an obscene phone call from a stranger? The availability and use of caller identification service has significantly reduced the number of such phone calls (Clarke, 1992; 1997). While the techniques that fall under the situational crime prevention umbrella may be a bit broader than what has been examined so far in the discussions of defensible space and CPTED, the criminal opportunities that these crime prevention strategies are designed to reduce are bit more narrow— as the name implies, situational crime prevention techniques are designed to reduce very specific criminal opportunities that arise in a particular situation.

What is situational crime prevention? According to Ronald Clarke (1983), a criminologist who has written extensively on this topic, situational crime prevention is defined in the following manner:

Situational crime prevention can be characterized as comprising measures (1) directed at highly specific forms of crime (2) that involve the management, design, or manipulation of the immediate environment in as systematic and permanent a way as possible (3) so as to reduce the opportunities for crime and increase the risks as perceived by a wide range of offenders (p. 225).

In a nutshell, situational crime prevention techniques are designed to reduce the opportunity for criminal acts by either (a) increasing the amount of effort a motivated offender must exert (b) increasing the level of risk of apprehension and detection or (c) reducing the potential reward. As noted by Murray (1995), situational crime prevention is not as concerned with the relationship between design changes and the impact on community life, such as increased social interaction, greater feelings of territoriality, and enhanced levels of informal social control. While these factors are important to the success of defensible space and CPTED strategies, they play a less important role in situational crime prevention. In this realm, the real cause of crime is opportunity—if you want to reduce crime, reduce the opportunities for crimes to occur.

Opportunity as a Cause of Crime

How does one go about reducing opportunities for crime? First, it might help to understand how crime and opportunity are linked. Felson and Clarke (1998) have outlined the following principles of opportunity and crime:

Opportunities play a role in causing all crime. While it has been argued that situational crime prevention places too much emphasis on property crimes that occur in public places (Crawford, 1998), Felson and Clarke maintain that opportunity causes all crimes—violent crimes, property crimes, white-collar crimes, and "victimless" crimes, like drug sales and prostitution. Even the occurrence of suicide has been linked to opportunity (Clarke & Mayhew, 1988).

Crime opportunities are highly specific. Consider for the moment the crime of burglary. Instead of all burglaries being lumped together, opportunities must be evaluated for very specific types of burglaries. The motives, risks, rewards, and techniques for residential burglary must be analyzed separately from commercial burglary. Even if only residential burglaries are considered, subcategories must also be considered with respect to the target type (such as single-family homes, apartment dwellings, duplexes, etc.) point of entry (windows versus doors, front or rear) or even time of day (daytime versus nighttime).

Since each offense is different, opportunity reduction strategies must be tailored to fit each specific offense.

Crime opportunities are concentrated in time and space. Crime is not randomly distributed in time and location. Certain locations and times are more dangerous than others. In the next chapter, "hot spots" and "burning times" are explored in greater depth. For now, suffice it to say that certain locations and certain times provide more opportunities for crimes to occur than other times and locations.

Crime opportunities depend on everyday movements of activity. Chapter 3 includes a discussion of routine activities theory, which argues that motivated offenders, suitable targets, and the lack of capable guardians converge in time and place as we conduct the business of our everyday lives. As we go to work, attend class, or partake in late night activities in our various activity nodes, our presence in these areas and our movements between them may provide opportunities for motivated offenders to come into contact with us.

One crime produces opportunities for another. A criminal may set out to commit one crime, but may end up committing many other offenses because of the other opportunities that arise. Felson and Clarke provide the example of a burglary. Once a burglar has entered a home, additional opportunities to commit crimes may develop. If the offender stumbles across a gun and chooses to take it, the offender has now committed armed residential burglary. If the homeowner suddenly returns to the residence, the burglar is now presented with the opportunity to commit a robbery, battery, or rape. The commission of the burglary may also lead to other opportunities, such as dealing in stolen goods.

Some products offer more tempting crime opportunities. Felson and Clarke argue that there are four characteristics that determine whether or not a target will be attacked: **Value, Inertia, Visibility,** and **Access** (**VIVA**). Some products are valued more than others, even though they may cost the same. For example, certain brands of tennis shoes, or compact disks by popular artists are more valued than other products of comparable price. Inertia refers to the weight of the item, which has to do with how easily the product can be transported. Visibility refers to the amount of exposure the target has to potential offenders. Access has to do with how easy the product is to get to. Items placed near open windows have easy access, while items carefully secured in a monitored showcase have less access. Therefore, certain products offer greater opportunities of theft than others, such as laptop computers or iPods.

Social and technological changes produce new crime opportunities. Felson and Clarke argue that mass-produced consumer goods pass through four stages: Innovation, Growth, Mass Market, and Saturation. New products are introduced during the innovation stage. For example, when home computers first came out, there was a very limited market. They were user hostile, expensive, and limited in their use. At the innovation stage, few home computers were stolen since not many people wanted them anyway. At the growth stage, thefts began to increase. During the growth stage, home computers became easier to use and less expensive. More and more people wanted home computers, which drove up demand. At the mass market stage, home computers became commonplace. Demand was high and many home computers were sold. The demand also fueled the theft of home computers, which was widespread. Finally, at the saturation stage, the price had dropped and most people who wanted to purchase the product have done so. Stealing a home computer now offers little potential reward, and thefts have declined. As technological innovations occur, the cycle starts again providing new opportunities for crimes to occur. Laptop computers, mp3 players, hand-held calculators, and airbags all follow the same cycle, providing different opportunities for theft at the various stages of market saturation.

Crime can be prevented by reducing opportunities. Felson and Clarke state that this assumption guides several crime prevention strategies, including defensible space, CPTED, problem-oriented policing, and situational crime prevention, which they argue is the best developed of the various strategies.

The Opportunity Reduction Techniques of Situational Crime Prevention: An Evolving Typology

Clarke and his colleagues (Clarke, 1983, 1992, 1995, 1997; Clarke & Homel, 1997; Clarke & Mayhew, 1980; Felson & Clarke, 1997; 1998; Newman, Clarke, & Shoham, 1997) continue to develop and expand on the notion of situational crime prevention. In his earlier writings, Clarke attempted to develop a classification scheme or typology that categorized twelve specific crime prevention strategies under three headings. These headings were based on rational choice theory: increasing the effort; increasing the risks; and reducing the rewards. The idea behind the development of such a classification scheme was to provide a framework for the ever-expanding number of situational crime prevention strategies. As argued by Lab (2000), without such an organizational framework, various techniques may be employed without any rationale or understanding of why the strategy should be effective.

In Clarke's original model, a great deal of emphasis was placed on modifications of the physical environment. However, as the popularity of situational crime prevention grew, researchers expanded the scope to include a greater emphasis on the social and psychological elements of committing crimes (Lab, 2000; Newman, et al., 1997). The second typology was modified from twelve techniques to sixteen. In the new classification scheme, the headings were changed to *perceived* effort, *perceived* risk, and *anticipated* rewards. While this modification may not seem major, it does reflect a greater emphasis on the psychological impact of environmental changes (Lab, 2000). In theory, seemingly minor alterations may result in great changes in the perception of effort, risk, and/or reward. Additionally, in the second version, a fourth category was added which was titled "Remove excuses for crime." The "new and improved" second typology, which includes examples of each technique, is presented in Box 5.1.

Box 5.1 Sixteen Opportunity Reducing Techniques of Situation Crime Prevention

Increase the perceived effort of crime

1. Harden targets:	Steering column locks, anti-robbery screens
2. Control access to targets:	Entry phones, electronic access to garages
3. Deflect offenders from targets:	Bus stop location, street closings, segregation of rival fans
4. Control crime facilitators:	Photos on credit cards, plastic beer glasses in pubs

Increase the perceived risks of crime

5. Screen entrances and exits:	Electronic merchandise tags, baggage screening
6. Formal surveillance:	Red light and speed cameras, security guards
7. Surveillance by employees:	Park attendants, CCTV on double deck buses
8. Natural surveillance:	Street lighting, defensible space architecture

Reduce the anticipated rewards of crime

9. Remove targets:	Phonecards, removable car radios, women's refuges
10. Identify property:	Vehicle licensing, property marking, car parts marking
11. Reduce temptation:	Rapid repair of vandalism, off street parking
12. Deny benefits:	Ink merchandise tags, PIN for car radios, graffiti cleaning

Remove excuses for crime	
13. Set rules:	Hotel registration, customs declaration, codes of conduct
14. Alert conscience:	Roadside speedometers, "idiots drink-and-drive" signs
15. Control disinhibitors:	Drinking age laws, car ignition breathalyzer, V-chip in TV
16. Assist compliance:	Litter bins, public lavatories, easy library check out

Source: Felson, M. & Clarke, R. (1998). Opportunity makes the thief: Practical theory for crime prevention. London, UK: Home Office.

As you can see, situational crime prevention includes many of the same strategies employed by defensible space and CPTED. We have already discussed many of these techniques including target hardening, various forms of surveillance, and access control.

The newer category, removing excuses for crime, includes strategies that make it more difficult for the offender to dismiss his or her involvement in criminal activity due to lack of knowledge of the violation, laziness, or other justifications. The setting of rules provides clear-cut definitions of what is and what is not acceptable behavior. People may be reminded of the rules (and possibly their violation of the rules) through the various "conscience alerts." Department stores often post signs reminding shoppers that read "Shoplifting is a crime." Some of these signs also include penalties for such violations of the law. These signs remind customers of the rules and hopefully make a rational person think twice before taking items from the store. In their writings, Clarke and Homel (1997) labeled the 'Removing excuses for crime' category as 'Inducing guilt or shame,' reflecting the social and psychology response that may arise when someone violates a rule or law. If expectations for behavior are clearly posted and conscience alerts provided, then people may be reminded of the guilt and shame they would feel if they did not comply with the posted rules.

Controlling disinhibitors refers to limiting access to alcohol, violent television, or other things that might free a person from their regular rational law-abiding state. By controlling disinihibitors, justifications for criminal activities may be removed (such as, "I was drunk and didn't know what I was doing"). Finally, strategies included in the category of assisting compliance make it easier to follow the law. For example, at a poorly planned outdoor event, with few trash cans and even fewer restroom facilities, a good deal of littering and public urination may occur (especially if there was heavy alcohol consumption at the event!).

The Third Evolution: Twenty-Five Techniques of Situational Prevention

In 2003, a third version of Clarke's original typology was introduced which was developed largely in response to a critique by Wortley, who brought in some concerns from the field of environmental psychology (Cornish & Clarke, 2003). Beginning in 1996, Wortley began a series of articles that examined the role of guilt, shame, and precipitating factors in crime causation (see, for example, Wortley 1996; 1997; 1998; 2001; 2002; 2008). Wortley felt that there was too much emphasis on the opportunity variables in Clarke's typology and not enough importance on precipitators that occur within the setting that may motivate potential offenders. Wortley argued that the term 'opportunity reduction' assumes that there is a motivated (or at least undecided) offender who is ready to take advantage of criminal opportunities when he/she comes across them. For Wortley, criminal motivation is not a given; motivation is situationally dependent. Wortley defined four precipitators that outline the ways in which situations might give rise to a criminal response even when there is no pre-existing motivation on the part of the offender: prompts, pressures, permissibility, and provocations.

First, **prompts** are environmental cues that trigger criminal behavior. Prompts may include such things as viewing erotic materials, coming across an unguarded, open door, or seeing others engage in criminal behavior (which may encourage an ambivalent person to do the same). **Pressures** are the situations that put social pressure on an individual to commit a crime. Pressures may include peer pressure from friends or acquaintances to engage in criminal or deviant acts, or following the directions of a boss or other authority figure who "orders" the individual to do something wrong. **Permissibility** situations are similar to the techniques of neutralization proposed by criminological theorists Sykes and Matza. Permissibility precipitators include the internal minimizing of a number of factors, such as the legitimacy of the moral principle, the degree of personal responsibility, the negative impact of the criminal act, or the worth or "clean hands" of the victim. Permissibility situations weaken the moral fiber of an individual, thereby freeing him or her to engage in the criminal act. Finally, **provocations** are situations that result in adverse emotional arousal, which can ultimately produce a criminal response. Frustration, crowding, lack of personal privacy, and environmental irritants, such as loud noise, may cause this. For Wortley, these precipitators create *motive* and open up a number of new considerations for situational crime prevention that previously were not considered. According to Wortley (1997), "Situations are conceived as not just engaging crime to occur, but as playing an active role in psychologically readying the individual to offend" (p. 74).

Cornish and Clarke (2003) responded to Wortley's critique and have now added a new category in their situational prevention typology: Reduce Provocations. The newest evolution in Clarke's typology is presented in Table 5.1. As you can see, Wortley's category of permissibility precipitators is addressed under the heading of "Remove excuses," where people are reminded of the rules and their conscience is alerted. Strategies related to Wordley's prompts, pressures, and provocations can be seen in the category "Reduce provocations," such as the need to reduce stress and emotional arousal.

There are a number of benefits in this newly evolved typology. First, because motivational factors are now considered, the strategies may be more useful in preventing crime across offenders with varying levels of motivation. A high level of motivation is no longer a given, and the precipitators that may increase an individual's motivation are now addressed. Second, the new typology encourages a broader understanding of why a certain technique does or does not work. For example, if a strategy is implemented without considering the motivational factors at work, the strategy could actually increase the level of crime if the strategy causes undue stress and aggravation on an individual in their efforts to comply (Cornish & Clarke, 2003; Lab, 2004).

Situational Crime Prevention in Practice

Situational crime prevention techniques have been applied in a seemingly endless variety of settings, including schools, jails, convenience stores, shopping malls, parking garages, public housing complexes, and even amusement parks (see Box 5.2 for an examination of Disney World's use of situational crime prevention techniques). Due to the successful implementation of various techniques in a number of different settings, situational crime prevention has been described as an area of promise in reducing crime (Barnes, 1995; Murray, 1995; Weisburd, 1997).

Table 5.1 Twenty-Five Techniques of Situational Prevention

Increase the Effort	Increase the Risks	Reduce the Reward	Reduce Provocations	Remove Excuses
1. Target hardening: • Steering column locks • Anti-robbery screens • Tamper-proof packaging	*6. Extended guardianship:* • Take routine precautions • Carry phone	*11. Conceal targets:* • Off-street parking • Gender-neutral phone directories	*16. Reduce frustration and stress:* • Efficient queues and polite service • Expanded seating • Smoothing music/lights	*21. Set rules:* • Rental agreements • Hotel registrations
2. Control access to facilities: • Entry phones • Baggage screening	*7. Assist natural surveillance:* • Improve lighting • Defensible space design	*12. Remove targets:* • Removable car radios • Women's refuges	*17. Avoid disputes:* • Separate enclosures for rival soccer fans • Reduce crowding in bars • Fixed cab fares	*22. Post instructions:* • "No Parking" • "Private Property"
3. Screen exits: • Tickets needed for exit • Electronic merchandise tags	*8. Reduce anonymity:* • Taxi cab IDs • School uniforms • "How's my driving?" stickers	*13. Identify property:* • Property marking • Cattle branding • Vehicle parts marking	*18. Reduce emotional arousal:* • Controls on violent pornography • Prohibit racial slurs	*23. Alert conscience:* • Roadside speed display boards • Signatures for customs declarations
4. Deflect offenders: • Street closures • Disperse pubs	*9. Utilize place managers:* • Two clerks at convenience stores • Reward vigilance	*14. Disrupt markets:* • Monitor pawn shops • Controls on classified ads • License street vendors	*19. Neutralize peer pressure:* • "It's OK to say, 'No.'" • "Idiots drive drunk."	*24. Assist compliance:* • Easy library checkout • Public lavatories • Trash cans
5. Control tools/ weapons: • Disabling stolen cell phones • Restrict spray paint sales to juveniles	*10. Strengthen formal surveillance:* • Burglar alarms • Security guards	*15. Deny benefits:* • Ink merchandise tags • Graffiti cleaning • Speed bumps	*20. Discourage imitation:* • Rapid repair of vandalism • Censor details of MO	*25. Control drugs and alcohol:* • Breathalyzers in bars • Alcohol-free events

Adapted from Cornish & Clarke (2003, p. 90).

Box 5.2   Situational Crime Prevention in Disney World

In what has become an oft-reprinted manuscript, Clifford D. Shearing and Phillip C. Stenning (1992) provide a guided tour of Disney World, which the authors describe as 'an exemplar of modern private corporate policing.' The strategies of crowd control, crime prevention, and discipline are built into the design of the park, with messages of safety and desired pathways of movement constantly being reinforced. The authors describe a typical visit:

> The fun begins the moment the visitor enters Disney World. As one arrives by car one is greeted by a series of smiling young people who, with the aid of clearly visible road markings, direct one to one's parking spot, remind one to lock one's car and to remember its location and then direct one to await the rubber-wheeled train that will convey visitors away from the parking lot. At the boarding location one is directed to stand safely behind guardrails and to board the train in an orderly fashion. While climbing on board one is reminded to remember the name of the parking area and the row number in which one is parked. Once on the train one is encouraged to protect oneself from injury by keeping one's body within the bounds of the carriage and to do the same for children in one's care ... (p. 250).

The authors point out that Disney World's success at handling huge crowds of people rests on its methods of anticipating problems and taking the necessary steps to prevent such incidents from occurring. Opportunities for rule violation and disruptive behavior are minimized by the constant messages from the staff directing the movement of the crowds. Physical barriers, such as fountains, flower gardens, and safety rails are used to limit the pathways that one would take. Surveillance is maximized by the roving Disney staff who, in addition to their various other duties, keep an ever-vigilant eye out for signs of disorder, stepping in immediately to politely (but firmly) request compliance. Those who choose to violate the rules are asked to leave the park.

—————

Source: Shearing, C.D. & Stenning, P.C. (1992). From the panopticon to Disney World: The development of discipline. In R. Clarke (Ed.) Situational crime prevention: Successful case studies (pp. 249–255). New York, NY: Harrow and Heston.

Successful applications of situational crime prevention techniques begin with a careful analysis of the specific crime problem. While issues related to crime analysis are discussed in later chapters, the specific context of the selected crime must be carefully examined. What is happening? Where is it happening? When? How? Why? What situation seems to be giving rise to the problem? Once full understanding of the situation surrounding the criminal event is reached, one can move on to consider various methods of limiting opportunities for the crime to occur. Once a technique has been implemented, the impact of the change(s) must be carefully monitored. If the technique has demonstrated success, the strategy may be tried in similar situations (Maxfield, 2001).

As an example, a municipal police officer was quite proud of a recent reduction in the number of automobile thefts that had occurred in the city in
recent months. About six months prior to this proclamation, the number of
auto thefts had been climbing quite dramatically and his agency was under
a good deal of pressure to get results. A number of officers had researched recent reports of auto thefts to see if there was any sort of pattern to the crimes.
What the officers found was quite interesting: In the majority of the car thefts,
the owner of the vehicle had left the keys in the ignition. Over the past ten
years or so the city had been experiencing dramatic growth and was changing from more of a rural town to a booming urban area. It is quite common
for people in small towns to leave their doors and windows unlocked and
their keys in their cars, a practice unheard of in larger metropolitan cities. After
their careful analysis of the situational conditions that contributed to the
stealing of cars, the agency implemented an educational campaign designed
to increase awareness. Billboards and public service messages broadcasted
on television and radio stations reminded drivers to remove their keys when
exiting their vehicles. Within a few months, the number of auto thefts had
declined.

This example illustrates one of the important considerations of situational
crime prevention: the technique used will vary with the particular circumstances of a specific type of crime. The educational campaign employed by
this agency might not work in other settings. Further, the billboards and other
reminders may no longer be as effective a few years (or even a few months)
later. While motivated offenders may no longer be able to easily open the door
and drive off using the keys, the car may still be stolen through the use of other
techniques that require a greater amount of effort, such as hotwiring. In situational crime prevention, each solution is tailor-made to fit the specific crime
problem, as it occurs in a single location, at a precise moment in time.

Box 5.3 Situational Crime Prevention on the Metro

The subway system running through the Washington, DC area is one of the safest systems in the country. Crime on the Metro is much lower than similar public mass
transit systems in Boston, Chicago, and Atlanta. The relative safety of the Metro is
attributed to the various situational crime prevention strategies that have been employed on the train. The opportunity reduction strategies include the following:

- Long, winding corridors and hidden corners were avoided in the design in
  order to reduce potential hiding places for offenders.
- Farecards may be purchased in any dollar amount at the vending machines,
  which reduces the amount of time that a passenger would have to fumble
  through his or her wallet searching out the correct currency to use.

- The exterior and interior surfaces are designed to be resistant to vandalism and graffiti.
- There are no restrooms or lockers available to the general public, which reduces places for offenders to loiter.
- There are no fast food restaurants, which serves to reduce the opportunity for litter as well as the potential for robbery or pick-pocketing of hungry, distracted customers.
- The area is under intense surveillance by staff, custodial workers, and closed-circuit televisions.

Adapted from La Vigne, N. (1997, November). Visibility and vigilance: Metro's situational approach to preventing subway crime. Washington, DC: NIJ.

Summary

Three related sets of policy recommendations that are derived from choice-based theories have been examined. Defensible space, CPTED, and situational crime prevention all rest on the assumption of a motivated rational offender. Proponents of these strategies argue that crime may be reduced through modifications that reduce the opportunity for a rational offender to commit a crime. Through the use of these various techniques a target may become less attractive to a motivated offender either by increasing the perceived risk of apprehension, increasing the perceived amount of effort, or reducing the anticipated rewards. These modifications may include changes in the physical environment, technological advancements (such as caller ID), or other strategies that will make an offender think twice before committing a crime.

Critiques and Concerns

While this family of crime prevention strategies has received a great deal of excited interest from some, others have voiced strong concerns over widespread implementation of these techniques. While these issues will be explored in greater detail in the final Chapter, it is important to briefly mention these critiques.

The most common critique of crime prevention strategies concerns the issue of **displacement**. In general, this argument claims that the various techniques explored in this chapter really have nothing to do with preventing crimes from happening—the crime simply moves. There are a number of different kinds of displacement and the most common forms are summarized in Box 5.4.

While proponents of crime prevention strategies must often defend their methods against charges of displacement, in actuality there is no empirical evidence that complete displacement has ever occurred. In the cases where some displacement has occurred, the overall crime level has been reduced (Barnes, 1995; Eck, 1993).

Box 5.4 Displacement Types

Displacement Type	Example
Temporal	Crime is moved to a different hour of the day or day of the week that is perceived to be less risky
Target	Crime is moved from a well-protected target to a more vulnerable one
Spatial	Offenders move from one location to another that is perceived to be a safer location
Tactical	Offenders change their methods of committing a crime to overcome the design modification
Perpetrator	As one offender becomes deterred from crime (either through their own choice or through arrest) another offender steps in
Type of Crime	Offenders deterred from one form of crime will now select an entirely new form of crime

Source: Adapted from Felson & Clarke (1998) and Barnes (1995).

There have also been a number of critiques raised on ethical grounds. It has been argued that the ability to implement crime prevention strategies is related to social class. Those with the resources to do so may turn their homes into fortresses. Poorer individuals cannot afford to move into gated communities and install expensive alarm systems. If you combine this argument with the notion of displacement, essentially the concern is that crime gets moved from the well-protected targets of the affluent to more vulnerable targets of the poor.

There have been other ethical and ideological charges against the various forms of crime prevention discussed in this chapter. For example, it has been argued that intensive video surveillance infringes on individual rights and personal freedoms. Others have charged that implementation of target hardening strategies and other tactics divert attention from the root causes of crime. Instead of investing in crime prevention strategies, we should be investing in social prevention—improving education, job training, and delinquency prevention programs (Felson & Clarke, 1997).

Since many of these same critiques could be leveled against other techniques explored in this text (crackdowns, directed patrol, even some community policing efforts), the final Chapter will include a more detailed discussion of these issues. For now, suffice it to say that not everyone is enamored by the success of the techniques presented in this Chapter.

Reclaiming Public Spaces

We close Chapter 5 with a reprint of an article by William Sousa and George Kelling. This study illustrates the effectiveness of problem-solving, order-maintenance, and situational crime prevention efforts on crime and public disorder problems in public places.

Spotlight on Research III

"Police and the Reclamation of Public Places:
A Study of MacArthur Park in Los Angeles"
William H. Sousa and George L. Kelling*

Abstract

Throughout the 1980s and 1990s, MacArthur Park—a 40-acre public park located near downtown Los Angeles—was widely known to be one of the largest open-air drug markets in Los Angeles. The Alvarado Corridor Initiative, a police-led initiative developed in 2003, was designed to address crime and disorderly behaviour in MacArthur Park through a combination of problem-solving, order-maintenance, and situational crime prevention efforts. This paper assesses the impact of the Alvarado Corridor Initiative using information from interviews and focus groups with neighbourhood residents, businesspeople, police officers, and other individuals familiar with MacArthur Park. The results suggest that many of the problems in MacArthur Park have been resolved and that the park experienced a turnaround that can be linked to the implementation of the Alvarado Corridor Initiative. In assessing the effectiveness of the Alvarado Corridor Initiative, this paper also provides a commentary on the evolution of public places in the United States and the role that the police can serve in terms of helping to preserve those public places.

* Reprinted with permission. *International Journal of Police Science and Management, 12*(1), 41–54.

INTRODUCTION

After his appointment as chief of the Los Angeles Police Department (LAPD) in November of 2002, William Bratton identified five high-profile areas of Los Angeles that were particularly troubled in terms of crime and disorder. Designating these areas as "Safer Cities" sites, the locations were to receive particular attention from police and other city agencies. MacArthur Park—a forty-acre public park located near downtown Los Angeles and within LAPD's Rampart Division—was identified as one of these "Safer Cities" sites.

The "Safer Cities" effort in the park, entitled the "Alvarado Corridor Initiative," marked a re-orientation of police philosophy toward a proactive, problem-solving approach. Combining innovative police work, community crime prevention, and assistance from other public agencies, the Alvarado Corridor Initiative attempted to address ongoing problems in MacArthur Park before they resulted in incidents of crime and violence. While elements of this initiative were clearly unique, the effort is based on similar programs in other cities that demonstrated success at reclaiming public spaces.

In this paper, we explore the impact of the Alvarado Corridor Initiative on crime and disorder in MacArthur Park. We begin by describing the decline of MacArthur Park as an example of the deterioration of public spaces in the United States. We then discuss the elements of the Alvarado Corridor Initiative, followed by a description of the information we use to determine its effectiveness at revitalizing MacArthur Park.

MacArthur Park and the deterioration of public spaces

Originally a place for diverse recreation and of physical beauty from its inception in 1885 until the 1940s, the story of MacArthur Park was one of general decline during the second half of the 20th century.[1] By 2002, it was widely acknowledged that MacArthur Park was lost to the criminal element. Four different gangs controlled the four quadrants of the park. Drug dealing was open and rampant. Public toilets were regularly used for prostitution. Vagrants set up camps both on the borders of the park as well as in its interior. Prostitution and drug dealing thrived in the tunnels under Wilshire Boulevard that connected the two sides of the park. A sense of physical disorder permeated the

---

1. The park was originally known as Westlake Park. It was renamed in 1942 in honor of General Douglas MacArthur of WWII fame.

park: graffiti, including gang graffiti, was widespread; trash containers over-flowed; lights were broken and unrepaired—all suggesting to citizens that the park was out of control. The *Los Angeles Times* regularly reported the deteri-orated condition of the park with story titles like "Former Place for Recreation Lost to Crime Culture" (Galarza, 2001).

In many respects, the story of MacArthur Park is an example of what has gone wrong in many urban parks and other public areas in the United States. Policy decisions made by courts, legislatures, and public policy makers in the US during the 1960s and 1970s gravely affected public spaces. Perhaps two of the most important policy innovations during this time were the decrim-inalization of minor criminal offences and the deinstitutionalization of the emotionally disturbed (Kelling & Coles, 1996).[2] Although these innovations were designed to address abuses and unfair treatment of individuals by gov-ernment, they had a detrimental impact on public spaces. Kelling and Coles (1996) describe several examples of the consequences of these policies. In New York City (NY), for instance, minor offenders, the mentally ill, and sub-stance abusers (often all one in the same) overwhelmed the subway, Grand Central Terminal, Bryant Park, and other public spaces. Similarly in Seattle (WA), where tourists, vagrants, business professionals, and shopkeepers had coexisted comfortably in and around Pioneer Square for decades, the influx of the mentally ill, substance abusers, and petty criminals turned a "quaint" and interesting neighbourhood into one that intimidated its users, under-mined commerce, and ultimately threatened its social and financial viability. It was often the case that vagrants who had inhabited the area were as vic-timized as others who lived in, used, and/or worked in the area. San Francisco (CA) had a like story: local neighbourhood parks became so infested with filth, condoms, and needles from "campers" that playground equipment was removed and the grounds were "bulldozed" and fenced in so that nobody could use them, especially sad circumstances for the children for whom they were intended.

Examples such as these could be given from virtually every large American city. In most cases, serious crime increased to intolerable levels as well. City and police attempts to manage street populations consistently were confronted with social and legal challenges as these attempts to restore order were characterized as either harassing or criminalizing the poor. Those who challenged city poli-

---

2. Although there are a myriad of discussions of the breakdown of order in American cities, one of the earliest and most trenchant was Jane Jacobs' *The Death and Life of Great American Cities* (1961).

cies often had a point. Many of the early attempts to restore order in public places were high handed, biased, and of marginal legality or morality. Many cities simply did not meet their responsibility to provide adequate shelter for those who needed it and could use it. Many police (officers and departments) confused status (genuinely homeless) with behaviour (unlawful conduct). Clumsy police "sweeps" often disregarded the rights (and property) of people living on the streets regardless of why they were there. Moreover, such sweeps had little long-term impact.

In many respects, it is not surprising that police and communities were ill prepared to deal with the consequences of deinstitutionalization and decriminalization and the associated legal and constitutional issues. The strategy police had in place, one largely conceived during the 1930s and 1940s and implemented during the 1950s and 1960s, was explicitly reactive and focused on "serious" crimes (Kelling & Moore, 1988). During this era, any suggestion that police had broader functions than responding to serious crime was met with police derision and indignation: they believed they were crime fighters, not social workers (Wasserman & Moore, 1988). Whatever street skills police developed over the generations, especially in dealing with unruly or disorderly persons, were lost as police were rapidly mobilized into cars. Police work in the United States became driving cars around city streets waiting for calls for service.

Moreover, the authority to deal with the problems of, and presented by, street people was inadequate. Courts deemed old vagrancy and loitering laws as too broad—a position largely justified given their widespread abuse by police. Many cities had to play "catch up" and enact new ordinances—ordinances that were routinely challenged by advocates and/or the American Civil Liberties Union, often successfully (see Kelling & Coles, 1996). Also compounding the problem was the initial reluctance of city or county prosecutors and the courts to take misdemeanours and minor offences seriously. While police were under considerable pressure in many communities to "do something" about the problem of street people, they had little support from either city or county attorneys. Just like police, most prosecutors preferred to deal with "serious" crime—again, the felonies. Likewise, judges believed that misdemeanours simply crowded their calendars with trivial matters.

While changing these patterns has been spotty and inconsistent across the United States, many communities have made considerable progress in reclaiming public areas such as city parks and playgrounds. Often these successes have been the result of a strong political demand that "something be done," as well as the evolution of community policing, situational crime prevention, and 'defensible space' strategies.

Framework for revitalisation

Beginning in the 1960s and 70s, a body of theoretical and empirical research began to emerge that provides a framework for the rejuvenation of public places. Jane Jacobs' (1961) commentary on urban life, for example, suggested how the layout of neighbourhoods and the design of streets could significantly impact citizens' use of public areas, including parks and sidewalks. According to Jacobs, urban planning that encourages the use of parks and sidewalks can help reduce fear, decrease crime and disorder, and promote feelings of shared ownership over public areas to a point where citizens 'self-police' those areas. Similarly, Oscar Newman's (1972) work on "defensible space" demonstrated the importance of building structure and spatial designs in terms of crime prevention in shared, urban spaces. Newman also proposed that the manipulation of architectural settings can promote positive social relationships, foster "limited friendships and the cognizance of neighbors," create "commonly shared effort[s] at maintaining ... facilit[ies]," and produce "areas for which people will adopt concern" (1972: 206).

More recent commentaries by urban planners have also examined the relationships between urban design, shared ownership of public areas, and community safety (see, in general, Oc & Tiesdell, 1997). Parker (2000), for example, discusses how the design and management of public places can promote a sense of propriety and increase natural surveillance performed by citizens, thereby decreasing crime and fear of crime. Accordingly, natural surveillance is a key component of situational crime prevention, which advocates for methods of improving a location's natural surroundings to increase the chances that criminals will be detected by citizens and other "place managers" (Clarke, 1997; Clarke & Eck, 2005; see also Jeffery, 1971).[3] Studies on situational crime prevention offer examples of reducing crime by manipulating the environmental features of places, such as improving street lighting, trimming shrubbery, and other methods designed to limit obstructed views in public places (Painter & Farrington, 1999; Casteel & Peek-Asa, 2000; see also Clarke, 1997).

As the ideas of defensible space and crime prevention through urban design developed, community policing emerged as the dominant police strategy in the United States. This strategy has at least two important characteristics that relate to the ability of police to improve public spaces. First, within the community policing model, police are more accountable to citizens and citizen concerns.

---

3. While situational crime prevention stresses the importance of methods designed to increase the risk of detection, it also argues for methods that increase the effort, reduce the rewards, remove the excuses, and reduce the provocations of criminal activity (see Clarke & Eck 2005).

Although police focused on serious felonies during the 1950s and 60s (Kelling & Moore, 1988), studies demonstrated that citizens are also greatly concerned with incivilities, minor offences, and disorderly people (Wilson & Kelling, 1982; Skogan & Maxfield, 1981; LaGrange, Ferraro, & Supancic, 1992). Police, therefore, can theoretically reduce fear and improve citizen quality-of-life in public locations by addressing minor offences.[4] Second, community policing is more proactive than past policing strategies that were distinctly reactive (Goldstein, 1979; Kelling & Moore, 1988). As such, police seek to prevent incidents of crime and disorder from occurring through more systematic methods of identifying, analyzing, and responding to underlying problems (Eck & Spelman, 1987). Recent research offers numerous examples of successful "problem-oriented" police tactics that are proactive in nature (see Braga, 2008).

Community policing, situational crime prevention, and the notion of defensible space combine to provide a framework for the revitalisation of public places. Taken together, they suggest that fear, crime, and disorder can be prevented if police and citizens proactively address ongoing problems (including minor offences), seek to "design out" crime, and promote a sense of shared ownership among people who use public areas. With this in mind, we now turn to the efforts designed to revitalise MacArthur Park in Los Angeles.

The Alvarado Corridor Initiative

Sporadic attempts had been made to deal with the escalating crime and disorder problems during MacArthur Park's decline, but most met with limited and/or only short-term success. As noted in a 2004 editorial in the *Los Angeles Times,*

> At least five times over the last 20 years, city leaders have hailed the renaissance of MacArthur Park. They've tried everything from police patrols to public art, with good results—until attention waned and crime waxed again along the palm-lined lake west of downtown Los Angeles, long known as a place to buy fake IDs, hire prostitutes and score drugs ("An Oasis," 2004, B-18).

Seeking a permanent, long-term solution to the problems in MacArthur Park, Chief William Bratton appointed a new command staff to LAPD's Rampart Division in May 2003, including Captain Charles Beck. Captain Beck began meeting regularly with community groups, neighbourhood stakehold-

---

4. Police efforts to reduce minor offences may decrease serious crime as well (Wilson & Kelling, 1982; Skogan, 1990; Kelling & Sousa, 2001).

ers, and city council members who represented the area. Key meetings were also held with officials from other city agencies. Captain Beck explained to them that he would be "asking for their help, but not now."[5] Only when it was apparent to all that he was serious about reclaiming the park for the long haul would he expect them to make investments. There simply had been too many "victories" in the past when special units would come into the park for a short period, sweep through with a series of arrests, and then go off to another assignment. The park, of course, would quickly revert to its disorderly crime ridden state.

By September of 2003, Rampart Division was ready to implement the "Alvarado Corridor Initiative." The targeted area included MacArthur Park and the area immediately surrounding it. The surrounding area was included to ensure that drug dealing and crime were not displaced to the neighbourhoods surrounding the park. The initiative consisted of the following elements:

- The contingent of officers directly assigned to the Alvarado Corridor area was increased from 12 officers and 2 sergeants to 16 officers and 2 sergeants. These officers had permanent assignments to the project, patrolled on foot and bikes, with the goal of "owning" the corridor.
- Emphasis was to be placed on all offences regardless of severity, misdemeanours as well as felonies.
- A "Mica Task Force" was established to address the counterfeit identification trade—an ongoing problem in and around MacArthur Park where dealers of counterfeit documents would actively solicit passersby—sometimes directly in front of police officers.
- The core of the Alvarado project was the patrol unit; however other special units supported patrol operations. For instance, undercover narcotics operations were conducted to reduce drug activity—both selling and buying. "Reverse buys," for example, focused on individuals who came to the park and its surrounding areas for the purposes of buying drugs.
- In January of 2004 closed circuit television cameras (CCTV) were installed that could monitor every area of the park. Experienced officers—often those trained in narcotics—regularly monitored the cameras and directed patrol officers to locations where illegal activity was underway.[6]
- Nearly 60 signs were erected (in both English and Spanish) posting the rules of appropriate behaviour in the park and giving notice that the police would enforce them. Since the police believed that it would be ini-

---

5. Personal communication with Captain Charles Beck on March 20, 2007.
6. Significant publicity accompanied the cameras. See, for example, Martinez (2004).

tially unfair to arrest or fine individuals for behaviour that was previously allowed, the signs were implemented in conjunction with a significant public education campaign to notify the public of increased enforcement efforts.

- Maintenance crews were able to improve maintenance of the park. No new personnel were assigned but one result of the enforcement effort was that litter and graffiti were substantially reduced. This reduction allowed maintenance staff to tend to other matters on a regular basis.
- The Department of Water and Power, recognizing the planned improvements in the park, doubled the amount of lighting in the park with attractive historic lights.
- The Forestry Department regularly trimmed trees and shrubbery thus reducing "hiding spots" and ensuring that the cameras could overlook all areas of the park.
- The Department of Parks and Recreation increased programming in MacArthur Park, including a summer concert by the Pasadena Symphony Orchestra.

Operational theory and previous research support the elements of the Alvarado Corridor Initiative. Attention to minor offences and improvements to park maintenance, for example, are supported by the "broken windows" hypothesis that advocates for the control of disorder as a method of reducing serious crime (Wilson & Kelling, 1982; Kelling & Coles, 1996; Kelling & Sousa, 2001). Efforts to improve lighting, trim shrubbery, install CCTV, and clearly post the acceptable rules of behaviour—all with significant publicity—are supported by research in the areas of situational crime prevention and defensible space (Clarke, 1997; Clarke & Eck, 2005; Newman, 1972). Increased communication with citizens, better coordination with city agencies, and increased foot and bike patrols to make officers more familiar with a specific geographic beat are all tactics that are consistent with the principles of community policing. Furthermore, understanding the problems in the park and taking these proactive steps to reduce lawlessness are inherent in the ideas of problem-oriented policing (Goldstein, 1979; Eck & Spelman, 1987).

METHODOLOGY

We had little influence over the implementation of the Alvarado Corridor Initiative. The priority on the part of LAPD was to regain order in MacArthur Park as quickly as possible—establishing experimental conditions for scientific purposes was not feasible. Despite the lack of experimental controls, information from several data sources can still be used to inform the impact of the Initiative on the quality of life in MacArthur Park. Specifically, we examine records of complaints for serious crime in MacArthur Park and its surrounding communities, as well as focus group and interview data concerning safety in MacArthur Park in recent years.

Crime trends in MacArthur Park

The Alvarado Corridor Initiative was designed to decrease minor offences in MacArthur Park, such as open-air drug and alcohol use, prostitution, public urination and defecation, littering, and other acts of public disorder. Unfortunately, we have no systematic method of determining the actual occurrences of minor offences in MacArthur Park around the time of the Alvarado Corridor Initiative. This is because of the manner in which minor offences are recorded in official statistics. Unlike a serious offence (i.e. felony) where a police report is generated whether or not it results in an arrest, a report for a minor offence is only generated if an arrest is made or if a citation is issued.[7] Determining the actual number of incidents of minor offences is therefore complex: shifting trends in official reports of minor offences may be a function of both changes in the actual incidents of those behaviours and/or changes in police activity directed at those behaviours.

Although we are not able to examine trends in minor offences using official data, we can examine trends in serious crime using official statistics. In fact, the tactics of the Alvarado Corridor Initiative were not only designed to impact minor offences—they were also designed specifically to prevent serious criminal activity by increasing the risks of detection and removing excuses for breaking the law (Clarke, 1997). If the tactics had their intended impact, we would expect to see a reduction in crime activity after the tactics were in place. To examine this outcome, we obtained data from LAPD on incidents of serious crime from 2001–2004. These include Part 1 violent offences (homicide, rape, robbery, aggravated assault) and property offences (burglary, larceny, and grand theft auto). The data include weekly crime counts for what we label

---

7. Felonies are typically brought to the attention of the police through citizen-initiated complaints—if an arrest is made, it is often done at a later time. Minor offences, however, are typically brought to the attention of the police through their own observation (and are thus police-initiated)—the complaint and arrest therefore occur at the same time.

Figure 1 Weekly Complaints for Serious Crime, MacArthur Park Area, 2001–2004

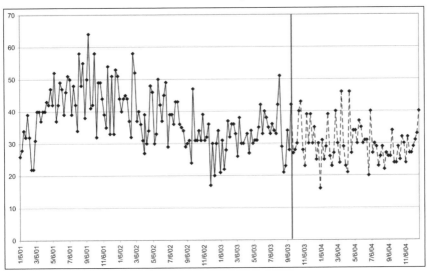

the "MacArthur Park Area"—a geographic area that includes MacArthur Park as well as the surrounding police beats.[8]

Figure 1 displays Part 1 offences in the MacArthur Park Area, per week, from 2001–2004. We indicate with a dashed line the period of the Alvarado Corridor Initiative, beginning in mid-September 2003. Over the entire four-year time period examined, MacArthur Park and its surrounding community averaged approximately 35 Part 1 offences per week, but fell from nearly 38 per week before the Initiative to just under 30 after it began (Table 1). Similar patterns hold for both violent and property offences.

Although serious crime decreased following the implementation of the Alvarado Corridor Initiative, at this point we are cautious in attributing the crime drop to the Initative's efforts. Crime reduction in MacArthur Park may have

---

8. MacArthur Park occupies Reporting District (RD) 245. An RD, which is roughly equivalent to a police beat, represents the smallest geographic unit within each LAPD command division. The MacArthur Park Area referred to in this paper includes the MacArthur Park RD (245), as well as the RDs surrounding the park: 246, 256, 264, 266, 267, and 275. The inclusion of the larger area is necessary because both monthly and weekly counts of Part 1 offences are typically low for the MacArthur Park RD by itself. In addition, although MacArthur Park is the focal point of the police and city activity, the Alvarado Corridor Initiative was intended to have an impact in the surrounding community as well.

Table 2　Average Number of Serious Offences per Week,
Pre and Post Initiative

	mean per week	
MacArthur Park Area	*pre intervention*	*post intervention*
Part 1 violent crime	14.35	10.89
Part 1 property crime	23.3	19.06
All Part 1 crime	37.65	29.95

been associated with the Initiative, but without proper statistical controls it is difficult to state whether the crime drop was a result of the Initiative or a result of extraneous factors.[9] For this reason we now turn to focus group and interview data to help determine the community's views of the Initiative's impact in MacArthur Park.

Information from interviews and focus groups

If the programs associated with the Alvarado Corridor Initiative had their intended impact, one would also expect to see positive reactions from public and private sector individuals who are in some way associated with MacArthur Park. Specifically, one might predict that neighbourhood residents, business-people, police, criminal justice officials, government officials, and other "users" of the park will note changes for the better in terms of perceptions of quality of life, fear of crime, disorder, and personal feelings of safety. One might also predict that these individuals will report more people using the park appropriately and for its intended purposes: recreation and relaxation.

To examine the extent to which these predictions are met, we conducted in-depth interviews and focus groups with MacArthur Park "stakeholders"— individuals who are familiar with MacArthur Park, who live and/or work in or near the park, and who represent a community, business, or government interest in the park. Asking questions of respondents such as these is an important method for gaining opinions about important events (Yin, 1994). Although focused interviews and focus groups have limitations of their own (bias, memory recall of respondents, inaccurate articulation of events, etc.), they repre-

---

9. Numerous factors have been linked to crime reduction, including shifts in local economic, demographic, and drug-use trends. For a recent discussion of these factors, see generally Blumstein & Wallman (2000).

sent significant sources of information, particularly if they corroborate each other and if they are corroborated by other sources of information (Yin, 1994).

We conducted six in-depth interviews with representatives from local businesses, local residents, park grounds keeping, and the police.[10] We also conducted three focus groups: a "community" group with five participants that included a representative from a neighbourhood school and a representative from a park volunteer group, as well as representatives from local citizens' groups and local business interests; a "government" group with five participants, including representatives from the Office of the US Attorney, Office of the Los Angeles City Attorney, Los Angeles City Council, Park Rangers, and City Parks and Recreation; and a "police" group with seven participants, all of which were police officers from LAPD's Rampart Division. The officers were either directly involved in the Alvarado Corridor Initiative or they had considerable experience in Rampart and could provide historical insight on police activity in MacArthur Park.

The questions posed to both the interviewees and the focus group participants were open-ended and designed to obtain opinions on several key issues related to MacArthur Park, including the park's recent history, recent changes (if any) in the park in terms of fear, safety, crime, and disorder, major reasons for these changes, and present and future concerns about the park. Our strategy was to achieve a "saturation point" with the data—the point at which additional interviews and focus groups were not yielding much new information about MacArthur Park. Ultimately, we sought to determine whether this information provided corroborative or contradictory evidence on the impact of the Alvarado Corridor Initiative.

The results of both the interviews and focus groups indicated strong consensus that the park experienced recent change. We focus on this change as we summarize the results of the interviews and focus groups into three categories: descriptions of change in MacArthur Park; contributing factors to the change; and the future of the park.

Descriptions of change

All individuals we spoke with, whether in interviews or focus groups, noted a positive change in MacArthur Park. Whereas respondents used terms such

---

10. Intensive interviews differ from structured interviews that require researchers to ask subjects to respond to precisely worded questions (see Berg, 2004). Rather, intensive interviews allow a researcher the flexibility to modify questions based on the direction of a subject's responses and probe beyond the subject's answers.

as "filthy," "unsafe," "crime-infested," "dirty," "open sewer," and "urban blight" to describe the park of the late 1990s, terms such as "serene," "safe," "clean," "vibrant," and "family-oriented" were used to describe the park as it is today. Although respondents described additional improvements that could be made, no one argued that the park has not dramatically improved. Individuals in the community focus group were the most vocal about these changes, describing the difference as "night and day."

Respondents recalled numerous examples to illustrate the change in the park. Some who reported witnessing strong-arm robberies, assaults, and blatant narcotics activity were no longer apprehensive about working in or walking through the park because they believe safety had greatly improved. What was once described by one interviewee as an "open hotel for the homeless, drug addicts, and prostitutes" was now a place where respondents saw many more families, joggers, and others using the park for recreational activities. In addition, respondents described a change in behaviour on the part of "transients" or "the homeless." One participant from the community focus group, for example, described a time when he and fellow co-workers found it impossible to have lunch in the park because vagrants would walk up and brazenly take food from benches and lunch tables. Other respondents reflected on similar stories, including watching vagrants routinely intimidate park visitors for money. These types of behaviours, however, are no longer common in the park as transients—while still present—abide by the park's rules. Respondents generally agreed that street people in the park are no longer threatening while civility is maintained.

Contributors to change

Interviewees and focus group participants acknowledged numerous contributors to the positive change in the park. These included strong support from city council and the US Attorney's Office, greater commitment from the City Attorney's Office in terms of the prosecution of minor offences, a greater presence of park rangers, improved programming from Parks and Recreation, overall better lighting, maintenance, and grounds keeping, and continuous support from local businesses and citizen groups. Respondents from all interviews and focus groups generally concurred, however, that LAPD was the catalyst for some of the more significant changes in the park in recent years.

A common suggestion provided—which was generally acknowledged by community, police, and government respondents—was that LAPD was the foundation for the change with other contributors providing important support services. Some of the police activities that were discussed during the interviews and focus groups included greater police visibility (such as bike patrols), increased attention to minor offences (such as public drug use/dealing, illegal vending, and violations of park rules and regulations), police undercover activity, and the installation and monitoring of surveillance cameras. Other respondents mentioned LAPD's prominent leadership role in the coordination of multi-agency efforts.

Respondents differed slightly in terms of which police tactics they believed were the most effective. Respondents representing the community and local businesses, for example, tended to agree that the surveillance cameras were a major contributor to crime reduction and prevention. One individual from the community focus group was adamant about the cameras' impact, stating that the cameras were "the best thing to happen to the park"—an opinion that was confirmed by the other focus group members. It was their belief that the cameras provided a constant police presence and therefore served as both a specific deterrent (catching *actual* wrongdoers in the act) and general deterrent (the certainty of being caught deters *potential* wrongdoers from attempting illegal activity).

Respondents representing government and police also acknowledged the contribution of the cameras, but were more likely to suggest that the overall police orientation in the park was the most important contributor from LAPD. In particular, they were more inclined to note police attention to minor offences and the police willingness to help (and be helped by) other city agencies. Several of the police respondents mentioned that the cameras were the most highly publicized portion of the initiative, and so much of the public may perceive them to be the major difference. The police however, tend to view the cameras as a method of reinforcing their overall attention to quality of life in the park.

Interestingly, respondents—especially those from the community focus group—discussed how the police contribution to the change has paved the way for additional contributors. Focus group participants sensed that now that the police had done much to gain control over the park, the demographics of the area had started to improve. This, they believed, was attracting the interest of private investors. Respondents suggested that the business community was beginning to respond to changes in the park, reacting to the growing markets for major retail stores and restaurants. In addition, respondents cited instances of discussions with major corporations over sponsorship of park activities—discussions that would have been unheard of several years ago. While the interest from the private sector has yet to be fully realized, respondents suggested that private interests have the potential of contributing to the park in such a way as to make it self-sustaining and a money "generator," rather than a burden to the city.

Future of the park

Although all respondents were generally optimistic, they voiced concerns about the future of MacArthur Park. A major concern deals with the park's reputation. While respondents report that criminals no longer believe the park is "the place to be" for illegal activity and that more families are beginning to use the park for its intended purposes, the challenge now is to convince many others that the park is a desirable place. Several respondents noted that a stigma is still attached to the park and that until the stigma is removed the area will remain unattractive to many. Respondents believe that the removal of this reputation is also necessary to make the park "self-regulating." Until this self-regulation begins and the community assumes more "ownership" of the park, the fear is that the park could begin to revert back to its former state. To prevent this, respondents emphasized the importance of continued activity from LAPD and other city agencies and continued support from LA government entities.

In summary, the data from the in-depth interviews and focus groups tend to support the idea that MacArthur Park looks and "feels" safer now than just a few years ago. This information also suggests that the police played (and continue to play) an important role in the reduction of serious crime in and around the park.

DISCUSSION AND CONCLUSION

In 2003, LAPD set out to reclaim a public space that had declined as a result of crime and disorder. The effort involved a series of steps: Chief William Bratton's commitment to restore order in MacArthur Park; a theory of action that was grounded in principles of community policing, situational crime prevention, and defensible space; the empowerment of a district captain and his ability to establish a foundation for other agencies to share "ownership" of the problem; innovative efforts that included identifying potential citizen uses of the park; the expansion of the park's capacity to make it consistent with those potential uses; and persistent oversight that remains to this day.

This effort—entitled the Alvarado Corridor Initiative—was the subject of this paper. Specifically, we examined the impact of the Alvarado Corridor Initiative on problems of crime and disorder in MacArthur Park. Results from interviews and focus groups with community stakeholders suggest that MacArthur Park was experiencing considerable problems related to quality-of-life and disorderly conditions throughout the 1990s and into the early years of this decade. Furthermore, community stakeholders believe that many of these problems have been resolved and that the park experienced a turn-around that can be linked to the implementation of the Alvarado Corridor Initiative.

Official crime data appear to support stakeholders' beliefs. Although these data are limited and proper experimental controls were not feasible at the time of the Initiative, a reduction in serious offences in and around the park did accompany the onset of the Initiative's tactics. We remain mindful that such a relationship could be one of chance—perhaps serious crime in the park would have decreased without the Alvarado Corridor Initiative in place. Additionally, to the extent that the Initiative was the impetus for positive change in the park, it is difficult to determine which of its numerous tactics were the most effective.

Nevertheless, public support for the Initiative's tactics remains high. Even media outlets (including the national media), which had previously been critical of city efforts in MacArthur Park, have generally touted improvements to safety in the park as a whole. A 2005 article in the real estate section of *The New York Times*, for example, discussed the revitalization and renaissance of MacArthur Park in Los Angeles, emphasizing the improved safety and increased desirability of the property surrounding it (Stevens, 2005).

To the extent that the park's improvements can be credited to the Alvarado Corridor Initiative, this study demonstrates the potential for police-led strategies at reclaiming public places. A question that arises, however, relates to what is required to maintain order in public places once it is re-established. In this MacArthur Park example, from LAPD's perspective, it seems that *law enforcement* (via arrest and citation) should appropriately decline after police efforts to gain control, but it is not clear that *policing* should decline, or if it should, by how much. The appropriate "dosage" of police required to maintain order in MacArthur Park is a critical question for LAPD and its community partners.

More important, however, involves the community's ability to assume shared ownership over the park to the point that it becomes 'self-policing' (Jacobs, 1961; Newman, 1972). The question of what makes a park (and other public spaces) "work well" has received a good deal of attention in the United States. Jacobs (1961) provides an interesting account of why and how parks are successful. Like sidewalks, parks only work well if they are used. Jacobs refers to unused sidewalks and parks as vacuums—relatively vacant spaces that can spiral into misuse and decay. Furthermore, the most successful public parks attract and are hospitable to a variety of users at various times throughout the day. Continuing to encourage individuals to use the park for its intended purposes, as well as encouraging greater private investment in the park and surrounding neighbourhoods, should therefore be critical goals for sustaining positive achievements.[11]

References

Berg, B. L. (2004). *Qualitative Research Methods for the Social Sciences* (5th ed.). Boston, MA: Pearson Education.

Blumstein, A. & Wallman, J. (Eds.). (2000). *The Crime Drop in America.* Cambridge: Cambridge University Press.

Braga, A. A. (2008). *Problem-Oriented Policing and Crime Prevention* (2nd ed.). Monsey, NY: Criminal Justice Press.

Casteel, C. & Peek-Asa, C. (2000). Effectiveness of crime prevention through environmental design (CPTED) in reducing robberies. *American Journal of Preventive Medicine,* 18, (4S), 99–115.

Clarke, R. V. (Ed.). (1997). *Situational Crime Prevention: Successful Case Studies* (2nd ed.). Monsey, NY: Criminal Justice Press.

Clarke, R. V. & Eck, J. E. (2005). *Crime Analysis for Problem Solvers in 60 Small Steps.* Washington, D.C.: Center for Problem Oriented Policing.

Eck, J. E. & Spelman, W. (1987). *Problem-Solving: Problem-Oriented Policing in Newport News* (Research in Brief). Washington, DC: National Institute of Justice.

Galarza, M. C. (2001, December 17). "Former place for recreation lost to crime culture." *Los Angeles Times.*

Goldstein, H. (1979). Improving policing: A problem oriented approach. *Crime and Delinquency,* 25, 236–258.

Jacobs, J. (1961). *The Death and Life of Great American Cities.* New York, NY: Random House.

---

11. Evidence of sustainment is clearly present in the park. On a recent visit to Los Angeles, for example, we noted the installation of a soccer field in MacArthur Park, as well as plans to restore the outdoor amphitheater for concerts—both of these efforts would not have been conceivable prior to the Alvarado Corridor Initiative. Additionally, LAPD continues its commitment and oversight. Deputy Chief Charles Beck, for instance, the former captain over Rampart Division who orchestrated the Alvarado Corridor Initiative, remains a regular visitor to MacArthur Park even though his promotion requires his assignment in a different part of the city.

Jeffery, C. R. (1971). *Crime Prevention through Environmental Design.* Beverly Hills, CA: Sage.

Kelling, G. L. & Coles, C. M. (1996). *Fixing Broken Windows: Restoring Order and Reducing Crime in Our Communities.* New York, NY: The Free Press.

Kelling, G. L. & Moore, M. H. (1988). *The Evolving Strategy of Policing* (Perspectives on Policing No.1). Washington, DC: National Institute of Justice.

Kelling, G. L. & Sousa, W. H. (2001). *Do Police Matter? An Analysis of the Impact of New York City's Police Reforms* (Civic Report No. 22). New York, NY: Manhattan Institute.

LaGrange, R. L., Ferraro, K. F., & Supancic, M. (1992). Perceived risk and fear of crime: Role of social and physical incivilities. *Journal of Research in Crime and Delinquency,* 29, 3, 311–334.

Martinez, A. (2004, March 11). "Cameras give park the once-over." *Los Angeles Times,* B-3.

Newman, O. (1972). *Defensible Space: Crime Prevention through Urban Design.* New York, NY: Macmillan Publishing.

"An oasis in L.A.'s core." (2004, June 19). *Los Angeles Times,* B-18.

Oc, T. & Tiesdell, S. (Eds.). (1997). *Safer City Centres: Reviving the Public Realm.* London: Paul Chapman Publishing.

Painter, K. & Farrington, D. P. (1999). Street lighting and crime: Diffusion of benefits in the Stoke-on-Trent project. In Painter K. & Tilley, N. (eds.), *Surveillance of Public Space: CCTV, Street Lighting and Crime Prevention.* Monsey, NY: Criminal Justice Press.

Parker, J. (2000, October). *Safer Spaces and Places: Reducing Crime by Urban Design.* Paper presented at the Council of Europe International Conference on the Relationship between the Physical Urban Environment and Crime Patterns, Szczecin, Poland.

Skogan, W. G. (1990). *Disorder and Decline: Crime and the Spiral of Decay in American Neighborhoods.* New York: The Free Press.

Skogan, W. G. & Maxfield, M. G. (1981). *Coping with Crime: Individual and Neighborhood Reactions.* Beverly Hills, CA: Sage Publications.

Stevens, K. (2005, April 17). "A new life for a park and its neighborhood." *The New York Times.*

Wasserman, R. & Moore, M. H. (1988). *Values in Policing* (Perspectives on Policing No. 8). Washington, DC: National Institute of Justice.

Wilson, J. Q. & Kelling, G. L. (1982). Broken windows: The police and neighborhood safety. *The Atlantic Monthly,* (March), 29–38.

Yin, R. K. (1994). *Case Study Research: Design and Methods* (2nd ed.). Thousand Oaks, CA: Sage Publications.

Authors Affiliation

William H. Sousa is an Assistant Professor in the Department of Criminal Justice at the University of Nevada, Las Vegas. His current research projects involve police order-maintenance practices, police management, and community crime prevention.

George L. Kelling is a Professor in the School of Criminal Justice at Rutgers University—Newark, the Faculty Chair of the Police Institute at Rutgers University, and a Senior Fellow at the Manhattan Institute for Policy Research. His most familiar publication, "Broken Windows: The Police and Neighborhood Safety" with James Q. Wilson, appeared in the *Atlantic Monthly* in 1982.

Acknowledgements

We thank those who made this project possible, LAPD Chief William Bratton, Deputy Chief Charles Beck, Los Angeles Mayor Antonio Villaraigosa, and former Mayor James Hahn. We also thank the Manhattan Institute for Policy Research for its support. The conclusions expressed in this paper are those of the authors and do not necessarily reflect those of the LAPD, the Manhattan Institute, or the Los Angeles Mayor's Office.

Chapter 6

The Analysis of Crime

Thus far, the examination of space, time, and crime has included an exploration of a number of theoretical explanations that have attempted to address why crime, disorder, and other social ills seem to be concentrated in certain geographic locations. Practical policies that have grown from these theoretical frameworks have also been studied. In this next section, the examination of a variety of tools available to law enforcement, private security agencies, local communities, government agencies, and other interested parties who are concerned with the study of patterns of crime and disorder is presented.

What Is Crime Analysis?

In its most rudimentary form, the term "crime analysis" has been applied to a patrol-oriented tool used by police agencies to identify patterns of criminal activity and to assist in a more rational deployment of patrol officers (Peterson, 1998). Through a careful analysis of police reports, calls for service, and other available data, police agencies may use crime analysis to concentrate their efforts where they are needed the most. While this is still an important aspect of crime analysis, there are many uses beyond this limited application.

Crime analysis is a broad term that is used to describe a number of different methods associated with the systematic examination of crime and crime-related data. According to Rachel Boba (2009), former Director of the Police Foundation's Crime Mapping Laboratory:

> Crime analysis is the systematic study of crime and disorder problems as well as other police-related issues—including socio-demographic, spatial, and temporal factors—to assist the police in criminal apprehension, crime and disorder reduction, crime prevention, and evaluation (p. 3).

This is a rather complicated definition, so the various components will be considered. First, crime analysis may use a variety of data sources in order to gain knowledge about a particular situation. **Qualitative data** is usually conceived of as non-numerical information. Qualitative studies include such things as a systematic observation of a problem location or neighborhood; careful examination of in-depth interviews with local residents, offenders, or victims; or a content analysis of various informational documents, such as property or real estate records or the narrative descriptions within arrest reports. On the other hand, **quantitative studies** usually involve number crunching of numerical data. For example, a crime analyst working in a police agency may calculate a range of times (such as 2:00 a.m. to 4:00 a.m.) in which a particular robber is likely to hit the next target or predict how many new officers will be needed given an increase in the population.

Depending on the specific situation or task, a crime analyst may use one or both types of data. It is important to remember that regardless of the data type, the crime analyst must carefully follow the rules associated with research methodology and statistical analysis. This is not "voodoo science," but a deliberate scientific examination of data carefully gathered, following the rules of social science research.

Boba's definition also includes a reference to socio-demographic, spatial, and temporal factors. According to Boba, socio-demographic factors include descriptions of individuals and groups, such as gender, race, income, age, and education level. On the individual level, these factors may assist law enforcement officers in the identification and apprehension of a specific suspect, such as "Be on the look out for a white male, age 27, with blonde hair and green eyes." On the group level, crime analysts may use socio-demographic information to try to explain why one neighborhood has a higher number of calls for service than another area. For example, census data may be used to compare the median income, proportion of renters, and race and ethnic composition of several different neighborhoods. This information may then be used to identify correlations or relationships between the number and type of calls for police services and these neighborhood characteristics. Spatial factors are important in the understanding of why certain locations seem to be more crime-ridden than others. Spatial factors include the location of a crime as well as other important considerations, such as street network patterns, zoning regulations, and locations of schools, liquor stores, or other places of interest. And finally, temporal factors include long-term patterns in criminal activity (i.e., over months or years), mid-length patterns (i.e., over weeks, days, or time of day), and short-terms patterns (i.e., time between events associated with a particular crime series).

Boba's definition ends with the four goals of crime analysis: apprehending criminals, reducing crime and disorder, preventing crime, and evaluation.

These goals are obviously centered on crime analysis in a law enforcement agency. While a great deal of this discussion will center on the use of crime analysis for police purposes, it is important to remember that members of the law enforcement community are not the only consumers of such information. Place managers, real estate speculators, academics, and program evaluations all make use of crime data and analysis for various purposes.

Historical Development of Crime Analysis

The information-gathering process associated with crime analysis may be traced back to ancient Chinese cultures and to Biblical times. According to Peterson (1998), historical references to the gathering, analysis, application, and use of information, especially during times of war, may be found dating back thousands of years. Crime analysis was also used during the feudal period of England. There is evidence that during this period "analysts" examined available data to specifically identify possible suspects and patterns of crime (Gottlieb et al., 1998).

In the United States, crime analysis—as a tool for law enforcement—has had a much shorter history. August Vollmer was Chief of Police in Berkeley, California, from 1905–1932. Vollmer was highly influential in his quest to professionalize policing. He advocated the hiring of college graduates to serve as police officers and was the first to establish college-level courses in police science at the University of California in 1916 (Walker & Katz, 2002).

As part of his professionalization agenda, Vollmer advocated a number of practices designed to make policing more effective and efficient. While the English had been using a systematic technique called modus operandi (MO) analysis to classify known offenders, Vollmer is credited with introducing this technique to the United States. In MO analysis, the peculiar aspects of an offender's actions in committing the crime are recorded. For example, a burglar may enter homes through sliding glass doors located in the rear of the home. Once inside, this particular burglar may ransack the home—taking televisions, stereos, and other electronic equipment, but leaving behind valuable jewelry. If this same MO is found in a number of different crime scenes, one can reasonably assume that the same person is committing these crimes. Through the use of MO analysis, police agencies may carefully examine other characteristics of crimes committed by this same offender in order to more efficiently identify and apprehend the suspect (Gottlieb et al., 1998; Haley, Todd, & Stallo, 1998).

In addition to the introduction of MO analyses, Vollmer is also credited with the development of more scientific patrol management procedures, such as examining calls for service in order to perform analyses based on "beats" or predetermined geographic zones. Vollmer used pin maps to identify the specific locations of crimes and/or calls for service. Through a visual examination of where the pins were clustered in the city, Vollmer was better able to deploy policing resources to the beats or locations where the crime and calls were concentrated (Gottlieb et al., 1998). Vollmer was quite a visionary for his time and his ideas of police management continue to impact contemporary law enforcement practices. Because of his influence, he has been called "the father of American police professionalism" (Walker & Katz, 2002, p. 33).

One of Vollmer's former students, Orlando W. Wilson, greatly expanded Vollmer's vision of policing as a modern professional science. Wilson held a number of influential positions, both in police agencies and in academia, serving as Chief in Wichita, Kansas, Superintendent of the Chicago Police Department, and as Dean of the University of California School of Criminology. Wilson wrote two widely read textbooks on police management principles, including *Police Administration* (1950). This textbook became known as the "bible" of police management, and although new contributors have been added, the text is still popular and influential in contemporary times (Cox, 1996; Walker & Katz, 2002).

Wilson contributed a number of revolutionary ideas to law enforcement. To enhance efficiency, Wilson developed an assignment allocation formula that provided an optimal number of patrol officers based on the level of criminal activity and calls for service in a specific area. Additionally, Wilson advocated the use of crime analysis, which he felt was an essential police function. In the second edition of his text, which was released in 1963, Wilson envisioned a crime analysis unit whose members would systematically review crime reports on a daily basis. From these reports, the crime analysts would categorize information on the location, time, MO, and other important factors in order to assist in the identification of crime patterns and/or offenders (Gottlieb et al., 1998; Walker & Katz, 2002).

The Growth of "Smart" Policing

The 1960s were a revolutionary time for the country and law enforcement. Police agencies were increasingly under attack for their heavy-handed tactics, especially among minority citizens. Riots rocked major cities where, oftentimes, the root cause was a real or perceived act of police misconduct that had involved a minority citizen. Crime rates were on the rise. A number of reports were released that criticized the police, calling for better hiring practices, improved training, more education, and greater professionalism (National Advisory Commission on Civil Disorders, 1968; President's Commission on Law Enforcement and Administration of Justice, 1967).

As a result of the intense interest in improving police practices, the federal government provided a great deal of money to fund policing-oriented research and to offer educational opportunities for police officers. The Law Enforcement Assistance Administration (LEAA) and the Police Foundation were born out of this era. The LEAA provided a billion dollars a year to improve the effectiveness of criminal justice agencies. Both the LEAA and the Police Foundation provided funding for research designed to study and improve police practices. Some of the research that was conducted during these times dramatically changed the way law enforcement services were provided (Swanson et al., 1998).

The Kansas City Preventive Patrol Experiment, which was funded by the Police Foundation, raised serious questions about the effectiveness of routine, random patrol on crime (Kelling et al., 1974). A study conducted by the RAND Corporation questioned the effectiveness of police investigations, reporting that many detective units were highly unproductive (Greenwood, 1975). The importance of faster response times, long heralded as being the key to effectively identify and arrest suspects, was also challenged by research findings (Department of Justice, 1978). As a result of these and other studies, police chiefs were under a great deal of pressure to alter their practices. The economy was also experiencing a downturn. No longer could police chiefs and sheriffs count on additional funds for the hiring of more police officers. Instead, administrators were forced to make better use of the resources that they already had. The need for more reliable and accurate information that could be used to assist law enforcement grew dramatically, as did interest in crime analysis.

In the mid-1970s, Robert O. Heck, a senior program specialist for the LEAA, developed the Patrol Emphasis Program (PEP). The goal of PEP was to provide a plan for police agencies to use crime analysis to assist in the management of calls for service and to enhance the quality of criminal investigations. The PEP plan did enjoy some success, and Heck expanded on these ideas to develop the Integrated Criminal Apprehension Program, or ICAP (Gottlieb et al. 1998). The importance of crime analysis was stressed once again in ICAP, especially in the identification of habitual offenders. The general assumption was that a small number of career criminals were responsible for a large number of offenses. This small group of offenders would, in all likelihood, have numerous recorded contacts with the police either through arrest reports, field interview reports, or other documents. Heck felt that if police agencies could somehow easily retrieve and categorize information that they already had within their grasp, the investigative process could be greatly improved. One of the changes recommended by ICAP was to improve the quality of record keeping, allowing for easier access to needed information.

Unfortunately, the popularity and utility of crime analysis in every-day operations was hampered by the available technology. Even with improved record keeping, the use of computers to retrieve needed information was extremely limited. For example, if a detective was looking for the name of a white male suspect with brown hair and brown eyes who had a tattoo of Mighty Mouse on his left shoulder, the information could not be readily accessed. In many agencies, important information was kept on note cards or paper reports that had to be searched by hand. In modern times, the task of finding a name, address, and other information on an individual based on a physical description would take a few seconds, assuming that the data had been entered into a computerized database.

During the 1970s, software applications were very complicated. Trained experts were needed to make modifications to Fortran-based programs that were housed on a mainframe system (Peterson, 1998). As a result of the "user-hostile" systems, as well as the expense, few agencies used computers for analysis. In 1980, a survey was conducted to investigate the level and sophistication of computer use by larger police agencies. A total of 122 agencies (out of 150 contacted) responded to the survey. The results revealed that only 12 of the 122 agencies that responded to the survey were using their computer systems for crime analysis related tasks (Tafoya, 1998). It was still a few more years before computer equipment and software applications had evolved to the point that many larger agencies could purchase and actually use the new tools (Peterson, 1998).

Contemporary Crime Analysis: The Building of a Profession

Interest in the analysis of crime continued to grow throughout the 1980s. More and more agencies began to develop crime analysis units, often with little or no idea of what, exactly, a crime analyst is supposed to do. In many cases, a person designated as a "crime analyst" received minimal (if any) training on analysis techniques. It was not unheard of for injured patrol officers to be assigned to the crime analysis unit before returning to full duty on the streets (a practice that continues today in some agencies, which we will discuss later).

In response to the demand for training and standards, a number of organizations were created in order to enhance professionalism in the field. In 1980, The International Association of Law Enforcement Intelligence Analysts (IALEIA) was created. **Intelligence analysis** is a special type of crime analysis. The use of this term usually refers to the analysis of data to solve major crimes or to assist in the investigation of organized criminal activity. The goal of the IALEIA organization was to develop professional standards for the growing field of intelligence analysis. Currently, the organization has members from around the globe and continues to provide training, career development, and technology awareness (Peterson, 1998). For more information, see Box 6.1.

In a formalized effort in 2004, IALEIA developed a set of minimum standards for intelligence analysis that attempted to codify the various processes. Standards were developed for employment consideration, continuing education requirements, and certification mandates. In addition to providing guidelines for maintaining a professional staff, the minimum standards also stressed the importance of accurate, timely and valid products and suggestions were provided for the preparation of documents from the intelligence analysis unit. Today, 362 law enforcement agencies have adopted the IALEIA standards (H. Dobbins, personal communication, January 26, 2011). While this may seem surprising low given the total number of agencies in the U.S. is around 18,000 (Reaves, 2007), as we shall see, there are many hurdles to overcome in the professionalization of this growing field.

**Box 6.1 The International Association of
Law Enforcement Intelligence Analysis (IALEIA)**

IALEIA, which was formed in 1981, provide services to law enforcement agencies interested in improving the skills of their analysts. According to the IALEIA (2010a) website:

> The purpose of IALEIA is to advance high standards of professionalism in law enforcement intelligence analysis at the local, state/provincial, national and international levels. Our aim is to enhance understanding of the role of intelligence analysis, encourage the recognition of intelligence analysis as a professional endeavor, develop International qualification and competency standards, reinforce professional concepts, devise training standards and curricula, furnish advisory and related services on intelligence analysis matters, conduct analytic-related research studies, and provide the ability to disseminate information regarding analytical techniques and methods.

For a nominal fee, you can join IALEIA to learn more about intelligence analysis, job opportunities, scholarships, and training materials. For more information, visit http://www.ialeia.org.

In 1989, the Society of Certified Criminal Analysts (SCCA) was created to complement the goals of IALEA. This organization has developed standards and testing for the professional certification of crime analysts and serves as the accreditation arm of IALEIA (see Box 6.2). Individuals who have attained certification as a crime analyst are held in high regard by their peers, and some agencies require certification for advancement. As of 2005, over 200 analysts from 11 countries including the U.S., U.K., South Africa, and Canada, have met the standards of this organization and are working as certified crime analysts. In order to become a certified criminal analyst, applicants must meet a number of criteria including the successful completion of a number of training courses, documented experience as a crime analyst, and the passing of an exam (for more information, see http://www.ialeia.org/scca).

Box 6.2 IALEIA Certification

The purpose of IALEIA Professional Certification is to foster and promote professional standards in analysis on an international level through continued training, education and career development. The following criteria are required to obtain IALEIA Certification:

1. Five years cumulative experience as an analyst, analytical supervisor or manager for law enforcement, a private corporation, or the military.

2. Completion of a minimum of 40 hours of basic analytical or intelligence training from an IALEIA recognized provider or agency. The training course(s) must encompass at least 9 of the 25 analytical standards as articulated in the Law Enforcement Analytical Standards (IALEIA, 2004).

3. A minimum of an Associate's Degree or the equivalent credits (generally 60), from an accredited academic or military program. The applicant must provide a copy of a transcript, or diploma or certificate earned.

4. Completion of the application form, submission of documentation of criteria met and payment of the non-refundable examination fee. If the applicant has been an IALEIA member for at least three years, the fee is $50. If the person is new to the association, the fee is $150, the equivalent of three years' membership.

5. Passing composite grade (70%) on the certification examination.

6. Membership in the International Association of Law Enforcement Intelligence Analysts.

7. If the applicant is not approved, the applicant will receive a letter outlining the supporting rationale for the decision.

8. Upon request and payment of a non-refundable $50 reexamination fee, the applicant may take the exam again in six months.

9. Analysts may apply only three times. If the applicant does not receive Professional Certification Committee approval on the third try, the individual is disqualified from any further IALEIA Professional Certification.

Source: IALEIA (2010b).

The International Association of Crime Analysts (IACA) was formed in 1990. The purpose of this organization is to encourage communication between crime analysts, so that they may learn from each other and improve their skills. The IACA maintains a "members only" list serve for the sharing of information and ideas. Students may join the organization and are then able to view employment opportunities, announcements of training courses, as well as to get a feel for the sorts of every day issues confronting crime analysts. This organization has around 1,500 members. Each year the organization holds an annual conference and offers many training and networking opportunities. Additionally, venders are on-hand to alert members to newly available technology and provide demonstrations.

Box 6.3 So You Want to Be a Crime Analyst?

As we tell our students, crime analysis is a great field to consider. The position can be very challenging and rewarding. Often, students wish to work in a law-enforcement related position but are put off by the odd working hours as well as the dangers associated with patrol. Crime analysis offers the best of all worlds. One can work on the identification and apprehension of criminals from the comfort of an air-conditioned office. Additionally, depending on the individual agency, crime analyst positions may be filled by non-sworn personnel. For those wishing to pursue a career as a crime analyst, the International Association of Crime Analysts offers a number of suggestions.

First, while there are few existing standards for employment and training, a degree in criminology/criminal justice, political science, or geographic information systems (GIS) may give an edge. When looking for an elective course, the IACA suggests the following areas:

- Criminology/Criminal Theory
- Geographic Information Systems (GIS)/Crime Mapping
- Criminal Justice/Social Science Research Methods & Statistics
- Improving your writing capabilities (creative and otherwise)
- The relationship between geographic and environmental factors and crime
- Police Science & Strategy
- Police Administration
- Desktop Publishing, Spreadsheet, and Database applications (especially Excel, Access, and similar applications)

Second, the options available to you locally should be explored. Some colleges and universities offer certification programs in crime analysis (e.g., University of Central Florida, Cal State Fullerton, Radford University, and Portland State University). Sign up for an internship with the crime analysis unit. Call your local Regional Community Policing Institute to see if there are any training courses you can take. There are also a number of private companies, such as the Alpha Group Center for Crime and Intelligence Analysis Training, which provide courses in crime and intelligence analysis at various locations throughout the country. Also, be aware that an in-depth background check will be required of applicants for crime analyst positions. This is true even for non-sworn personnel.

Sample Job Description/Position Announcement

CRIME ANALYST—Milwaukee Police Department

THE PURPOSE of this position is to collect, collate, analyze, disseminate, and evaluate crime data to discover developing trends, patterns, and changes in criminal activity, using mapping and other analytical software. The Crime Analyst works within the Intelligence Fusion Center of the Milwaukee Police Department.

ESSENTIAL FUNCTIONS:

- Produce information related to crime trends to assist the department's operational and administrative personnel in preventing and suppressing criminal activities, aiding the investigative process, increasing apprehension of offenders and clearing cases.

- Prepare data used to make recommendations on manpower deployment and resource allocation.

- Maintain statistical reports that detail the results of analysis, conclusions, and recommendations; prepare periodic statistical reports for department commanders and the Fire and Police Commission.

- Measure and forecast long-term public safety activity related to problem solving, intervention, and crime reduction efforts.

- Maintain databases on probation and parole information provided by the Wisconsin Department of Corrections and United States District Court.

- Collect, analyze and interpret data received from various departmental units and other law enforcement agencies.

- Maintain proficiency with GIS software and crime analysis methods and tools.

- Analyze crime information from Federal, State and local law enforcement agencies.

- Assist members of the department, elected officials and community members in obtaining data from systems to which they have access.

- Train department members on access to and analysis of data.

- Maintain maps for active court cases for use at trials.

- Perform other related duties as assigned or required.

MINIMUM REQUIREMENTS:

- Master's Degree in Geography, Public Policy, Public Administration, or other related fields of study with a concentration in statistics, research methods, intermediate or higher quantitative or qualitative methods from an accredited college or university AND at least one year of experience conducting research using complex statistical analysis and statistical computer programs

OR

- Bachelor's Degree in an academic field similar to the above from an accredited college or university and at least two years of experience conducting research using complex statistical analysis and statistical computer programs.

- Experience with the use of statistical computer programs, such as SPSS or SAS and experience working with GIS software, computer databases, spreadsheets, and Microsoft Office.

- Valid driver's license at time of appointment and throughout employment.

- Residency in the City of Milwaukee within six months of appointment and throughout employment.

PREFERRED QUALIFICATIONS:

- Knowledge of law enforcement computer systems (i.e., RMS, CAD).

- IACA certification desirable.

KNOWLEDGE, SKILLS, AND ABILITIES REQUIRED:

- Ability to collect, analyze, and interpret data and statistics using quantitative and qualitative methodology.

- Ability to prepare and present complex statistical reports.

- Ability to effectively participate in team efforts to improve/develop departmental programs and services.

- Ability to exercise judgment and discretion in completing assigned tasks.

- Ability to communicate orally and in writing to effectively prepare and present findings to Command-level officers and other local, State and Federal law enforcement officials.

- Knowledge and experience with computer systems in conducting research, analyzing data, and presenting and communicating findings.

THE CURRENT ANNUAL SALARY RANGE is $52,170–$63,366 annually with excellent benefits. Recruitment may be above the beginning of the range depending on experience.

Source: http://www.milwaukee.gov/jobs/CA.

Challenges with Crime Analysis: The "Haves" versus the "Have-Nots"

Crime analysis is a rapidly evolving field with a great deal of potential. While some agencies have enthusiastically embraced crime analysis, others seem to purposely resist the introduction of this new crime-fighting tool, dismissing it as a "fad" that is nothing more than formalized common sense. It is truly fascinating to see the great disparity in the funding, support, and respect given to different crime analysis units, some within the same jurisdiction. In Box 6.4, Haley et al. (1998) describe three stages of evolution of crime analysis units. While some agencies are outstanding examples of sophisticated units, others agencies do not have the capabilities (or perhaps the interest) to provide even the most rudimentary crime analysis.

Box 6.4 Stages of Development of Crime Analysis Units

I. Informal

- Based on an officer's memory and past experience
- Hampered by officer's limited duty time and interest and large volume of crime
- Subjective, biased, and out of date
- Time consuming
- Limited MO storage, analysis, and ability to recognize patterns
- Uncoordinated and ineffective communications

II. Formal Crime Analysis: Basic Operations

- Staffed by one or two people
- Normal business hour operations
- Analyzes three or four crime categories
- Manual filing and storage with limited cross-referencing
- Lacks crime prediction and known offender/MO analysis
- Limited visual geographical analysis, usually pin maps

III. Formal Crime Analysis: Advanced Operations

- Rapid correlations among offenses involving expanded numbers of crime categories
- Names of suspects provided for operational units
- Computer storage database with rapid searching criteria
- Large staff with a twenty-four hour operation
- Crime reports reviewed for quality before entered into database
- Complex storage of known offender information, including descriptions, vehicles, and MOs

Source: Haley, K., Todd, J., & Stallo, M. (1998). Crime analysis and the struggle for legitimacy. Presented at the annual meeting of the Academy of Criminal Justice Sciences in Albuquerque, NM, March 10–14, 1998.

As amazing as it might sound, it has been estimated that as many as one-third of law enforcement agencies still do not have computers (Pilant, 1999). Even when the agencies do have computers, there are no guarantees that the technology is being used efficiently. Kim worked with one local law enforcement agency that had no access to the Internet or email. At this same agency, she was told to never ask for the same information twice, since there would be no correspondence between the data. While attending a training session for crime analysis in the summer months of 2000, Kim met one crime analyst who was not provided with a desktop computer of her own and an agency statistician who had never taken a course in statistics. While there are still some crime analysts who have only a high school education (that may have been earned many, many years ago), other agencies have employed individuals with doctorate degrees in statistics to crunch their numbers.

Challenges with Crime Analysis: The Problem of Data

Even for the agencies that are truly committed to professional crime analysis, there are difficulties that must be dealt with especially with respect to data quality. One of the more serious problems is the fact that criminals do not respect jurisdictional boundaries. A robber may regularly seek out targets in areas that are policed by several different local agencies. The actual number of agencies with responsibility within a specified geographic area, say a county, may vary wildly. Currently, in Leon County, Florida, there are only three primary agencies that investigate crimes: Leon County Sheriff's Office, Florida State University Police Department, and Tallahassee Police Department. Conversely, in Miami-Dade County, Florida there are 36 different agencies! These totals do not include the various federal agencies that may be conducting investigations within the county. As we will see, this is a serious problem on several different levels.

In order to perform meaningful crime analysis, the analysts must have access to all of the incidents that occurred, not only within the bounds of his or her agency, but neighboring agencies as well. It can be very difficult for an analyst to gain access to the data gathered by a neighboring agency. In some areas there are very real "turf wars" between the various agencies and very little cooperation exists. Even if data sharing were possible, the animosity can be very strong between some agencies, precluding any meaningful cooperation. In areas where the relationships may be very good, agencies still may not be able to share information because of software compatibility issues. Different agencies may use different record management software programs that run on different operating systems. For example, in the state of Massachusetts there are many different data collection systems in use, from four major software vendors, with no easy method for the systems to communicate with each other (Bibel, 2000).

Now, the critical reader may have picked up on another point regarding the necessity for an analyst to have access to data from all crime incidents. You may recall our discussion of the dark figure of crime in Chapter 1. The analysts will only have access to incidents that are known to the police. If no one calls the police, then the analyst could be missing out on critical information. This can be even further complicated when one adds the additional layer of

data availability

complexity associated with multiple agencies. There may be differential rates of event-reporting between neighboring agencies. As described by Eck (2002), consider the case where citizens in one jurisdiction report 65% of the sexual assaults to their local police. However, in a neighboring jurisdiction, only 30% of the sexual assaults are reported. This different reporting rate can lead the analyst down the wrong road when trying to identify meaningful patterns in the data. It could very well be that the problem is more concentrated in the area with fewer reported rapes.

Types of Crime Analysis

What does a crime analyst have to do with our broader discussion of space, time, and crime? Crime analysts are asked to perform a variety of different tasks, not all of which are directly related to our immediate concerns. For example, one form of crime analysis is called **administrative crime analysis**. This type of crime analysis involves the provision of crime data to administrators, city council members, and citizens. The crime analyst may be asked to prepare a report for the city council on the feasibility and potential impact of a juvenile curfew ordinance; provide crime data for the preparation of grants; or maintain a crime analysis website for local citizens to access (Boba, 2009; Gottlieb et al., 1998).

We have also previously mentioned intelligence analysis, which is a specialized type of crime analysis. Intelligence analysis involves the study of "organized" criminal networks. Movies often portray a crime family or other criminal network in the form of a pyramid, with the kingpin or don at the top, followed by a layer of lieutenants, then a layer of lower-level people. This is an example of intelligence analysis. Intelligence analysts may use such tools as telephone toll analyses (to monitor who is connected to whom), financial or tax analyses, or various methods to study family or business relationships. In light of the September 11th attacks on the World Trade Center and the Pentagon, intelligence analysis has been used to monitor terrorist networks both domestically and abroad (Boba, 2009).

Criminal investigative analysis is often associated with the investigation of serial murders and is often known as "profiling." While this type of analysis was made wildly popular by the movie "Silence of the Lambs," in actuality, analysts at the local level rarely perform this function. Since serial murderers rarely respect jurisdictional lines, this type of analysis is normally conducted by federal law enforcement agencies. A victim may be picked up in one state, murdered in another, and the body recovered elsewhere (Boba, 2009; Gottlieb et al., 1998).

Of greater interest to our discussion of space, time, and crime are **tactical crime analysis** and **strategic crime analysis**. Tactical crime analysis is focused on more immediate concerns. On a daily basis, the analyst reviews available crime data gathered from arrest reports, field interview reports (FIRs), calls for service, trespass warnings and other available information to identify how, when, and where criminal activity has occurred. After reviewing this information, the analyst attempts to identify a potential **crime pattern** or **crime series**. Gottlieb et al. (1998) define a crime pattern as "the occurrence of similar offenses in a defined geographic area, either a single reporting district, a beat, or an entire jurisdiction" (p. 17–18). In a crime pattern, there is no evidence that the same person or persons committed the crimes. Conversely, a crime series is a type of crime pattern where there is evidence to believe that the crimes were committed by the same person or persons.[1] Tactical crime analysis also involves the identification of "hot spots" and "burning times," issues discussed at length in the next section.

While tactical crime analysis is primarily used to make more informed decisions regarding the deployment of policing resources, strategic crime analysis is more focused on long-term issues (Velasco & Boba, 2000). An easy way to keep the definitions of strategic versus tactical crime analysis separate is to focus on the timeliness of the information used. Tactical crime analysis uses data that have been collected over the past several days, while strategic crime analysis uses information that has been collected over a much longer period of time, normally a year or more (Canter, 2000). According to Boba (2009) strategic crime analysis is "the study of crime problems and other police-related issues to determine long-term patterns of activity as well as to evaluate police responses and organizational procedures" (p. 346). Along with crime data, the analyst also considers neighborhood characteristics such as the race, education level, family structure, and income level of local residents.

Space, Time, and Crime Analysis: Hot Spots, Hot Routes, and Burning Times

The analysis of hot spots has been described as the new "catchphrase" of research on crime (Swartz, 2000). The study of hot spots is, well, hot. Branti-

---

1. At this point, it is important to mention that definitions of "crime patterns" and "crime series" may vary between agencies. Some agencies will flip the definitions of these terms, while others will assign completely different definitions to the terms. Please bear in mind that crime analysis is an emerging profession with no standardized vocabulary.

Figure 6.1

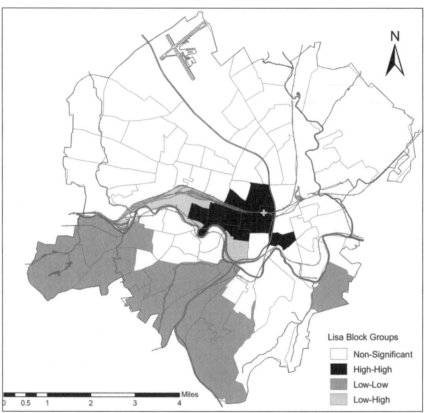

ngham and Brantingham (1999) argue that the study of hot spots has evolved
into "one of the most important contributions of environmental criminology
both to contemporary criminological research and to criminal justice practice" (p. 7). The Brantinghams define a hot spot as the concentration or cluster of crimes in space. In other words, crime event locations are not distributed
randomly in space. Hot spots are usually differentiated from high crime areas.
Hot spots are typically small geographic locations, such as an intersection or
even a single address, while a high crime area is geographically larger than a
hot spot (Farrel & Sousa, 2001). For example, Figure 6.1 illustrates the spatial
clustering of robbers in the city of Roanoke, Virginia at the Census block level
(Van Patten, McKeldin-Coner, & Cox, 2009).

Although various techniques can be used to identify hot spots on a planar surface, not all crimes occur in these locations. Some crime events take place along a linear network such as a street or a bus route. These areas are known as hot routes and have become the focus recent research efforts (see for example, Tompson, Patridge, & Shepherd, 2009; Van Patten, 2007). Finally, burning times are defined as "temporal clusters of crimes at specific, repeated moments in some temporal cycle" (Brantingham & Brantingham, 1999, p. 8).

It is important to recognize a few points regarding high crime areas, hot spots, hot routes, and burning times. First, not every target (i.e., individuals, homes, or businesses) in a high crime area will experience crime. No matter how large or small the area, some locations will have a higher number of crimes than others (Block & Block, 1995; Eck & Weisburd, 1995). Second, a hot spot may not be hot all of the time—you need to consider both the location and time of day. For example, there is a relatively small entertainment district in the Tampa, Florida area known as Ybor City. Without fail, when the bars close on Friday and Saturday nights at 3:00 a.m., the number of assaults, acts of vandalism, and incidents of driving under the influence predictably increase. However, during the day, the area reports far fewer criminal events when the streets are filled with business people and a few tourists looking for a quick bite for lunch.

A third point concerns the state of our knowledge regarding the temporal dimension of crime. While a good deal of research has been conducted on geographic hot spots, relatively little effort has gone into the examination of hot routes and burning times (Morgan, 2009; Ratcliffe, 2004; Youstin & Nobles, 2009). Part of the reason for this lack of attention concerns the relatively complex techniques for conducting hot route analysis and the fuzzy nature of the measurement of time by police agencies, respectively. Recall our discussion of exact time versus split time crimes in Chapter 1. For some types of crimes, it is relatively easy to get a good estimate for the time that a crime actually occurred. For other types of crimes, especially property crimes, the time of occurrence must be estimated. Crime analysts and researchers have a variety of ways to calculate their 'best guess' to estimate the actual time of the crime. These techniques have varying levels of sophistication. The strategies are impacted by the size of the time span between known events: i.e., when you left your house and when you returned to find your home had been burglarized. It is one thing if you ran down to the store for a few items and returned within a matter of minutes. It is quite another issue if you were gone for four days. This lack of a definitive measure is problematic for researchers and crime analysts, and has hindered the advancement of knowledge in this important area.

Causes of Hot Spots

How does a hot spot become hot? To answer this question, we will return to our earlier discussion of crime pattern theory in Chapter 3. Recall that according to the Brantinghams, nodes were defined as areas where people travel to and from, such as work, school, entertainment districts, or shopping areas. Nodes have the potential for becoming hot spots of criminal activity. The Brantinghams (1995) have defined three different kinds of hot spot places: crime generators, crime attractors, and crime enablers. Each type of hot spot evolves for very different reasons. Understanding the underlying causes is essential for successfully reducing crime in a hot spot area (Clarke & Eck, 1995).

Crime generators are places that attract large numbers of both offenders and victims, such as shopping malls, sporting events, parades and other festivities. Some areas, such as bus/subway interchanges or huge 'park and ride' parking lots, may become crime generators due to the large number of people that come and go. These locations have a high number of criminal incidents simply because of the sheer volume of people interacting in one area. Large numbers of potentially unprotected targets mingle with motivated offenders, creating many opportunities for crimes to occur. One possible solution to curbing crime at this type of hot spot is to increase the level of protection, possibly through increased police or security presence.

Crime attractors are a bit different than crime generators. Crime generators are places that are attractive to offenders simply due to the nature of the activity that occurs at that particular location—offenders are looking to have a good time and not really actively searching out a potential target to victimize. Conversely, a crime attractor location is known to provide many criminal opportunities and motivated offenders are drawn to these locations for the purpose of committing crimes. Areas with open-market drug sales, bar districts, large unsecured parking areas, or known prostitution strolls would be examples of crime attractor hot spots. To reduce crime at these locations, offenders must somehow be discouraged from coming to the location

Crime enablers are locations that have little or no regulation of behavior. The lack of control increases the likelihood for crime to occur. According to Clarke and Eck (2005), changes in the level of guardianship may be abrupt (such as when the services of a bouncer at a bar are eliminated) or may be gradual over time, as the level of monitoring slowly erodes. Because of the unsavory reputation, many victims tend to avoid going to these locations. Unknowing or unwitting attendees tend to put themselves at high risk because there are relatively few targets for the motivated offenders to prey upon. Crime may be reduced at these locations by reinforcing the level of guardianship.

Identifying Crime Hot Spots

There are different types of hot spot analysis (Eck et al., 2005). Deciding on which approach is best depends in large part on the size of the geographic area of concern, which can vary from a small geographic location, like a specific address, to larger area like Census blocks, block groups, or tracts. The geographic level of analysis will correspond to the particular question that the analyst is trying to answer.

A wide range of different methods and techniques can be used to characterize crime hot spots (Eck et al., 2005). These techniques fall into three different categories; and although an in-depth discussion of the statistics behind each method is beyond the scope of this text each approach is presented below:

1. *Global statistical tests* such as mean center, standard deviation distance and ellipse, and global tests for clustering, including the Nearest Neighbor Index, Moran's I and Geary's C statistic;
2. *Hot spot mapping techniques* such as point mapping, spatial ellipses using hierarchical or K-means clustering, thematic mapping using enumeration areas, quadrat mapping, and kernel density estimation; and
3. *Local indicators of spatial association statistics* such as the Gi and Gi* statistics.

While the hot spot techniques listed above serve a somewhat different purpose, they are all concerned with characterizing hot spots in an effort to develop a better understanding of where crimes occur, which can ultimately lead to the design of intervention strategies and the development of prospective crime mapping. No single technique has emerged as the "best" one for crime hot spot mapping, and there has been surprisingly little comparative research on their strengths and weaknesses, with some notable exceptions (Chainey, 2005; Chainey, Tompson, & Uhlig, 2008; Grubesic, 2006).

Regardless of technique, most crime hot spot analyses are based on the same thing: a dataset of individual locations, with each point representing one or multiple crime incidents. The dataset of crime incidents is *assumed* to be a very good representation of the actual crime incidents (i.e., the sample is complete or very close to complete and the locations are accurate). These locations are usually pulled from an agencies records management system geocoded.[2] As noted above, the comparison of different hot spot analysis tech-

---

2. In a Geographic Information System (GIS), addresses are converted to features on a map through the geocoding process. Geocoding is the process of assigning an X-Y coordi-

niques has received some attention from researchers; however, far less attention has been paid to the quality of the geocoding process and its effect on
hot spot analysis.

Types of Hot Spots: Ratcliffe's Hot Spot Matrix

Jerry Ratcliffe has done a good deal of research on hot spots of criminal activities and is one of a handful of researchers who has incorporated temporal
dimensions with spatial analysis (see, for example, Ratcliffe 2000; 2002; 2004;
2006). Ratcliffe has developed a classification scheme that incorporated both
the spatial and temporal aspects of hot spots. Using this scheme, he then proposed a practical matrix outlining strategies used to combat crime that address
spatio-temporal considerations.

First, we begin this discussion with a description of Ratcliffe's classification
schemes. Once an agency has identified a hot spot, the actual criminal events
contained within this hot spot can take on a few different patterns based on time
and location. With respect to spatial considerations, there are three broad categories: dispersed, clustered, and hotpoint. **Dispersed** hot spots contain criminal events that are fairly evenly spread throughout the hot spot. Obviously,
the locations for these events are still clustered geographically (hence its identification as a hot spot of crime), but it is within this area defined as a hot spot
that the relatively even dispersion of criminal events takes place. **Clustered** hot
spots contain one or more specific places that account for the majority of the
criminal events. Ratcliffe uses the example of a hot spot that includes a sports
stadium within its geographic bounds. Criminal events tend to cluster at the
location of the stadium, but other areas surrounding the stadium also contain
high crime areas. Finally, a **hotpoint** hot spot has one single location that trig-
gers the hot spot. All crimes are located at a single, identifiable location. Returning to the Brantingham's discussion, this single hotpoint location would
best be described as a crime attractor or crime generator.

Ratcliffe further defined hot spots based on their temporal dimension. Criminal events within a hot spot may be classified into three temporal categories:
diffused, focused, and acute. **Diffused** hot spots contain crimes that happen
at any time during the day or night; there is no identifiable peak clustering of
crimes within the hot spot. This could be a "real" diffusion, or one that is an

---

nate pair to the description of a place by comparing the descriptive location-specific elements
to those in reference data. The geocoding process is defined as the steps involved in trans-
lating an address entry, searching for the address in the reference data, and delivering the
best candidate or candidates as a point feature on the map.

Figure 6.2

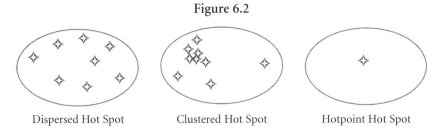

| Dispersed Hot Spot | Clustered Hot Spot | Hotpoint Hot Spot |

Adapted from Ratcliffe (2004).

artifact of the problematic nature of time. That is, if the time span is too great, one cannot determine with any confidence whether or not a peak exists within the hot spot. **Focused** hot spots contain certain blocks of time that have more criminal activity than others. While crime events do occur throughout the 24-hour period, significant clustering of events can be identified. Last but not least, **acute** hot spots contain criminal events that are clustered within a relatively small window of time. The difference between a focused and an acute hot spot is really one of degree. In an acute hot spot, there are very, very few crimes that occur outside of the acute time to the point where there may be some time periods in which no crimes occur. In a focused hot spot, the temporal clustering of criminal events is not quite as pronounced.

So far in this discussion we have treated the spatial and temporal aspects of hot spots as separate entities. While this provides a good starting point for our discussion, Ratcliffe's intention was to classify hot spots on both dimensions. For example, you could have a hot spot with criminal events that are dispersed spatially but exhibit focused temporal clustering. In order to mount a defense against criminal events, the analyst must not only recognize that there is a hot spot, but he or she must also have a strong understanding of both the temporal and spatial dimensions of what is actually happening within a hot spot.

In a nice transition to our next section on directed patrols, Ratcliffe then incorporated the various spatial and temporal dimensions of hot spots into a practical matrix of use to law enforcement professionals, providing suggestions for strategies that vary based on the type of hot spot problem. At one extreme of the table are hot spots that are dispersed spatially and diffused temporally—criminal events are clustered within a relatively small hot spot, but the events are spread evenly by time and place throughout this geographic area. At the other end we have hot spots that are best described as hot points spatially and acute temporally. This would mean that there is a single location

Table 6.1 Ratcliffe's Policing Hotspot Matrix

	Spatial Dimensions		
Temporal Dimensions	Dispersed	Clustered	Hotpoint
Diffused	Uniform vehicle patrols, architectural changes, public education campaign	Random breath tests, foot patrols, architectural changes, publicity campaign	Roadblocks, plain clothes patrols, breath tests, use of private security
Focused	Uniform vehicle and foot patrols, enhanced lighting, public education campaign	Vehicle and foot patrols, random breath tests, private security, improved lighting	Surveillance units, plain clothes foot patrols, CCTV
Acute	Unmarked vehicle patrols, private security, improved lighting	Surveillance and plain clothes patrols, CCTV	Surveillance, arrest squads, CCTV, unmarked police units

Adapted from Ratcliffe (2004, p. 17).

within a hot spot that is only hot for a relatively short time period. The actual strategy employed by an agency or place manager needs to carefully consider when and where the criminal events occur within the hot spot. As noted by Ratcliffe, as crime becomes more concentrated both spatially and temporally, law enforcement tactics move from more highly visible strategies (such as unformed patrols, or roadblocks) to strategies that are much more likely to result in detection and apprehension, such as the use of aggressive arrest squads. Ratcliffe's Policing Hot Spot Matrix for possible use at a problem housing complex is presented in Table 6.1.

Targeting Hot Spots: Directed Patrols

Lawrence Sherman and his colleagues have done a great deal of research on hot spots and the distribution of crime in urban areas (see, for example, Sherman, 1995; Sherman, Gartin, & Buerger, 1989; Sherman, Schmidt, & Velke, 1992; Sherman, Shaw, & Rogan, 1995; Sherman & Weisburd, 1995). In one study, Sherman et al. (1989) conducted an analysis of the calls for service to the police in the city of Minneapolis. The researchers found that half of the 323,000 calls could be traced to only 3% of the addresses in the city. The concentration was even greater if one only considered predatory crimes such as robbery, auto theft, and criminal sex acts. A single address accounted for 810 calls for police service over a one-year period. Conversely, no calls for service were received from 60% of the addresses in the city. If police efforts could be concentrated to target these "repeat customers," both the crime rate and the workload of the police could significantly be reduced.

Sherman, et al. (1995) tested the impact of concentrated police efforts in a hot spot area. In beat 144 located in Kansas City, the homicide rate was nearly 20 times greater than the national average. Additionally, there were 14 rapes, 72 armed robberies, and 222 aggravated assaults in this single, relatively small beat. Drive-by shootings were also common in this relatively small area. In this particular study, a technique called **directed patrol** was used to target gun crimes in hot spot locations within beat 144 during the burning times of 7 p.m. to 1 a.m., seven days a week.

In contrast to random patrol, directed patrol provides officers with specific instructions on who or what they should be focusing their attention on. Some agencies employ directed patrol plans for the officers to use in their uncommitted time (when they are not responding to a call, for example), while other agencies free officers from responding to 911 calls, making directed patrol activities their sole responsibility. In the Kansas City study, additional officers assigned to the hot spot areas did not answer calls for service, but were expected to focus exclusively on gun detection and gun seizures. Sherman and his colleagues found that the directed patrol efforts were successful. Significant reductions were found in the number of gun-related crimes, including homicides and drive-by shootings. Additionally, citizens living in the target area reported lower levels of fear, greater neighborhood satisfaction, and lower perceptions of social and physical disorder. The researchers concluded that directed patrol efforts targeted at hot spots was a cost-effective means of fighting gun-related crime. Successful directed patrol efforts have also been noted in targeting drug markets (Weisburd & Mazerolle, 2000), high crime taverns (Sherman et al., 1992), arson (Martin, Barnes, & Britt, 1998), residential burglary (Reno, 1998), and even serial rapists (LeBeau, 1992).

There appears to be a law of diminishing returns at work with respect to the length of time a patrol officer remains in a hot spot for the purpose of deterring crime and the amount of time that the hot spot remains crime-free. In the late 1980s, the Minneapolis Police Department initiated directed patrols at hot spot locations during burning times. Patrols were shifted from low-crime areas to provide targeted police presence at 55 street corner hot spots during peak crime times. Koper (1995) found that the longer the police remained at a specific location, the greater the length of time until the first criminal incident occurred—up to a point. The correlation remained strong for each minute of police presence up to 15 minutes. At that point, the relationship between police presence and crime incidents began to reverse itself. Therefore, according to Koper, the most effective amount of time for a patrol officer to remain at a hot spot for the purpose of deterring criminal activities is no more than 15 minutes. At that point, the patrol officer should move on to another hot spot location.

It is the responsibility of the crime analyst to gather the daily reports of criminal activity, identify potential hot spots, burning times, or other patterns that may exist, and assist in the development of directed patrol plans to resolve the crime problem. In this next section, one example of the use of hot spot analysis in identifying precursors to terrorism is provided. At the end of this Chapter, in a second Spotlight on Practice, you will read over a description of a typical day in the life of a tactical crime analyst.

Spotlight on Practice II

Crime Analysis Group/Analytical Section
Las Vegas Metropolitan Police Department
Intelligence Led Policing Bureau
Patrick Baldwin, Shannon Smith, and Marina Gonzalez

Crime Mapping and Criminal Precursors to Terrorism

Terrorist precursor crimes are defined as unlawful acts that could facilitate a terrorist attack, or campaign. The extent of terrorist precursor criminal activity in the United States is unknown. There are some indications that it may be widespread. Some have suggested that given the high per capita income of United States citizens, an open society, and the presence of terrorist groups that criminal precursor crime may be worse in the United States compared to other locations. The American Terrorism Study found that approximately one-third of the various activities that terrorists engage in to facilitate an attack were criminal and that these crimes could be taken into account when trying to isolate potential terrorist activity from all other activities.

Another study focused on identifying and analyzing hostile surveillance activity using suspicious activity calls for service (CFS) data. Hostile surveillance is a preparatory behavior and is defined as selecting targets, asking probing questions, observing and testing security measures. The study suggests that these activities offer the best opportunity for local law enforcement agencies to prevent and deter terrorist attacks by identifying "potential vulnerabilities or

Figure 6.3

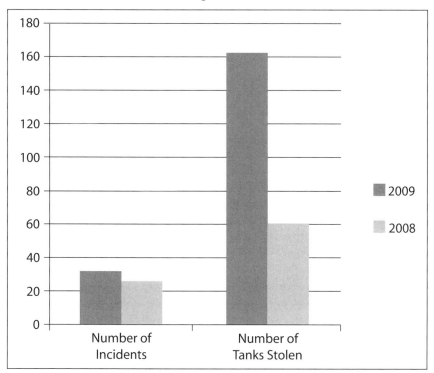

areas of interest to likely terrorists, including the times and locations of pre-planning activity".

In December 2009, using a CFS data-mining query developed by Southern Nevada Counter-Terrorism (SNCTC) analysts, a significant increase in the number of stolen propane tanks was identified. The number of incidents did not increase significantly; however, the number of tanks taken more than doubled when compared to the previous year (Figure 6.3).

Propane tank thefts are of concern to fusion center analysts and personnel based on their potential use in terrorism. In 2004, Dhiran Barot plotted to use limousines packed with flammable gas cylinders (propane, acetylene, and oxygen) and explosives to blow up underground parking garages in Britain—known as the "Gas Limos Project." In a manuscript, found in an al Qaeda safe house titled "Rough Presentation for Gas Limos Project," the choice of using gas cylinders was made based on availability and because they could be obtained without attracting much attention from security: "The cylinders are easily available to the general public without requiring illegal activities, licenses, or hijacking etc. (We can achieve similar results from a large grouping of gas cylinders as we would from a gas tanker.)" Throughout the manuscript the importance of appearing innocuous while planning and testing the attack is stressed.

The incidents of stolen propane tanks were mapped to identify any spatial relationships and to determine proximity to any critical infrastructure, especially near Las Vegas Boulevard South (The Strip). Many of the world's largest hotels, resorts, and casinos reside on the Strip. The Strip is also one of the most visible tourist destinations in the world. Using ESRI's Arc 9, hotspots were generated using the Kernel Density tool that is part of the Spatial Analyst extension. Overall, the maps revealed a strong correlation to industrial land use areas. The business types victimized most often were construction, industrial, and propane supply companies located in industrial land use areas. Retail chain stores such as Walmart, CVS Pharmacy, Walgreens, as well as gas stations and grocery stores, were also victimized; however, these locations were victimized much less frequently.

Further analysis revealed that the number of tanks taken was to some extent correlated to the business type. As one might expect, more tanks were taken per incident from retail stores and gas stations where the tanks are easily accessible—kept together in a "cage"—than from industrial type businesses. In 2008, three incidents of propane tank theft were linked to a chain retail store, compared to six incidents in 2009. Furthermore, the incidents of propane theft from retail stores in 2009 were localized to a single area that can be clearly seen in the hotspot analysis map (Figures 6.4 and 6.5).

Once the source of the propane tank theft increase was identified, analysis was conducted to identify why the increase occurred. Several hypotheses were developed and investigated including: terrorism, recycled/scraped propane tanks, use in the production of methamphetamines, and black market activity.

There was no intelligence that indicated that the tanks were taken to be used as an improvised explosive device (IED) for terroristic activity. Operators of local recyclers and scrap yards were interviewed and it was found that they only accept used tanks and that they would not recycle a new tank. There was also no increase of used propane tanks at any of the interviewed scrap yard/recycling centers.

Local narcotics units and DEA representatives were interviewed and it was their opinion that the tanks were not associated with methamphetamine production. Finally, intelligence gathered from arrests in other jurisdictions led to the conclusion that the increase in propane tank thefts was due to black market activity. Local retailers were charging $40–$50 per tank, while the tanks were being sold on the street for about $20.

Figure 6.4

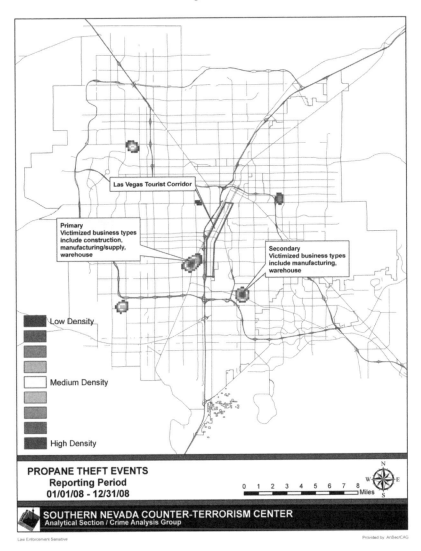

Although black market activity was determined to be the cause of the increase, SNCTC personnel continue to analyze propane thefts and advise local law enforcement on their potential use in terrorist activity.

Figure 6.5

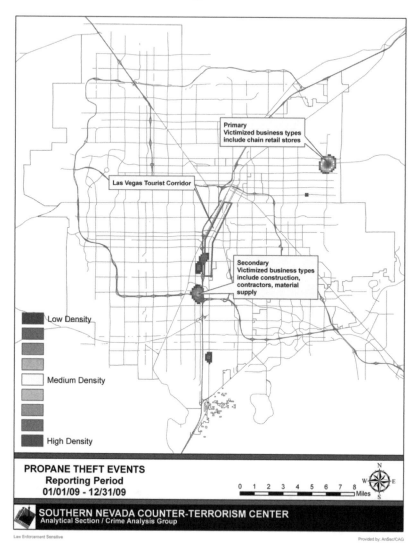

Another use of CFS data mining and mapping in preventing terrorism is the proliferation of false 911 calls. In 2010, the Las Vegas Valley began to experience 911 calls claiming there was a shooting or a fight. These calls were

Figure 6.6

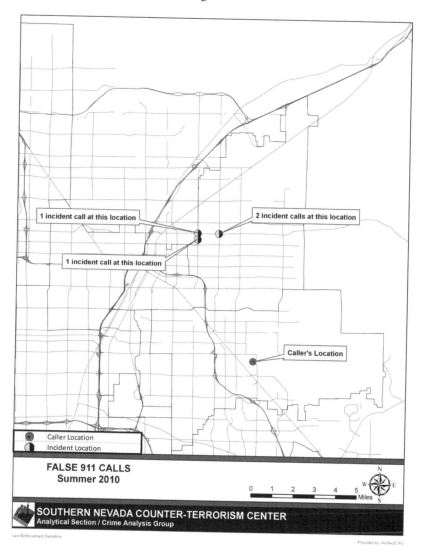

frequently made from cell phones. When officers arrived, there was no such activity. In a few instances, the caller would claim to be watching the police officers respond. This type of activity is of great concern as it may identify pre-operational surveillance of police responses or procedures.

During one scenario, a caller was claiming there was an officer involved shooting and when officers arrived there was no criminal activity or crime scene. The Las Vegas Metropolitan Police Department's Computer-Aided Dispatch (CAD) tracked the caller to the nearest cell tower to get an approximate location of the caller. The calls received were all made from the same cell phone number. The caller's location and the CFS locations were then mapped using ESRI's Arc 9 for comparison (Figure 6.6). There was no correlation between the caller's location and the CFS locations. However, mapping did reveal that the caller's cell phone number plotted in the same location and all of the CFS locations occurred within close proximity to each other. Once this was determined an officer safety advisory was released and CFS in the area were closely monitored. These false 911 calls stopped shortly thereafter. This has become a nationwide trend and SNCTC analysts continue use of CFS data mining queries to identify these types of CFS and use mapping to locate the cell phone callers in relation to the CFS.

Authors Affiliation

Baldwin is the manager of the Crime Analysis Group at the Southern Nevada Counter-Terrorism Center. A member of the Las Vegas Metropolitan Police Department for nine years, his previous assignments were as the gang criminal intelligence analyst and a patrol bureau crime analyst. Mr. Baldwin also has worked as a senior research analyst and program manager for the Illinois Criminal Justice Information Authority and as an analyst for the Schaumburg Police Department, Schaumburg Illinois. He is an alumnus of the University of Illinois, Chicago.

Shannon Smith is a crime analyst assigned to the Southern Nevada Counter-Terrorism Center where she is the liaison analyst between the Crime Analysis Group and the Counter-Terrorism Analysis Group. A member of the Las Vegas Metropolitan Police Department for four years, she is a graduate of Boise State University.

Marina Gonzalez is a crime analyst assigned to the Southern Nevada Counter-Terrorism Center where she is responsible for crime series and crime trends. A member of the Las Vegas Metropolitan Police Department for four years, she is a graduate of New Mexico State University.

Strategic Crime Analysis: The Next Step

As phrased by Bruce (2000, p. 10), tactical crime analysis is described as "where the action is," "urgent *and* important," and "dealing with the immediate, the critical, the here and now." When you read Bruce's daily journal, you get a feel for the almost frenzied flurry of activity surrounding the efforts in quickly gathering, analyzing, and disseminating timely information to the troops. When working in the tactical dimension, crime analysts are under great pressure to quickly identify patterns, series, and hot spots for activity. The strategic analysis of crime is a more reflective process. For example, in an analysis of the calls for service data, the tactical analysts may identify a specific neighborhood as having a higher than normal level of requests for police services. However, the analysts may not have the time (or all of the necessary information) to develop a long-term solution to this problem. One of the important elements of strategic analysis is to use the tactical data to identify problems and develop innovative solutions to these problems. Strategic crime analysis is an essential component of problem-oriented policing.

Wolves and Ducks and Dens: Oh My!

The most important conclusion of this book is that crime is not evenly distributed among persons, places, or times. It has been argued that 10% of the offenders committing the most crimes are responsible for about 50% of all crimes; 10% of the most victimized people are involved in about 40% of all crimes; and that 10% of the locations with the most crime are responsible for about 60% of all crime (Eck, 2001; Sacco & Kennedy, 2002).

Tactical crime analysts may determine that a neighborhood has a high level of criminal activities. However, one cannot be sure whether or not the high rate of crime is due to a problem with "ravenous wolves," "sitting ducks," or a "den of iniquity" (Clarke & Eck, 2005; Eck, 2001). A wolf problem involves a high number of motivated offenders who attack different targets at different locations. The guardianship of these locations is weak, leaving the target vulnerable for attack. A sitting duck problem involves a rather small number of victims who are repeatedly targeted by different offenders. A good example of a sitting duck is a taxi driver, who is repeatedly robbed by different offenders at different places. Taxi drivers are particularly vulnerable because they often come into contact with motivated offenders at many different locations and the guardianship at these locations may be questionable at best. Finally, a den of iniquity occurs when different offenders and different victims, or targets, converge at the same location. A shopping mall that has many criminal incidents involving different offenders and different targets is a good example of a den problem. How effectively a police agency responds to a troubled area will depend on careful analysis of the data. Does the agency have a wolf problem, a duck problem, a den problem, or some combination of the three?

Additionally, the police may not have access to all of the necessary information to accurately diagnose the problem. It is important to keep in mind that even the best crime analysis is based on the data that police have access to. If citizens do not call the police to inform them of a crime problem, then there are no reports of the incident. If there are no reports, then crime analysts do not have the input to identify possible patterns of criminal activity. While a police officer may possess a good deal of familiarity with his or her beat, the quality and quantity of this information cannot compare to the intimate knowledge held by a local resident. In order to correctly identify problematic conditions and develop successful plans to address these problems, police need to tap into the informal database of the local community.

Strategic Crime Analysis and Community Policing Problem Solving Efforts

In Chapter 4, the underlying concepts of community policing and problem oriented policing were discussed at length. Under a community policing philosophy, local law abiding residents are viewed as partners in the safeguarding of their neighborhood. Police cannot successfully reduce crime and improve the quality of life in a neighborhood without the cooperation and input of the people who live there.

Crime analysis has been described as the most important element of the problem-solving process (Bynum, 2001). Gotleib et al. (1998) assert that it is "incomprehensible" to believe that problem solving community policing programs can be successful without the input of crime analysis. Problem-solving policing assumes that patterns and trends in community problems may be detected. "Community problems" may involve criminal activity or quality of life issues, or some combination of both. Correct identification of patterns and trends will lead the police and the community to understand why these conditions exist and ultimately develop methods to resolve the problems (Bynum, 2001).

The SARA Model: Analysis in Action

The SARA model is the most commonly used course of action in the process of problem solving. This four-step model involves scanning, analysis, response, and assessment (Eck & Spellman, 1987). Data recently collected from law enforcement agencies with more than 100 full-time sworn officers indicates about 1-in-5 actively encourages patrol officers to engage in SARA-type problem-solving projects on their beats (B. Reaves, personal communication, January 26, 2011).

Scanning is the first step in the problem-solving process. During this phase, the actual problem is identified through a preliminary review of available information. Data from a variety of sources are considered, such as calls for service, reports of criminal incidents, perceptions of patrol officers assigned to the area, and citizen input. At this stage, the goal is to try to move beyond the rather simple conceptualization of singular incidents. Instead, scanning involves standing back and trying to see "the big picture." For example, a patrol officer may move from one call for service to another, viewing each call as a singular, isolated incident. The purpose of the scanning phase is to move beyond this level and identify clusters or groups of similar, related, or recurring problems (Boba, 2009). Once the clusters or groups have been identified, the agency must prioritize these problems for consideration and select which issues will be addressed.

The **analysis** phase involves careful consideration of a variety of data sources in order to answer the questions of what, where, when, how, and why the problem has developed. While police agencies have demonstrated success in the identification of problems, proficiency during the analysis stage has proven to be more challenging (Bynum, 2001). One of the problems is that agency personnel may *assume* they already know what the "true" nature and cause of the problem is. As a result, an agency may feel that an exhaustive analysis of the problem is a waste of time (Boba, 2001). However, data collected during the analysis stage can provide information that the agency may not have considered important or relevant.

During the analysis stage, it is important to solicit input from as many sources as possible. Full knowledge of an area's problems cannot be gained from a single source (Block, 1998). For example, a patrol officer working in a specific geographic area may have a different view than an officer assigned to a gang or narcotics unit working in the same zone. A local resident may offer additional information, as can the owner of a neighborhood business. Community social service workers may also provide relevant input. This becomes even more important when one considers the element of time: The manager of a local bank may have a much different perspective than the owner of a convenience store that is open 24 hours a day.

During the **response** phase, the police agency solicits input from local residents, business owners, various community groups, schools, churches, and other interested partners to develop innovative solutions to the problem (Gotlieb et al., 1998). If a neighborhood problem involves a large number of juveniles hanging around on local street corners with nothing to do, the agency would be wise to include representatives from this group in the development of possible solutions. If an agency requests input from a number of different sources, then the agency will (hopefully) end up with a larger number of possible solutions from which to choose the best course of action. Some of the action plans will not be feasible due to financial or legal constraints. Once the police and their new partners have agreed on the best course of action, the plan should be implemented.

Finally, the **assessment** phase involves an evaluation of the effectiveness of the chosen response. The assessment phase allows the agency to determine whether or not the action plan worked as planned. In some cases, the assessment may show that the initial problem was misidentified during the scanning phase, or that more detailed analysis was needed. As an example of the SARA process in action, I (Kim) will walk you through an experience I had with the City of Pensacola, Florida Police Department.

The SARA Process: One Agency's Experience

A few years ago I (Kim) was asked by the Pensacola Police Department to assist them with a Community Oriented Policing Services (COPS) grant. As per the requirements of the grant, the agency used the SARA model to identify a community problem, perform careful analysis, develop innovative solutions to the problem, and assess their efforts.

Prior to the application for the funds, agency personnel set up the scanning phase in order to identify the problem that would be targeted by the grant funds. Based on a preliminary evaluation of the data available to the PPD, a relatively small lower income area known as the East King Tract was selected as the targeted neighborhood. The area had recently experienced an increase in the number of calls for service, and local residents were repeatedly calling in complaints to the police regarding the open sales of drugs. The PPD was also aware of a number of law abiding elderly residents who resided in the area for a number of years and had previously been active in a local Neighborhood Crime Watch Program. Conditions in the neighborhood had deteriorated to the point where the Crime Watch members were so afraid of being victimized that they no longer held meetings. More and more renters moved into the area and a number of run-down uninhabited homes were being used as crack houses. A number of vacant lots were overgrown with weeds and strewn with garbage. It was not uncommon to see inoperable vehicles parked in driveways and on unkempt lawns without a current license plate. Based on the preliminary scanning meetings with community leaders, neighborhood watch organizers, patrol officers, supervisory personnel, elected officials, and local business owners, the grant was written to develop innovative strategies to curb the open drug sales and to improve the quality of life for residents in the neighborhood.

During the analysis phase, the PPD tried to gather information about problems in the East King Tract from a variety of sources. The agency analyzed its own internal sources of data, looking back at calls for service, field interview reports, arrest records, and crime reports for the past 12 months. Additionally, specialized units in the PPD were asked for their input. The agency also turned to external sources for information. A telephone survey of local residents was conducted in order to solicit their opinions regarding the conditions in their neighborhood and possible suggestions for improvement. Meetings were scheduled with local residents to discuss possible solutions to the problems. Community outreach workers at the local recreation center were contacted as well. Based on the data collected during the analysis phase, it was determined that what had appeared to be two separate problems—drug dealing and the deteriorating physical appearance of the neighborhood—were actually part of the same problem. Drug dealers were hiding their cache of drugs in the overgrown vacant lots and the abandoned vehicles. If these convenient hiding places could be eliminated, then the drug dealers would (hopefully) stop selling drugs in the neighborhood.

The initial response phase involved a virtual frenzy of activity. Agency personnel videotaped the area, carefully noting the locations of unsightly vacant lots, abandoned houses, and dilapidated cars. Officers went door-to-door, alerting residents to the agency's efforts and asking for their help. The PPD also contacted the Codes Enforcement Department and the Litter and Sanitation Department, asking for their assistance. Owners of rental properties, who often resided out of state, were alerted to problems with their properties and provided with a number of options to assist the police in correcting them, such as allowing the police to issue trespass warnings to unauthorized individuals loitering on the properties. Dozens of vehicles were towed from the area, and several abandoned houses were scheduled to be condemned. A major clean-up effort was scheduled, with representatives from the PPD, various community groups, local church members, volunteers from the University, and local elected officials all chipping in to help remove more than 13 tons of trash from this neighborhood. The physical appearance of the neighborhood greatly improved.

The PPD also conducted a number of undercover drug sweeps in the area, targeting local street dealers. Local residents were encouraged to contact the PPD when they witnessed drug activity and were provided with the pager numbers of the crime analysts to alert the unit when, where, and how such activities were taking place. The crime analysts kept a careful record of each call, and quickly fed the information back to the patrol officers and specialized units responsible for the area.

Several months later, an assessment of the PPD's efforts was conducted. While drug-related arrests and calls for service were down, unfortunately, the deteriorated conditions of the neighborhood had returned. Much to the distress of the PPD, many of the vacant lots were again strewn with garbage. The agency had felt that they had successfully repaired this "broken window," but obviously there was still a problem, and an unsightly one at that. Residents were frustrated with the police, and felt that the neighborhood looked worse now than when the grant had begun. The agency personnel were quite discouraged and scheduled a second clean up. Once again local residents and volunteers from a variety of community programs worked to pick up the lots, throwing out several tons of trash, abandoned sofas, and even a discarded toilet. The agency personnel recognized that these cleanups provided a temporary solution. A long-term solution to this problem was needed.

The agency personnel then went back to the drawing board, or in SARA terms, returned to the analysis phase. Why did the level of trash return so quickly? Where had they gone wrong? It was brought to the attention of the PPD that local residents could be seen dumping their trash in the vacant lots in the wee hours of the morning. Additionally, local residents also reported that people would "steal" water from their neighbors, filling up gallon jugs with water from a garden house. Based on the information provided by the local residents, the PPD began to do a little homework.

The PPD contacted several county records offices and was able to determine that a sizeable number of residents living in the East King Tract had no regular trash removal service. In this particular area, residents could choose from a number of different trash removal companies and were independently responsible for contracting and paying for these services. The East King Tract was a lower income community and many of the residents simply could not afford to pay for such services. Since these residents had no way to legally dispose of their trash, they would simply wait until late at night and dump the trash in the vacant lots. The PPD also determined that several homes did not have their water activated, thereby necessitating the theft of water from other sources. Thus, the PPD set out to identify charitable organizations or other funding sources to provide trash service and water to those families who could not afford to pay for such amenities.

The experience I gained by working with the PPD on this project was truly invaluable. I was able to observe crime analysts perform tactical crime analysis as they prepared timely reports for the patrol officers and narcotics unit, based on daily internal crime data and the input of the concerned citizens. I was also able to watch as a strategic crime analysis function unfolded. The East King Tract problem solving effort was an informative exercise in how a law enforcement agency uses various sources of input to detect long-term patterns of activity, develop responses to these patterns, assess the effectiveness of the response, and modify the response as needed.

I also saw how input from the crime analysts contributed to the quality of data that was collected by the line officers. For example, a call for service is initially classified based on the information provided by the complaining citizens. This initial classification may be different from the actual situation. Often, residents would phone in complaints about drug dealers hanging out on the corner. When the officer responded, the "perpetrators" (1) may have left the area; (2) may have turned out to be completely innocent teenagers who were bored and had nothing better to do; or (3) were actually drug dealers who fled the scene once they saw the patrol car approaching. Unfortunately, for the crime analysts, all three of these situations were closed out with no report written. In fact, prior to the intensive scrutiny given to the data generated by the patrol officers as part of the East King Tract problem solving effort, the majority of calls for service were disposed of with no final report completed by the patrol officers. The crime analysis unit was able to convince the supervisors that follow-up data from the patrol officers was invaluable, and the agency modified its report writing policies to assist in the data collection efforts.

Summary

The analysis of crime data has become an important tool for many law enforcement agencies in their efforts to reduce crime and improve the quality of life for community residents. Crime analysis can provide answers to such questions as who, what, where, when, and how criminal acts and other problematic conditions have occurred. In this chapter, the various types of crime analysis have been discussed with a focus on tactical and strategic crime analysis. In the next chapter, crime mapping will be introduced, one of the specialized tools available to the crime analyst.

Spotlight on Practice III

Tactical Crime Analysis
Musings from the Cambridge Police Department*
Christopher Bruce

Tactical crime analysis is the meat and drink of a crime analyst's life. It is fast-paced and exciting, dealing with the immediate, the critical, the here and now. It's dirty, grueling, arms-in-the-mud work that has to be done every day. There is no rest for tactical crime analysts, no breaks. Strategic crime analysts can stay in their ivory towers, dithering with their inferential statistics and longterm trends, afraid to get their hands dirty. They can work on the new redistricting plan for next year; we'll be identifying, analyzing, and putting an end to that robbery pattern that's happening right now. Tactical crime analysis is where the action is—which is why it's also called "action-oriented analysis." Both urgent and important, tactical crime analysis is the crime analyst's A-1 priority. When it's effective, it's done first—before you answer your e-mail, before you make those phone calls, before your morning break. No time to mull over coffee: Read! Analyze! Disseminate! Such, anyway, is the philosophy of the Cambridge Police Department's Crime Analysis Unit, which is proud of its fierce dedication to this process. Consequently, we've developed a number of procedures and policies to help us optimize this vital job.

The Day Begins with the Reports

We have written a document called The Ten Commandments of Crime Analysis. Commandment #2 is: "Thou shalt read thy agency's crime reports every day." This means reading the physical copy of the written report, not the RMS or CAD Entry. There's just something about poring over those actual carbon copies, with a blue pen and a caffeinated drink close at hand, that embeds the crime in your mind—so that when you come across a related incident, you're likely to identify a pattern instantly. Plus, it avoids the timeliness, accuracy, and other data quality problems inherent in many records management systems. Calls for service are important, too—and many of them don't result in written reports, at least in our department. Thus, while one analyst works his way through the pile of crime reports, the other reviews the non-crime entries in the CAD system.

---

* Source: Bruce, C. (Spring, 2000). *Crime Mapping News*, 2, 10–12. Reprinted with permission.

The analyst with the reports cross-checks each one against the crime analysis database for any related incidents. The nature by which each report is checked varies from report to report. For a regular housebreak, for instance, the analyst may look for all housebreaks in the same neighborhood for the past month. A housebreak with a peculiar M.O. may warrant a check of all housebreaks, going back several months, for a similar M.O. If the report lists a suspect or an arrested person, the name will be checked for any previous reports. In this manner, we try to catch any pattern, series, or hot spot within two or three incidents.

A Database for Crime Analysts

The Cambridge Police Department's quest to procure a "new" records management system—now in its tenth year—is a comedy of errors that we won't bore you with here. But it has indirectly benefited the Crime Analysis Unit because, faced with no adequate commercial system, we were forced to design our own—and, of course, we designed it to be of optimal use to crime analysis.

As masters of this system—created in Microsoft Access—we assumed data entry responsibility for crime incidents, hiring a full-time data entry clerk for this task. A lot of units might balk at the idea of taking on Records Unit responsibilities like this, but we feel that the confidence we can feel in the accuracy and timeliness of the information outweighs the six to eight hours a week we have to spend on it.

One field in particular makes this database unique: the "analysis" field. It allows the analyst to enter his or her own notes and thoughts about a crime and the likelihood that it's connected to a pattern. A note on a housebreak might read, for example, "Two blocks away from break yesterday, but significant differences; probably no pattern." Or: "One of two breaks in this building this date. Such incidents unusual for this building on such a high floor—maybe inside job?"

The "analysis" field for an acquaintance house burglary reviews the history of the parties involved: "Suspect and victim go way back. Suspect used to live in the building, and had some kind of relationship with VI, producing several assault reports. Since suspect moved out some time in 1999, she has tried to break into victim's apartment twice.

Of course, a large number of reports simply read, "No history on suspect," or "No patterns in the area." Overall, this system makes it easy to keep track of patterns, and to provide investigators a way to look up a quick analysis on their assigned cases.

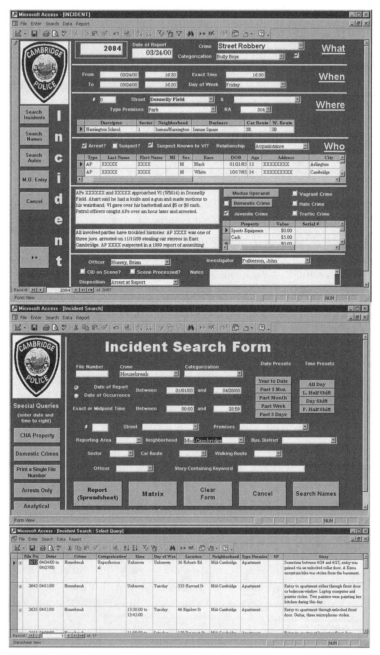

The Cambridge Police Department's Crime Analysis Database entry, incident search, and incident search result screens. This is a Microsoft Access database developed by the Crime Analysis Unit over the course of several years.

Mapping

Because our jurisdiction is geographically small (6.2 square miles), and because both analysts have been working here for many years, we rarely use crime mapping to help identify crime patterns—we can usually assess geographic proximity just by looking at the addresses.

Once a pattern is found, of course, mapping helps us analyze it and provides a visual aid for the written analysis published in the Daily Crime Bulletin.

(Just in case we've missed something in our daily review of crime reports, however, we map and review each of our five "target crimes"—street robberies, housebreaks, larcenies from motor vehicles, auto theft, and commercial breaks—once per week. Occasionally, we catch a pattern during this review process that we originally missed. An example of one of these reviews appears below.)

Geography being one of two ways that potential crime patterns are initially identified (the other is modus operandi), many agencies do map crimes on a daily basis to find patterns. These agencies need to be aware that a cluster of crimes does not necessarily signify a pattern of crimes. The map is never the end product, and any apparent cluster needs to be analyzed more thoroughly before the existence of a pattern can be ascertained. Geographic coincidences occur far more often than one might expect, so that four housebreaks that occur over the course of a week within two blocks of each other may be obviously and entirely unrelated (e.g., one is a professional job, another amateur, the third between warring acquaintances, and the fourth a landlord/tenant matter).

Tactical crime mapping, like tactical crime analysis, can be a down and dirty process. The annals of etiquette in crime mapping go out the window: when you're trying to quickly find or display a crime pattern, elements like scale bars, legends, layout windows, tables imported from your RMS, and other frilly GIS features take more time than they're worth. It's a thirty second process: CTRLF a dozen locations on the street layer, choose a symbol, zoom in, and maybe drop some text, circles, lines or arrows on the cosmetic layer to highlight certain features. Then copy the entire mess to the clipboard and paste it into your word processing application. Sure, it's only a few degrees removed from paper maps and push pins, but it gets the job done fast. (Incidentally, for this type of "down and dirty" crime mapping, we find MapInfo to be a more user-friendly, adaptable application than ArcView, though we own and use both applications.)

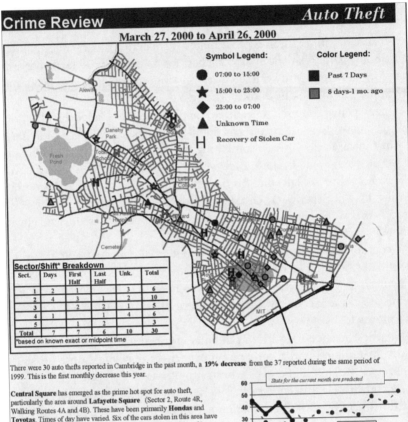

There were 30 auto thefts reported in Cambridge in the past month, a **19% decrease** from the 37 reported during the same period of 1999. This is the first monthly decrease this year.

Central Square has emerged as the prime hot spot for auto theft, particularly the area around **Lafayette Square** (Sector 2, Route 4R, Walking Routes 4A and 4B). These have been primarily **Hondas** and **Toyotas**. Times of day have varied. Six of the cars stolen in this area have since been recovered, all of them in the north shore communities of Lynn, Revere, and Chelsea. Chelsea Police, while making the most recent recovery of a 1998 Honda Accord stolen from Washington Street, chased two white males in their 20s, both over six feet tall. Neither was caught. The most recent three thefts have been off of **Main Street**.

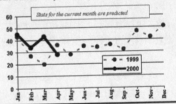

Above: A Target Crime Review for auto theft. Each of five target crimes is reviewed once per week in the *Daily Crime Bulletin*.

Left: The *Daily Crime Bulletin*.

Dissemination

Since the Crime Analysis Unit's inception more than 20 years ago, the primary means of dissemination of crime and pattern information has been the Daily Crime Bulletin. In the early days, we used a typewriter and a drafting table; now we use Microsoft Word. Among other things, the Bulletin contains:

- a review of all target crimes since the previous bulletin
- an analysis of any current crime patterns and trends
- a comprehensive review of that day's target crime
- a list of recently issued warrants
- abstracts of articles from various newspapers
- interdepartmental memoranda and notices

Creating a four-page bulletin for your department every day can be a grueling, repetitive process. This is why we recommend interns. We employ a full-time and a part-time intern from Northeastern University to edit and publish the Daily Crime Bulletin.

More recently, we've availed ourselves of technology to put this information out faster. A daily e-mail goes out to all command staff members and superior officers as soon as we've finished going through the crime reports for the day. This e-mail serves as a pre-Bulletin: a way to get pattern information out in a timelier manner.

The next step, of course, is live, interactive information via an intranet, currently under development. This may serve to replace the paper Bulletin entirely, once it's accessible from the MDT's in the cruisers.

The End of the Day

By two o'clock, the Bulletin is done, and we have moved into the stage of the tactical crime analysis process—strategy development—that we no longer directly control. The Crime Analysis Unit can now focus on other projects, including the occasional strategic crime analysis.

But tactical crime analysis is like garbage collection: there's always more waiting for you the next day; and if you don't do anything about it, it gets out of control real fast. Our nights are filled with tortuous dreams of the insidiousness occurring in our jurisdictions while we sleep; our mornings brim with nervous anticipation until we hold a new, fresh stack of poorly-written, illegible, coffee-stained reports once again.

Chapter 7

The Mapping of Crime

Chapter 6 introduced the importance of crime analysis for fighting crime, identifying high crime areas and problem locations, and developing responses to improve the quality of life in these problem areas. In this Chapter, a specialized tool used by many crime analysts called crime mapping will be explored.

The Growth of Computerized Crime Mapping: From Push Pins to PCs

While the use of crime mapping in the form of pin maps has been traced back to the early 1900s, computerized crime mapping through the use of powerful geographic information systems (GIS) is becoming more and more popular. In the early 1900s, August Vollmer advocated the use of more scientific methods in police practices, including the use of pin maps to identify the locations of criminal activity. There is evidence that the New York City Police Department was using manual pin maps as early as 1900 (Harries, 1999). In contemporary times, chances are many police agencies still use pin maps displayed prominently in their briefing rooms. Different color push pins may be used to depict the location of different categories of crime, time of occurrence, or beat. The pin map might include incidents that had occurred over the past 24 hours, week, month, or other meaningful units of time. Pin maps might include crimes for an entire jurisdiction, or may be based on small units, such as beats or reporting districts. While some agencies still use pin maps to assist in the identification of crime patterns, there are a number of drawbacks to their use.

A crime analyst in a small agency who has painstakingly created a pin map for his or her agency's jurisdiction, carefully color-coding criminal offenses that have occurred over the past month may run into a problem on the first day of the new month. A picture of the previous month's map could be taken to "store" the data; pins could be continually added (perhaps in different shades?) to the old map; or the pins could be removed all together. As one can imagine, pin maps are difficult to continually update with new information.

Once the pins are removed, it is difficult to keep track of previous crime patterns that may continue into the new month. Month to month comparisons of crime data are difficult to make, if not impossible. One cannot "ask" the map to store information, nor can the pins be easily manipulated (Boba, 2009; Harries, 1999).

Additionally, pin maps can become quite large and cumbersome. For example, the jurisdiction of Baltimore County covers 610 square miles. In order for a pin map of the entire area to be viewed, 12 different maps have to be joined together. The final map takes up 70 square feet of wall space (Canter, 1997, cited in Harries, 1999).

Overcoming the Obstacles

Much of the same can be said for the integration of GIS technology in law enforcement as was true for the discussion of the technological impediments that challenged the growth of crime analysis. Early software programs were slow and user-hostile, and hardware systems were cost prohibitive. The first computer-generated maps of crime were made during the 1960s and 1970s. In 1967, the St. Louis, Missouri Police Department used computer generated maps to depict the frequencies of larcenies from automobiles (Weisburd & McEwen, 1998). Despite the appeal of automatic crime mapping, the technological challenges were great and only a few agencies incorporated mapping technology into their operations.

Interest in crime mapping was fueled in the late 1980s, when the National Institute of Justice established a program called the Drug Market Analysis Program. This program provided federal grants to establish partnerships between law enforcement agencies and academic researchers. The goal of the partnerships was to use innovative analytic methods to identify and track drug markets. Five awards were made, marking some of the first crime mapping projects funded by the federal government. The success and publicity surrounding these projects resulted in great interest among law enforcement and researchers alike, in the use of GIS as a new tool to explore crime patterns and trends (LaVigne & Groff, 2001).

In the 1990s, even more federal funding was provided to allow law enforcement agencies to purchase crime mapping hardware and software. The Community Oriented Policing Services (COPS) Office provided funds to agencies to enhance and improve their community policing activities through the use of the new technology. Agencies could apply for grants from the Making Officer Redeployment Effective (MORE) program, which had a budget of one billion dollars. Additionally, since 1995 the COPS Office has provided funding for the Police Foundation's Crime Mapping Laboratory, which provides technical assistance and advice for agencies wishing to incorporate crime-mapping technologies into their operations (Boba, 2009). The National Institute of Justice continues to actively encourage the use of crime mapping by offering grants, fellowships, and other forms of assistance to agencies wishing to adopt the new technology, although the available funding has been significantly reduced in the wake of September 11th.

Box 7.1 Information Clearinghouses for Crime Mapping Issues

The Crime Mapping Laboratory of the Police Foundation offers a number of services to agencies interested in crime mapping technology. Laboratory personnel will provide training, technical support, and consultation services to law enforcement personnel, especially to those agencies that have received COPS funding to purchase crime mapping technology to enhance their community policing efforts. Additionally, the Crime Mapping Laboratory publishes a regular newsletter, the *Crime Mapping News*, which provides a wealth of information on training opportunities, upcoming conferences, successful stories from the field, web site reviews, and information on new software and crime mapping analysis techniques. For more information, please check out their web site at: http://www.policefoundation.org and follow the links to the Crime Mapping Laboratory.

The National Institute of Justice Mapping and Analysis for Public Safety (MAPS) Office was established in 1997. Formerly known as the Crime Mapping Research Center, the goal of MAPS is to promote the use of GIS technology for applications in criminal justice research and practice. Over the past few years, the MAPS program has funded several geospatial technology research projects with the goal of advancing the collection and geographical analysis of crime data. The range of these projects spans from simple to advanced. MAPS also offers the Crime Mapping Research Conference, which brings together researchers and practitioners in advance our understanding of crime, criminal justice, and public safety from a spatiotemporal perspective. Finally, in conjunction with the COPS Office, the bulletin *Geography & Public Safety* is published for practitioners and researchers. The bulletin provides examples of how geographic principles may be applied to real-life crime problems. Students may access this bulletin free of charge at http://www.ojp.usdoj.gov/nij/maps/bulletin.htm.

The Crime Mapping and Analysis Program (CMAP) provides technical assistance and training to law enforcement agencies in the use of GIS as well as crime and intelligence mapping. Funded by the National Institute of Justice's Office of Science and Technology, CMAP provides a number of useful resources including publications, a crime analysis unit developer kit, free software downloads, and free crime mapping and analysis manuals. For more information, please visit their website at http://www.justnet.org/Pages/cmap.aspx.

Today, the use of crime mapping is still in its infancy, but there are signs that it is a growing area of interest among law enforcement agencies. For example, a 1997 survey of 2,004 law enforcement agencies conducted by the Crime Mapping Research Center (CMRC) found that while most agencies (73%) use some form of crime analysis, only 261 (13%) use computerized crime mapping (Mamalian & Lavigne, 1999). Ten years later, data collected from large law enforcement agencies (i.e., agencies with 100 or more full-time sworn officers) indicated that about 1-in-4 use computers to map crime (B. Reaves, personal communication, January 26, 2011).

The critical reader may have noted that the results of these surveys are (at this writing) several years old. Unfortunately, more recent data regarding the utilization of crime mapping do not exist. While it may very well be that more agencies have adopted the technology, as argued by Boba (2009), more than likely the rate of growth has slowed quite a bit in recent years. This is due to two factors. First, larger agencies that want to use the technology have already adopted it. Smaller agencies that do not have crime mapping capabilities may never choose to purchase the technology, either due to personal preferences or personnel and/or budgetary limitations. Second, as noted earlier in this text, funding for projects to assist local law enforcement agencies has been cut significantly since September 11, 2001. More and more funding has been shifted to Homeland Security and the prevention of terrorist attacks. While it could be argued that local agencies can and do play an important role in preventing terrorism on our soil, it is difficult to justify the expense of establishing a crime mapping unit for a small policing agency when many of the larger cities still do not have necessary basic tools to adequately respond to or prevent terrorist attacks.

Uses of Crime Mapping

Just what is computerized crime mapping, and how can agencies use this tool? In its most basic function, computerized crime mapping allows agencies to create high-tech pin maps. Crimes, calls for service, arrests, or other incidents may be plotted on a digitized map of a reporting district, beat, neighborhood, or entire jurisdiction. However, because the information is stored in a computerized database, the "pins" can be easily saved from month to month. The "pins" can also be manipulated to display specific incidents for the previous shift, day, week, month, or year. As a result, visual detection of crime patterns may be easier than with a traditional pin map (LaVigne & Groff, 2001). According to the previously mentioned 1997 survey, the use of computerized pin maps was the most common application of crime mapping technology (Mamalian & LaVigne, 1999). This type of mapping is sometimes referred to as **descriptive mapping.**

Box 7.2 How Are Computerized Pin Maps Created?

In order for a computerized pin map to be generated, the location of a crime incident must be **geocoded**, or assigned an x and y coordinate, so that it may be placed on a map. In the course of their duties, police officers regularly collect data that include an address: location of the call for service, arrest, field interview report, or accident. One of the primary jobs of an analyst using a geographic information system (GIS) is to convert these addresses to an x and y coordinate, usually in latitude and longitude decimal degrees, and identify its geographic location on a map. In practice, this can be a very painful process.

The most widely employed method for geocoding crime event data is to use street centerline data that can be purchased, borrowed from local agencies (i.e., a city planning office or GIS office), or accesses through the US Census Bureau. These data contain street network information represented as street line segments that hold street names and the range of house numbers and block numbers on each side of the street. Address geocoding is accomplished by first matching the street name, then the segment that contains the house numbers and finally placing a point along the segment based on a linear interpolation within the range of house numbers. This approach to geocoding an address is referred to as "street geocoding" and has become the most widely used form of geocoding.

Crime event data can also be geocoded using reference data that contain property boundary information that represents a plot or parcel of land. Parcels are traditionally the most spatially accurate data with address information available. Geocoding against parcels allows one to match against individual plots of land rather than interpolating against a street centerline. This is particularly useful in areas where parcels are not regularly addressed or those parcels that may be quite a distance from the centerline. Parcel geocoding typically results in a lower match rate in part because a single parcel can be associated with many addresses. Despite these lower match rates, parcel geocoding is considered more spatially accurate and is now becoming widespread given the development of parcel level databases by many cities and counties in the US.

The third approach to geocoding involves the use of address point reference data. Address points are commonly created from parcel centroids (i.e., the center) for all occupied parcels. This is supplemented with address points for sub-addresses such as individual apartment units, condominium units, or duplexes. Field data collection or verification of building locations using digital aerial imagery can be used to further supplement the address point file. Address point data sets are of great value to local government, in particular emergency services. When used as reference data for geocoding, address points data help produce very spatially accurate crime maps.

For information contained on a crime map to be meaningful, the geocoding process needs to meet certain quality expectations. The overall quality of any geocoding result can be characterized by its *completeness, positional accuracy* and *repeatability*. Completeness is the percentage of records that can reliably be geocoded, also referred to as the match rate or hit rate. Positional accuracy indicates how close each geocoded point is to the "true" location of the crime event. And repeatability indicates how sensitive the geocoding results are to variations in the street network input, the matching algorithms of the geocoding software, and the skills and interpretation of the analyst. Geocoding results of high quality are complete, spatially accurate and repeatable. So as a consumer of map information, it is important to recognize how computerized maps are created.

For more information, see the following sources:

Clarke, K. (2010) Getting started with geographic information systems *(5th ed.). Upper Saddle River, NJ: Prentice Hall.*

Harries, K. (1999) Mapping crime: Principle and practice. *Washington, DC: National Institute of Justice.*

In addition to automated pin mapping, computerized crime mapping also allows agencies to compare their in-house crime data against various community-level characteristics. External data bases, such as census data, property assessment data, city planning data, parks and school data, utilities data, and even digital images and photographs can become part of the agency's database, allowing the analyst to consider spatial relationships between crime problems and various demographic characteristics (Boba, 2009; Mamalian & LaVigne, 1999). This powerful analysis tool requires a bit more technical and statistical expertise and, as a result, only about half of the police agencies that employ crime mapping reported using these advanced features (Mamalian & LaVigne, 1999). This more advanced type of mapping is one form of **analytical mapping.**

Box 7.3 Incident Mapping and Analysis on the North Carolina State University Campus*

Our Vision

The North Carolina State University Police Department (NCSUPD) is introducing incident mapping to make information accessible to officers so they can conduct more problem solving. We are designing our system so that patrol plans can be more officer-driven versus middle management-driven. When patrol officers return to work after normal days off, they will be able to print a map of their assigned area and see specifically where incidents have occurred to help them determine the next appropriate action. Officers will also be able to map calls-for-service and conduct further analysis to determine specific causes for similar and/or repeat calls. Finally, we want officers to be able to run a query when they do problem solving so they can see what kind of effect their response has on a particular problem.

With 55 officers, the NCSUPD patrols the largest university in North Carolina with a community of approximately 35,000 students, staff, and visitors. Crime rates are generally low compared with other communities of our size and scope, and we are fortunate to be experiencing a downward trend in our overall crime. To better predict where incidents are going to occur, however, requires precise and accessible information on both criminal and non-criminal incidents and has driven us to conduct crime analysis using GIS mapping.

The Beginning

Prior to 2003, the extent of crime mapping at the NCSUPD consisted mainly of generating simple pin maps. When the department's patrol lieutenants and chief investigator enrolled in a crime-analysis course offered by the university, they learned to look beyond the incident and understand how analysis could help the department reduce crime, decrease calls-for-service, and solve community problems. These department supervisors started to look at crime problems proactively, using analysis to provide their officers with more comprehensive information, such as the number of similar incidents, dates, times, victims, locations, and offenders. They also acquired specific information on campus lighting, landscaping, and building design that would aid university police in their crime prevention efforts and be helpful to victims.

Information for NIBRS Versus Information for Problem Solving

In the spring of 2004, the department became a research site for Enhancing Community Policing: Institutionalizing Problem Analysis, a grant that provided expert technical assistance and funding to assist us with problem solving. Working with these experts, we discovered early on that our incident and crime data—calls for service, citations, motor vehicle accidents, general police information, and criminal reports—were not conducive to in-depth analysis. Like most departments, we collect data electronically but data formats were designed for reporting to NIBRS, not for crime analysis. In addition, the few people in our department who had the expertise to link our databases and run meaningful queries also had other duties; thus, it was often difficult to get the information in a timely fashion or in a format that was user-friendly. We also had a problem with our old data collection methods because they did not provide enough accuracy, such as exact location, about incidents. There are, for example, 16,000 parking spaces on campus but they are identified only by the parking lot address. In order to know exactly where a car break-in occurred in a parking lot, officers needed to collect better information that would enable them to analyze environmental factors. To accomplish this, we upgraded our software capabilities.

Information and Access

We looked for a user-friendly, computer program that would be compatible with our current databases and decided the Crime View 2000 software program would fit our needs. The Huntersville (NC) Police Department was currently using Crime View and gave us a demonstration allowing us to observe first-hand the program's capabilities and compatibility with our needs.

The software would enable officers, supervisors, and administrators to access our criminal and incident data and assist them in compiling reports and gathering information that could be used proactively. It also gave patrol officers the ability to query data and produce a visual display of all the activities in their districts, such as crimes reported, motor vehicle stops, field interviews, and calls-for-service.

Partnerships

While cleaning up our data for better information, including an accurate geocoding service, and to facilitate implementation of the Crime View program, we discovered that much of the information we needed already existed in other campus departments. The College of Natural Resources, for example, provided us with street centerlines, building foot plans, digital orthophotos, playing fields, and water features. The Department of Transportation provided parking lot data, emergency callbox locations, bus stops, and streetlights. Facilities Operations provided building floor plans and correct addresses. Obtaining the data from these departments and making it available to patrol officers will assist them in problem-oriented policing by providing precise information. Being able to show exactly where crime occurs in large open areas will lead to information-driven solutions. Making recommendations to other departments based on information instead of hunches will be critical as they budget for crime prevention.

We also found that several university departments had some type of GIS or GPS information we could use so we set up a meeting with these different departments to review what information we were capable of sharing. As a result of this project, we were able to establish a university GIS users group, which enabled us to more precisely locate and map street addresses, trees and shrubs, future construction sites, sewers, electric services, water lines, and tunnels under the university. Both academic and support departments come together monthly to develop guidelines and protocols for data collection. The project has the support of the campus community and the university's chancellor. It has expanded to include several other campuses within the University of North Carolina system that use GIS. Finally, our partnerships with other departments have resulted in the discovery of several software site licenses that already existed on campus, reducing our implementation costs.

Next Steps

We were initially recording the location of incidents by building name, followed by a specific description of a more exact location. Changes in building names and occupants required us to make duplicate searches to accurately record all incidents occurring at a location. The rapid growth of the university and the implementation of mapping made us recognize the need for static locations. We now use street names and addresses for locations and add symbols to the location field that marry up to the mapping system to produce exact locations. This allows accurate mapping to pinpoint problem areas to address. Report data entry now provides more useful information. Police officers have been assigned to geographic areas, and graduate students have loaded PDAs with floor plans so that officers can map exact locations in both internal and external open areas to include with their reports. The Crime View mapping software is projected to come online in July 2005. We will provide problem-solving training to the officers and are depending on our supervisors to teach them how to conduct the appropriate kinds of analyses using more robust information and geographic references. It has taken the NCSUPD, technical experts, and other members of the university community over one year to develop our mapping program and we believe that the long-term benefits of improved information for problem solving are worth it.

This article was co-authored by Lt. Col. John Dailey, Assistant Chief, Sgt. Jon Barnwell, Crime Prevention Division, and Ed Farmer, Special Events/Crime Stats, North Carolina State University Police Department.

* *First appeared in* Crime Mapping News, *Volume 7, Issue 1, 2005, pp. 6–7.*

Descriptive Mapping: Computerized Pin Maps and More

As previously noted, the use of computer generated pin maps is by far the most popular, and most rudimentary, use of crime mapping technology. According to the 1997 survey of law enforcement agencies conducted by the Crime Mapping Research Center (now known as MAPS), among the agencies that actually used a crime mapping or a GIS program, the most commonly used mapping application was automated pin maps. While agencies that use their system solely to create pin maps are barely scratching the surface of the potential of their crime mapping system, this basic application is still a very useful, flexible, and somewhat powerful tool.

In practice, law enforcement agencies can use descriptive mapping in a variety of ways. The article on tactical crime analysis written by Christopher Bruce in Chapter 6 described the use of descriptive mapping by the Cambridge, Massachusetts Police Department. One of the primary advantages of using computerized crime mapping techniques is that the maps can be easily printed and distributed to all concerned parties—patrol officers, detectives, and community crime watch groups. Instead of having to discern and memorize the information presented on a wall pin map, computerized crime maps can focus the reader's attention on very specific pieces of information, such as a rash of residential burglaries that have occurred in a specific area over the past several days.

Police agencies can also use descriptive mapping to assist different neighborhood problems and for outreach efforts. For example, City of Henderson Police Department (HPD), Nevada uses descriptive mapping to convey information about neighborhood problems and concerns to their constituents. Both the Calls for Service (CFS) information and Offense Reports (REPORTS) taken in the specific neighborhood are displayed in Figure 7.1. One of the concerns for the neighbors in the area was the possible crime attractor factor for the newly built Trailhead. Based on the analysis of the numerous CFS and offenses reported in the buffer area, the crime analysts from HPD were able to determine that nearly all of the CFS and reported offenses were unrelated to the Trailhead and its impact to the neighborhood was very minimal. Analysts also recommended revisiting the study on an annual basis in order to make sure that there was no increase in the crime activity in the neighborhood, attributed to the trailhead in the future.

Mapping can also be used to better allocate resources to fight crime. For example, mapping software can provide information on the exact locations of patrol cars and other units. It is becoming more common for patrol vehicles to have global positioning system (GPS) receivers installed, which allows dispatchers to have real-time location data for the vehicle. When a call comes into the com-

Figure 7.1

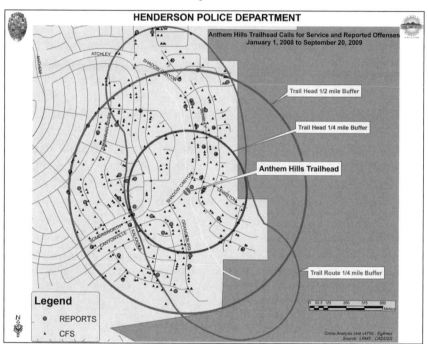

munications center, the dispatchers are able to assign the call to the closest patrol vehicle to the incident. This ability reduces the response time and also allows
the dispatcher to better estimate the response time to the caller (Rich, 1995).

In a rather innovative twist, mapping systems are being used to triangulate
the exact location of gunfire. The ShotSpotter Gunshot Location System (GLS)
is one product that uses acoustic sensors that are spread over a geographic area
to detect the source of gunfire. The system is integrated with 911 dispatch centers so that when the sound of a gunshot is picked up by the sensors, dispatchers are notified of the location of the shots within seconds of their occurrence.
The ShotSpotter system can detect shots of within a two-mile radius of the individual sensors and can even tell if the suspect was in motion (i.e., a drive-by
shooting). The Redlands, California, Police Department used this technology
in their attempt to reduce gunfire. The city was having a serious problem with
"celebratory" gunfire on holidays and weekends. After installing the system, the
city experienced a 75% reduction in gunfire in their jurisdiction (for more information, please see the ShotSpotter website at http://www.shotspotter.com).

Other agencies regularly use crime mapping to display the home addresses of sexual predators living within their jurisdiction. After the brutal rape and murder of 7-year-old Megan Kanka in 1994, President Clinton signed Megan's Law into effect. Megan's Law requires that all sex offenders convicted of crimes against children be registered and their personal information be made available in a publicly accessible database (for more information, see http://www.klaask-ids.org). Police agencies may then use this information to assist in their criminal investigations. Citizens may also use this information to see if any registered sex offenders reside in their neighborhoods. For example, in my (Kim) home state of Florida, the Florida Department of Law Enforcement maintains such a database. When I typed in my old St. Petersburg address (which is one block away from an elementary school) I found that there were 113 registered sexual offenders/predators living within a one-mile radius of my home. The FDLE database provides pictures of the registered offenders, their names and physical descriptions, and information on the nature of their offense (please see http://offender.fdle.state.fl.us/offender/homepage.do).

Box 7.4 Geocoding Accuracy Considerations in Determining Residency Restrictions for Sex Offenders

In this piece of applied research, Paul Zandbergen and Timothy Hart (authors of this spotlight) used crime-mapping technology to examine how specific geocoding techniques can affect analysis of sex offender residency restriction violations for registered sex offenders*

Law enforcement agencies throughout the United States rely on Geographic Information Systems (GIS) as a valuable tool in combating crime. Results from a government survey show that nearly two-thirds of the nation's largest law enforcement agencies use GIS to map reported crimes, more than one-half use GIS to map calls for service, and more than two-in-five use GIS to map arrest data. GIS is also used by law enforcement for the monitoring and tracking of registered sex offenders, especially within jurisdictions that have enacted laws that prohibit registered sex offenders from living within a specified distance of places where children congregate (i.e., residency restrictions laws).

Many GIS application by law enforcement agencies include the use of address geocoding, a technique that assigns coordinates to a street address. The use of geocoding has become widespread and it is arguably a successful application of GIS. As with other techniques used to create spatial data, however, there is some uncertainty associated with the results of geocoding, which may affect its usefulness. Our paper explored the positional error of geocoding and its impact on the analysis of residency restrictions for registered sex offenders using Orange County, Florida as a case study.

Our study investigated how the positional error in street geocoding affects the determination of residency restrictions of registered sex offenders. Two research objectives were undertaken in particular: 1) Determine the positional error in street geocoding of sex offenders' residences, and the locations of schools and day care facilities; and 2) Determine the degree to which geocoding inaccuracies introduce error and bias in the results of the analysis of sex offender residency restrictions. Results of our research have very direct implications for how residency restrictions are determined and enforced as well as for assessing the utility of street geocoding for these types of applications.

In order to answer our two research questions, we used a subset of sex offender data (n=623) that contained the complete list of registered sexual offenders for the State of Florida for 2003. We limited our analysis to Orange County, Florida. We also obtained the address information for 261 schools and 498 day care facilities within our study area. For our analysis, three versions of geocoded locations for sex offenders, schools, and parcels were produced: 1) points of street geocoded locations; 2) centroids of parcel geocoded locations; and 3) polygons of parcel geocoded locations.

We addressed our first research objectives by measuring the Euclidean distance (i.e., straight line distance) between street geocoded location and the nearest boundary and centroid of the corresponding parcel polygon. In order to assess the extent to which geocoding inaccuracies introduced error and biased assessments of residency restriction violations for registered sex offenders, we buffered the street and parcel locations of sex offenders' residences, schools, and daycares. We used the buffering information to help us to determine the number of locations that should have been considered a violation of Florida's 1,000-foot rule but weren't (i.e., a Type I error) as well as those that appeared to be a violation, but truly were not (i.e., a Type II error). Figure 7.2 provides a visual representation of our methodology.

Our results indicated that street geocoding of the locations of schools, day care facilities, and sex offenders' residences was found to result in substantial positional errors. The distribution of the positional errors precluded the use of conventional error estimates (i.e., averages). In addition, the use of street geocoded locations results in substantial underestimates of the true number of offenders living within the 1,000-ft restricted zone around schools and day care facilities. Finally, the use of street geocoded locations results in a small number of Type II errors.

Using parcel centroid instead of the parcel boundary didn't make things much better. For example, the use of parcel centroids instead of property boundaries results in substantial underestimates of the number of offenders residing within a 1,000-ft zone but no Type II errors. In fact, we recommended that the use of centroids be avoided not only for the locations represented by large parcels but also those represented by small parcels due to the amount of error introduced by using these locations.

In the end, our study found that typical street geocoding was of insufficient positional accuracy to allow for spatial analysis at relatively short distance like those involving assessments of Florida's 1,000-foot rule for registered sex offenders. We cautioned law enforcement assessing residency restriction law violations for Florida's sex offenders not to use this particular geocoding technique.

---

* *For more information, please see Zandbergen, P. & Hart, T. C. (2009). Geocoding accuracy considerations in determining residency restrictions for sex offenders.* Criminal Justice Policy Review, 20(1), 62–90.

Figure 7.2. Example Analysis of 1,000 Feet Residency Restrictions
Using Parcel and Street Geocoding.

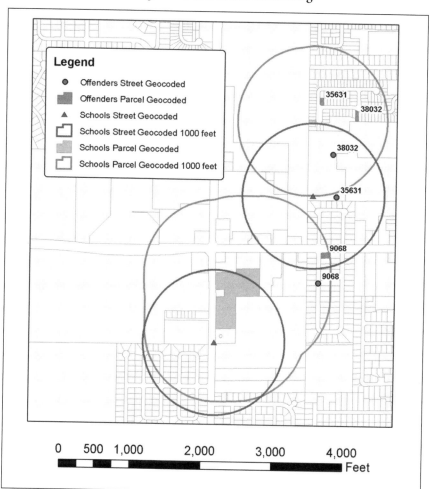

Law enforcement agencies can also use descriptive computerized pin maps
to visually demonstrate the effectiveness of an intervention strategy. For example, if an agency has been concentrating its efforts on street level drug dealing in a specific neighborhood, the agency can create a map that displays the
number of drug related calls for service before and after their intervention

(McEwen & Taxman, 1995). This visual depiction can be quite useful (and dramatic), especially when interacting with community members and local government officials. No special training or lengthy explanations are needed to decipher the movement of the data points.

The usefulness of descriptive mapping does have its limits. While computerized crime mapping can be useful in allowing agency personnel to detect patterns and trends in the data points, there is still a great deal of subjective interpretation (McEwen & Taxman, 1995). What one person identifies as an important pattern in the data points may be completely dismissed by another.

This subjectivity can be especially problematic in the identification of hot spots. The vast majority of agencies that use crime-mapping technology (86%) have indicated that hot spots of criminal activity were identified by visual inspection (Mamalian & LaVigne, 1999). As discussed in the previous chapter, understanding and controlling a hot spot can be very effective in reducing the overall level of crime in a jurisdiction. Before attempting to address a hot spot, one has to know exactly where it is located. Identifying a hot spot simply through visual inspection can lead to errors.

There are a number of different analytical methods for identifying a hot spot. In one relatively basic technique, called **repeat address mapping,** only those addresses that meet a pre-set minimum criteria (called a **minimum plotting density**) are shown on a map. For example, an agency may wish to identify the "worst of the worst" crime locations in the city. In an analysis of data provided from the New York City Police Department, researchers mapped addresses in the Bronx that had four or more crimes occur over a 13-month period. By using this criterion, the researchers limited the number of mapped addresses to less than 7% of all locations and were able to account for nearly a quarter of all of the crimes that had occurred. The researchers could then concentrate on what was happening at this relatively small number of locations that caused them to be hot spots for crime (Eck, Gersh, & Taylor, 2000).

Other types of analyses exist for identifying hot spots. In one type of analysis, called **kernel smoothing,** the individual data points depicting crime locations are "smoothed out" to create an image that shows the areas with the highest density or concentration of crime. Another type of analysis uses what are called **standard deviation ellipses.** A free computer program called STAC— Spatial and Temporal Analysis of Crime—is available to law enforcement agencies and other interested parties from the Illinois Criminal Justice Information Authority. This program (as well as other programs on the market) will automatically analyze individual geocoded addresses and identify clusters. The location and size of the hot spots are clearly identified by an ellipse that is drawn around the areas with the highest concentration of criminal activity (Rich, 1999).

A detailed discussion of these techniques requires more statistical expertise and is really beyond the scope of this text (see, for example, Eck et al., 2005; the Crime Mapping Research Center, 1998; Langworthy & Jefferis, 2000; or McLafferty, Williamson, & McGuire, 2000 for more information on these and other techniques). Oftentimes these techniques (i.e., Nearest Neighbor Index, Moran's I, Geary's C statistic, K-means clustering, kernel density estimation Gi and Gi* statistics) can be quite confusing for practitioners to employ, and researchers disagree on which method is the best (LaVigne & Groff, 2001). Part of the problem is that since crime mapping is still in its infancy, even the most basic spatial analysis techniques are beyond the comfort level of many law enforcement personnel. Hence, at this point in time, the use of descriptive mapping is much more popular than analytical mapping, which requires more advanced skills.

Analytical Mapping: Beyond the Individual Crime Incident Locations

Analytical mapping is a bit more complex than descriptive mapping. While descriptive mapping focuses on the visual presentation of individual data points, analytical mapping displays the results of data analysis. Data points are analyzed and the results of the analysis are then mapped. Analytical mapping allows for better understanding of the trends and patterns of criminal events than does descriptive mapping (McEwen & Taxman, 1995).

Analyzing Domestic Violence in Baltimore

The Baltimore County, Maryland Police Department used analytical mapping techniques to gain a better understanding of the county's spouse-abuse problem. The agency wanted to know the addresses and areas that experienced a high number of spousal abuse calls. Additionally, the agency wanted to locate areas of under-reporting; that is, where incidents of spousal abuse may be taking place but were not reported to the police.

Using the agency database, it was relatively easy to identify the locations with high volumes of calls related to spousal abuse. However, the identification of under-reporting areas was a bit more complex. The agency added social and demographic information broken down by census tracts to its database that already included the locations of spousal abuse incidents. The goal was to develop a mathematical equation where the number of spousal abuse calls could be predicted based on the area's demographic characteristics. This equation, called a multiple regression model, represented the best fitting model for all of the data values. The agency then compared the actual number of spouse abuse calls with the number of calls expected, using the regression model. In some of the areas, the number of spousal abuse cases that was predicted using the model was much higher than the actual number of cases. This provided evidence of under reporting.

Through their detailed analysis of the combined databases, the agency was able to identify five possible areas where victims were not reporting cases of spousal abuse. These areas were highlighted on a map of the entire county, thereby easily allowing consumers of this information (social service providers, domestic violence counselors) to see the areas that were possibly in need of victim assistance (for a more detailed and statistically advanced discussion of this project, see Canter, 1990, 1998; McEwen & Taxman, 1995). These maps, therefore, provided the results of the analysis, as opposed to a more rudimentary pin map display of where the spousal abuse calls had taken place.

Geographic Profiling: Hunting Serial Criminals

Geographic profiling is an advanced form of analytical crime mapping. Drawing heavily on crime pattern theory, routine activities theory, and other environmental criminology principles, geographic profiling assists in the investigation of criminal activities by identifying the most likely location where a serial criminal lives. In this type of analysis, information concerning the location of a number of crimes in a series is carefully examined. The goal is to create a map that displays the most probable location of the home or workplace of a serial offender (Rich, 1999; Rossmo, 1995). It is important to note that not all crimes are appropriate for geographic profiling. According to Rossmo (1998; 2004) the crime must be serial in nature and involve violent, predatory acts (such as murder, rape, robbery, arson, bombings, and child molestation) that exhibit hunting behavior on the part of the offender.

Dr. Kim Rossmo, a former detective in the Vancouver, Canada Police Department, developed geographic profiling in the early 1990s. Dr. Rossmo studied criminology at Simon Fraser University in Vancouver under the tutelage of Patricia and Paul Brantingham, noted environmental criminologists. Rossmo, formerly the Director of Research for the Police Foundation, has been instrumental in training detectives in the strategies of hunting serial offenders based on geographic indicators. His work led to the development of a software program called RIGEL Profiler. Geographic profilers in the United States, Canada, and Europe use this program to identify the most likely home address of serial offenders (Laverty & MacLaren, 2002).

According to routine activities theory, crime tends to cluster in areas where motivated offenders come into contact with suitable targets. The Brantingham's notions concerning crime pattern theory added the concepts of activity spaces and awareness spaces. An offender's activity space consists of the areas he or she regularly travels to and between: work, school, home, or recreational areas. Awareness spaces are usually much larger, and may include locations in the city where one rarely visits. Both activity spaces and awareness spaces together form a cognitive map of the city or area in which one lives.

According to Rossmo, within the regularly traveled activity space there is one point that can be described as the most important place in one's spatial life (1995, p. 223). For the majority of people, their home is the most important anchor point in their activity space. For criminals, it would follow that their crimes would be centered near their home addresses, following a **distance-decay function**. That is, the further you get away from the regular activity space of an offender, the less likely that person is to engage in predatory criminal activity. Suitable targets will be hunted close—but not too close—to the home or spatial anchor point. An offender may avoid locations that are too close to the home, so as to avoid detection by neighbors who may recognize him or her as the perpetrator (Rossmo, 1995; 2000). Using this theoretical basis, Rossmo and his colleagues developed a criminal geographic targeting (CGT) model. This model analyzes the geographic coordinates of criminal events that are part of a series in order to produce an image that depicts the likelihood that an offender resides within a specific hunting area. Consider the following case:

In October 1995, two teenage girls in the municipality of Abbotsford, British Columbia were attacked on the street at night, by a man, with a baseball bat. One victim was murdered and dumped in the Vedder Canal, some 20 miles away; the other was left for dead, but she somehow managed to survive and make her way to a nearby hospital. A few days later, the Abbotsford Killer began a series of bizarre actions starting with several taunting 911 telephone calls. He then stole and defaced the murder victim's gravestone and dumped it in the parking lot of a local radio station. Finally, he threw a note wrapped around a wrench through a house window; in the note, he admitted to other sexual assaults. These actions provided 13 different sites for the geographic profile. He was eventually caught through a local-based strategy initiated by the Abbotsford Police Department. His residence was in the top 7.7% of the geoprofile (Rossmo, 2000, p. 215).

The easiest way to imagine how the program works is to use the example of an arsonist who has set fires at eight different businesses around his home.

The best guess of where the arsonist lived would be to find the exact center point of the eight known crime locations, a sort of spatial average or mean. Of course, the development of a real geographic profile that identifies the home of a serial offender is much more complex. In developing a geographic profile, Rossmo (2004) argues that there are three considerations that are of the utmost importance: **crime locations**, **target backcloth**, and **offender hunting style**. With respect to crime locations, Rossmo notes that most literature on the geography of crime often discusses the concept of a crime location as a single place. This is not always so. Some crimes may have multiple location points that must be considered. For example, a homicide may have four separate locations including where the victim was encountered, where the attack occurred, where the murder took place, and where the body was finally dumped. These events may in fact all take place at a single location, or they may occur at two or more spots. Generally speaking, if an offender employs more locations in committing a crime, then this would suggest a higher level of organization and offender mobility. It should also be noted that in an ongoing investigation, the police may only know one or two locations: the dump site for the victim and/or where the victim was last seen.

The target backcloth may best be defined as the spatial opportunity structure that is formed by the temporal and geographic distribution of appropriate crime targets. It is important to recognize that an "appropriate" target may vary greatly from offender to offender, and that this definition of an appropriate target may impact the amount of searching required on the part of the offender. Rossmo provides the example of an arsonist. Let's say an arsonist has a preference for warehouses. Warehouses tend to be clustered together in areas of a city where the zoning permits their existence. If the arsonist limits her target selection to warehouses, then it is not all that difficult to figure out where the potential attack sites are. However, if the arsonist likes to start fires in a random selection of residential and non-residential locations, then the target backcloth is relatively uniform across the city. In the case where the spatial distribution of victims is uniform, the locations of the crimes are determined to a greater extent by the activity space of the offender.

Finally, the hunting style utilized by an offender will also impact the spatial distribution of the crime sites. For serial murderers, the hunting process may be divided into two parts: the search for a victim and the method of attack. In searching for a victim, Rossmo identified four different methods. **Hunters** are offenders who set out from their home to intentionally search for a target. Crimes of the hunters are usually confined to their own city of residence, as the victims are hunted within the offenders' awareness space. **Poachers** also intentionally search out victims, but in this case the offender begins the search from a location other than his/her home and travels to another city to find a victim. **Trollers** find their victims quite by accident, as they are moving through the legitimate activities of their day. Trollers are not actively searching for a target. Instead, they have a chance encounter with a potential victim, as they move through their activity space. **Trappers** are defined as offenders who take on a specific role or occupation that will provide them with opportunities to encounter victims. Custodial killers (such as nurses or home health care workers who poison their patients) would fall into this category.

With respect to the method of attack, Rossmo defined three different categories: raptor, stalker, and ambusher. **Raptors** attack their victim almost immediately upon first encounter. **Stalkers** follow their victims, waiting for an opportune time to attack. For stalkers, the attack, murder and body dumpsite are influenced to a greater extent by the activity space of the victim. **Ambushers** are defined as those offenders that attack a victim who has been lured to a location, such as the residence or workplace of the offender. Oftentimes, the bodies of the victims are found hidden somewhere on the offender's property. Generally speaking, the victim search type impacts the location of the victim encounter sites, while the method of attack influences the location of body dump sites.

In addition to crime locations, target backcloth, and hunting style, Rossmo (2000, p. 213) lists a number of factors that should also be considered when building a profile. These factors include the type of offender (single versus multiple offenders), street layout patterns, bus stops and other public transportation hubs, zoning and land use, and the demographic characteristics of various neighborhoods—that is, a white serial rapist may not venture into Hispanic neighborhoods to search out a potential victim, etc. To make the situation even more complex, an offender may very well have multiple spatial anchor points, such as the home, workplace, or the residence of his/her significant other. Ultimately, the geographic profile may be used by law enforcement agencies to prioritize suspects, develop directed patrol plans, and optimize the use of door-to-door canvasses.

If crime mapping is in its infancy, then geographic profiling is at the embryo stage. This is an area of great excitement, and is truly at the cutting edge of analytic crime mapping technology. While it is still relatively rare to find a resident geographic profiler working at a large agency (especially in the United States), more and more criminal investigators are being trained in geographic profiling techniques. While initially these techniques were reserved for more serious serial murder, rape, arson, robbery or terrorism cases, the techniques may also be used in identifying the home address of serial burglars, auto thieves, and credit card fraud offenders (Laverty & MacLaren, 2002). For more information on geographic profiling, visit the website for Environmental Criminology Research Inc. at http://ecricanada.com.

The Geography of Time: Spatio-Temporal Considerations

As noted previously in our discussion of hot spots in Chapter 6, the temporal analysis of crime has lagged behind spatial considerations. While a good number of law enforcement agencies have embraced crime mapping and the analysis of the locations of crimes, relatively few have really taken a hard look at temporal dimensions (Helms, 2003). Similarly, few academic researchers have tackled the issue. One of the pioneers in this area is Jerry Ratcliffe from Temple University. In a recent work, Ratcliffe (2006) has drawn from the field of time geography and Miller's (2005) measurement theory to develop a temporal constraint theory to explain offending patterns. This next section draws heavily on their works.

We begin our excursion into spatio-temporal considerations with a discussion of what Miller and Ratcliffe call Classical Time Geography. It begins with the idea that activities occur at specific locations for relatively limited periods of time. The shopping mall is only open for so many hours a day, the university only has classes during specified hours of the day and evening, a football game is scheduled for a Saturday afternoon, etc. How efficiently you can move between these various locations and times depends on your mode of transport. In most cases, if you have a car you can get from Point A to Point B a whole lot faster than if you are on foot.

A very important key to time geography is the concept of **constraints**. A constraint limits your opportunity to travel to events and participate in activities. There are a number of different kinds of constraints. First, if you do not have access to public or private transportation, then your ability to go to certain locations that are beyond a reasonable walking distance is restricted. Second, if you have obligations such as work, school, meetings, or other events that you must attend then this limits your ability to do other things; you cannot be at two places at the same time. A third type of constraint, known as an authority constraint, has to do with your ability to freely enter some locations whenever you want. Your access to some areas may be restricted by public or private authorities, such as a gated community. Last but not least, you also have personal constraints, such as the need to eat or sleep, that limit your ability to be at any place at any time. In Ratcliffe's analysis, he bundles all of the various constraints into one general category called **temporal constraints**.

Time geography also makes a distinction between **fixed** and **flexible** activities. Fixed activities cannot be easily rescheduled. You essentially must be there at a specific time or else there may be some consequence. If you miss a doctor's appointment, for example, it could be days or weeks until the appointment can be rescheduled. Conversely, flexible activities are just that—flexible obligations that can be moved about throughout the day or week. Grocery shopping is a good example of a flexible activity, especially if there is a 24 hour market nearby. The distinction between fixed and flexible activities can get a bit fuzzy at times. Studying for an exam that is weeks away can be a flexible activity, but as the exam approaches you may guard the time you need to study and treat the activity as fixed (especially the night before, for many!). Also, a fixed activity for one person (such as attending class and arriving on time) may be a flexible activity for someone who is not so conscientious about attending class.

The need to be at a location for a specified block of time is called a **coupling constraint**. Because the obligations are more rigid in time and place, fixed activities have strict coupling constraints. On the other hand, because the events can be moved around rather freely, flexible activities have a more fluid coupling in time and location.

In addition to the idea of constraints, the **space-time path** and the **space-time prism** are central to the concept of time geography. The space-time path is the movement of an individual through time and place as they travel through their day. Paths tell us about an individual's activity space and also about the fixed activities that make up the anchor points of their lives. A space-time prism is basically an extension of the space-time path. The prism allows us to visually map an individual's ability to reach locations in space and time given their fixed activities; that is, when and where the individual *could* be based on when and where that individual *has* to be. Hopefully this will make more sense in a few moments.

In Figure 7.3, you will see a simple space-time prism. A space-time prism may be drawn between any two points that are adjacent in time if there is some temporal interval between the two points to allow for movement. Let's say that Location X is your workplace and that you are working a split-shift. You have to be at work from 11:00 a.m. until 2:00 p.m. and return at 5:00 p.m. For sake of illustration, let's also say that being at work is a fixed temporal constraint—you have to be there and you cannot be late. The potential path area is that area that you can access during your available time budget, or the time between when your first shift ends and when your second shift begins. The size of the potential path area will depend on your maximum velocity as you move through space—that is, the size of the area will be different if you on foot, skateboard, bike, car, etc. You can only travel so far within the amount of free

Figure 7.3 A Sample Space-Time Prism

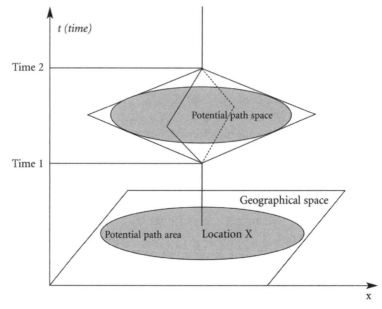

Adapted from Miller (2005) and Ratcliffe (2006).

or discretionary time that you have between the shifts. The potential path space shows all of the locations and all of the times that you can actually occupy during the specified time budget.

The potential path area is more of a 2-dimensional portrayal of the geographical space you could cover; the potential path space considers both location and time. Now, this "simple" space-time prism can get a lot more complicated if we add additional locations (like home, work, class, work, class, bar, home) and if some of these activities become flexible activities rather than fixed. The general idea is that you can only be at certain places given the amount of free time you have. Also, it is important to note that where you are in space and time is controlled by your fixed temporal constraints. For example, at 4:45 p.m. you can only be so far away from work as you must be there in 15 minutes. You will need to be much closer to work at 4:45 p.m. than you would at say, 2:30 p.m. That is why the figure of a prism is used—the area gets much smaller as you get closer to the location of your temporal constraints.

Let's say you know that your friend Joe has to be at class at 2:00 p.m. At 1:40 p.m. you can actually have a fairly good idea of where Joe might be given this temporal constraint. He may be in the parking lot on campus, he may be in line for coffee at the kiosk next to the classroom building, or he may be sitting outside of the building killing some discretionary time before class. You also have a fairly good idea where Joe probably would not be, such as sitting at his apartment that is 45 minutes away from campus. If you know the location of a time constraint, one can map out the relative probability or risk of where a person might be in time and place.

Right about now you might be asking yourself what all of this has to do with criminal behavior. Well, offenders have time constraints just like non-offenders. They have to sleep, eat, visit with their mothers, or even go to school or work. They must fit in their criminal activities between the time constraints of their day, just as we would work in legitimate activities.

Ratcliffe provides the example of a child who walks to school every morning. For purposes of illustration, let's say that the walk to school for little Steve takes 20 minutes and that school starts at 9:00 a.m. If Steve does not wish to be late, then he must leave his house by 8:40 a.m. at the absolute latest. Steve's time budget for the trip has both a *journey time*, which is the time it actually takes him to walk from home to school, and a *reserve time*, which is the time that is left over just in case he runs into unexpected delays. Leaving at 8:40 a.m. would be cutting the time budget very closely and would not allow for any unanticipated events, such as running into a convenience store along the way for an early morning treat. Steve just has enough time to walk at a normal pace to school.

Now, let's say that Steve fancies himself a graffiti artist and enjoys tagging things. If he wishes to paint a tag or two before school he needs to increase his time budget to include not only the travel time required to walk to school, but also the reserve time needed to find an appropriate location, paint his tag, and still make it to school on time. This scenario is dependent on the fact that Steve really wants to make it to school on time, i.e., he views the 9:00 a.m. arrival time as a fixed temporal constraint.

Ratcliffe points out the fact that as Steve walks to school, the relative risk for various targets changes as Steve moves through space and time. As the time draws closer to 9:00 a.m., targets closer to school are at greater risk than those targets closer to his home. Again, assuming that Steve wants to be on time at 9:00 he must be geographically closer to the school than his home. Ratcliffe argues that if Steve's temporal constraints are known, then the potential risk to targets can be mapped both spatially and temporally. This has implications for situational crime prevention strategies. It may be more important (and provide greater monetary savings) to protect a target only during peak at-risk times given the movement of an offender through time and place.

This discussion has provided a very basic overview of this exciting, new area in the geography of space and time. Ratcliffe has been quite prolific in this area, and has provided detailed procedures for the modeling of relative risk for targets in time and place. For more advanced technical reading, you are encouraged to review Ratcliffe's recent works (see, for example, Morgan, 2009; Ratcliffe, 2000; 2002; 2006).

Crime Mapping for Police Operations: The COMPSTAT Model

Arguably, one of the most exciting trends in law enforcement circles today is the incorporation of the COMPSTAT model for managing patrol operations. Depending on which source you look at, COMPSTAT either stands for "Compare Stats" (Silverman, 1999) or "Computer-Driven Crime Statistics" (McDonald, 2002). No matter the source of the acronym, the central meaning is the same: police decision-making should be driven by timely, accurate data. The program began in New York City and, based on their widely publicized success, has quickly expanded across the country to an ever-growing number of municipal and county law enforcement agencies.

When Commissioner William Bratton assumed his duties as the new head of the New York City Police Department (NYPD) in 1994, one of his first policies was to hold weekly meetings with a commanding officer from each of the City's eight bureaus. The goal of these meetings was to discuss the current levels of crime in each area. Quite to Bratton's surprise, the bureau representatives did not have a clue to what their current crime statistics were. It was not uncommon for the data to have a time lag of three to six months. Bratton set out to change this trend, demanding that accurate and timely crime statistics be gathered and distributed. Precinct commanders were held accountable if data from their zone were in error. The importance of geographic accountability cannot be stressed enough in the COMPSTAT model. Instead of being confined to the comfort of their offices, patrol commanders and higher level supervisory personnel were now required to be intimately familiar with the inner workings of their zone, as much as the patrol officers assigned to the area. A clear message was sent to the 31,000 sworn officers that a new era had arrived—the COMPSTAT era (Silverman, 1999).

The Principles of COMPSTAT

As described by McDonald (2002), the COMPSTAT model is based on five principles: (1) specific objectives; (2) timely and accurate intelligence; (3) effective strategies and tactics; (4) rapid deployment of personnel and resources; and (5) relentless follow-up and assessment. In this next section we will spend some time discussing each of these principles, especially as they relate to the use of crime statistics, crime mapping, and geographic accountability.

Specific Objectives: Defining Priorities

When he took office in 1994, Bratton defined a number of specific objectives that needed to be addressed. By clearly identifying these areas of emphasis, Bratton sent out a message to his patrol officers and command staff stating which problems were important and worthy of attention and effort, and which were not. Bratton's objectives included reducing the number of crime incidents in a variety of categories, including youth violence and delinquency, domestic violence, and auto-related crime. Additionally, the availability of guns, street level drug dealing, and public disorder crimes were also elevated to primary importance. Once the specific objectives or areas of importance were identified, the NYPD set out to address these problem areas.

Accurate and Timely Intelligence

The central component of COMPSTAT is the scientific analysis and use of quality, timely crime data. The data are drawn from a variety of sources, including both internally and externally generated information. Internal data include such things as calls for service, arrests, field interview reports, and crime reports. External data can come from a variety of sources, including information that is gathered from other law enforcement or correctional agencies, interviews with arrestees, or even tips from private security firms. The underlying assumption is that without accurate data, the police cannot develop an effective response.

The NYPD relies heavily on the use of crime mapping technology to identify crime patterns and hot spots of criminal activity. In fact, the ability to utilize crime mapping is viewed as an essential component for any agency wishing to adopt a COMPSTAT model (McDonald, 2002). Brightly colored maps that display locations of criminal acts are projected on a large overhead screen in weekly COMPSTAT meetings, providing an important (and dramatic) visual tool for fighting crime.

Once a pattern or hot spot has been identified, the heat is on patrol commanders to do something to address the problem(s). Responsibility for crime in one's assigned area is a key component to the success of COMPSTAT. If a hot spot is identified, the commander is challenged to explain why the hot spot developed and to provide a clearly articulated tactical plan for dealing with the hot spot.

Effective Tactics

One of the more interesting components of the COMPSTAT model is that effective tactics are developed based on a geographic area, not a specific specialized unit or shift. All units assigned to an area, including narcotics, gang units, community policing, crime prevention, and major crimes are expected to work together to assist the patrol division in developing and implementing effective crime fighting strategies. This spirit of cooperation within and between the units is a dramatic change from the way traditional law enforcement is often carried out. Even in relatively small agencies, a robbery detective may not know the patrol officers working in the area. He or she may not be familiar with other detectives assigned to property crimes or other violent crimes, even though they may be looking for the same criminal working in the same area. Additionally, many times these specialized units work in competition with each other for case clearances and resources, which may further erode cooperation. COMPSTAT is designed to alter the independent nature of the various specialized units in order to get them organized around fighting crime in a specific geographic location.

In order for this strategy to be successful, the lines between divisions become blurred. If a lieutenant or patrol commander feels that the problems in his area could be reduced if the narcotics unit conducted an undercover sting operation in a hot spot location, then he should have the authority and influence to get the needed assistance. Under traditional policing strategies, the lieutenant may not be made aware of the undercover operations of the narcotics unit, even if the narcotics officers were working in the lieutenant's own zone. In some cases, this sort of tactical information is provided on a need-to-know basis only. In traditional law enforcement, the unit of analysis is the specialized unit, not the geographic area. Under COMPSTAT, all specialized units work together to develop innovative strategies to reduce crime in their assigned area.

In addition to the emphasis on specialized units, in many cases traditional policing has been focused on shifts. The day commander is aware of all crimes that occurred during his or her assigned time. However, the day commander may not be aware of crimes that occurred outside of the time window of responsibility (like the night or afternoon shift). Geographic accountability makes patrol commanders responsible for reviewing all crime reports that occur within their assigned zone, regardless of the time of occurrence. This is very important in the identification of patterns and trends of criminal activity—criminals do not confine their activities to coincide with a patrol commander's shift.

Rapid Deployment of Personnel and Resources

Once a plan of action has been developed, it is essential that the strategy be implemented as soon as possible. Once again, the key to this component is coordination of various specialty units, along with patrol operations, in order to achieve a common goal. One of the important points of COMPSTAT is accountability. Once a problem has been identified and a strategy is developed, it is the responsibility of a command supervisor to ensure that the appropriate steps are taken. If not, that individual may be humiliated, reassigned, or demoted due to their lack of attention to the COMPSTAT process.

Relentless Follow-Up and Assessment

Once a strategy has been implemented, the COMPSTAT process does not mark the end of an investigation. In fact, it is really only the beginning of the process of relentless follow-up and assessment. Though *"relentless"* is a very powerful word it truly captures the spirit of COMPSTAT. As phrased by McDonald (2002, p. 21), "The term *relentless* is an emotionally charged adjective that encapsulates several forces—determinism, doggedness, urgency, energy, and single-mindedness. These are all forces that improve performance by virtue of the fact that relentless or consistent follow-up increases alertness, productivity, and attention to detail."

Once again, the responsibility falls on the patrol commanders to discuss the success or failure of their intervention strategy. If a tactical plan has proved to be successful in one particular area, then a similar strategy may be used in similar areas to address comparable problems. If the assessment shows that a strategy was not effective, it is the responsibility of the patrol commander to explain why the strategy failed and to develop new alternatives. As an additional source of pressure, these new alternatives need to be developed in a timely manner for presentation and discussion at the next COMPSTAT weekly meeting.

A Note on Strategies within COMPSTAT

The goal of COMPSTAT is not simply to move crime into someone else's backyard, but to solve the crime problem. For this reason, the COMPSTAT management system of patrol operations seems to dovetail well with the community policing philosophy. The goal is to reduce crime within a specific geographic region, calling in whatever resources necessary to develop strategies in order to achieve the goal. Many elements of the principles of COMPSTAT do not sound that much different from the SARA model of community policing (Scanning, Analysis, Response, Assessment).

It should be noted that in some circles, COMPSTAT has become synonymous with zero tolerance policing, though this is not always the case. **Zero tolerance policing** is an aggressive form of law enforcement that emphasizes the "broken windows" philosophy. By focusing attention on relatively minor offenses, the quality of life for area residents will be improved and ultimately, major crimes will be reduced (Walker & Katz, 2002). The reason that COMPSTAT and zero tolerance policing are tied together is that the NYPD adopted both strategies at the same time, leading the media to conclude that the approaches were the same (McDonald, 2002). Within a COMPSTAT model, an agency can adopt any number of strategies to reduce the level of crime in a geographic area. An agency may adopt zero tolerance policing as part of its COMPSTAT model, or may decide that a community policing strategy would be best (or even some combination of the two).

It should be noted that Willis, Mastrofski, and Kochel (2010) have noted a number of differences between the philosophy of community policing and the COMPSTAT model. First and foremost is the difference between the missions of the two strategies. Under community policing, the mission of the police is very broad; the police are expected to address a variety of community concerns and quality of life issues. The mission of the COMPSTAT model is much more focused: the primary goal is to reduce crime, especially serious offenses. The different core missions between these two philosophies highlight other important considerations. For example, since COMPSTAT focuses on crime, the strategy is heavily reliant on official police statistics for data (i.e., field interview reports, arrest data, calls for service, etc.). Because the community policing model is broader, agencies seek information from local residents on a variety of crimes and quality of life concerns. There are organizational differences as well. While community policing focuses on the involvement of lower level patrol officers and sergeants in the identification of local problems, COMPSTAT is more of a top-down organizational model, where it is the responsibility of command staff and crime analysts to identify and analyze community crime problems. Finally, with respect to assessment, under the COMPSTAT model, strategies are reviewed and critiqued at regularly scheduled meetings. Conversely, community-policing strategies look at a variety of indicators to evaluate the success or failure of an intervention (such as citizen surveys that measure changes in levels of fear), as opposed to concentrating on reductions in calls for service or other direct measures of crime. As a result of these varied differences, Willis and his colleagues found that agencies that implemented both the community policing and COMPSTAT strategies tended to keep the strategies separate and independent of each other.

The Future of COMPSTAT

The COMPSTAT model has been given a great deal of credit as a contributing factor in the dramatic reduction in crime rates in New York City. As a result of the positive publicity, larger agencies across the country are jumping on the COMPSTAT bandwagon. Many agencies have already replicated the system or plan to do so in the future. Agencies that have already adopted the COMP-STAT model include Boston, Massachusetts Police Department; New Orleans, Louisiana Police Department; Los Angeles, California Police Department; Maryland State Police; as well as Sheriff's Departments in Broward County and Sarasota County, Florida. While the available data are a bit dated, in a 1999 survey of over 1,000 municipal police agencies, more than half reported that a COMPSTAT model was in the works (Weisburd, Mastrofski, McNally, & Greenspan, 2003). McDonald (2002) similarly noted that as many as two-thirds of police chiefs in major cities planned on adopting a similar system in the very near future. As noted by Dabney (2010), one can reasonably assume that the interest in adopting a COMPSTAT model has continued over the past decade. It should follow that as agencies adopt a data-driven management tool, greater emphasis will be placed on the importance of crime analysis and crime mapping technology.

Predictive Policing:
The PAI and RRI ... FYI

While most applications of crime mapping are retrospective, there is a growing interest in using crime mapping techniques for predicting future crime events in space and time, with the ultimate goal of informing a proactive approach to crime prevention. While the field of predictive crime mapping is relatively new, the interest is clearly growing and there have been a number of recent publications (e.g., Bowers, Johnson, & Pease, 2004; Chainey, Tompson, & Uhlig, 2008; Christens & Speer, 2005; Groff & LaVigne, 2002; Johnson & Bowers, 2004; Johnson, Bowers, Birks, & Pease, 2008; Johnson, Lab, & Browers, 2008). The reliability of these techniques, however, also depends heavily on the accuracy of the retrospective hot spot maps created from past events.

Several general approaches exist in predictive crime mapping, including the use of temporally aggregated hot spots, individual-level analysis of repeat victimization, and various univariate and multivariate analysis of area level data (see, for example, Groff & LaVigne, 2000 for a review). While there is no agreement on which general approach is most reliable for crime prediction, the research appears to suggest that the "best" method is likely to depend on the type of crime. For example, Johnson et al. (2008) successfully developed a predictive individual-level model based on optimal foraging behavior of repeat offenders, but the approach was specifically designed for burglaries and may not apply to other types of offenses. Similarly, Johnson et al. (2008) determined substantial variation in the stability of crime hotspots and this is expected to vary by type of crime.

Among the various approaches to predictive crime mapping, hot spot analysis has received the most attention—in part because many hot spot techniques are in widespread use, in part because of their versatility across spatial-temporal scales and across types of crime. Spencer Chainey and his colleagues (2008) provided one of the first comparative analyses of a range of hot-spot techniques for predictive crime mapping and introduced the concept of a Predictive Accuracy Index (PAI). This index provides a measure of how reliable a retrospective hotspot is able to predict future crime events relative to the size of the hotspots. In a response to Chainey's PAI, Ned Levine (2008) introduced the Recapture Rate Index (RRI). Together, these two indices provide a solid foundation for a more comprehensive comparison of predictive hot spots methods across study areas.

Summary

Crime mapping allows interested parties to clearly identify the geographic location for criminal offenses, monitor the effectiveness of crime intervention strategies, and assist in the deployment and management of police operations. More advanced crime mapping techniques allow researchers and agency personnel to move beyond the identification of individual crime locations to a deeper analysis of crime trends and patterns. Interest in crime mapping appears to be growing, as more and more agencies express interest in adopting the new technology. In addition, crime-mapping technologies are advancing other criminal justice-related efforts outside law enforcement (see Spotlight on Practice III) and becoming more accessible to the general public (see http://projects.latimes.com/ mapping-la/crime).

Using GIS to Improve Probation and Parole Workload Efficiency

This final Spotlight on Practice, which is reprinted from the Fall 2010 edition of TechBeat, the quarterly newsmagazine of the National Law Enforcement and Corrections Technology Center System, describes how the corrections departments in Colorado and Rhode Island are finding that mapping software is making their jobs much easier and efficient as well as allowing better supervision of offenders.

SPOTLIGHT ON PRACTICE IV

Rhode Island Mapper

Rhode Island, the nation's smallest state, has a large probation and parole caseload, with approximately 27,000 individuals on probation or parole. To make tracking of officers' caseloads and offenders more efficient, the Department of Corrections is using the Community Supervision Mapping System.

The Web-based computer software system was developed by the Providence Plan, a nonprofit community organization, and the Urban Institute with funding from the Office of Justice Programs' National Institute of Justice (NIJ). The Providence Plan developed the system using open source software and the Urban Institute conducted an evaluation. The aim of the program is to enable corrections, public safety and social service agencies to better supervise and assist offenders returning to or already in the community.

The system allows users to query locations of released prisoners and map the results at the street level using Google Maps. Users can click on an address and pull up a photo, name, date of birth and case information of the probationer. The system automatically updates the database each night with changes of address and with new offenders on probation or parole.

Christine Imbriglio, supervisor of probation and parole in Kent County, says in addition to helping organize workloads, when probation and parole officers are planning home visits, the system will alert them about offenders living in the same area, so visits can be better coordinated.

"The mapper figures out who lives where and figures out logistics. It really makes it more efficient for an officer," Imbriglio says. The Probation and Parole division has about 76 officers. System users can search by name, city, assigned caseload, supervision level, offense type, distance from a particular address or for individuals recently released into a specific community, and obtain probation and parole officer contact information.

In addition, the system enables officers to plan and conduct compressed, targeted visits in one area in a short period of time. In conjunction with the police department, officers identify communities that have had a recent spate of crime. Two-person teams of probation and police officers map locations of parolees and probationers and spread out, covering 100 home visits in four hours.

In addition, the mapper has been an excellent tool for sex offender supervision by providing users the ability to layer the offender's address in relation to school locations. Rhode Island law currently prohibits any sex offender who is required to register from residing within 300 feet of school.

"Rhode Island has some of the largest caseloads in the country so it is difficult to plan home visits without a tool such as the mapper," Imbrigilo says, adding that the present sentencing system in the state does not provide the courts with many sentencing alternatives besides probation.

The system makes it easier for Imbriglio to track the cases of the officers she supervises. She can also query the system to find out who has been released back into a specific community within the past week, month or year and share discharge planning information with law enforcement as well as community support agencies.

"It automates what people were trying to do manually," says Jim Lucht, information group director for the Providence Plan. "Their existing system is extensive but they have to dig through multiple screens to get information. Our system contains a subset of the most important elements and allows users to rapidly query. It also adds geographic capability."

The system currently has about 700 users, including police officers, according to Lucht. The system also can help social service agencies such as the Family Life Center of Rhode Island better coordinate services to offenders and their families.

Colorado C-WISE

Colorado parole officers have a tool to map caseloads and plan home visits more efficiently. The capability comes through an addition to the existing Colorado WebBased Integrated Support Environment (C-WISE) system used by the Colorado Department of Corrections, Division of Adult Parole, Community Corrections and Youthful Offender System.

C-WISE is a system for electronically entering case contact, surveillance and supervision information. It provides more accurate, quicker access to information and easier statistical tracking. It uses geographic information system (GIS) technology to map officer caseloads, prepare for home visits and provide outside agencies with the locations of offenders living near a crime location.

The division wanted to expand its current GIS technology to allow parole officers to produce maps independently and set up a routing system for planning visits to offenders' homes.

Elisa DiTrolio, division crime analyst, says equipment, software and programming costs to add the mapping and routing component were funded by a U.S. Department of Justice Anti-Gang Initiative grant.

"It presents the officer with a way to view their caseloads in real time instead of just on paper," says DiTrolio. "We have about 300 officers statewide and all have access and all have been trained on the system."

Chapter 8

Some "Radical" Closing Thoughts

The journey through space, time, and crime is almost complete. This text began with several families of theories that have been used to try to explain the geographic concentration of crimes in certain places and spaces, namely Positivism and Classical criminology. It then examined a number of policy recommendations that were derived from these families of theories. Finally, it introduced crime analysis and crime mapping, tools that are used by law enforcement agencies and other interested parties to identify patterns and locations of criminal activities. Today, the study of space, time, and crime is generating a great deal of excitement and energy among law enforcement practitioners and researchers alike. There has been a virtual explosion of interest in these topics over the past several decades. However, it must be noted that not all of this interest has been positive.

Not all researchers share the same level of enthusiasm regarding the study of crime and space. In fact, some are downright critical of the topics explored in this text. In order to understand the criticisms that have been made, the theory behind the negative reactions must be explored. Specifically, the ideas of **radical criminology**, a third family of criminological theory that is closely associated with the writings of Karl Marx, needs to be discussed.

Radical Criminology

Theoretical Assumptions

A number of different but related theoretical perspectives are contained under what I will define as "radical criminology." These various viewpoints on the nature of the law, crime, and society are known by a number of different names—conflict theory, critical criminology, Marxism, feminist theory, post-modern criminology, to name a few. While each of the subgroups has their own distinct arguments, all share a few common threads. The similarities between these various perspectives and then the important differences between a few of the subgroups, specifically conflict criminology and Marxist criminology, will be examined.

First, radical criminologists maintain that inequality of power is at the very root of the crime problem in the United States. While the various radical theorists may debate over who actually holds the ultimate power and why, one cannot escape the issues of power, domination, and control in the radical perspective. Radical criminologists force attention on disadvantaged, less powerful groups in our society such as the poor and/or members of racial and ethnic minority groups. Second, since inequality of power causes crime, the only way to reduce crime is to change the existing power structures. Hence, this family of theories is "radical"—crime and other social problems will be reduced only through the advancement of political initiatives that involve real and lasting changes in our social structure (Bohm, 1997; Curran & Renzetti, 2001; Vold, et al., 2002).

Conflict criminology begins with the assumption that society is comprised of a number of different groups, all of which are vying for control and power. These various groups have competing ideas of what is right and what is wrong, hold different values, and push their own individual political agendas that are designed to further the self-interests of the particular group. The group that is in power has the ability to control the actions of the state, which includes directing the content of the laws as well as the behavior and functions of the court system and the police. Less powerful groups in society are more likely to have the "normal," everyday expected behaviors of their group defined as criminal. Less powerful group members are thus more likely to find themselves caught up in the formal processing of the criminal justice system (Vold et al., 2002).

To help illustrate this point, consider the beliefs of Christian Scientists. Growing up in Detroit, my (Kim) neighbors were members of this religious group and I was often invited to attend church functions with the family. Since my parents were happy to get me out of the house, I attended a number of these events and became somewhat familiar with their beliefs. One of these excursions involved a trip to Cedar Point, an amusement part in Ohio. "Jungle Larry," who hosted the wild animal shows and was a Christian Scientist himself, met with our group of about 30 kids and chaperones. Jungle Larry told us a story about how he had been seriously injured by a lion while he was on safari. Jungle Larry had been mauled by the animal, and was left to die in the wilderness with several broken bones and open gaping wounds. But there he was—fully healed and back at Cedar Point. In keeping with the beliefs of his religion, it was the power of prayer (and prayer only) that ultimately healed Jungle Larry.

You see, Christian Scientists do not endorse the use of what most folks in our society would deem "normal" medical practices. It is this aspect of their beliefs that lands Christian Scientists in the news occasionally. From time to time, you may hear cases in which parents have been brought up on criminal charges of neglect for not seeking medical attention for their sick children. Instead of injecting their child with insulin to counteract the effects of diabetes for example, a Christian Scientist parent may follow what is normal, expected behavior for their group—they pray for their child. Indeed, seeking out medical treatment would violate the beliefs of the group and would be viewed as an act of deviance among Christian Scientists. Since a minority of individuals in our society holds these beliefs, the group does not have a great deal of power and influence. Therefore, what is considered to be normal behavior for the group of Christian Scientists has been defined by more powerful groups in society as "wrong" and "criminal."

Think about how different our society would be if Christian Scientists held power and were able to have their beliefs, values, and norms translated into law. Blood transfusions, organ transplants, the use of prescription drugs, and other medical practices would be outlawed. We would see news reports of parents brought up on criminal charges for seeking black market chemotherapy treatments for their seriously ill child. Society at large would scratch their heads and wonder how parents could subject a child to such horrible, seemingly abusive treatments. It is very important to keep in mind that for conflict theorists, what is "right" and what is "wrong" is completely relative—it is the definitions of the group in power that get translated into what is and is not acceptable behavior for society. As phrased by Chambliss and Seidman (1971, p. 473–474), "the higher a group's political and economic position, the greater is the probability that its views will be reflect in the laws." The definitions of the more powerful groups ultimately become the law of the land—even though these definitions are no better or worse than the definitions held by less powerful groups.

Conflict Criminology and the Control of Public Space

Principles of conflict criminology have been used to analyze the enactment and enforcement of laws designed to control the activities of less powerful groups in society, especially in public spaces. Jeff Ferrell (2001) adopted a conflict stance in his analysis of laws and police practices designed to control the behavior of African Americans, Hispanics, and other less powerful groups as they conduct the everyday business of their lives in public areas. According to Ferrell, public space is a battleground for the control of less powerful groups in society. The presence of racial and ethnic minorities, the poor, and other groups defined as threats to the safety and status of public spaces must be closely monitored and regulated. To illustrate his point, Ferrell describes several case studies involving laws designed to control the behavior of minority group members in public spaces, specifically street cruising and hip hop graffiti.

Controlling Street Cruising

Street cruising is a popular, positive cultural event in Hispanic and Mexican-American communities. Younger men and women take great pains to customize their cars with brightly painted murals that symbolize their cultural heritage. Many of these vehicles are also converted into "lowriders." The proud car owners and their passengers cruise around the city streets in what has been described as a positive, constructive alternative to gang membership, an important source of shared cultural pride, and an integral step in the building of a public ethnic identity.

Unfortunately, not all share the same level of enthusiasm for the street cruisers. Neighborhood activists in a number of cities brought pressure against City Councils and their local police, demanding that something be done to eliminate cruising. Instead of describing the activity as a celebration of ethnic heritage, a Phoenix newspaper described street cruising as "a slow-moving parade of noise, litter, vandalism and violence" (Konig, 1997, p. B1, cited in Ferrell, 2002).

Since the street cruisers are members of a less powerful group in society, their activities have been defined as improper and illegal. The more powerful community activists have been successful in their mission to remove the cruisers from public space, drawing on the power of the legal system. Popular cruising areas have been blocked with barricades, curfews have been enacted, traffic fines have been increased, and laws that regulate the volume of car stereos have been enforced. Hundreds of arrests have been made in the newly designated "no cruising" zones. Ferrell (2002) closes this case study with the following observations of the impact of the anti-street cruising campaign in Denver, Colorado:

> In the years following the erasure of cruising from the streets of north Denver, the neighborhoods there have continued to see skyrocketing housing prices, a steady influx of middle class Anglo homeowners

eager to live near Denver's revitalized downtown, and thus the steady flushing out of north Denver's largely working class, Hispanic population from these newly upscale areas (p. 60).

By controlling the behavior of the largely Hispanic street cruisers, wealthier Whites were able to drive the "less desirable" element from their newly claimed territory.

Outlawing Hip Hop Graffiti

While Ferrell described street cruising as an important source of cultural identity and pride in Hispanic communities, hip hop graffiti provides a similar avenue for African Americans to display their ethnic character and individuality. Graffiti writers display their works in a variety of locations: subways, trains, and exterior walls of buildings. While graffiti art or "tagging" is sometimes confused with gang-related graffiti, it should be noted that hip-hop graffiti developed as an alternative to gang membership and conflict.

Unfortunately for the hip-hop graffiti writers, their particular form of artistic presentation has been defined as one of the early, very negative signs of a community spiraling out of control. Following the "broken windows" philosophy, cities have aggressively targeted any evidence of graffiti, removing the paintings as soon as they are discovered. In what has become described as a racialized panic over hip hop graffiti, an all out war has been launched in many cities to apprehend the writers. Harsher penalties have been enacted and enhanced enforcement methods have been employed, including citizen surveillance teams, infrared video cameras, night vision goggles, and helicopter patrols. What is defined by the writers and members of the hip hop culture as a positive activity that expresses their cultural identity has been effectively criminalized by the larger society. Since the writers and their supporters are a subordinate group in society, their views do not carry any weight. The more powerful groups in society define the actions of the writers as "bad," and ultimately the apprehended writers find themselves caught up in the criminal justice system.

Of course, it must be pointed out that not all graffiti is labeled as bad. Once again, "bad" is a relative term. In the city of Tampa, Florida, a team of "graffiti busters" aggressively targets any signs of graffiti, removing the murals, tags, and other painted messages within 24 to 48 hours of their discovery. However, the graffiti busters have been ordered to leave one form of graffiti alone. Visiting college crew teams regularly come to the Tampa area for rowing practice along the Hillsborough River. These team members—many of them from Ivy League schools—paint their school emblems on sea walls in the downtown area (Morgan, 2002). These "tags" of the wealthy and powerful are viewed as perfectly acceptable and not really graffiti at all. In fact, the spray painted college emblems have been described as part of the city heritage and tradition; the emblems of the less powerful are defined as criminal. If you stand back and view this objectively, is there really any difference between the two forms of graffiti — other than who has painted it?

Who's Got the Power?
Conflict versus Marxist Perspectives

Central to the arguments of conflict criminology is the issue of power. Some groups will have the power to influence our political and legal systems, while most groups will not. Members of less powerful groups are really at the mercy of the powerful groups, as these more powerful groups have the ability to advance and promote their values and norms through the legal system. In effect, crime is directly caused by relative powerlessness (Bohm, 1997). Crime results when the actions of a subordinate group violate the values and norms of another group that has control of the law and the legal system (Akers, 1994). While conflict criminology does focus our attention on how the law and the police may be used against subordinate groups in society, a few important points are missing. Where does the power come from? How did one group rise to power over all others? Conflict criminology does not directly address the questions of where the power came from or how the power structure evolved (Vold et al., 2002). Conversely, these questions are central to the assumptions of Marxist criminology, another radical perspective.

While conflict criminology dodges the issue of how power became so unequally distributed, Marxist criminology addresses this point head on. Marxist criminology focuses on class-based struggles between the rich and the poor and is premised on the works of Karl Marx. The writings of Karl Marx were greatly impacted by the Industrial Revolution, which had literally turned the world upside down. The manners, customs, and traditions that had been in place for a thousand years had changed suddenly and dramatically. Marx set out to analyze what had happened, why the changes had taken place, and to predict what changes would follow. His theories are very complex, drawing on history, economics, political science, and other disciplines. Since Marx did not directly address the issue of crime at any length, different criminologists have developed very different interpretations of what Marx really meant in his writings. The result is a number of related, but competing, theories that fall under the umbrella of Marxist criminology (Bohm, 1997; Taylor, et al., 1973; Vold et al., 2002).

Marx argued that power was concentrated in the hands of a relatively small group of ruling elites. While conflict criminology rested on the idea of a number of competing groups in society struggling for power, Marx saw a single power-elite that had control of the real power in society—social power, political power, and economic power were all concentrated in the hands of the elite. This ruling elite had evolved through the workings of the capitalist system. Capitalism is a highly competitive economic system in which only the strongest survive. Through the competitive process, the **bourgeoisie** class (owners of the means of production, like factories, businesses, etc.) becomes smaller and smaller. Less successful businesses fail, and the former business owners fall into the much larger **proletariat** class. The proletariat is comprised of large numbers of oppressed, working class people whose only choice for survival is to sell their labor to the bourgeoisie. While the proletariat is virtually powerless, the power of the bourgeoisie is derived from their monopoly ownership of the means of production.

According to Marx, this small ruling elite not only controls the economic system, but the political system as well. This implies that the bourgeoisie is able to control the laws, the police, and the entire criminal justice system to further their own interests. The capitalist class holds all real power. Their primary goal is to maintain their position of dominance in society at the expense of the proletariat. Following this argument, we would expect to find members of the proletariat over-represented in all stages of the criminal justice system, including official police contacts, arrests, prosecution, and incarceration. Since the rich and the powerful control the criminal justice system, crimes that are more likely to be committed by the poor are defined as more serious, elicit greater fear, receive greater levels of attention by the police (the social control agents of the state), and carry harsher penalties than crimes committed by the affluent.

To help illustrate this point, consider the crime of robbery. Robbery has been defined as a very serious crime of personal violence. The FBI has deemed this crime as one of the Part I crimes, which would imply that the vast majority of police agencies pay careful attention to the number of robberies occurring in their jurisdiction. After all, the total number of robberies appears on the front page of the local newspaper and is often used as an indicator of public safety. Back when I (Kim) used to own a carry-out pizza shop, the threat of an armed robber entering the business was always very real. The fear associated with a stranger entering my shop, threatening my crew (and me, of course!) with violence, and taking the hard earned cash was very unsettling.

Objectively speaking, what is robbery? Someone wants or needs more of something (usually money), so they take it from someone else. Who commits robbery? A typical offender is poor, young, male, and disproportionately African American (Miethe & McCorkle, 2001; Wright & Decker, 1997). Why are robberies committed? In a qualitative study of active robbers, Wright and Decker found that the vast majority of the robbers that they interviewed noted a need for cash as a primary motivation. Consider the following responses noted by the interviewees (Wright & Decker, 1997):

> Being broke [gets me to thinking about doing an armed robber] ... cause being broke, man, you don't feel good. You ain't got nothing in your pocket, so you want to take something out of someone else's pocket. (Bill Williams—No. 78)
>
> [The idea of committing an armed robbery] comes into your mind when your pockets are low; it speaks very loudly when you need things and you are not able to get what you need. It's not a want, it's things that you need, basic things that if you don't have the money, you have the artillery to go and get it. That's the first thing on my mind; concentrate on how I can get some more money. (Black—No. 79)
>
> [Armed robbery] was a big joke more or less when I was younger. It ain't no joke now. It's survival. That's how I look at it now. (James Minor—No. 14) (p. 33).

So, viewed objectively, robbery is a crime committed by less powerful individuals in society. Robbers want money. However, given their occupational and social status, they have a rather limited range of opportunities from which to choose just how they will get the money. Compare the situation of a robber from that of a physician, an accountant, a stockbroker, a banker, or the Chief Executive Officer of a large corporation. Greed, need, and want are not confined to lower socioeconomic classes. If a physician feels that she wants money, then the opportunities available to act on this want are very different. A physician may turn to other means to acquire money through illegal means, such as defrauding Medicaid, engaging in tax evasion, or possibly embezzlement.

Kim recalls taking a group of students to a Federal Correctional Facility in Florida for a tour. The prison inmates had put together a program called "Life Talks" where they discussed their involvement in various acts of crime. When the class arrived, there was a well-groomed Caucasian man sitting at one of the tables. He was extremely articulate, pleasant, and spoke at length to several of the students in the class. The students were shocked to find out that this "nice man" was actually a convicted criminal who had engaged in real estate fraud in Texas. During a question and answer session with the correctional staff, the students went so far as to say that this "nice man" did not belong in prison and should be transferred to some other type of facility or released outright. The staff responded very harshly to these comments, indicating that this inmate had bilked families out of their entire life savings by promising to build them new homes in developments that did not exist. For whatever reason, even future criminal justice leaders define crimes of greed committed by the privileged very differently.

Consider the case of Bernie Madoff, the architect of a $65 billion Ponzi scheme. In his quest to accumulate vast wealth, Madoff engaged in the largest act of fraud in the history of the U.S. Thousands of individuals lost their entire life savings based on Madoff's promises of investment returns as high as 46% (Gloven, Larson, & Voreacos, 2009). While Madoff ultimately plead guilty to nearly a dozen different criminal charges related to his pyramid scheme, many view this type of criminal act of greed differently than they would a crime of greed committed by a robber or "street criminal." People do not lie awake at night fearful of their investment banker, but the cost to the victim can be just as devastating.

Thinking Outside of the Box: The Radical Perspective

Some time has been spent discussing two specific types of radical criminological theories: conflict theory and Marxist theory. To help keep them separate, conflict theory tends to be used to help us better understand cases of culture conflict while Marxist theory is usually employed when analyzing rich-versus-the-poor type issues. Sometimes the distinction can get a bit blurred. However, the important thing to remember is that this family of theories forces us to think about "crime," "criminals," and crime reduction strategies in a much different way. The rest of this chapter will be devoted to a critical evaluation of the various intervention strategies that were previously presented in this text. As this discussion will suggest, there is often more to consider than what immediately meets the eye.

Radical Critiques

First and foremost, radical criminologists would charge that too much emphasis is focused on crimes committed by individuals from lower socioeconomic classes. Indeed, the focal point of our entire criminal justice system places far too much weight on "street crimes" and not enough importance on crimes of the powerful. Crime analysis, crime mapping, and other high tech enforcement tools of law enforcement are used to better control the "dangerous classes" of society. Consider the cases of corporate greed exhibited by the companies Enron, Worldcom, and Bernard Madoff. Thousands of employees and investors lost everything due to the deceptive accounting practices used by these corporate giants. The individuals responsible for these crimes will never show up on any crime analysis bulletin, nor will their homes be identified on a crime map. Local police agencies do not monitor the criminal actions of the wealthy or privileged. This is in spite of the fact that one is at least as likely to be injured or killed due to an occupation injury or disease, unnecessary medical procedures, or poor emergency medical services as being the victim of aggravated assault or a homicide. Further, society has lost more money from embezzlement, price fixing, and consumer deception than the combined losses of all of the property crimes included in the all-important list of FBI Part I crimes (Reiman, 1998). A number of crime reduction policies have been discussed in this text. Regardless of the specifics of the policy, all target the everyday behaviors and criminal actions of the less powerful.

What Could Be Wrong with Rebuilding Communities?

In the previous discussions of criminological theory, two other schools of thought were presented: Positivism and Classical criminology. Just as a point of review, a Positivist assumes that human behavior is not a matter of free choice. One's actions are, at least to some extent, determined by factors beyond one's immediate control. These factors may include both internal and external influences, such as psychological or biological defects, poor socialization within the family, or growing up in a low income, high crime neighborhood. Positivists believe that differences between criminals and non-criminals can be clearly identified.

The quality of the environment in which people live is an important difference between criminals and non-criminals. Certain communities have higher levels of crime than others. Poverty, social disorganization, higher levels of residential turnover, greater racial and ethnic diversity, higher number of single parent households, and lower levels of informal social control are oftentimes associated with high crime spaces. To reduce crime in these areas, the sense of community must be strengthened, educational and job opportunities improved, and the level of both formal and informal social control increased.

How would a radical criminologist view such community-building initiatives? You might recall our discussion of the Urban Jobs and Enterprise Zone Act, which was heralded as a cure for unemployment and urban decay. The program was designed to provide tax incentives to small business that would operate in designated areas and employ local residents. The goal was to encourage entrepreneurs to open new businesses, expand their operations, or relocate their operations from other areas to the economically challenged neighborhoods. New jobs would be created and the local economy would improve, ultimately improving the quality of life for the local citizens. In a critical review, Walton (1982) argued that because of the way the tax incentives were structured, large firms who were least in need of tax breaks were much more likely to reap the rewards, while "Mom and Pop" small businesses would not see the benefits of the program. The rich would get richer, and the poor would be no better off. Furthermore, the types of jobs created by this program have been criticized. The positions tend to be low paying jobs that require low skills. Some have argued that enterprise zones serve to "bring the Third World home" and offer a future of economic stagnation in the targeted areas (Goldsmith, 1982; cited in Walton, 1982). Critics argue that the program simply cannot work in the long term and local residents will ultimately pay the price of degraded labor, unmet expectations, and even greater class division and income inequality (Walton, 1982).

What about programs like the Chicago Area Project? The CAP, which is still in operation today, is based upon the work of Shaw and McKay. Designed to improve conditions in troubled neighborhoods and reduce social disorganization, the CAP advocated after school and weekend recreational, educational, and vocational programs. Local youths were provided with opportunities to engage in positive activities, such as sports programs and other structured events. Local business owners joined the executive boards of the CAP, providing financial support, volunteer hours, and other forms of philanthropy. What could possibly be bad about that?

A radical criminologist would attack such measures, arguing that these sorts of "feel good" programs are nothing more than a band-aid designed to make the rich feel better about themselves, with little or no real concern given to the plight of poorer people in society. By focusing attention on social disorganization as a cause of delinquency, the real causes of crime and other social problems—the inequality and exploitation that are part and parcel of our capitalist system—were completely ignored. Of course the wealthy would support CAP programs that were designed to improve the living conditions of the poor— they would be crazy not to. These programs did alleviate some of the problems of the less fortunate. However, most importantly, these programs deflected attention away from the real problems and allowed the unequal distribution of wealth and resources to continue (Krisberg & Austin, 1978; Sheldon, 2001; Snodgrass, 1976).

Bear in mind that when thinking like a Marxist, violent revolution is always a possibility. Even though they may not have any real power, when one considers the sheer number of warm bodies, the proletariat is a much larger class than the ruling elite. The threat of an uprising, in which the proletariat seizes power and redistributes wealth and resources, is very real. Therefore, the proletariat must be pacified in some manner. It is not in the best interests of the bourgeoisie elite to have the proletariat dwell on their poor lot in life and blame the elite for their impoverished situation. By donating some money here and there, holding a charity banquet, or volunteering a few hours a month to some sort of cause, the bourgeoisie give the illusion that they are the "good guys." Anger, blame, and outrage are diverted away from the powerful elite, even though it is their everyday business practices that have caused the neighborhoods to deteriorate and ensure that the impoverished conditions will continue.

The Dark Side of Community Policing: A Wolf in Sheep's Clothing?

What about community policing initiatives? Isn't community policing a better way for police officers to conduct themselves in lower income neighborhoods than say, zero tolerance policing? Well, yes and no. Zero Tolerance Policing (ZTP) is an aggressive, pro-active policing strategy that encourages police officers to target relatively trivial criminal offenses. In the City of New York, Rudolph Guiliani abandoned community policing, which he viewed was too soft on crime, in favor of ZTP. Hispanics, African Americans, and members of various immigrant groups have borne the brunt of these new aggressive tactics (Bass, 2001; Chambliss, 1994). The number of minorities stopped and frisked by the police has increased sharply, especially in neighborhoods where they constitute a clear minority. For example, in communities where African Americans and Hispanics comprise less than 10% of the population, Blacks comprised 30% of those stopped by the police and Hispanics accounted for another 23.4% (Bass, 2001). It should come as no surprise that complaints filed against the NYPD have risen 41% since ZTP became the norm. Most of these complaints have been filed by racial and ethnic minorities (Bass, 2001; Greene, 1999).

While not all of these encounters with police end with a formal arrest, many of the encounters do. Even in cases where no formal arrest is made, the stop provides a great opportunity for the police to embark on a fishing expedition to gain valuable intelligence concerning "dangerous" individuals. One of the goals of zero tolerance policing is to have a record of the formal contact with the individual who has been stopped. This information gathering exercise assists in crime analysis—data gathered during the encounter is passed along to the crime analysis unit. The location and time of the stop, name, address, and identifying characteristics (scars, tattoos) of the individual stopped, and any known acquaintances are entered into a searchable database. If the police ever need to find the individual in the future, they have a good place to start. While law enforcement personnel herald the field interview report as an essential tool in fighting crime, a radical criminologist would attack this practice, arguing that the government is monitoring the comings and goings of innocent people who have been defined as potential criminals. Since a disproportionate number of minorities and lower income residents find themselves stopped and interviewed by the police, this practice is viewed as just another tool of exploitation designed to keep less powerful groups in check.

If an arrest is made, then the individual is fingerprinted (more data for crime analysts) and gets a formal arrest record. Since it is much easier to plead guilty to a minor offense than to fight the charge in court, more than likely the individual will have a criminal conviction (Walker, 1998). Now, if this same individual is ever arrested and convicted on a more serious charge, it will not be their first encounter with the criminal justice system. This removes the possibility of the arrestee being offered the opportunity to participate in various diversion programs for first time offenders and increases the likelihood of more serious sanctions being handed down. Once again, the issue of power and who gets targeted for arrest enters into the picture. The data suggest that under ZTP, minorities have been disproportionately arrested for less serious misdemeanor offenses (Harcourt, 1998). Given the problems associated with ZTP, some have gone so far as to label the practice "harassment policing" (Panzarella, 1998; Walker & Katz, 2002).

Since Zero Tolerance Policing has been criticized so heavily, is community policing better? Not exactly. Community policing has a bit of a dark side. In a documentary on the Arts and Entertainment channel (A&E), on the history and changing role of the police, community policing was compared to vigilante justice. Under a system of vigilante justice, local residents monitor the behavior of those defined as criminal and often take the law into their own hands. While this sort of policing system is usually associated with the historical era of the frontier and the "Wild West," the concern is that this sort of "justice" is being replicated in many contemporary neighborhoods. Under the warm and fuzzy guise of community policing, some questionable tactics may be utilized to monitor and control the behavior of those defined as dangerous, different, or undesirable (A&E Home Video, 1996).

For example, my (Kim) father lives in a neighborhood that has a rather strong neighborhood watch and community policing organization. The group holds regular meetings, distributes a newsletter, organizes various dinners and other community events, and even developed a rather complex communication system to report criminal activities in the neighborhood. When I visit, sometimes there is a crime watch sign posted at the main entrance to the neighborhood with a ribbon attached. Sometimes the ribbon is green; other times it is blue. This is a message to members of the neighborhood watch. A green ribbon indicates that a burglary had taken place, and a blue ribbon means that there was some sort of problem with juveniles. There are other codes, but the newsletter is needed to figure out what sort of incident had occurred.

In one unfortunate incident, one of the community watch members discovered that a local resident had a *15-year-old* conviction for exposing himself in public. Now, this sort of conviction can result from a number of different scenarios other than the image of a child molester driving around a playground in a trench coat. Perhaps he had been skinny-dipping, or had been caught parking with his girlfriend—even public urination could fall under this sort of charge. Based on the age of the man, the incident probably occurred during his college-age years. The exact circumstances surrounding the incident did not matter to the community watch, who distributed "important alert" fliers to all of the people in the neighborhood informing them that a "sexual predator" lived in their midst. Not surprisingly, he did not live there much longer.

The strongest community organization efforts tend to arise in neighborhoods dominated by white, older, middle class homeowners who perceive some sort of threat to their way of life. Oftentimes, this threat is centered on changes in the racial composition of the neighborhood, as members of racial or ethnic minorities purchase or rent homes in the area (Skogan, 1986). Under these sorts of conditions, community-policing efforts may be utilized to legitimize and support a system of racism. Neighbors are encouraged to monitor the actions of "criminals" in their community, in order to help the police in their war on crime. Additionally, community efforts to reduce decline and maintain neighborhood racial stability have been most successful in areas where the residents' mission was supported by what Skogan described as "large but immobile corporate actors (e.g., hospitals, banks, and universities) with a sunk investment to protect" (1986, p. 222). In the words of a radical Marxist, the capitalist elite had a stake in ensuring that the "dangerous classes" of individuals be driven out of "their" neighborhood; thereby making sure that their real estate investments and personal safety remained undisturbed.

Too Much Weeding and Not Enough Seeding?

As noted earlier, community policing programs are most successful in white, middle class neighborhoods. In areas with high number of working and lower class minority residents or areas where a sense of community does not exist, community policing efforts are not as successful. In keeping with our radical critique, given the emphasis that the police and the criminal justice system places on street crimes, it should come as no surprise that minority, lower income areas tend to have higher rates of crime. In higher crime neighborhoods, another more aggressive law enforcement tactic has been used that is packaged as an offshoot of community policing: Operation Weed and Seed.

Operation Weed and Seed (OWS) started in 1991 when the United States Department of Justice provided grant opportunities to law enforcement agencies to target high crime neighborhoods. The program initially began in about 18 communities and by the year 2000 had expanded to 200 projects throughout the United States (Dunworth & Mills, 1999). Today, Weed and Seed sites number over 250, serving neighborhoods across the country that range in size from 3,000 to 50,000 residents. The goal of OWS is based on its name: First, violent offenders and drug dealers are "weeded out" through aggressive, pro-active law enforcement and dogged prosecution. The weeding phase is a coordinated effort between federal, state, county, and local police departments along with their prosecutor's offices. The underlying philosophy is that the neighborhoods cannot be improved without removing the dangerous elements from circulation. Then, after the criminal offenders have been removed, the area is "seeded" with various programs designed to improve the quality of life for the local residents, including: economic opportunities, drug and alcohol treatment programs, juvenile intervention and diversion programs, community enrichment, and crime prevention strategies (Roehl, Huitt, Wycoff, Pate, Rebovich, & Coyle, 1996; Simons, 2002). Unfortunately, the seeding portion of the program has taken a back seat to weeding; the emphasis of the Weed and Seed programs has been on law enforcement (Bridenball & Jesilow, 2005; Miller, 2001)

While the National Institute of Justice has heralded Operation Weed and Seed as a success, not all community members share the same level of enthusiasm. And, once again, the disparate evaluations often fall along race and class lines. "Regular" community policing projects are used in white, middle class neighborhoods, while OWS projects are more likely to be used in poorer, minority communities. It is the weeding phase of the projects that has raised concerns among residents of the communities targeted for such efforts. In an evaluation of a Weed and Seed program in Seattle, Reed (1999) found that local residents were afraid that the program served to extend the power of the police in their community. Bridenball and Jesilow (2005) found that a Weed and Seed program in Santa Ana, California actually increased the residents' fear of gang activity and crime in their neighborhood. Consider the following statements by Elijah Gosier, an African American columnist, as he voices his concerns about a Weed and Seed project:

> No one argues with the seed portion of the equation. Who could argue with the prospect of federal money supporting jobs and businesses and other community enhancements? The only argument with the *seeding* is that it can be viewed as a bribe to coerce a hurting community to submit to the *weeding*. [emphasis in original] The weeding is the sticking point. Some perceive it as granting the police permission to trample the provisions of the constitution that are intended to protect citizens from police and governmental excesses. They see it as something just short of martial law.... There is a history of mistrust—even enmity—between police and communities like the one targeted for St. Petersburg's Weed and Seed program, communities that are poor and black. [Officers in charge of the project] said little to dispel those sentiments among those who have acquired them over years of experience ... If police in a Weed and Seed do the same thing they do in the rest of the city, why bother calling it something other than policing, especially when that something is as *tactless and dehumanizing* as weeding? Why couple the weed with the seed? [emphasis added] If you're looking to arrest major drug figures, why waste time mining for them in the poorest part of town, where only their flunkies work? (Gosier, 1997, p. C1).

Unfortunately, the concerns voiced by Gosier have not been unfounded in many communities. While weeding efforts have been successful, the seeding efforts have proven to be much more of a challenge. Police agencies and their community partners either do not know exactly what to do to increase education, vocational, and other quality of life measures, or, in other areas there simply is not enough funds left to do any seeding in the newly-weeded areas (Kennedy, 1996; Tien & Rich, 1994). In sum, police agencies are good at the weeding phase, but not so good at the seeding component.

The net effect is that poor and minority residents may experience a very different form of community policing than more affluent, white residents. While white residents interact with "Officer Friendly" at community meetings and neighborhood picnics, many minorities experience aggressive law enforcement tactics, including increased "stop and frisks," crackdowns, heightened surveillance, undercover stings, and other intensive operations. It should also be noted that if federal law enforcement agencies get involved, drug cases may then be moved to federal court. Federal drug convictions carry much harsher penalties than state convictions. No matter which jurisdiction eventually tries the case, arrest and prosecution are the keys to success in the OWS areas.

Conversely, success in community policing efforts in more affluent, white neighborhoods is measured by the *absence* of arrests. An arrest is viewed as the last resort, since an arrest does nothing to address the underlying problems in a community. So, in the eyes of a radical criminologist, community policing is nothing more than an excuse to unleash an army of occupation on minority communities, whose residents will once again experience the full weight of the criminal justice system. In practice, community policing becomes indistinguishable from zero tolerance policing—though it may *sound* better. Wealthy business owners can support OWS efforts and appear charitable and caring—all the while supporting a system that emphasizes greater social control over less powerful groups in society.

In closing, radical criminologists would argue that community building efforts have a much darker agenda than assisting the less fortunate. But what about policies based on choice theories? Would a radical criminologist view these programs as potential harmful to less fortunate groups in society?

Radical Critiques of Choice-Based Policies

As a point of review, choice-based policies are based on the theoretical perspective of Classical Criminology. A Classical Criminologist assumes that human beings exercise free will in making rational decisions. After careful consideration of a number of factors, including perceived effort, reward, risk of apprehension, and alternative courses of action, a rational offender selects the "best" location and time to commit a crime as well as the best form of crime to commit (robbery versus burglary, for example). In this text we have discussed a number of policy recommendations based on this school of thought, including various target hardening strategies such as defensible space, crime prevention through environmental design, and situational crime prevention.

It is important to mention that a radical criminologist would attack one of the core, basic assumptions held by a Classical Criminologist: the issue of free choice. Radical criminologists focus on issues related to the unequal distribution of power in our society. An affluent white male has much different choices and opportunities than an African American female born in a family of poverty. In order to understand how choices are structured, it is absolutely essential to consider how differently people are treated based on social class, race, gender, and other social and demographic characteristics. A radical criminologist would argue that the assumption of free choice for all members in our society, given the inequalities of our social structure, is absurd.

Monopoly, Anyone?

If it helps to understand what a radical criminologist is talking about, consider the game of Monopoly. The object of the game is to become the richest player by buying, selling, or renting properties. A player travels around the game board, landing on various properties. If someone else has not already purchased the property, the player may buy the property. Then, when another player lands on the property, that player must pay the owner of the property rent. The owner can improve the property by building houses and hotels, which allow the owner to charge even more rent. When you are broke, you are out of the game.

Monopoly can be viewed as a miniature replication of our capitalist system. Of course, there is one important consideration: In Monopoly, all players are essentially equal. Everyone starts out the game with the same amount of money. Then, based on the luck of the dice, draw of the card, and individual strategy, the winner is decided. Both luck and skill enter into the equation of who will ultimately be the most successful.

Now, let's make the game more accurately reflect the realities of American society. The person who draws the shoe game piece is given $500 to start the game. The person who is the thimble is given $1,500, and the person with the dog starts the game with $5,000. Now, the person with the hat begins the game with $50,000 and ownership of Park Place and Boardwalk (the two most valuable properties). On top of that, the "hat" person also controls the bank and is allowed to set interest rates for loans and dole out money as they see fit. Also, the hat person may send other, less powerful pieces to jail, if they complain too much or otherwise disturb the game.

As the game begins, who really has "free" choice? Would you be shocked if the "shoe" person grabbed some cash when the banker got up to use the restroom? A radical criminologist would argue that this unequal situation more accurately reflects the class-based realities of our society. Also, bear in mind that in the Monopoly illustration, we have not considered issues of discrimination based on gender, race, or ethnicity. What if the thimble person were not allowed to collect $200 upon passing "Go" for no reason other than being a thimble?

Because of the unequal nature of our society, the assumption of free choice is not a given for radical criminologists. Instead of free choice, minority citizens and members of lower socioeconomic classes experience **structured choice**. Proponents of this perspective argue that an individual's circumstances may be best understood when one considers how often meaningful, positive life chances and opportunities are made available to that individual (Lynch & Patterson, 1996; Stretesky & Lynch, 1999a). In our current social structure, one's race and social class factor heavily into how often positive life chances are presented. Greater constraints are placed on the choices available to minorities and less affluent individuals. For example, if a neighborhood begins to deteriorate, a more affluent white family has more choices than a less affluent minority family. The minority family may not have the financial resources to leave. Furthermore, due to discrimination in housing and employment, the minority family may experience greater difficulty in finding a new home and a new job. These constraints further limit the choices that are available to the minority family. Radical criminologists would argue that structured choice more accurately describes our class and race-based social system. Therefore, any policies based on flawed theoretical assumptions are doomed to failure.

Beyond the debate surrounding free choice, radical criminologists would have other concerns regarding choice-based policies. One of the more serious critiques surrounds the issue of displacement, or simply moving crime from one target to another. To summarize, radical criminologists would argue that the location where the crime ultimately moves might be linked to social class. Individuals with more money will be able to utilize target hardening strategies, hire security consultants, or even have their own private police force, while the poor will not. Targets that are not well protected are viewed as easier to violate, so it would follow that poorer people and their homes, cars, and businesses will experience higher levels of victimization.

Crime Displacement: Is the Glass Half Empty?

As mentioned in Chapter 5, displacement occurs when crime simply moves or changes its form as a result of a crime fighting strategy. The specifics of the crime fighting strategy can take on a variety of forms: enhanced efforts by law enforcement, situational crime prevention, or various target hardening techniques. In their evaluations of the effectiveness of these strategies, researchers have identified a number of different types of displacement. Criminals can move from one location to another (called **spatial** or **territorial displacement**); move from one time to another (**temporal displacement**); select a more vulnerable target (**target displacement**); change their methods to adapt to the new design modification (**tactical displacement**); or change to a completely new form of crime. Regardless of the type of displacement, the important point is that there is no net reduction in the level of crime—the criminals have simply adapted to the heightened level of risk, modifying their behavior to reduce the threat of apprehension.

Of the various forms of displacement, spatial displacement is the most prevalent (Lab, 2000). Interestingly enough, individual police agencies may not be very concerned with spatial displacement, as long as the crime moves out of their jurisdiction. Over the years of my (Kim) research on various police issues, I have interacted with a number of officers from many different agencies. Occasionally, the issue of displacement has come up, especially if an agency's crime fighting efforts have been well publicized in the media. One municipal agency had received a great deal of positive publicity after their FBI UCR numbers experienced a dramatic drop. I asked an agency representative about his perception of the drop, and he began to laugh quite heartily. Apparently a large lower income housing project had been deemed uninhabitable and was demolished. The former residents—predominately poor and minority—had a great deal of difficulty finding landlords who would accept their housing vouchers within the city limits. The displaced residents ultimately found new housing—in the county, outside of the city limits. While the official crime statistics for the city experienced a sharp decline, the numbers from the county sheriff 's department reported a similar increase. The displacement of the local residents—and the crime problems that followed them— was quite a source of amusement for the municipal police officers.

Illustrations of calculated displacement are not difficult to come by. In one-on-one conversations, I (Kim) have been told that it is relatively common for police personnel to pick up vagrants in their jurisdiction, only to drop them off in a nearby city. The neighboring city will then return the favor. The "sport" in this activity is not to get caught in the act. Prostitution stings chase women and their customers out of one area and into another agency's space. Of course, it is much easier to make an arrest than it is to try to address the underlying root cause of why the women have turned to prostitution in the first place. When planning various evaluation studies, I have been met with incredulous stares and told not to worry about measuring displacement. The police knew where the crime would move. In some cases, agency personnel provided me with the specific cross streets where the crime would be channeled. As long as the crime was out of their jurisdiction, the project was to be labeled a success.

Law enforcement agencies are not the only guilty parties with respect to a lack of concern over the issue of displacement. As noted by Lab (2000), there are not many studies of various crime fighting efforts that explicitly address the issue of displacement. One of the reasons for this omission is the fact that displacement is not a primary concern of the law enforcement agency, business, commercial development, or apartment complex that has initiated the crime prevention effort. As long as the crime problem was moved out of their realm of concern, the effort was a victory. Even now, as I reflect back on my previous life as a private business owner, I would share in this guilt. If I had spent several thousands of dollars in surveillance cameras, locking devices, safes, increased lighting, and other target hardening measures, I would not be concerned with whether or not the robbers had decided to go down the street to victimize a less protected target. My only concern was whether or not my chances of becoming a victim had been reduced. So what if the robbers drove by my place of business to hit the more vulnerable local 7-11; as long as it was NIMBY—not in my back yard. This, of course, is a very selfish, shortsighted view, but most business owners are not interested in changing the world— only their little part of it.

In a review of the issue of displacement, Lab (2000) summarizes with the following:

> These studies find that displacement is a viable concern for discussions of crime prevention. Although the list of studies supporting each type of displacement is limited, this is probably due to the failure of most evaluations to consider displacement. In many other studies, displacement of one type or another is a realistic rival hypothesis to the claims of crime prevention. Interestingly, two reviews that claim to find little evidence of displacement argue that it should not be a major concern (Eck, 1993; Hesseling, 1994) actually uncovered a significant level of various forms of displacement. Both Hesseling's (1994) and Eck's (1993) analyses show that roughly one-half of the studies show evidence of displacement, particularly territorial and target forms. The fact that the authors do not find 100% displacement, or displacement in all studies, leads them to conclude that it is not a major problem. This is an unrealistic criterion and any evidence of displacement is a concern that should be addressed (p. 88).

A proponent of various crime prevention and target hardening strategies would probably argue that while half of the studies reviewed did show evidence of displacement, that would imply that half did not. The glass is half full, not half empty. Felson (1998, p. 141–142) goes so far as to describe displacement as an "illusion," stating that the displacement model is "extremely dubious." Felson further argues, "it is a disgrace to use 'displacement' as an excuse to hold back creativity in preventing crime" (1998, p. 142).

The Ethics of Crime Prevention

Part and parcel of the displacement debate is where and against whom crimes are displaced. A radical criminologist would argue that wealthy people, who can afford protections, deflect crime and criminals into less powerful communities. Therefore, minorities and people from lower socioeconomic communities will experience heightened levels of crime. The wealthy will enjoy greater safety and protection at the expense of the poor.

Felson and Clarke (1997), both supporters of routine activities theory and situational crime prevention, recognize the issues surrounding the displacement of crime into less powerful communities. In order to ensure equal protection from crime to all members of society, Felson and Clarke (1997, p. 200) provide the following principles that they feel should guide crime control policy:

1. Situational prevention should not serve as a means for one segment of the community to displace its crime risk onto another element.
2. Situational prevention should not serve just one social class, nor should its costs be borne by another social class or stratum of society.
3. Situational prevention should be attentive to the victimization risks of minorities and disempowered segments of society.

These are truly noble goals that radical criminologists would embrace wholeheartedly. However, it should also be noted that Felson and Clarke (1997) do not perceive that situational crime prevention disproportionately favors the wealthy. According to Felson and Clark, individuals who argue that the rich reap greater benefits than the poor do not fully understand the basic principles of situational crime prevention. The poor can benefit from crime prevention efforts just as the wealthy can—the positive successes of the various strategies are not confined solely to affluent residents. Less affluent communities can experience a **diffusion of benefits**, a sort of spillover of the positive effects of crime-prevention strategies.

Furthermore, Felson and Clarke argue that policies that appear to disproportionately target individuals from lower socioeconomic classes are not really hurting the poor. For example, if the police stop and question teenagers in lower income areas when they are out late at night, enforce curfews, or otherwise restrict the teens' freedom, this official action by the police should not be viewed as a bad, discriminatory action. In fact, this form of social control is quite helpful in lower income communities. According to Felson and Clark (1997),

> ... wealthier groups tend to restrict more closely the freedom of their children to wander, especially at night, thus containing the amount of trouble they get into. If we wish to treat equally those lower in income, especially those living in inner cities, *facilitating equality of supervision* is one method" [emphasis added] (p. 204).

So, it is really in the interests of equality that the police pick up, question, gather intelligence data, and monitor the actions of lower income kids. By now, you should be able to recognize that a radical criminologist would take great issue with this assertion. A radical criminologist would argue that there really is no difference between wealthy teenagers and poor teenagers— except in how their very similar behaviors are defined. Poor kids hanging out on a street corner are viewed as dangerous potential criminals and are more likely to be picked up by the police (who are disproportionately assigned to poor and minority communities). Teens from wealthy families are more likely to have cars and hence be mobile and less obvious to the eyes of the public and the police. Further, fewer police patrols in wealthy neighborhoods leads to fewer official contacts. The assertion that more aggressive monitoring of teens in lower income neighborhoods enhances equality of supervision provides even greater justification for police to stop and question poorer youths.

A radical criminologist would argue that the answer to the crime problem is not to engage in various crime prevention strategies, but instead to provide a more level playing field for poor and minority youths. Improve educational, vocational, and occupational opportunities for residents of our inner cities. Change the existing social structure to ensure that all members of society, regardless of race, ethnicity, or socioeconomic class truly do have free choice, and not just structured choice. Inequality is the root cause of all crime. Without addressing this basic issue, any crime control effort will fail.

Felson and Clarke (1997) argue that pursuing these sorts of programs may very well be a waste of time and effort. In their words (1997, p. 205), "However liberal and attractive [social improvement programs] might sound, it violates our basic notion that people are not very prone to long-term improvement. Social prevention implies improving people, which we regard as a goal almost sure to produce frustration." Social prevention programs designed to improve education, recreation, and employment opportunities must take a back seat to situational crime prevention in any serious discussion of crime prevention. In this view, programs advocated by radical criminologists will certainly fail. You cannot change people by increasing their education levels or improving their economic status. This charge goes back to the very basic principles of Classical Criminology: People are basically evil. Left to our own devices, we will return to our evil nature. If you want to control crime, you need to go back to certain, swift, and proportionate punishments. If people perceive that they will get caught and punished, they will not commit crimes. For a Classical Criminologist, the answer to the crime problem is quite simple. To a radical criminologist, the answer is also quite simple—it is just a very different answer.

And so the debate continues. Before the close of this Chapter, it is important to recognize a new movement that is slowly picking up speed among more traditional criminologists: the study of environmental justice. Research in this area forces one to consider new issues in the study of crime and space.

Is There Something Truly Sinister Going on in Lower Income Communities? The Issue of Environmental Justice

Environmental justice puts a new spin on why crime and other social problems are concentrated in lower income and/or minority communities. Thus far, various policies designed to improve the quality of life in higher crime areas have been examined, such as community building efforts. Various crime prevention strategies that attempt to increase the perception of effort and risk of apprehension, thereby encouraging a rational potential criminal to rethink his or her actions have also been discussed. In this section, it is suggested that something much worse is happening in some communities that may lead the local residents to engage in impulsive, antisocial behavior. Without addressing these underlying conditions, even the best policy will be ineffective.

The study of environmental justice really began to take off in the late 1970s (Stretesky & Lynch, 1999a). Environmental justice is a rather broad area that includes study of the relationship between social demographic characteristics (such as race, ethnicity, income, and education levels) and exposure to various environmental hazards. These environmental hazards may include such things as the geographic locations of storage and dump sites for hazardous wastes, accidental chemical releases, lead poisoning, and various forms of pollution (air, water, soil). The principles of environmental justice argue that all things being equal, these environmental hazards should be distributed equally across society. One should be just as likely to find a hazardous waste dump site in an affluent white neighborhood as in a poorer community inhabited by racial and ethnic minorities (Bullard, 1994; Stretesky & Lynch, 1999a). No one group should be exposed to higher concentrations of air pollution than another.

As one might suspect, this is not the case. Exposure to various pollutants and environmental hazards has been linked to the demographic characteristics of a community. Higher levels of exposure to various environmental hazards and risks are much more likely to be found in less affluent African American and Hispanic neighborhoods than in more affluent white neighborhoods (Krieg,

1995; Reiman, 1998; Stretesky & Lynch, 1999a, 1999b; United Church of Christ, 1987). The concentration of pollutants in these neighborhoods has a number of implications for the residents. Depending on the nature of the toxin, local residents may experience higher levels of various forms of cancer, respiratory diseases, cardiovascular disease, miscarriages, birth defects, and other health problems (Edelsein, 1988; Gould, 1986; Lave & Seskin, 1970; Morello-Frosch, Pastor, & Sadd, 2001). It should also be noted that the quality of health care that one receives varies with race and social class. If a less affluent minority resident contracts a life threatening disease like cancer, then he or she is less likely to have health insurance and ready access to state of the art medical treatments. Not surprisingly, the mortality rate for African Americans diagnosed with cancer is higher than the mortality rate for whites (for a more detailed discussion, see Reiman, 1998).

Lead Exposure and Crime

Environmental pollutants have also been linked to various behavioral changes. In particular, exposure to lead has been studied by criminologists and other behavioral researchers. While lead exposure is detrimental at any age, it is particularly harmful to the developing brains of small children, especially children age five and under. Lead exposure may lead to irreversible brain injuries which impact social and behavioral development, including: language acquisition, attention, memory, sensory perception and fine motor processes (Lidsky & Schneider, 2000). In a review of the medical literature, Stretesky (2003) reports that lead exposure has been linked to lower IQ scores, lower educational success, higher levels of hyperactivity and impulsive behaviors, and delinquency (see, for example, Banks, Ferretti, & Shucard, 1997; Bellinger, Stiles, & Needleman, 1992; Needleman & Gatsonis, 1990; Needleman, Riess, Tobin, Biesecker, & Greenhouse, 1996). It has been argued that as much as 20% of all crime may be linked to lead exposure (Needleman, 1990).

The issue of lead poisoning becomes particularly troubling when considering that exposure to lead is not distributed equally across all segments of society. According to the Centers for Disease Control (1997, cited in Stretesky, 2003), minority children are much more likely to be exposed to lead than white children. African American children suffer from lead poisoning at a level that is over five times the rate for white children. Lead poisoning also appears to be concentrated among those living in our inner city, urban areas. Whereas 21% of inner city youths had levels of lead in their blood that were above the CDC's maximum allowable level—only 5.8% of youths residing in rural and suburban areas had high levels of lead in their blood (Lidsky & Schneider, 2000).

Social class also appears to be related to lead exposure. While 16% of children from low-income families were found to have high lead blood levels, the percentage was lower in more affluent families: only 5.4% of middle class children and 4% of high income children were found to have blood lead levels above the maximum recommended amounts (Lidsky & Schneider, 2000).

Furthermore, as argued by Stretesky (2003), the detrimental effects of lead poisoning are often wrongly attributed as characteristics of individuals. Consider for a moment the debate surrounding intelligence scores and race. It has been argued by some researchers that certain racial and ethnic groups are less intelligent than other groups based on their IQ scores. Since these same researchers also argue that IQ has a genetic component, it would follow that they would make the argument that certain groups are inherently intellectually inferior (Herrnstein, 1988; Herrnstein & Murray, 1994). However, because of social inequalities in our society, minority children are exposed to higher rates of lead. Lead exposure has been linked to lower intelligence scores. Therefore, it would follow that minority children would have lower IQ scores—not because of inherent racial differences, but because of their exposure to lead.

Lead and Space: Hot Spots of Crime, or Hot Spots of Lead?

Just as crime is not equally distributed across all geographic areas, risk for lead exposure is concentrated in certain places. For most of us, the most commonly thought-of source of lead poisoning is lead-based paint. Before the harmful effects of lead exposure were known, it was common for homes to be decorated using lead-based paint. As the paint cracked and peeled the small pieces were often eaten by children, who then suffered lead poisoning. People living in newer homes do not have to concern themselves with exposure to lead-based paint. However, people who live in older housing units are more likely to be exposed to lead, especially in inner city areas. Since many minorities and/or less affluent individuals tend to be concentrated in communities with older rental units, it would follow that children growing up in these areas are exposed to higher levels of lead.

Furthermore, exposure to lead and other toxins can also occur through the air. Stretesky (2003) reported that black youths were much more likely than white youths to live in counties that have higher concentrations of lead in the air. In effect, there are identifiable lead "hot spots" that are often found in lower socioeconomic areas, with a higher number of minority residents. The higher concentration of lead in these communities causes irreversible biochemical changes in the residents. These changes may lead to concentrated geographic patterns of crime, delinquency, and other social problems. Since lead exposure has been linked to higher levels of aggression, violence, and delinquency, it would follow that geographic areas with high levels of lead would have high levels of crime (Klug, 2000; Lidsky & Schneider, 2000). For example, Stretesky and Lynch (2001; 2004) found a positive relationship between air lead concentrations and the occurrence of homicides and other violent crimes, and property crimes: Geographic areas, with higher levels of lead in the air, also reported higher levels of criminal activities, even when controlling for rival causes. Assuming that there is a relationship between lead exposure and crime, individuals who are exposed to lead suffer irreversible brain damage that leads to various behavioral problems including: impulsive behaviors, poor school performance, memory problems, violence, and aggression.

Certain neighborhoods experience higher levels of exposure than others, which would imply that certain areas have higher numbers of exposed individuals than others. If a community with high levels of lead exposure is targeted with a few of the policies explored in this text, will even the best community building efforts have any impact in areas in which the very air that the residents breathe is poison? Can a policy based on the assumption of a rational offender have any effect if many of the residents suffer from a condition that causes impulsive, aggressive behavior? Probably not.

Unfortunately, while interest in the area of environmental justice is growing, there are very few criminologists who study the link between exposure to environmental contaminants and crime. Clearly, this is an area of great importance with implications for any crime control policies that our society chooses to enact. A crime hot spot may actually be deflecting our attention away from something much worse. While people can certainly be arrested, addressing the underlying cause of the problem is a much more difficult process.

Summary

We do hope that this closing Chapter has encouraged you to take a closer look at some of the various theories and policies that have been discussed in this text. Nothing is ever simple. Even the most carefully considered policy driven by the best of intentions might backfire, causing even more problems for residents living in high crime areas. You, the reader, may very well be the next police chief, city council representative, mayor, or governor. You may hold an influential office where your opinions and actions truly have an impact on the lives of other people. We hope that in some small way, this text has helped to sharpen your critical thinking skills regarding crime, criminals, and public policy.

Not In My Backyard: Using Laws to Push out Registered Sex Offenders

In this final Spotlight on Research, Tasha Youstin and Matt Nobles use GIS to examine the impact that legislation designed to restrict where sex offenders may live in a Florida county impacts their movement over time. Although sex offender residency restriction laws are popular legislative responses to dealing offenders released back into society, mounting research shows that the unintended consequences of these laws might be outweighing their benefit.

Spotlight on Research IV

Residency Restrictions
A Geospatial Analysis of Sex Offender Movement Over Time
Tasha J. Youstin and Matt R. Nobles*

This study assesses the geospatial effects of sex offender residency restrictions in one Florida county at two time points. Data were used to determine if sex offenders were spatially clustered, if tougher restrictions increased clustering, and how residency restrictions affected areas with high concentrations of children and areas of low income. Findings indicate that while minor offender clustering is occurring, in general offenders became more widely dispersed throughout the county as a result of a more restrictive residency ordinance. Results demonstrate that current restrictions do not prevent convicted offenders from living in areas with the highest concentrations of children under age 18 and that a large number of offenders were not in compliance with current restrictions, indicating difficulties with implementation of enforcement.

Since the early 1990s, sex offender policies have focused on protecting the public against sexual victimization by unknown offenders, also known as "stranger danger." Despite studies that show that the majority of sexual crimes are committed by offenders who are known to their victim (Snyder, 2000), researchers have been able to do little to alleviate the public fears about stranger-related sexual crimes. Whereas once sex offenders were viewed as needing treatment to help cure their disordered behavior (Jenkins, 1998), the pendulum has now swung to an environment where there is an overwhelming public and political need for protection against these deviants. This atmosphere of fear has led to post-release requirements for convicted sex offenders such as mandatory registration, community notification and residency restrictions. These policies were implemented to help protect the public from future victimization by convicted offenders, though there is little if any empirical evidence of their effectiveness (Levenson, 2005). The relative paucity of research into the effects of residency restrictions leaves many questions unanswered. The aim of the current study is to determine how sex offender residency restrictions have changed the spatial dispersion of sex offender residences in one county in Florida using Geographic Information System software. The theoretical and empirical rationale for examining potential relationships between sex offender residency and crime is partially established by a strong literature relating crime and geographical space generally. For example, some research finds a direct link between crime-related decision making and geographical patterns of individual-level offending, perhaps involving a rational calculus to evaluate factors such as target attractiveness and spatial opportunity in the urban context (Brantingham & Brantingham, 1984; Capone & Nichols, 1976). The remaining rationale comes from the strong policy implications frequently championed in the residency restriction movement. Both of these rationales are addressed. While not intended as an explicit assessment of the ability for residency restrictions to reduce recidivism, this study looks at the potential clustering effects that may be caused by residency restrictions due to the limited housing options available to sex offenders. In addition, this study explores how patterns of sex offender residency relate to areas that may possess a high risk of victimization, particularly areas of low income and areas densely populated with children age 17 and under. Given that main premise of residency restrictions is to decrease contact between offenders and potential victims, the results of this investigation can inform more effective policies for reducing sexual recidivism.

LITERATURE REVIEW

Sexual offenders are the only class of felons required to register their location and have their names and photos accessible to the general public. Further, policies that increasingly limit the freedoms of these offenders even after they have served their court mandated sentences continue to be enacted (Durling, 2006). Residency restrictions seek to control where sex offenders can and cannot live when reentering the community post-conviction and are among the newest restrictions implemented. As of 2008, thirty states and hundreds of smaller jurisdictions have enacted laws that prohibit convicted sexual offenders from living within a specified proximity to "sensitive" areas, and bills to establish residency restriction are currently pending in 12 states (Meloy, Miller & Curtis, 2008). These sensitive areas generally include parks, schools, and day care facilities, but can encompass many more areas that fall within the prohibition of "areas where children congregate" (Stromberg, 2007). Currently, the least restrictive distance requirement is 500 feet, though the standard for many states is to restrict offenders from living within 1,000 feet of designated areas (Levenson, 2005; Levenson & Cotter, 2005). In the last few years, many individual jurisdictions have increased the buffer zones to 2,500 feet, which is the most restrictive distance requirement to date (Levenson, 2005).

Most sex offender policies are based on three assumptions: 1) "All sex offenders reoffend", 2) "Treatment does not work", and 3) "There is a pervasive threat of stranger danger" (Levenson, 2005, p. 3). Research on these three assumptions shows them to be flawed (Levenson, 2005; Zimring, Piquero, & Jennings, 2007). In regards to the first assumption that all sex offenders inevitably reoffend, a recent study by Sample and Bray (2003) found that although sex offenders are more likely to be rearrested for a new sex crime than non-sexual offenders, sexual offenders still recidivate at lower rates than other violent offenders, with an overall rearrest rate for any offense of 45.1% within five years. Compare this to a rearrest rate of 74.9% for those whose most serious offense was robbery, 66% for burglary, 58% for non sexual assault, and 52.9% for larceny. Complimenting this study, a meta-analysis by Hanson and Bussiere (1998) found that sex offenders recidivate at a rate of about 13% within 5 years from release. These studies indicate that it is incorrect to assume that sexual offenders inevitably reoffend.

Perhaps exacerbated by the overall belief in criminology that rehabilitation does not work (Martinson, 1974), sexual offender policies shifted away from rehabilitative programs from the 1970s through the 1990s (Jenkins, 1998). A recent meta-analysis of sex offender treatment programs challenges the assumption that rehabilitation does not work for sexual offenders. Findings show that cognitive-behavioral treatment programs can reduce recidivism by as much as 40% (Hanson et al., 2002). These findings clearly refute the idea that sex offenders cannot be successfully treated.

Finally, the fear of stranger victimization, or "stranger danger," is difficult to assuage in light of highly publicized accounts of heinous sexual crimes of children by strangers. Still, according to a study from the Bureau of Justice Statistics on the sexual assault of young children, over 90% of child victims of sexual abuse are victimized by a family member or an acquaintance (Snyder, 2000). In contrast, 7% of child victims of sexual assault (those age 17 and under) were victimized by a stranger (Snyder, 2000). Although a 7% victimization rate by strangers is certainly worth acknowledging, these statistics illustrate the need for the public to understand that sexual victimization is more likely be perpetrated by someone known to the victim.

Another main assumption specific to residency restriction is that proximity to potential targets, such as children, increases the likelihood of recidivism.

This assumption is supported by research suggesting that proximity to an offender increases the likelihood of victimization, identified as distance decay (Rengert, Piquero & Jones, 1999). However, peer reviewed research has not demonstrated that proximity to places where children congregate increases recidivism or that housing restrictions reduce recidivism (Levenson, 2005). Looking at the potential efficacy of residency restrictions, Duwe, Donnay and Tewksbury (2008) examined sexual offenders who recidivated in Minnesota from 1990 to 2002 and found it was unlikely that any of the 224 new sex crimes that involved an arrest, conviction, and reincarceration would have been prevented had residency restrictions been in place. This is because most of the crimes did not involve strangers, and most occurred within a mile of the victim's home, a school, park, or a playground. The authors concluded that there is little evidence to suggest that residency restrictions are a viable method for preventing future sex crimes by released sex offenders. Coming to the same conclusion, a review of the frequency of charges for sex crimes in Iowa before and after the implementation of a 2,500 foot residency restriction showed the number of charges to be increasing, instead of decreasing after the restriction was put in place (Blood, Watson & Stageberg, 2008).

Research examining the relationship between proximity to areas where children congregate and recidivism rates found conflicting results. A study done by the Colorado Department of Public Safety (2004) found that child molesters who recidivated did not live any closer to schools or day care centers than molesters who did not commit a new sexual offense. Colorado researchers concluded that residency restrictions should not be considered as an efficacious mechanism for mitigating sex offender recidivism. An analysis of the reoffense patterns of 224 recidivist sexual offenders released between 1990 and 2002 indicated that a residency restriction law would have deterred none of the 224 recidivistic sexual crimes (Minnesota Department of Corrections, 2003).

While the studies by the Colorado Department of Public Safety and the Minnesota Department of Corrections indicate that proximity to targets does not influence recidivism, some research shows the opposite to be true. Walker, Golden and VanHouten (2001) analyzed the residential locations of sex offenders in Arkansas and found that 48% of registered sex offenders with minor victims lived within 1,000 feet of schools, parks and day care facilities, versus only 26% of registered sexual offenders with adult victims. Though this study did examine recidivism, the authors argued from a Routine Activities perspective that sex offenders with minor victims might be situating themselves to be in close proximity to potential targets. Maghelal and Olivares (Unpublished Manuscript) reinforced the belief that sex offenders reside close to potential targets when they determined that 55.4% of sexual offenders living in Brazos County, Texas lived within 1,000 feet of schools, parks, day care facilities. Questioning whether the percentages of sexual offenders living in close proximity to areas of interest mirrors that of the general population, Zgoba, Levenson and McKee (2008) demonstrated that 88% of sexual offenders and 80% of non offending citizens lived by schools, parks, churches, or day care facilities. Chajewski and Mercado (2008) also found that while sex offenders tended to live closer to schools than randomly selected members of the community, sex offenders with adult victims lived closer to schools than sex offenders with child victims.

Looking at offenders' residences and distance to crime, Beauregard, Proulx, and Rossmo (2005) performed a meta-analysis of literature on various types of crimes and found that most offenders commit their crimes in close proximity to their home base. However, only one study examined by the authors looked specifically at offenses against children (homicides of children) and that particular study found that 91% of offenses occurred within 5 miles of the offender's home. Overall, the relationship, if any, between proximity to targets and offense rates, as well as the difference between sexual offenders and non-sexual offenders in residential distance to schools, parks and day care facilities is still unclear. Ultimately, more research needs to be undertaken before any definitive conclusions can be made.

While researchers continue to explore the relationship between proximity to targets and offense rates, literature has also focused on the general effects of these policies. Studies show that as the distance requirements for residency restrictions increase, housing options for offenders become seriously limited (Barnes, Dukes, Tewksbury & DeTroye, 2008; Chajewski & Mercado, 2008; Levenson & Cotter, 2005; Mustaine, Tewksbury & Stengel, 2006; Zandbergen & Hart, 2006; Zgoba et al., 2008). In some cases, sex offenders can essentially be prohibited from living in entire cities or counties, leading scholars to question whether current residency restrictions are the equivalent of societal banishment seen throughout history (Petracca, 2006; Yung, 2007). In one extreme example, sex offenders in Miami, Florida were forced to take permanent refuge under a bridge because they could not find adequate housing due to the city's 2,500 foot residency restrictions (Zarrella & Oppmann, 2007).[1] Although these laws infringe on basic freedoms of sex offenders, courts

---

1. As of February 6, 2008, those sex offenders residing under the Julia Tuttle Causeway were ordered by local law enforcement to leave the premises and find actual housing, though the 2,500 foot restrictions are still in place (Fox News, 2008).

have ruled that such infringements are superseded by the compelling interest of the state to protect its citizens (Doe v. Miller, 2005). The American Civil Liberties Union has asked the U.S. Supreme Court to rule on this issue, but the court has declined (Levenson, 2005). However, despite the lack of a widespread ban on residency restrictions, some individual jurisdictions, such as Jacksonville, Florida, recently ruled residency restrictions to be unconstitutional (Florida v. Schmidt, 2007).

Researchers have examined the extent to which residency restrictions limit housing options for sexual offenders in various locations. A study of residency restrictions in Orange County, Florida revealed that 95.2% of all residential land fell within a 1,000 ft prohibitive buffer zone, and 99.7% of residential land fell within a 2,500 ft buffer zone when including schools, parks, day care facilities, and bus stops as restricted areas (Zandbergen & Hart, 2006). Chajewski and Mercado (2008) found that if implemented, 1,000 foot and 2,500 foot residency restriction in New Jersey would create residency shortages for sex offenders, with 2,500 foot boundaries in urban areas leaving virtually no available space for sex offenders to live. In response to pending legislation of a 1,000 foot residency restriction, or a one mile restriction from areas where children congregate in South Carolina, Barnes et al. (2008) examined the effects that implementing the suggested residency restrictions would have in four counties in the state. The authors found that if the legislation required sex offenders to move out of restricted areas (making the policy retroactive), 19.5% of the offenders would be required to move, and 45.6% of the available residential area would be off limits under a 1,000 ft. residency restriction. Should the 5,280 ft. (1 mile) residency restriction be enacted, 80.9% of the sample would be required to move, and 81.3% of the available residential area would be restricted for these offenders. Consequently, researchers have questioned whether these restrictions will lead offenders to cluster in the limited residential areas available to them (Levenson & Cotter, 2005).

Given the limited housing options available to released sex offenders, Mustaine et al. (2006) found that most sex offenders live in areas that contain at least one trait consistent with social disorganization. The findings of this study raise questions as to whether or not sex offenders are being forced into areas with high concentrations of structural disadvantage, as areas of low socioeconomic status are more likely to be socially disorganized (Sampson & Groves, 1989; Shaw & McKay, 1942). Aside from the challenges for sex offenders to locate stable jobs and maintain a high quality of life, the implications of residents living in areas in which sex offenders take up residence is unknown. One possibility is that children in socially disorganized areas could be increasingly at-risk for sexual victimization due to the preponderance of known sex offenders residing next door and throughout these neighborhoods if the aforementioned theory of distance decay is true (Rengert et al., 1999). In contrast to the finding by Mustaine et al., recent research shows that in Hamilton County, Ohio, areas prohibiting sex offenders due to residency restrictions were actually more disorganized than other areas (Grubesic, Murray & Mack, 2008). While the authors found no support for the assumption that residency restrictions force sex offenders to live in undesirable areas, they contend that just because an area is not off limits to offenders, it does not mean that offenders will be able to find affordable housing in those areas, or won't face community bylaws prohibiting their residency.

Levenson and Cotter (2005) surveyed 135 sex offenders from Florida about their perceptions of residency restrictions and reported that the majority of offenders were unable to live with supportive family members due to residency restrictions. The results also indicated that many offenders suffered financial and emotional hardships due to the restrictions. Further, Mercado, Alvarez and Levenson (2008) found that 34% of respondents sampled from New Jersey reported being unable to live with supportive family members. Each of these studies concurred with prior research on other sex offender policies in reporting that offenders suffered emotional and financial hardships due to the restrictions, which led to decreased stability for the offenders (see e.g., Tewksbury, 2005). Another finding of the study discussed earlier by the Colorado Department of Public Safety found that offenders who had social and family support in their lives were significantly less likely to recidivate (Colorado Department of Public Safety, 2004). Barnes et al. (2008) found that implementing the pending legislative policy of a one mile residency restriction in South Carolina would increase the distance of offender to treatment facilities by 14.2% (approximately 29,000 feet) creating additional burdens to helping offenders successfully rehabilitate. Thus, concern is rising that residency restrictions may be creating environments that are detrimental to offenders' successful reintegration into the community. As residency restrictions limit the ability of released sexual offenders to live with supportive friends and family members, they may lack the support shown to be a significant predictor of successful probation survival for sexual offenders (Hepburn & Griffin, 2004).

Aside from the difficulties created by limited housing options for sexual offenders, there may be difficulties implementing and enforcing residency restrictions themselves. Tewksbury and Mustaine (2006) concluded that one-half of their sample of offenders from Seminole County, Florida was in compliance with local residency restrictions. These findings bring to light the need for research investigating how law enforcement agencies are handling the increased workload associated with record-keeping, home visits, community notification, and other surveillance logistics. Another issue creating problems for law enforcement agencies is the problem of losing track of sexual offenders because they have absconded from registration and effectively disappeared (Human Rights Watch, 2007). As one sheriff in Iowa reported, "We went from knowing where about 90% of them were. We're lucky if we know where 50 to 55% of them are now ... because what the law did is it created an atmosphere that these individuals can't find a place to live. So what that causes them to do is come in and lie about where they're at or maybe they just don't come in at all" (Stachura, 2006).

In sum, research on sexual offender residency policies suggests that while these policies represent an attempt to prevent sexual offenders from reoffending, research has not verified that residency restrictions reduce recidivism. Furthermore, research suggests that residency restrictions are based on flawed assumptions, create difficulties for offenders trying to find housing, and may actually be contributing to sex offender recidivism by increasing hardships on released sexual offenders attempting to reintegrate into the community (Levenson & Cotter, 2005; Mercado et al., 2008).

As residency restrictions continue to be implemented in jurisdictions throughout the United States, it is important to understand the consequences of these restrictions on communities. Research on residency restrictions raises the question of whether offenders are clustering together residentially due to limited housing options (Levenson & Cotter, 2005), and whether sex offenders are moving disproportionately into areas of low socioeconomic status (Mustaine et al., 2006). Also, there is increasing concern over the ability of law enforcement to correctly and consistently implement these policies (Human Rights Watch, 2007; Stachura, 2006; Tewksbury & Mustaine, 2006)

The study at hand attempts to answer several of these questions and to determine the nature and magnitude of geospatial effects of residency restrictions. The area of focus for the analysis is Alachua County, Florida, a medium sized, semi-rural county located in central Florida. The analysis examines the residential movement of released sexual offenders over a four-year period from 2003 to 2007. During this period the residency restrictions for the county seat, Gainesville, were increased from the statewide standard (for sex offenders who victimized minors) of 1,000 feet from schools, parks and day care facilities to a citywide ordinance restriction of 2,500 feet from the same areas. It was believed that this increased restriction would illustrate a higher intensity of geospatial effects, if any, of residency restrictions. This study focuses on four main research questions:

1. Are sex offender residences clustered in space?
2. Does the spatial distribution of sexual offenders change with the implementation of more restrictive residency restrictions?
3. How do residency restrictions relate to areas that may be at heightened risk of victimization, such as low income areas and areas densely populated with children under age 18?
4. Do offenders move into areas that are subject to residency restrictions?

It is hypothesized that low income areas may be at increased risk of victimization not only because more offenders may be living there (Tewksbury & Mustaine, 2006), but because areas of low income tend to have higher proportions of single parent households, which may lead to decreased supervision of children in the area. It is hypothesized that areas densely populated with children age 17 and under may be at heightened risk of victimization due to the increased number of potential targets.

DATA & METHODS

Data

Data for the present study were collected from several official sources. First, residential addresses and criminal history data for sex offenders as of March 2007 were provided by the Florida Department of Law Enforcement (FDLE) via public records request. Second, residential addresses and criminal history data for sex offenders as of May 2003 were obtained from the Florida Geographic Data Library, a data warehouse maintained at the University of Florida's Geo-Plan Center. In both cases, the data contained fields that included the physical address and victim type for registered sexual offenders located in Florida. Next, a variety of supplemental layers were acquired from the City of Gainesville's Planning Department. These layers included locations of schools, daycare facilities, and public parks, all of which are relevant to city ordinances restricting sex offender residence.[2] Finally, standard layers for the county boundary and

---

2. Some studies on sex offender residency restrictions incorporate public school bus stops in analyses of geographical proximity. However, under Florida law, bus stops are considered restricted places as a special condition of release supervision that only applies to certain offenders as determined by the Florida Department of Corrections. Our data do not feature details on specific conditions of release, and as such, we have excluded these locations from this analysis.

block group divisions were acquired from the 2000 U.S. Census in order to map patterns of economic distribution and residential distributions of children younger than 18 years of age.

Methods

Exploratory spatial data analysis begins with locating the phenomena of interest. To this end, we employed ESRI's ArcGIS 9.1 software together with the two sex offender datasets to geocode physical locations and to filter offenders based on whether the victim was a minor. Geocoding is an iterative process whereby a test address is spatially located through matching to a reference layer containing addresses of known locations (e.g., land parcels) or street segments representing address ranges. In this case, a county-wide street centerline was utilized for geocoding. Results were highly accurate, with a 95% successful geocoding rate.[3] This yielded an overall N of 236 for the 2003 list and 249 for the 2007 list. After geocoding, sex offenders were further filtered according to whether they were convicted of a crime involving a minor victim. This division yielded an N of 178 for the 2003 list (75.4%) and 197 for the 2007 list (79.1%).

The layers for schools, daycare facilities, and parks were used to create spatial buffers as specified in the ordinance, a nominal radius of 2,500 feet. Although centroids and polygons were both available for buffer creation, the preferred basis is polygons, because it is conceivable that the perimeter of a very large park or school may fall outside of the radius extending outward from the centroid. By selecting polygons, we conservatively display the minimum distance from any portion of the relevant parcel, not just the minimum distance from the center of that parcel. Finally, buffers were joined to

---

3. Geocoding rates can be somewhat misleading. For example, it is possible to configure ArcGIS to match addresses that are less than perfect in order to account for variations and human error in data entry (e.g., transposition of digits) or address standardization (e.g., "STREET" instead of "ST"). Furthermore, the positional accuracy of certain geocoding techniques introduces additional error into street-level spatial analyses (see e.g., Zandbergen & Hart, 2009, for a full discussion). For the present analysis, the criteria specified were only addresses that were 100% matches to our reference centerline. "Ties," which occur when one test address can be plotted in two different spatial locations, were excluded. Also, the authors attempted to manually match records in instances where automated geocoding failed; this resulted in a slight improvement to the overall success rate, from approximately 92% successful with fully automated matching to 95% successful with a combination of automated and manual matching.

create a contiguous "no residence" layer showing areas within the city and county off-limits to sex offenders. This buffer area can be overlaid with the geocoded sex offender residence locations to show how many registered offenders are living in areas that are prohibited under county ordinance or state law. It is important to state that the 2,500 foot residency restriction imposed in 2005 only supplanted the state imposed 1,000 foot residency restriction in the city of Gainesville, not the entire county of Alachua. Though this study mapped 2,500 foot residency restrictions throughout the entire county for the second time period (2007), the result of the study should not be compromised because the majority of the restricted areas (schools, parks and day care facilities) fall within Gainesville city limits, and only one offender in the sample who relocated between the two time periods fell within a 2,500 foot buffer zone that was outside of the city limits. Additionally, this one offender relocated within a 1,000 foot restricted area, and therefore the fact that the buffer is established at 2,500 feet should not unduly influence the results of the analysis.

The 2000 U.S. Census layers were used to identify clustering of household income and population age. Specifically, maps were created using GeoDa 0.9.5-i (Anselin, Syabri, & Kho, 2006) at the block group unit of analysis to show spatial concentrations of three key measures. The basis for each of the maps is the local indicators of spatial autocorrelation, or LISA, which demonstrates statistically significant values for the measure of choice in relation to neighboring units (Anselin, 1995). In this example, each block group (N =121) may be assigned one of four LISA categories: high-high, low-low, high-low, or low-high, depending on the value for the variable of interest for that block group as well as the range of values for all of the block groups that share a common border. Examinations of spatial processes are partly contingent upon the definition of neighboring units included in the analysis, as well as their hypothesized relationships. Defining a systematic proxy for these relationships is necessary because the precise relationships between all observed units are unknown (see Baller, Anselin, Messner, Deane & Hawkins, 2001). The present study utilizes the queen criterion, which specifies that neighbors are defined as those units sharing a border and a common corner. This method provides a common and reasonable approximation of physical neighborhoods. The LISA maps presented here exhibit univariate comparisons across geography rather than bivariate associations; the comparisons that form the basis for LISA categories are between a given block group and neighboring block groups rather than between two separate variables in the dataset. Thus, LISA maps in this analysis not only identify block groups that have significantly high or low values for social variables like socioeconomic status, they also depict the spatial concentration of those block groups relative to the range of values for neighboring block groups. The measure of income selected was median family income. Two separate age measures were used: percentage of residents under age five and percentage of residents between ages 5 and 17. Because residency restrictions are intended to provide protection to children and adolescents under age 18, both of these categories were deemed relevant to our research questions and used in the analysis. Hypothetically, by identifying where younger children are more densely clustered, it may be possible to test whether residency restrictions for registered sex offenders are preventing the offenders from living in areas that contain more potential victims.

Extant research suggests that sex offenders face a variety of challenges resulting from increasingly punitive residency restrictions (Levenson & Cotter, 2005; Mustaine et al., 2006; Tewksbury & Mustaine, 2006; Zandbergen & Hart, 2006), but the aggregate spatial effects have not been examined in great detail. A full examination of the residency restriction effects requires both a spatial analysis and a temporal analysis to ascertain changes in spatial patterns over time. This analysis incorporates both aspects by providing exploratory spatial data analysis for the residential locations of registered sex offenders before and after a local ordinance went into effect in November of 2005 which increased residency restrictions from 1,000 feet to 2,500 feet for registered offenders convicted of sexual crimes against minors. The location selected for this analysis provides an interesting case study because one would expect that any effects on the residential locations of sexual offenders due to residency restrictions would be exacerbated by more restrictive residency restrictions due to the decreased residential areas available to sexual offenders. While there is a limited amount of time between the analysis and the implementation date, the analysis can still provide valuable insight into the spatial effects of this policy, even if the study can only provide conservative results.

The primary objective for exploratory spatial data analysis is to map physical locations and observe spatial relationships between potentially related phenomena (see Anselin, 1995; Messner et al., 1999). More specifically, this exploratory spatial data analysis offers insight into sex offender residency restrictions by revealing four trends of interest. First, identifying the basic residential tendencies of sex offenders can be illustrative—whether they are, in fact, clustered tightly together or more randomly distributed in space is pertinent for a variety of theoretical and policy-oriented reasons. To address this question, we present maps depicting spatial concentrations of the proportion of registered sex offenders relative to the population within a given block group. Proportions were calculated by dividing the number of registered sex offenders with minor victims[4] per block group by the general population of the block group.[5] Using proportions helps to alleviate problems that would be found comparing sparsely populated areas to densely populated areas.

Identifying any potential changes in the spatial distribution of registered sex offenders over time, the second research question, is important to better understand the effects of increasingly punitive residency restrictions. We present evidence in the form of mean interpoint distances from 2003 and 2007 and subject these measures to significance testing.

Another critical issue in the management of released sex offenders is addressed in the third research question, which explores the relationships between the locations of registered sex offenders and areas that may be at heightened risk of victimization. We demonstrate these relationships with maps showing the proportions of sex offenders with minor victims to children under age 18, as well as the proportions of sex offenders to the general population, stratified by median income. Proportions were calculated to compare areas densely populated with children to sex offenders by dividing the number of sex offenders with minor victims in a block group by the number children under age 18 in the same block group. These proportions were created for both 2003 and 2007 and were used to create maps illustrating spatial densities for each of the proportions in each block group relative to neighboring groups. Census block groups were then split into three categories: low population of children under age 18, medium population of children under 18, and high population of children under age 18. Statistical tests were employed to compare the proportion of sex offenders to the population for all three groups. Mean income was used to separate the block groups into low income, middle income, and high income, as provided by the Census.[6] One block group (of 121

---

4. Sex offenders with adult victims are excluded from this analysis as residency restrictions in the county of Alachua, Florida, as well as the entire state are only imposed on offenders with minor victims.

5. Calculating these proportions using general population values rather than the number of adults 18 years or older per block group is conceptually appropriate, since some sexual offenders may themselves be juveniles. For a comprehensive discussion of juvenile sexual offenders, including policy considerations, see Barbaree and Marshall (2008).

6. The proportions were created by dividing the range of existing values for each of the census variables (median family income, children under age 5, children ages 5 to 17) into three approximately equal terciles, with each level containing 40 census block groups. The division into equal terciles is imperfect, but our belief is that separating block groups using alternatives (e.g., standard deviations from the mean across all block groups) impairs the analysis because the intrinsic ordering into "high, medium, low" categories is lost when relying on central tendency. For example, using standard deviations could naturally result in

block groups) was removed from this part of the analysis because there was no mean family income provided in the Census data. Each income category (low, medium, and high income) contained 40 block groups. After separating the block groups, the proportion of sex offenders with minor victims was compared for each category of block groups using significance tests to determine if there were differences in the proportion of sexual offenders based on the socioeconomic status of the block group. This analysis was performed for both time periods.

Finally, to answer the question of whether offenders are moving into restricted areas, maps showing the locations of offenders with minor victims were examined. The number of offenders moving into a 1,000 foot buffer zone as well as the number of offenders moving into a 2,500 foot buffer zone was divided by the total number of offenders who moved between 2003 and 2007 to determine the percentage of offenders not in compliance with the residency restrictions. Only offenders who moved between the two time periods were included in this part of the analysis because residency restrictions are not retroactive, and therefore an offender may be living in a restricted area but still be compliance with the law because they acquired their residence before the areas was restricted to them. It is possible that increasing the restricted areas from 1,000 feet from areas where children congregate to 2,500 feet from these areas will increase the total number of offenders in restricted areas, but the phenomenon will not impact the result found here, because only offenders with minor victims who moved between the time points are analyzed.

RESULTS

Residential Clustering

Geocoding the residential locations of sex offenders with minor victims showed that these individuals were distributed widely throughout Alachua County, with denser concentrations within the incorporated urban area of the county seat, Gainesville (see Figure 1). Within the urban area, there was a somewhat tighter concentration of sex offenders living within the city core,

---

too few observations (block groups) in a given category, because using categorizations based on mean or median values rather than terciles or other "cut point" methods places great emphasis on the normality (or lack thereof) of the distribution for the census measures under study. While median family income was somewhat normally distributed across block groups in this county for the 2000 census, the distributions for children under age 5 and for children age 5 to 17 were highly skewed.

while points were more widely distributed at the fringes. Proportions of sex of-fenders with minor victims in relation to the overall population were created for each block group. LISA maps showed some clustering of sex offenders with minor victims in the Northwest area of Alachua County in 2003, an area char-acterized as a middle class suburban area (see Figure 2a). Figure 2b displays clus-tering of offenders in the center of Alachua County in 2007. This area is characterized by lower socioeconomic status on the east side of the Gainesville, the most populous city in the county. The figures show clustering of sex offenders in a small number of census blocks. This clustering effect changed over time from the suburban middle class area of the northwest to a few, lower income, more urban areas in the center of the county. However, despite these few areas with a higher proportion of sexual offenders, overall there did not appear to be well-defined clustering within the county.

Changes in Spatial Distribution of Sexual Offenders

We next examined patterns of movement for registered sex offenders with minor victims who relocated within the county between 2003 and 2007. Out of the original sample of correctly geocoded registered sex offenders in Alachua County, 40 were identified as relocated between the two time periods.[7] These offenders were mapped and the resulting layers indicated that residential mo-bility among registered sex offenders did not increase clustering or geograph-ical concentration. To complement the visual assessment provided by Figure 3, interpoint distances between the residential locations of all sex offenders with minor victims were calculated for each time period. The mean interpoint distance between offenders in 2003 of 13793.72 feet (standard deviation = 6671.21) and a mean interpoint distance in 2007 of 51110.48 feet (standard deviation = 19174.23) indicated that offenders were further apart in 2007 than in 2003. To determine if the mean interpoint distances were significant, a t-test was performed. Levene's test was significant, indicating that equality of vari-ance for the two time periods could not be assumed. Results showed that the mean interpoint distances in 2003 (N = 178) and 2007 (N = 197) were signif-icantly different from one another (t = -25.625, df = 247.12, p < .001), sug-

---

7. Relocation is operationalized here as an individual offender present in both the 2003 and 2007 datasets with different residential addresses at time 1 and time 2. Offenders were matched on FDLE ID number to ensure accuracy. Offenders whose residential address cor-responded to a correctional facility (e.g., currently incarcerated) in one or both datasets were removed from the analysis, as they were unaffected by residency restriction policy changes.

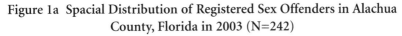

Figure 1a Spacial Distribution of Registered Sex Offenders in Alachua County, Florida in 2003 (N=242)

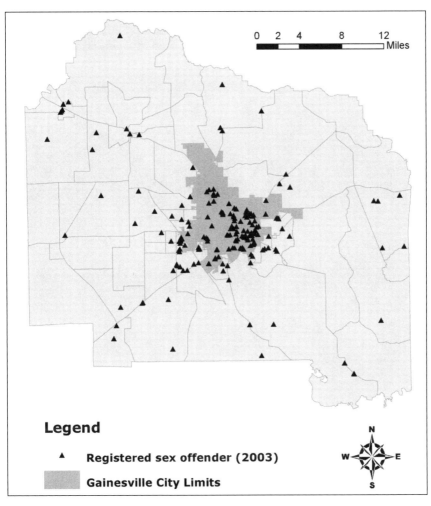

gesting that offenders were more dispersed throughout the county as opposed to clustered closer together.

Relationship to Population Demographics

Exploratory spatial data analysis of the social variables from the U.S. census showed the percentage of minors and median family income were highly

Figure 1b Spacial Distribution of Registered Sex Offenders in Alachua
County, Florida in 2007 (N=249)

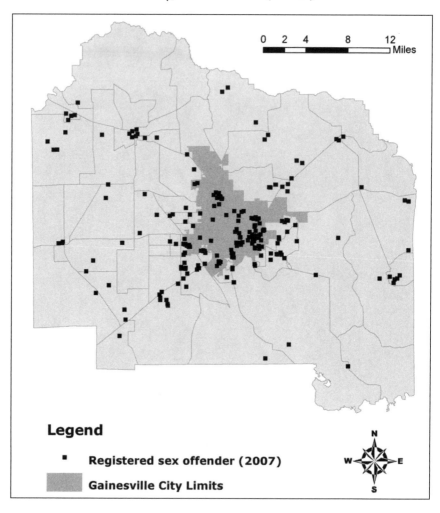

concentrated in space. Because the unit of analysis here was block groups rather
than individual points, we utilized a standard indicator of spatial autocorrelation, global Moran's I, to determine the degree to which these social variables were concentrated in space. Importantly, the use of global Moran's I
provided a means of identifying spatial autocorrelation across all block groups
in the county. This conceptualization was appropriate because the analysis was
limited to only block groups within a single county, and the analysis itself concerned the spatial distribution of registered offenders within the county as a func-

**Figure 2a Spacial Concentration of Proportion of
Sex Offenders to Total Population in 2003**

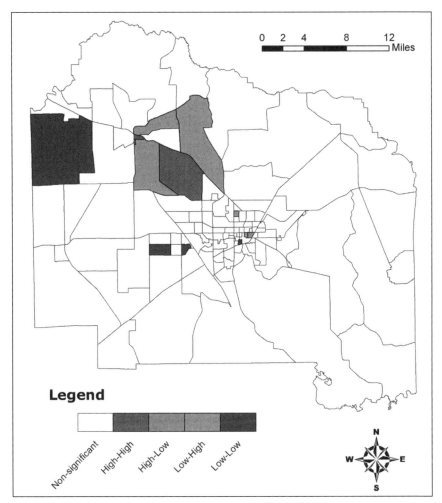

tion of increasingly punitive residency restrictions. Calculation of Moran's I
for median family income showed highly significant spatial autocorrelation (I
= 0.4806, p < 0.0001). Thus, Alachua County residents were highly concentrated in terms of socioeconomic status, both at the low and the high ends of
the range. Results are displayed in Figure 4a. Further, Moran's I values also indicated highly significant spatial autocorrelation for the concentration of children under 18 years of age (I = 0.7240, p < 0.0001) within the county. These
concentrations are depicted in Figure 4b. Maps of the restricted areas created

**Figure 2b Spacial Concentration of Proportion of
Sex Offenders to Total Population in 2007**

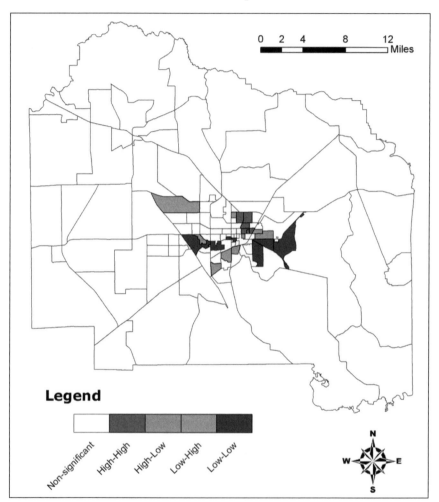

by residency restrictions showed the restricted areas to be equally distributed, among areas of high income and low income (see Figures 4a and 5). Because of this finding, it was not expected that sex offenders would cluster in areas of low income as opposed to areas that are more affluent as a direct result of residency restrictions.

To verify this hypothesis, block groups were separated into three categories (high income, medium income, and low income) of 40 block groups each based upon the mean family income per block group (see Table 1). An ANOVA

Figure 3a Intra-county Registered Sex Offender
Relocations between 2003 and 2007 (N=40)

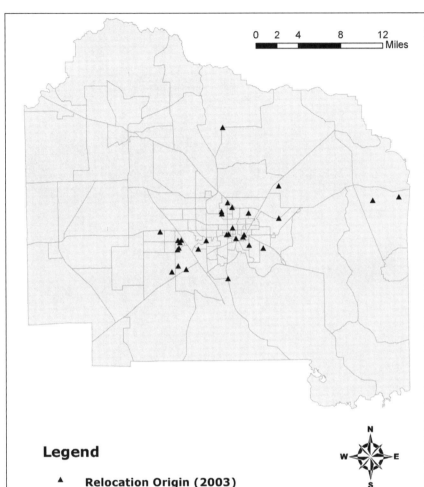

compared the proportion of sexual offenders in each block group by income groups for 2003 and 2007. Results of the ANOVA were not significant.[8]

The geospatial analyses at both time periods showed that the residency restrictions did not cover large areas highly populated with children younger

---

8. Tables displaying the ANOVA results were omitted due to non-significance, but they are available upon request from the authors.

**Figure 3b Intra-county Registered Sex Offender
Relocations between 2003 and 2007 (N=40)**

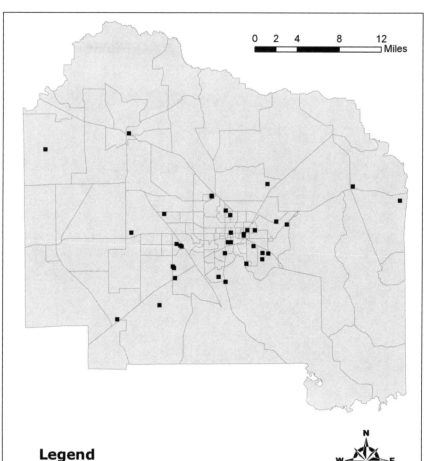

than 18 years of age. Still, while sex offenders were shown to live in close proximity to these areas of high concentration of minors, they did not seem to congregate or cluster there in a systematic or intentional fashion (see Fig. 4b and
Fig. 5). Block groups were divided into three groups by the mean number of
children younger than 18 years of age (see Table 1). To determine if the proportion of sex offenders to the population differed significantly for the three
groups, ANOVA tests were performed for each time period. Again, the ANOVA
tests for 2003 and 2007 were not significant. Given these tests, we conclude

Figure 4a Spacial Concentration of SES in Alachua County, Florida (2000 Census)

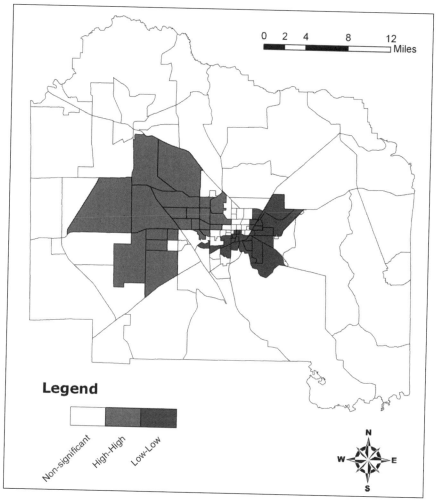

that sex offenders were not more concentrated in areas of low socioeconomic status or areas densely populated with children under age 18. In contrast, the proportion of offenders was equally dispersed throughout the county, both before and after the implementation of the harsher residency restriction policy.

Additionally, the observed counts of sex offenders residing within each of the geographic buffer zones (within 1,000 feet of a restricted location, between 1,000 and 2,500 feet of a restricted location, within 2,500 feet of a restricted lo-

Figure 4b Spacial Concentration of Children under Age 18 in
Alachua County, Florida (2000 Census)

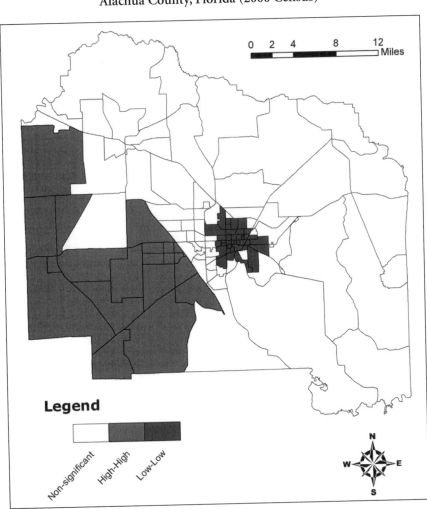

cation, and outside 2,500 feet of a restricted location) were tabulated for each
time period (see Table 2). Although the more punitive 2,500 foot restriction
ordinance was not in effect in 2003, identifying the number of offenders who
would have been subject to its enforcement provides a useful contrast. The differences in counts between Time 1 and Time 2 illustrate that the number of offenders in each restricted zone decreased substantially, although the overall
number of offenders in Alachua County remained relatively constant from
2003 to 2007. This demonstrates that offenders reside increasingly outside of

Figure 5 Residency Restriction Buffers

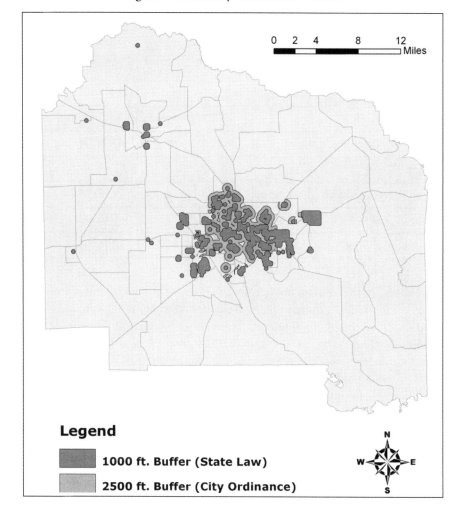

Legend

1000 ft. Buffer (State Law)

2500 ft. Buffer (City Ordinance)

the buffered areas, and it also suggests that the spatial distribution of offender residences in 2007 became increasingly scattered rather than concentrated in the densely populated urban center.

Residential Mobility Over Time

A more interesting trend was illustrated when the sex offender residential movement points were overlaid with the 2,500 ft. buffers specified in county

Table 1 Descriptive Statistics for Census (2000)
Block Groups in Alachua County, Florida

	N	Min	Max	Mean	Std. Dev.
Mean Income					
Group 1: Low Income	40	$4,821	$31,750	$22,193.50	$6,933.74
Group 2: Med. Income	40	$33,036	$48,576	$39,817.55	$4,519.34
Group 3: High Income	40	$48,750	$98,959	$66,078.87	$14,705.11
Children Under 18					
Group 1: Low Population	41	0	180	99.76	55.04
Group 2: Med. Population	40	191	386	275.77	57.261
Group 3: High Population	40	390	1915	716.03	366.676

ordinances. In this case, results show that many offenders relocated into "off limit" areas under the more punitive residency restrictions. The analysis indicated that 27 of the 40 sexual offenders with minor victims (72.5%) who moved between 2003 and 2007, moved into a 2,500 ft. restricted buffer area. Because actual move dates were not provided in the available data, it is possible that all 40 offenders could have moved before the more stringent 2,500 foot residency restrictions were put in place. As such, the movement of offenders was also analyzed using 1,000 foot buffer zones. This analysis indicated that 40% (N = 16) of offenders moved into restricted areas. The nature and circumstances of

Table 2 Tabulation of Sex Offender Locations
by Geographic Proximity to Residency Restriction Zones
in Alachua County, Florida, 2003 and 2007

	2003	2007	Difference $(T_2\text{-}T_1)$
Within 1,000 feet (state law)	106	80	-26
Between 1,000 feet and 2,500 feet	39	27	-12
Within 2,500 feet (city ordinance)	116	73	-43
Outside 2,500 feet	126	176	50
Total	242	249	7

**Figure 6 Intra-county Registered Sex Offender Relocations
with Residency Restriction Buffers in 2007 (N=40)**

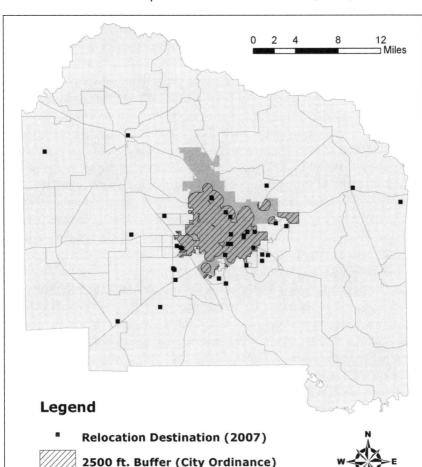

these movements was beyond the scope of the present analysis, but it appeared that in some cases, more punitive ordinances were not effective in preventing registered offenders from relocating into restricted areas. Results are shown in Figure 6. It should be noted that at the 2007 time period, 108 sexual offenders with minor victims were living within the 2,500 foot buffer zones. This is not unexpected, however, because residency restrictions in this area were not retroactive, and therefore offenders who maintained a residence within a restricted area before the restrictions were put in place were not required to move.

DISCUSSION

This study's primary objective is to examine the effects of sex offender residency restrictions on the spatial distribution of registered sex offenders over time. In regards to the question raised by prior researchers that residency restrictions may lead to clustering (Levenson & Cotter, 2005), data from both time points show concentrations of sexual offenders with minor victims in several block groups throughout the county. However, when using mean interpoint distances to examine the influence of increasing the residency restrictions from 1,000 feet to 2,500 feet, results show that offenders became more dispersed throughout the county, as the mean distance increased from 13793.72 feet in 2003 to 51110.48 feet in 2007. The discrepancy between the apparent clustering found in the LISA maps and the dispersion effect found through interpoint distances may be explained by the small number of offenders with minor victims in the county. There were 121 Census block groups in the analysis and between 178 and 194 offenders with minor victims in 2003 and 2007 respectively. Because of this, each offender moving into or out of a block group can have a significant influence on the spatial autocorrelation of sexual offenders. While clustering increased in a few block groups between the two time periods, the general trend indicated by the interpoint distances reveals that offenders are being more widely distributed throughout the county. As we find clustering in both time periods, it is unclear if the clustering is solely caused by residency restrictions. It is possible that the residential clustering is due to the increased hardships placed on sex offenders resulting from the combination of policies enacted against them, including registration and notification, which may contribute to decreased financial stability (Levenson, 2008; Levenson & Cotter, 2005; Levenson & Hern, 2007; Tewksbury, 2005). This relationship needs to be fully explicated through future research.

One potential concern casting doubt on this finding is that offender clustering may be driven largely by the shape and orientation of the incorporated city limits, which in this study represent the jurisdictional limits of the harsher 2,500 foot restrictions. The conventional logic behind this supposition is that as buffered restriction zones grow, the number of available domiciles for registered sex offenders decreases. Our perspective is that the opposite finding, namely those more punitive restrictions may result in greater dispersion, is equally plausible. This supposition is partially supported by our analyses, which indicate that the number of sex offenders residing outside of the 2,500 foot buffered areas (representing most of the Gainesville city limits) increased dramatically from 2003 to 2007 despite relative stability in the overall number of offenders in Alachua County (see Table 2).

The third research question for this study investigated how residency restrictions related to areas that might be at heightened risk for victimization, such as areas of low mean family income, or areas densely populated with children under age 18. Statistical tests showed no significant differences between the proportions of sexual offenders in areas of low, medium, or high income, as well as no significant differences between the proportion of sexual offenders in areas of low, medium, and high populations of children under age 18. While it was anticipated that the proportion of offenders would not differ based on mean family income because it was shown that the residency restrictions in Alachua County were evenly dispersed between areas of high income and areas of low income, it was noteworthy that offenders were not more concentrated in areas densely populated with children under age 18, even though maps indicated that the majority of these areas were not restricted by residency restrictions. This finding adds to extant research which found that sex offenders do not live significantly closer to areas where children congregate than members of the general population (Zgoba et al., 2008), further discrediting the assumption at the heart of residency restrictions that offenders place themselves near potential victims in a systematic way.

Finally, this study looked at the number of offenders moving into areas restricted by residency restrictions. By mapping the locations of the 40 offenders who moved between 2003 and 2007, it was shown that 72.5% (N = 27) moved into a 2,500 foot restricted buffer area. In the event that all 40 offenders who moved did so before the 2,500 foot restriction was implemented in 2005, the locations were reanalyzed using the original 1,000 foot buffer zones. The results of this reanalysis showed that 40% (N = 16) moved into restricted areas.

While this study offers a valuable addition to what is known about the effects of residency restrictions, the analyses are not without limitations. First, these results are based on a single county. This concerns both the study's sample size, which is relatively small, as well as the overall generalizability of the findings. We believe that the present analysis could provide a model for further extension of this line of inquiry, and fully support replication in different regions with larger datasets, including those featuring yearly observations. Our view is that further replication is a necessary and an inevitable step needed to forward this growing sub-field. Also, while we have no reason to believe that the results of this study are widely or perfectly generalizable, we contend that Alachua County represents an interesting test case that offers certain environmental advantages such as highly pronounced class-based segregation. More importantly, the phenomenon of increasingly punitive residency restrictions observed in Alachua County is being repeated and modeled all over the country. Second, our data do not permit fully robust conclusions about some trends that we identify. For example, although it seems unlikely, it is possible that all offenders in the sample who relocated between 2003 and 2007 could have done so prior to 2005, when the 2,500 ft. restriction ordinance went into effect. Thus, some offenders who were observed as relocating into the larger "no access" buffer zones may have been in compliance with state law at the time of their move. It should be noted, though, that a large portion of the offenders who relocated between 2003 and 2007 (40%, N = 16) would have still fallen within the previous 1,000 foot buffer zones under state law. Unfortunately, retrospective offender location data was unavailable for additional years within the study timeframe for use in our analysis, as the official data source maintained by Florida Department of Law Enforcement is continually updated, and old files are not stored for researchers to access. We hope that future studies involving replication with larger datasets can help to understand the trends in offender movement over time.

Finding that a large number of sex offenders were in violation of the residency restriction points to an additional limitation of the study. While the purpose of this study was to assess the overall effects of residency restrictions on the spatial distribution of sex offenders, this study cannot give an accurate depiction of those effects because it is apparent that the restrictions were not working as intended. It is possible that in an area were there is 100% compliance with residency restrictions, residential clustering, dispersion, or relationships between offenders and areas of low mean income or high populations of children may be different. Still, the results offered by this study are valuable as they provide a look into the effects of these restrictions as they are being implemented by counties. There is no reason to suspect that the implementation of residency restrictions in Alachua County, Florida is different from other jurisdictions with residency restrictions, as the rate of non-compliance in this study was comparative to previous studies looking at residency restrictions (Tewksbury & Mustaine, 2006). Another limitation of the study is the use of static figures for area characteristics. While this study utilized data from the 2000 Census at the block group level, variables such as population, mean family income, and number of children under age 18 remained constant at both time periods. Unfortunately, data on these variables was not available on a year to year basis, forcing this analysis to use these static figures. Finally, while we illustrate trends in spatial concentration for two time periods surrounding the more punitive residency restriction intervention, we cannot reliably make inferences about potential effects before residency restrictions of any type were made effective. Doing so would require, at minimum, a third time point with residency data for sex offenders before any residency restrictions were put in place in order to compare all three levels of restriction. Unfortunately, we were unable to locate this data for our analysis, as Florida instituted residency restrictions for sexual offenders in 1997, but the state does not retain residency records for sexual offenders at different time periods. The registry in Florida is updated from a master list, thus the FDLE was unable to trace back to 1997 to determine where sex offenders were living at that time. With the appropriate data, we regard this additional analysis as a valuable future research direction.

Exploratory spatial data analysis shows limited residential clustering of registered sex offenders in Alachua County. This may be viewed as supportive of the currently underdeveloped literature on criminological theories that might potentially explain sexual offending as a function of geography and social structure (e.g., social learning, routine activities, etc.), because those theoretical orientations might predict spatial concentration of offenders. Our analysis is not intended to assess any theoretical suppositions about the etiology of the behavior, but this study and others like it may be instrumental in constructing theoretical models that could better account for this class of offenders. These results may differ in other areas, however, if residency restrictions are not equally distributed in space between areas of high socioeconomic status and areas of low socioeconomic status.

When considering potential theoretical relationships between the variables under study, many questions remain largely unresolved. For example, although geographic proximity is supposed to relate to sexual offender recidivism and/or the risk of victimization for children under age 18, thus, residency restrictions are widely popular, the nature of that relationship is tenuous. One line of reasoning suggests that smaller geographic areas present more risk than larger areas when holding the number of potential victims constant; however, it is at least conceivable that the opposite could be true, and that victims could be sought out when they were less numerous for any number of logistical and practical reasons (victims' social isolation, restricted patterns of movement, greater predictability, etc.). Ultimately, this is an empirical question that we cannot address in this analysis because we lack victimization data. Notably, developing this line of reasoning and empirical inquiry would also have implications for methodology, as future studies could use geographic area to adjust proportions as a function of the hypothesized relationship between area and risk in this population.

Examining the spatial clustering of offenders has implications for policy as well. From a policing perspective, information pertaining to the spatial distribution of registered sex offenders may aid in routine patrols, preventive techniques such as neighborhood watch programs, pursuing technical parole/probation violations through regular address verification, and a variety of other concerns. However, results from this study suggest that the workload and administrative responsibilities for police may actually be increased by harsher residency restrictions, because offenders are dispersed more widely, making coordination of prevention and monitoring programs more difficult and labor-intensive. This is to say nothing, of course, about the increasingly demanding workload resulting from "net-widening" and broader classification schemes in Florida as well as many other states.

Our analysis also identified two demographic properties potentially relevant to policies affecting sex offender residency restrictions. First, it appears that socioeconomic status is highly spatially autocorrelated in Alachua County. If residency restrictions were differentially affecting offenders based in some way on their income level, these trends should have been apparent in the maps showing the spatial distribution of offender residences. Examples of this type of potential effect include class bias or a differential effect whereby offenders are relegated to lower-socioeconomic status areas due to fewer opportunities to relocate into middle-class or upper-class neighborhoods. However, it appears that the spatial distribution of registered sex offenders both before and after the more punitive 2,500 ft. residency restrictions is relatively unrelated to income.

Second, our analysis suggests that residency restrictions in Alachua County may not be protecting the children under age 18. Many of the 2000 Census block groups identified as having a high-high concentration of residents under age 18 had few or no residency restriction buffers whatsoever. This occurs because schools in Alachua County are centrally located, for the most part, but aggressive expansion and annexation of the city of Gainesville has meant a great deal of growth in the northwest and southwest quadrants of the urban area. Gainesville's schools remain fixed in the urban core, while many residents who have young families relocate to the unincorporated fringes where new, primarily middle-class neighborhoods are being developed. Construction of new schools, parks, and daycare facilities has not kept pace with housing, rendering residential restrictions essentially meaningless in certain areas characterized by a high density of families with young children.

With respect to the residential mobility trends over time, our analysis suggests questions about the efficacy of residency restrictions. For example, many offenders relocated into "off limit" areas within Alachua County between 2003 and 2007. Some ordinances restricting residency also feature exemptions usually enacted by judges to alleviate hardship in cases where a registered offender has searched unsuccessfully for a suitable place of residence outside the restricted areas (Levenson & Cotter, 2005). It is unclear how many cases in

Alachua County were accompanied by such exemptions, or the precise nature of the requests. These questions should be addressed in future research investigating court decisions involving sexual offenders. It is possible that offenders are unable to locate suitable residences due to their own socioeconomic background or income potential, but a trend of this nature should have resulted in a clustering effect in the highly polarized low-socioeconomic status areas of Alachua County. No trend is evident.

One of the most alarming findings from this study is that residency restrictions are not covering areas highly populated with children less than 18 years of age. This finding gives reason to criticize the locations selected for residency restrictions that appear arbitrary (schools, parks and day care facilities). While offenders may not be able to live near a school where children congregate under constant supervision, convicted sexual offenders may live next door to a family with small children who play unsupervised outside their home. Also, as results show at both time periods, many sexual offenders with minor victims live within restricted areas because they secured that residence before restrictions were implemented. These nuances may give provide a false sense of security that could possibly contribute to future victimization if parents are less diligent in monitoring their children because they believe they are living in an area "off limits" to sexual offenders. Even if research showed evidence that residency restrictions could be effective, a finding unsupported in the literature to date, these laws would not be a panacea for parents.

CONCLUSION

Addressing policy issues pertaining to sexual offenders is a delicate matter at best. Many policymakers are well-intentioned when championing sex offender policies, such as residency restrictions, that are presumed to be clearly and definitively in the best interests of the public. However, evolving research on these measures suggests that they may have no effect at all; even worse, that they may aggravate the problem. This study shows limited clustering of the residential locations of sex offenders with minor victims. Furthermore, increasingly harsh residency restrictions resulted in the dispersion of offenders throughout the county. In addition, offenders did not appear to be moving disproportionately into areas of low socioeconomic status, or areas densely populated with children younger than age 18. Finally, results suggest that residency restrictions are not functioning as intended as indicated by the number of offenders moving into restricted areas. Unfortunately, the politics of sex offender policy, which can scarcely be separated from logical or legal rationale, makes comprehensive reform in the near term unlikely. One of the greatest challenges moving forward will be to remember that the best intentions must be tempered with objective, systematic analysis in order to guide future policy.

References

Anselin, L. (1995). Local indicators of spatial association—LISA. *Geographical Analysis, 27*, 93–115.

Anselin, L., Syabri, I., & Kho, Y. (2006). GeoDa: An introduction to spatial data analysis. *Geographical Analysis, 38*, 28–35.

Baller, R., Anselin, L., Messner, S., Deane, G., & Hawkins, D. (2001). Structural covariates of U.S. county homicide rates: Incorporating spatial effects. *Criminology, 39*, 561–590.

Barbaree, H.E., & Marshall, W.L. (Eds.). (2008). *The juvenile sex offender* (2nd ed.). New York: Gulliford Press.

Barnes, J.C., Dukes, T., Tewksbury, R., & DeTroye, T. (2008). Predicting the impact of a statewide residence restriction law on South Carolina sex offenders. *Criminal Justice Policy Review, Online First.* doi:10.1177/0887403408320842.

Beauregard, E., Proulx, J., & Rossmo, D.K. (2005). Spatial patterns of sex offenders: Theoretical, empirical, and practical issues. *Aggression and Violent Behavior, 10*, 579–603.

Blood, P., Watson, L., & Stageberg, P. (2008). *State legislation monitoring report.* Des Moines, IA: Criminal and Juvenile Justice Planning.

Brantingham, P.L., & Brantingham, P.J. (1984). *Patterns in crime.* New York: MacMillan.

Capone, D.L., & Nichols, W.W. (1976). Urban structure and criminal mobility. *American Behavioral Scientist, 20*, 199–213.

Chajewski, M., & Mercado, C.C. (2008). An evaluation of sex offender residency restriction functioning in town, county, and city-wide jurisdictions. *Criminal Justice Policy Review, Online First.* doi:10.1177/08874 03408320845.

Colorado Department of Public Safety. (2004). *Report on safety issues raised by living arrangements for and location of sex offenders in the community.* Denver, CO: Sex Offender Management Board.

Doe v. Miller, No. 04-1568 (8th Cir. April 29, 2005).

Durling, C. (2006). Never going home: Does it make us safer? Does it make sense? Sex offenders, residency restrictions, and reforming risk management law. *The Journal of Criminal Law and Criminology, 97*, 317–363.

Duwe, G., Donnay, W., & Tewksbury, R. (2008). Does residential proximity matter? A geographic analysis of sex offense recidivism. *Criminal Justice and Behavior, 35*, 484–504.

Florida v. Schmidt, No. 16-2006-MO-010568-AXXX (4th Cir. October, 11, 2007).

Fox News. (2008). *Florida orders sex offenders living under Miami bridge to find permanent housing.* Retrieved March 4, 2009 from http://www.foxnews.com/story/0,2933,328827,00.html.

Grubesic, T.H., Murray, A.T., & Mack, E.A. (2008). Sex offenders, housing and spatial restriction zones. *GeoJournal, 73*, 255–269.

Hanson, R.K., & Bussiere, M.T. (1998). Predicting relapse: A meta-analysis of sexual offender recidivism studies. *Journal of Consulting and Clinical Psychology, 66*, 348–362.

Hanson, R.K., Gordon, A., Harris, A.J.R., Marques, J.K., Murphy, W., Quinsey, V.L., et al. (2002). First report of the collaborative outcome data project on the effectiveness of treatment for sex offenders. *Sexual Abuse: A Journal of Research and Treatment, 14*, 169–194.

Hepburn, J.R., & Griffin, M.L. (2004). The effect of social bonds on successful adjustment to probation: An event history analysis. *Criminal Justice Review. 29*, 46–75.

Human Rights Watch. (2007). *No easy answers: Sex offender laws in the U.S.* New York: Human Rights Watch. Retrieved March 4, 2009 from http://www.hrw.org/en/reports/2007/09/11/no-easy-answers.

Jenkins, P. (1998). *Moral panic: Changing concepts of the child molester in modern America.* New Haven: Yale University Press.

Levenson, J.S. (2005). Sex offender residence restrictions. *Sex Offender Law Report.* Civil Research Institute.

Levenson, J.S. (2008). Collateral consequences of sex offender residence restrictions. *Criminal Justice Studies, 21*, 153–166.

Levenson, J.S., & Cotter, L.P. (2005). The impact of sex offender residence restrictions: 1,000 feet from danger or one step from absurd? *International Journal of Offender Therapy and Comparative Criminology, 49*, 168–178.

Levenson, J.S., & Hern, A. (2007). Sex offender residence restrictions: Unintended consequences and community re-entry. *Justice Research and Policy, 9*, 59–73.

Maghelal, P., & Olivares, O. (Unpublished Manuscript). Critical risk zones: Violators of Megan's Law.

Martinson, R. (1974). What works? Questions and answers about prison reform. *The Public Interest, 35*, 22–54.

Meloy, M.L., Miller, S.L., & Curtis, K.M. (2008). Making sense out of nonsense: The deconstruction of state-level sex offender residence restrictions. *American Journal of Criminal Justice, 33*, 209–222.

Mercado, C.C., Alvarez, S.A., & Levenson, J.S. (2008). The impact of specialized sex offender legislation on community re-entry. *Sexual Abuse: A Journal of Research and Treatment, 20,* 188–205.

Messner, S.F., Anselin, L., Baller, R.D., Hawkins, D.F., Deane, G., & Tolnay, S.E. (1999). The spatial patterning of county homicide rates: An application of exploratory spatial data analysis. *Journal of Quantitative Criminology, 15,* 423–450.

Minnesota Department of Corrections (2003). *Level three sex offenders residential placement issues.* St. Paul: Minnesota Department of Corrections. Retrieved March 4, 2009 from http://www.leg.state.mn.us/docs/2003/mandated/030175.pdf.

Mustaine, E.E., Tewksbury, R., & Stengel, K.M. (2006). Social disorganization and residential locations of registered sex offenders: Is this a collateral consequence? *Deviant Behavior, 27,* 329–350.

Petracca, M. (2006). Banished! New Jersey's municipalities' unconstitutional trend of banishing sex offenders. *Seton Hall Legislative Journal, 31,* 253–285.

Rengert, G.F., Piquero, A.R., & Jones, P.R. (1999). Distance decay reexamined. *Criminology, 37,* 427–446.

Sample, L.L., & Bray, T.M. (2003). Are sex offenders dangerous? *Criminology and Public Policy, 3,* 59–82.

Sampson, R.J., & Groves, W.B. (1989). Community structure and crime: Testing social-disorganization theory. *The American Journal of Sociology, 94,* 774–802.

Shaw, C.R., & McKay, H.D. (1942). *Juvenile delinquency in urban areas.* Chicago: University of Chicago Press.

Snyder, H.N. (2000). *Sexual assault of young children as reported to law enforcement: Victim, incident, and offender characteristics.* (Bureau of Justice Statistics Publication NCJ 182990). Washington, D.C.: U.S. Government Printing Office.

Stachura, S. (2006). *The consequences of zoning sex offenders.* Retrieved April 8, 2008 from http://minnesota.publicradio.org/display/web/2006/04/21/sex offconsequences.

Stromberg, M. (2007). Locked up, then locked out: Residency restrictions for sex offenders may create more problems than they solve. *Planning, 73,* 20–25.

Tewksbury, R. (2005). Collateral consequences of sex offender registration. *Journal of Contemporary Criminal Justice, 21,* 67–81.

Tewksbury, R., & Mustaine, E.E. (2006). Where to find sex offenders: An examination of residential locations and neighborhood conditions. *Criminal Justice Studies, 19,* 61–75.

Walker, J.T., Golden, J.W., & VanHouten, A.C. (2001). The geographic link between sex offenders and potential victims: A routine activity approach. *Justice Researcher and Policy, 3,* 15–33.

Yung, C.R. (2007). Banishment by a thousand laws: Residency restrictions on sex offenders. *Washington University Law Review, 85,* 101–160.

Zandbergen, P.A., & Hart, T.C. (2006). Reducing housing options for convicted sex offenders: Investigating the impact of residency restriction laws using GIS. *Justice Research and Policy, 8,* 1–24.

Zandbergen, P.A., & Hart, T.C. (2009). Geocoding accuracy considerations in determining residency restrictions for sex offenders. *Criminal Justice Policy Review, 20*(1), 62–90.

Zarrella, J., & Oppmann, P. (2007). *Florida housing sex offenders under bridge.* Retrieved April 6, 2007 from http://www.cnn.com/2007/LAW/04/05/bridge.sex.offenders/index.html.

Zgoba, K.M., Levenson, J.L., & McKee, T. (2008). Examining the impact of sex offender residence restrictions on housing options. *Criminal Justice Policy Review, Online First.* doi:10.1177/0887403408322119.

Zimring, E., Piquero, A.R., & Jennings, W.G. (2007). Sexual delinquency in Racine: Does early sex offending predict later sex offending in youth and young adulthood? *Criminology and Public Policy, 6,* 507–534.

Bibliography

A&E Home Video (1996). *Police* [Film]. (Available from New Video Group, 126 Fifth Avenue, New York, NY 10011).

Akers, R. (1992). *Drugs, alcohol, and society.* Belmont, CA: Wadsworth.

Akers, R., & Sellers, C. S. (2009). *Criminological theories: Introduction and evaluation* (5th ed.). Los Angeles, CA: Roxbury.

Banks, E., Ferretti, L., & Shucard, D. (1997). Effects of low-level lead exposure on cognitive function in children: A review of behavioral, neuropsychological and biological evidence. *Neurotoxicology, 18*, 237–282.

Barnes, G. (1995). Defining and optimizing displacement. In J. Eck & D. Weisburd (Eds.) *Crime and place* (pp. 95–114). Monsey, NY: Willow Tree Press.

Barnes, H., & Teeters, N. (1959). *New horizons in criminology* (3rd ed.) Englewood Cliffs, NJ: Prentice Hall.

Bartollas, C., & Hahn, L. (1999). *Policing in America.* Boston, MA: Allyn and Bacon.

Bass, S. (2001). Out of place: Petit apartheid and the police. In D. Milovanovic & K. Russel (Eds.) *Petit apartheid in the U.S. criminal justice system: The dark figure of racism* (pp. 43–55). Durham, NC: Carolina Academic Press.

Baum, K., & Klaus, P. (2005). Violent victimization of college students, 1995–2002 (NCJ-20636). Washington, DC: BJS.

Beccaria, C. (1963). *On crimes and punishments.* (H. Paolucci, Trans.). Indianapolis, IN: Bobbs-Merrill. (Original work published 1764).

Becker, H. (1963). *Outsiders: Studies in the sociology of deviance.* New York, NY: The Free Press.

Bellinger, D., Stiles, K., & Needleman, H. (1992). Low-level lead exposure, intelligence and academic achievement: A long-term follow-up study. *Pediatrics, 90*, 855–861.

Bennett, J. (1981). *Oral history and delinquency: The rhetoric of criminology.* Chicago, IL: University of Chicago Press.

Bibel, D. (2000). Statewide crime analysis and mapping: An on-going project. *Crime Mapping News, 2*, 1–4.

Blau, J., & Blau, P. (1982). The cost of inequality: Metropolitan structure and violent crime. *American Sociological Review, 47,* 114–129.

Block, C. (1998). The geoarchive: an information foundation for community policing. In D. Weisburd & T. McEwen (Eds.). *Crime mapping and crime prevention* (pp. 27–82). Monsey, NY: Willow Tree Press.

Block, R., & Block, C. (1995). Space, place and crime: Hot spot areas the hot places of liquor-related crime. In J. Eck & D. Weisburd (Eds.) *Crime and place* (pp. 145–184). Monsey, NY: Willow Tree Press.

Boarnet, M., & Bogart, W. (1996). Enterprise zones and employment: Evidence from New Jersey. *Journal of Urban Economics, 40,* 198–215.

Boba, R. (2001). *Introductory guide to crime analysis and mapping.* Washington, DC: COPS.

Boba, R. (2009). *Crime analysis and crime mapping.* Thousand Oaks, CA: Sage.

Bohm, R. (1997). *A primer on crime and delinquency.* Belmont, CA: Wadsworth.

Bowers, K. J., Johnson, S. D., & Pease, K. (2004). Prospective hotspotting. The future of crime mapping? *British Journal of Criminology, 44,* 641–658.

Bracey, D. (1992). Police corruption and community relations: Community policing. *Police Studies, 15,* 179–183.

Brantingham, P. J., & Brantingham, P. L. (1981). *Environmental criminology.* Prospect Heights, IL: Waveland Press.

Brantingham, P. J., & Brantingham, P. L. (1991). *Environmental criminology* (2nd ed.). Prospect Heights, IL: Waveland Press.

Brantingham, P. J., & Brantingham, P. L. (2008). Crime pattern theory. In R. Wortley & L. Mazerolle (Eds.) *Environmental criminology and crime analysis.* Portland, OR: Willan Publishing.

Brantingham, P. L., & Brantingham, P. J. (1998). Planning against crime. In M. Felson (Ed.) *Reducing crime through real estate development and management* (pp. 23–28). Washington DC: Urban Land Institute.

Brantingham, P. L., & Brantingham, P. J. (1999). A theoretical model of crime hot spot generation. *Studies on Crime and Crime Prevention 8,* 7–26.

Bridenball, B., & Jesilow, P. (2005). Weeding criminals or planting fear: An evaluation of a Weed and Seed project. *Criminal Justice Review, 30*(1), 64–89.

Brooks-Gunn J., Duncan G. J., & Aber, J. L. (1997). *Neighborhood Poverty: Vol. I: Context and consequences for children* (Eds.). New York, NY: Russell Sage.

Browning, C. R., Feinberg, S. L., & Dietz, R. D. (2004). The paradox of social organization: Networks, collective efficacy, and violent crime in urban neighborhoods. *Social Forces, 82*(2), 503–534.

Browning, C. R., Burrington, L. A., Leventhal, T., & Brooks-Gunn, J. (2008) Neighborhood structural inequality, collective efficacy, and sexual risk behavior among urban youth. *Journal of Health and Social Behavior, 49*(3), 269–285.

Bruce, C. (2000, Spring). Mapping in action. Tactical crime analysis: Musings from the Cambridge, Massachusetts Police Department. *Crime mapping news, 2*, 10–12.

Bullard, R. (1994). *Dumping in dixie: Race, class and environmental quality.* Boulder, CO: Westview.

Bureau of Justice Assistance (1997). *Crime prevention and community policing: A vital partnership.* Washington, DC: USGPO.

Burgess, E. (1925). The growth of the city. In R. Park, E. Burgess, & R. McKenzie (Eds.) *The city* (pp. 47–62). Chicago, IL: University of Chicago Press.

Bursik, R., Jr. (1986). Delinquency rates as sources of ecological change. In J. M. Byrne & R. J. Sampson (Eds.) *The social ecology of crime* (pp. 63–76). New York, NY: Springer-Verlag.

Bursik, R., Jr. (1988). Social disorganization and theories of crime and delinquency: Problems and prospects. *Criminology, 26*(4), 519–551.

Bursik, R., Jr., & Grasmick, H. (1993). *Neighborhoods and crime: The dimensions of effective community control.* New York, NY: Lexington Books.

Butler, S. M. (1980). *Enterprise zones: Pioneering in the inner city.* Washington, DC: Heritage Foundation.

Bynum, T. (2001). *Using analysis for problem-solving: A guidebook for law enforcement.* Washington, DC: COPS.

Byrne, J., & Sampson, R. (1986). Key issues in the social ecology of crime. In J. Byrne & R. Sampson (Eds.), *The social ecology of crime* (pp. 1–22). New York, NY: Springer-Verlag.

Canter, P. (1990). *Baltimore County Police Department spousal abuse study.* Towson, MD: Baltimore County Police Department.

Canter, P. (1998). Geographic information systems and crime analysis in Baltimore County, Maryland. In D. Weisburd & T. McEwen (Eds.) *Crime mapping and crime prevention* (pp. 157–92). Monsey, NY: Willow Tree Press.

Canter, P. (2000). Using a geographic information system for tactical crime analysis. In V. Goldsmith, P. McGuire, J. Mollenkopf, & T. Ross (Eds.) *Analyzing crime patterns: Frontiers of practice* (pp. 3–10). Thousand Oaks, CA: Sage.

Centers for Disease Control and Prevention (1997). *Screening young children for lead poisoning: Guidance for state and local public health officials.* Atlanta, GA: CDC.

Center for Problem-Oriented Policing (2010). *A theory of crime problems.* Retrieved September 3, 2010, from http://www.popcenter.org/learning/pam/help/theory.cfm.

Chambliss, W. J. (1994). Policing the ghetto underclass: The politics of law and law enforcement. *Social Problems, 41*(2), 177–194.

Chambliss, W. J. (1996). The Saints and the roughnecks. In R. Berger (Ed.), *The sociology of juvenile delinquency* (pp. 43–54). Chicago, IL: Nelson-Hall.

Chambliss, W. J., & Seidman, R. (1971). *Law, order, and power.* New York, NY: McGraw-Hill.

Chainey, S. (2005). *How accurate is my hotspot map?* Eighth Annual Crime Mapping Research Conference, September 7–10, 2005. Savannah, GA.

Chainey, S., Tompson, L., & Uhlig, S. (2008). The utility of hotspot mapping for predicting spatial patterns of crime. *Security Journal, 21,* 4–28.

Christens, B., & Speer, P.W. (2005). Predicting violent crime using urban and suburban densities. *Behavior and Social Studies, 14,* 113–127.

Clarke, R. (1983). Situational crime prevention: Its theoretical basis and practical scope. In M. Tonry & N. Morris (Eds.), *Crime and justice: A review of research* (pp. 225–256). Chicago, IL: University of Chicago Press.

Clarke, R. (1992). *Situational crime prevention: Successful case studies.* New York, NY: Harrow and Heston.

Clarke, R. (1995). Situational crime prevention. In M. Tonry & D. Farrington (Eds.) *Building a safer society: Strategic approaches to crime prevention.* (pp. 91–150). Chicago, IL: University of Chicago Press.

Clarke, R. (1997). *Situational crime prevention: Successful case studies Volume 2.* New York, NY: Harrow and Heston.

Clarke, R., & Cornish, D. (1985). Modeling offenders' decisions: A framework for research and policy. In M. Tonry & N. Morris (Eds.), *Crime and justice: An annual review of research, volume 6* (pp. 147–185). Chicago, IL: University of Chicago Press.

Clarke, R., & Eck, J. (2005). *Crime analysis for problem solvers in 60 small steps.* Washington DC: NIJ.

Clarke, R., & Felson, M. (1993). *Routine activity and rational choice: Advances in criminological theory volume 5.* New Brunswick, NJ: Transaction Publishers.

Clarke, R., & Harris, P. (1992). A rational choice perspective on the targets of automobile theft. *Criminal Behavior and Mental Health, 2,* 25–42.

Clarke, R., & Homel, R. (1997). A revised classification of situational crime prevention techniques. In S. Lab (Ed.) *Crime prevention at a crossroads.* Cincinnati, OH: Anderson Publishing.

Clarke, R., & Mayhew, P. (1980). *Designing out crime.* London, UK: HMSO.

Clarke, R., & Mayhew, P. (1988). The British gas suicide story and its implication for prevention. In M Tonry & N. Morris (Eds.), *Crime and justice: A review of research.* Chicago, IL: University of Chicago Press.

Cohen, L., & Felson, M. (1979). Social change and crime rate trends; A routine activity approach. *American Sociological Review, 44*, 588–608.

Cook, P. (1980). Research in criminal deterrence: Laying the groundwork for the second decade. In N. Morris & M. Tonry (Eds.) *Crime and justice: An annual review of research volume 2*, (pp. 211–268). Chicago, IL: University of Chicago Press.

Coordinating Council and Juvenile Justice and Delinquency Prevention, (1996). *Federal efforts to prevent and reduce juvenile delinquency: FY 1995*. Washington, DC: USGPO.

Cordner, G. (2004). The survey data: What they say and don't say about community policing. In L. Fridell & M. Wycoff (Eds.) *Community policing: The past, present, and future* (pp. 59–72). Washington, DC: PERF.

Cornish, D., & Clarke, R. V. (1986). Introduction. In D. Cornish & R. V. Clarke (Eds.). *The reasoning criminal: Rational choice perspectives on offending* (pp. 1–16). New York, NY: Springer-Verlag.

Cornish, D., & Clarke, R. V. (1987). Understanding crime displacement: An application of rational choice theory. In S. Henry & W. Einstader (Eds.). *The criminology theory reader.* (pp. 45–56). New York, NY: New York University Press.

Cornish, D., & Clarke, R. (2003). Opportunities, precipitators, and criminal decisions: A reply to Worley's critique of situational prevention. In M. Smith & D. Cornish (Eds.) *Theory for practice in situational crime prevention* (pp. 41–96). Monsey, NY: Criminal Justice Press.

Cox, S. (1996). *Police: Practices, perspectives, problems.* Boston, MA: Allyn and Bacon.

Crawford, A. (1998). *Crime prevention and community safety: Politics, policies and practices.* London, UK: Longman.

Crime Mapping Research Center (1998). *Hotspots: An exploration of methods.* Available online at www.usdoj.gov/cmrc.

Cromwell, P., Parker, L., & Mobley, S. (1999). The five-finger discount: An analysis of motivations for shoplifting. In P. Cromwell (Ed.) *In their own words: Criminals on crime* (pp. 57–70). Los Angeles, CA: Roxbury Publishing.

Cromwell, P., Olson, J., & Avery, D. (1991). *Breaking and entering: An ethnographic analysis of burglary.* Newbury Park, CA: Sage.

Crowe, T. (2000). *Crime prevention through environmental design: Applications of architectural design and space management concepts* (2nd Ed.). Boston, MA: Butterworth-Heinemann.

Crowe, T., & Zahm, D. (1994, Fall). Crime prevention through environmental design. *Land Development*, 22–27.

Curran, D., & Renzetti, C. (1994). *Theories of crime.* Boston, MA: Allyn and Bacon.

Curran, D., & Renzetti, C. (2001). *Theories of crime* (2nd Ed.). Boston, MA: Allyn and Bacon.

Dabney, D. (2010). Observations regarding key operational realities in a Compstat model of policing. *Justice Quarterly, 27,* 28–51.

Davis, P. (1998, September 18). Altering the landscape for criminals. *The Washington Post,* pp. B1, B5.

DeLeon-Granados, W. (1999). *Travels through crime and place.* Boston, MA: Northeastern University Press.

Department of Justice (1978). *Response time analysis.* Washington, DC: USGPO.

Dunworth, T., & Mills, G. (1999). *National evaluation of Weed and Seed.* Washington, DC: USGPO.

Durkheim, E. (1965). *The division of labor in society* (G. Simpson, Trans.). New York, NY: Free Press. (Original work published 1893).

Eck, J. (1993). The threat of crime displacement. *Criminal Justice Abstracts, 25,* 527–546.

Eck, J. (2001). Problem-oriented policing and crime event concentration. In R. Meier, L. Kennedy, & V. Sacco (Eds.), *The process and structure of crime.* Piscataway, NJ: Transaction Press.

Eck, J., Chaney, S., Cameron, J., Leitner, M., & Wilson, R. (2005). *Mapping crime: Understanding hot spots.* Washington, DC: NIJ.

Eck, J., Gersh, J., & Taylor, C. (2000). Finding crime hot spots through repeat address mapping. In V. Goldsmith, P. McGuire, J. Mollenkopf, & T. Ross (Eds.) *Analyzing crime patterns: Frontiers of practice* (pp. 49–64). Thousand Oaks, CA: Sage.

Eck, J., & Spellman, W. (1987). *Problem solving: Problem oriented policy in Newport News.* Washington, DC: PERF.

Eck, J., & Weisburd, D. (1995). Crime places in crime theory. In J. Eck & D. Weisburd (Eds.) *Crime and place* (pp. 1–34). Monsey, NY: Willow Tree Press.

Edelstein, M. (1988). Contaminated communities: The social and psychological impacts of residential toxic exposure. Boulder, CO: Westview.

Einstadter, W., & Henry, S. (1995). *Criminological theory: An analysis of its underlying assumptions.* Fort Worth, TX: Harcourt Brace College Publishers.

Elliott, D., & Huizinga, D. (1983). Social class and delinquent behavior in a national youth panel. *Criminology, 21,* 149–177.

Evans, J. R., & Mathur, A. (2005). The value of online surveys. *Internet Research, 15*(2), 195–219.

Faggiani, D., & Hirschel, D. (2005). The impact of information technology on crime reporting: The NIBRS process. In A. Pattavina (Ed.) *Informa-*

tion technology and the criminal justice system (pp. 101–124). Thousand Oaks, CA: Sage.

Farrel, G., & Sousa, W. (2001). Repeat victimization and hot spots: The overlap and its implications for crime control and problem oriented policing. In G. Farrel & K. Pease (Eds.). *Repeat victimization* (pp. 221–240). Monsey, NY: Willow Tree Press.

Feagin, J., & Feagin, C. (1993). Racial and ethnic relations (4th ed.). Englewood Cliffs, NJ: Prentice Hall.

Federal Bureau of Investigation (1975). *Crime in the United States.* Washington, DC: USDOJ.

Federal Bureau of Investigation (2000). National Incident-Based Reporting System Volume I: Data Collection Guidelines. Washington, DC: USDOJ.

Federal Bureau of Investigation (2001). *Crime in the United States.* Washington, DC: USDOJ.

Federal Bureau of Investigation (2004). *Uniform Crime Reporting Handbook.* Washington, DC: USDOJ.

Federal Bureau of Investigation (2009a). *Crime in the United States, 2008— Offense definitions.* Retrieved August 20, 2010, from http://www.fbi.gov/ucr/ cius2008/ about/offense_definitions.html.

Federal Bureau of Investigation (2009b). *Crime in the United States, 2008— Table 1.* Retrieved August 20, 2010, from at http://www.fbi.gov/ucr/cius2008/ data/ table_01.html.

Federal Bureau of Investigation (2009c). *Crime in the United States, 2008— Table 5 data declaration.* Retrieved August 20, 2010, from http://www.fbi.gov/ucr/cius2008/ data/table_05_dd.html.

Federal Bureau of Investigation (2009d). *National Incident Based Reporting System—Frequently asked questions.* Retrieved on August 20, 2010, from http://www.fbi.gov/ucr/downloadables/ nibrs_general_2008.pdf.

Feins, J. D., Epstein, J. C., & Widom, R. (1997). *Solving crime problems in residential neighborhoods: Comprehensive changes in design, management, and use.* Washington, DC: NIJ.

Felson, M. (1986). Linking criminal choices, routine activities, informal control, and criminal outcomes. In D. Cornish & R. Clarke (Eds.) *The reasoning criminal* (pp. 119–128). New York, NY: Springer-Verlag.

Felson, M. (1998a). *Crime and everyday life.* (2nd ed.). Thousand Oaks, CA: Pine Forge Press.

Felson, M. (Ed.). (1998b). *Reducing crime through real estate development and management.* Washington D.C.: Urban Land Institute.

Felson, M. (2002). *Crime and everyday life.* (3rd Ed.). Thousand Oaks, CA: Pine Forge Press.

Felson, M. (2006). *Crime and nature.* Thousand Oaks, CA: Sage.

Felson, M., & Boba, R. (2010). *Crime and everyday life.* (4th ed.). Thousand Oaks, CA: Sage.

Felson, M., & Clarke, R. (1995). Routine precautions, criminology, and crime prevention. In H. Barlow (Ed.) *Crime and public policy: Putting theory to work* (pp. 179–190). Boulder, CO: Westview Press.

Felson, M., & Clarke, R. (1997). The ethics of situational crime prevention. In G. Newman & R. Clarke (Eds.), *Rational choice and situational crime prevention: Theoretical foundations* (pp. 197–218). Brookfield, VT: Ashgate Publishing.

Felson, M., & Clarke, R. (1998). *Opportunity makes the thief: Practical theory for crime prevention.* London, UK: Home Office.

Ferrell, J. (2001). Trying to make us a parking lot: Petit apartheid, cultural space, and the public negotiation of ethnicity. In D. Milovanovic & K. Russell (Eds.) *Petit apartheid in the U.S. criminal justice system: The dark figure of racism* (pp. 55–68). Durham, NC: Carolina Academic Press.

Fleming, Z. (1999). The thrill of it all: Youthful offenders and auto theft. In P. Cromwell (Ed.) *In their own words: Criminals on crime* (pp. 71–79). Los Angeles, CA: Roxbury Publishing.

Flynn, D. (1998). *Defining the "community" in community policing.* Washington, DC: Community Policing Consortium.

Fricker, R. D., & Schonlau, M. (2002). Advantages and disadvantages of Internet research surveys: Evidence from the literature. *Field Methods, 14*(4), 347–367.

Fridell, L. (2004). The results of three national surveys on community policing. In L. Fridell & M. Wycoff (Eds.) *Community policing: The past, present, and future* (pp. 39–58). Washington, DC: PERF.

Foucault, M. (1977). *Discipline and punish: The birth of the prison.* New York, NY: Pantheon.

Fowler, F., Jr., & Mangione, T. (1982). *Neighborhood crime, fear, and social control: A second look at the Hartford program.* Washington, DC: USDOJ.

Gibson, C., & Lennon, E. (1999). Population division working paper No. 29. Washington, DC: United States Bureau of the Census.

Glovin, D., Larson, E., & Voreacos, D. (March 10, 2009). Modoff to plead guilty in largest US Ponzi Scheme. Retrieved on January 31, 2011 from http://www.bloomberg.com/apps/news?pid=20601087&sid=awXqT47 DqXZo&refer=home.

Goddard, H. (1914). *Feeblemindedness: Its causes and consequences.* New York, NY: Macmillan.

Gold, M. (1987). Social ecology. In H. Quay (Ed.) *Handbook of juvenile delinquency* (pp. 62–105). New York, NY: John Wiley & Sons.

Goldsmith, W. (1982). Bringing the Third World home. *Working Papers, 9*, 25–30.

Goldstein, H. (1979). Improving policing: A problem-oriented approach. *Crime and Delinquency, 25*, 236–258.

Goldstein, H. (1987). Toward community-oriented policing: Potential, basic requirements, and threshold questions. *Crime and Delinquency, 33*, 6–30.

Goldstein, H. (1993). *The new policing: Confronting complexity.* Washington, DC: NIJ.

Gosier, E. (1997, August 20). 'Weeding' might sow more seeds of distrust. *St. Petersburg Times*, 1C.

Gordon, M. (1964). *Assimilation in American life.* New York, NY: Oxford University Press.

Gottfredson, M. R., & Hirschi, T. (1990). *A general theory of crime.* Stanford, CA: Stanford University Press.

Gottlieb, S., Arenberg, S., & Singh, R. (1998). *Crime analysis: From first report to final arrest* (2nd ed.). Montclair, CA: Alpha Publishing.

Gould, J. (1986). *Quality of life in American neighborhoods: Levels of affluence, toxic waste, and cancer morality in residential zip code areas.* Boulder, CO: Westview.

Gould, S. (1981). *The mismeasure of man.* New York, NY: W.W. Norton.

Greek, C. (1992). *Religious roots of American sociology.* New York, NY: Garland.

Greene, J. (1999). Zero tolerance: A case study of police policies and practices in New York City. *Crime and Delinquency, 45*, 171–187.

Greenwood, P. (1975). *The criminal investigation process.* Santa Monica: RAND Corporation.

Groff, E. R., & LaVigne, N.G. (2002). Forecasting the future of predictive crime mapping. *Crime Prevention Studies, 13*, 29–57.

Grubesic, T. H. (2006). On the application of fuzzy clustering for crime hot spot detection. *Journal of Quantitative Criminology, 22*(1), 77–105.

Haley, K. Todd, J., & Stallo, M. (1998). Crime analysis and the struggle for legitimacy. Presented at the annual meeting of the Academy of Criminal Justice Sciences in Albuquerque, New Mexico, March 10–14, 1998.

Hanson, E. T. (2004). Community policing during a budget crisis: The need for interdisciplinary cooperation, not competition. In L. Fridell & M. Wycoff (Eds.) *Community policing: The past, present, and future* (pp. 151–158). Washington, DC: PERF.

Harcourt, B. (1998). Reflecting on the subject: A critique of the social influence conception of deterrence, the broken windows theory, and order maintenance policing New York style. *Michigan Law Review, 97*, 291–389.

Harries, K. (1999). *Mapping crime: Principles and practice.* Washington, DC: NIJ.

Hart, T. C. (2003). Violent victimization of college students (NCJ-196143). Washington, DC: BJS.

Hart, T. C. (2007). Violent victimization of college students: Findings from the National Crime Victimization Survey. In J. Sloan & B. Fisher (Eds.), *Campus crime: Legal, social, and policy perspectives* (2nd Ed.), pp. 129–146. Springfield, IL: C.C. Thomas.

Hart, T. C., & Miethe, T. D. (2011). Violence against college students and its situational contexts: Prevalence, patterns, and policy implications. *Victims and Offenders, 6*(2), 157–180.

Hart, T. C., & Rennison, C. (2003). Reporting crime to the police, 1992–2001 (NCJ-195710). Washington, DC: BJS.

He, N., Zhao, J., & Lovrich, N. (2005). Community policing: A preliminary assessment of environmental impact with panel data on program implementation in U.S. cities. *Crime and Delinquency, 51*(3), 295–317.

Herrnstein, R. (1988). Crime and human nature revisited: A response to Bonn and Smith. *Criminal Justice Ethics, 7,* 10–15.

Herrnstein, R., & Murray, C. (1994). *The bell curve: Intelligence and class structure in American life.* New York, NY: The Free Press.

Helms, D. (2003). Whendunnit: Unraveling the hidden patterns in the timing of serial crime. *Law Enforcement Technology, 30*(7): 144–147.

Helms, D. (2004). Temporal analysis. In C. Bruce, S. Hick, & J. Cooper (Eds.) *Exploring crime analysis: Readings on essential skills* (pp. 220–262). North Charleston, SC: Booksurg LLC.

Hesseling, R. (1994). Displacement: A review of the empirical literature. In R. Clarke (Ed.), *Crime prevention studies, volume 3.* Monsey, NY: Criminal Justice Press.

Hibbert, C. (1966). *The roots of evil: A social history of crime and punishment.* London, UK: Weidenfeld and Nicolson.

Hirschi, T. (1969). *Causes of delinquency.* Berkeley, CA: University of California Press.

Hirschi, T. (1986). On the compatibility of rational choice and social control theories of crime. In D. Cornish & R. Clarke (Eds.) *The reasoning criminal* (pp. 105–118). New York, NY: Springer-Verlag.

Hope, T. (1995). Community crime prevention. In M. Tonry & D. Farrington (Eds.), *Building a safer society: Strategic approaches to crime prevention* (pp. 21–90). Chicago, IL: University of Chicago Press.

Howell, J., & Hawkins, J. (1998). Prevention of youth violence. In M. Tonry & M. Moore (Eds.), *Youth violence,* (pp. 263–316). Chicago, IL: University of Chicago Press.

International Association of Law Enforcement Intelligence Analysts, Inc. (2004). *Law Enforcement Analytic Standards.* Washington, DC: USDOJ.

International Association of Law Enforcement Intelligence Analysits, Inc. (2010a). *About us.* Retrieved September 25, 2010 from http://www.ialeia.org/aboutus.

International Association of Law Enforcement Intelligence Analysits, Inc. (2010b). *IALEIA certification process and criteria for designation as criminal intelligence certified analyst (CICA).* Richmond, VA: IALEIA.

Jacobs, J. (1961). *Death and life of great American cities.* New York, NY: Vintage Books.

Jeffery, C. (1971). *Crime prevention through environmental design.* Beverly Hills, CA: Sage.

Johnson, S. D., & Bowers, K.J. (2004). The burglary as clue to the future. The beginnings of prospective hot-spotting. *European Journal of Criminology, 1*(2), 237–255.

Johnson, S. D, Bowers, K.J., Birks, D. J., & Pease, K. (2008). Predictive mapping of crime by ProMap: Accuracy, units of analysis and the environmental backcloth. In D. Weisburd, W. Bernasco, & G. J. N. Bruinsma (Eds.). *Putting crime in its place: Units of analysis in geographic criminology.* (pp. 171–198). New York, NY: Springer.

Johnson, S. D., Lab, S. P., & Browers, K .J. (2008). Stable and fluid hotspots of crime: Differentiation and identification. *Built Environment, 34*(1), 32–45.

Kappeler, V. Sluder, R., & Alpert, G. (1994). *Forces of deviance: Understanding the dark side of policing.* Prospect Heights, IL: Waveland Press.

Katz, J. (1988). *Seductions of crime.* New York, NY: Basic Books.

Kelling, G., Pate, T., Dieckman, D., & Brown, C. (1974). The *Kansas City preventive patrol experiment: A summary report.* Washington, DC: Police Foundation.

Kennedy, D. (1996). Neighborhood revitalization: Lessons from Savannah and Baltimore. *National Institute of Justice Journal, 231,*13–17.

Klug, E. (2000). Lead poisoning may be linked to delinquency. *Corrections Today, 62,* 14.

Kobrin, S. (1959). The Chicago Area Project—A 25 year assessment. *Annals of the American Academy of Political and Social Science, 322,* 20–29.

Koper, C. (1995). Just enough police presence: Reducing crime and disorderly behavior by optimizing patrol time in crime hot spots. *Justice Quarterly 12*(4), 649–672.

Kornhauser, R. (1978). *Social sources of delinquency.* Chicago, IL: University of Chicago Press.

Krieg, E. (1995). A socio-historical interpretation of toxic waste sites. *The American Journal of Economics and Sociology, 54,* 1–14.

Krisberg, B., & Austin, J. *Children of Ishmael.* Palo Alto, CA: Mayfield Publishing Company.

Lab, S. (2000). *Crime prevention: Approaches, practices and evaluations* (4th ed.). Cincinnati, OH: Anderson.

Langworthy, R., & Jefferis, E. (2000). The utility of standard deviation ellipses for evaluating hot spots. In V. Goldsmith, P. McGuire, J. Mollenkopf, & T. Ross (Eds.) *Analyzing crime patterns: Frontiers of practice* (pp. 87–104). Thousand Oaks, CA: Sage.

Lave, L., & Seskin (1970). Air pollution and human health. *Science, 169,* 723–733.

Laverty, I., & MacLaren, P. (2002, Summer). Geographic profiling: A new tool for crime analysts. *Crime Mapping News, 4,* 5–8.

LaVigne, N., & Groff, E. (2001). The evolution of crime mapping in the United States: From the descriptive to the analytic. In A. Hirschfield & K. Bowers (Eds.) *Mapping and analyzing crime data: Lessons from research and practice* (pp. 203–222). New York, NY: Taylor & Francis.

LeBeau, J. (1992). Four case studies illustrating the spatial-temporal analysis of serial rapists. *Police Studies, 15,* 124–145.

Lee, M., Maume, M., & Ousey, G. (2003). Social isolation and lethal violence across the metro/nonmetro divide: The effects of socioeconomic disadvantage and poverty concentration on homicide. *Rural Sociology, 68,* 107–131.

Lidsky, T. & Schneider, J. (2000). Evaluating the poisoned mind. *Trial, 36,* 32–40.

Lynch, M., & Patterson, E. (1996). *Justice with prejudice.* Boston, MA: Harrow and Heston.

Lundman, R. (1993). *Prevention and control of juvenile delinquency* (2nd ed.). New York, NY: Oxford University Press.

Mamalian, C., & LaVigne, N. (1999). *The use of computerized crime mapping by law enforcement: Survey results.* Washington, DC: NIJ.

Martin, D., Barnes, E., & Britt, D. (1998). The multiple impacts of mapping it out: Police, geographic information systems (GIS) and community mobilization during Devil's Night in Detroit, Michigan. In N. Lavigne & J. Wartell (Eds.) *Crime mapping case studies: Successes in the field* (pp. 3–14). Washington, DC: PERF.

Martin, R., Mutchnick, R., & Austin, W. (1990). *Criminological thought: Pioneers past and present.* New York, NY: Macmillan Publishing Company.

Martinson, R. (1974). What works? Questions and answers about prison reform. *The Public Interest* (Spring), 25.

Maxfield, M. (2001). *Guide to frugal evaluation for criminal justice: Final report.* Washington, DC: NIJ.

Maxfield, M., & Babbie, E. (2011). *Research methods for criminal justice and criminology* (6th ed.). Belmont, CA: Wadsworth.

Mayhew, P., Clarke, R., & Elliot, D. (1989). Motorcycle theft, helmet legislation and displacement. *Howard Journal, 28,* 1–8.

McDonald, P. (2002). *Managing police operations: Implementing the New York Crime Control Model-CompStat.* Belmont: Belmont, CA: Wadsworth.

McEwen, T., & Taxman, F. (1995). Applications of computerized mapping to police operations. In J. Eck & D. Weisburd (Eds.) *Crime and Place* (pp. 259–284) Monsey, NY: Criminal Justice Press.

McGahey, R. (1986). Economic conditions, neighborhood organization, and urban crime. In A. Reiss, Jr. & M. Tonry (Eds.) *Communities and crime* (pp. 231–270). Chicago, IL: University of Chicago Press.

McLafferty, S., Williamson, D., & McGuire, P. (2000). Identifying crime hop spots using kernel smoothing. In V. Goldsmith, P. McGuire, J. Mollenkopf, & T. Ross (Eds.) *Analyzing crime patterns: Frontiers of practice* (pp. 77–86). Thousand Oaks, CA: Sage.

Merry, S. (1981). Defensible space undefended: Social factors in crime control through environmental design. *Urban Affairs Quarterly, 16,* 397–422.

Michalowski, R. (1985). *Order, law and crime: An introduction to criminology.* New York, NY: Random House.

Miethe, T., & McCorkle, R. (2001). *Crime profiles: The anatomy of dangerous persons, places, and situations* (2nd ed.). Los Angeles, CA: Roxbury.

Miethe, T., & McCorkle, R. (2006). *Crime profiles: The anatomy of dangerous persons, places, and situations* (3rd ed.). Los Angeles, CA: Roxbury.

Miller, H. J. (2005). A measurement theory for time geography, *Geographical Analysis, 37,* 17–45.

Miller, L. (2001). *The politics of community crime prevention: Implementing Operation Weed and Seed in Seattle.* Burlington, VT: Ashgate.

Miller, W. (1962). The impact of a "total community" delinquency control project. *Social Problems, 10,* 168–191.

Morello-Frosch, R., Pastor, M., & Sadd, J. (2001). Environmental justice and southern California's riskscape: The distribution of air toxics exposures and health risks among diverse communities. *Urban Affairs Review, 36,* 551–578.

Morenoff, J., Sampson, R., & Raudenbush, S. (2001). Neighborhood inequality, collective efficacy, and the spatial dynamics of urban violence. *Criminology, 39,* 517–560.

Morgan, J. D. (2009). Hot routes: Developing a new technique for spatial analysis of crime. *Crime Mapping: A Journal of Research and Practice, 1*(2), 8–39.

Morgan, P. (2002, December 3). Fighting urban scrawl. *The Tampa Tribune,* Baylife 1, 5.

Monachesi, E. (1955). Pioneers in criminology IX: Cesare Beccaria (1738–1794). *Journal of Criminal Law, Criminology and Police Science, 46*, 439–449.

Moore, M., & Tonry, M. (1998). Youth violence in America. In M. Tonry & M. Moore (Eds.) *Youth violence* (pp. 1–26). Chicago, IL: University of Chicago Press.

Mosher, C. J., Miethe, T. D., & Hart, T. C. (2011). *The Mismeasure of Crime* (2nd Ed.). Thousand Oaks, CA: Sage.

Murray, C. (1995). The physical environment. In J. Wilson & J. Petersilia (Eds.), *Crime* (pp. 349–362). San Francisco, CA: Institute for Contemporary Studies.

Mumola, C. J., & Karberg, J. C. (2007). Drug use and dependence, state and federal prisoners, 2004 (NCJ-213530). Washington, DC: BJS.

Myers, R. (2004). What future(s) do we want for community policing? In L. Fridell & M. Wycoff (Eds.) *Community policing: The past, present, and future* (pp. 169–182). Washington, DC: PERF.

National Advisory Commission on Civil Disorders (1968). *Final Report.* New York, NY: Bantam Books.

National Advisory Commission on Criminal Justice Standards and Goals (1973). *Report on police.* Washington, DC: USGPO.

National Institute of Justice, (2000). *Excellence in Problem-Oriented Policing: The 1999 Herman Goldstein Award Winners.* Washington, DC: NIJ.

Needleman, H. (1990). The future challenge of lead toxicity. *Environmental Health Perspectives 89*, 85–90.

Needleman, H., & Gatsonis, C. (1990). Low-level lead exposure and the IQ of children: A meta-analysis of modern studies. *Journal of the American Medical Association, 263*, 673–678.

Needleman, H., Riess, J., Tobin, M., Biesecker, G., & Greenhouse, J. (1996). Bone lead levels and delinquent behavior. *Journal of the American Medical Association, 275*, 363–369.

Newman, G., Clarke, R., & Shohan, S. (1997). *Rational choice and situational crime prevention: Theoretical foundations.* Brookfield, VT: Ashgate Publishing Company.

Newman, O. (1972). *Defensible space.* New York, NY: Macmillan.

Newman, O., & Franck, K. (1980). *Factors influencing crime and instability in urban housing developments.* Washington, DC: USGPO.

Office of Juvenile Justice and Delinquency Prevention, 1995. *Matrix of Community-Based Initiatives.* Washington, DC: OJJDP

Panzarella, R. (1998). Bratton reinvest 'harassment model' of policing. *Law Enforcement News*, June 15/30, 13–15.

Papke, L. (1994). Tax policy and urban development: Evidence from the Indiana Enterprise Zone Program. *Journal of Public Economics. 54*, 37–49.

Paternoster, R. (1987). The deterrent effect of perceived certainty and severity of punishment: A review of the evidence and issues. *Justice Quarterly, 42*, 173–217.

Patillo, M. D. (1998). Sweet mothers and gangbangers: Managing crime in a black middle-class neighborhood. *Social Forces 76*, 747–774.

Peak, K., & Glensor, R. (2002). *Community policing and problem solving: Strategies and practices* (3rd ed.). Upper Saddle River, NJ: Prentice Hall.

Pease, K., & Laycock, G. (1996). Revictimization: Reducing the heat on hot victims. Washington, DC: NIJ.

People.com (2010). Celebrity Central/Top 25 Celebs—Lindsay Lohan. Retrieved November 15, 2010 from http://www.people.com/people/lindsay_lohan.

Peterson, M. (1998). *Applications in criminal analysis: A sourcebook* (2nd ed.). Westport, NY: Praeger.

Phillips, P. (1980). Characteristics and typology of the journey to crime. In D.E. Georges-Abeyie & K.D. Harries (Eds.), *Crime: A spatial perspective* (pp. 167–180). New York, NY: Columbia University Press.

Pilant, L. (1999, January). Going mobile in law enforcement technology. *National Institute of Justice Journal, 238*, 11–17.

Plaster, S. & Carter, S. (1993). *Planning for prevention: Sarasota, Florida's approach to crime prevention through environmental design*. Tallahassee, FL: Florida Criminal Justice Executive Institute.

Poyner, B. (1983). *Design against crime: Beyond defensible space*. London, UK: Butterworths.

President's Commission on Law Enforcement and Administration of Justice (1967). *The challenge of crime in a free society*. Washington, DC: USGPO.

Rand, M. & Rennison, C. (2002). True crime stories? Accounting for differences in our national crime indicators. *Chance, 15*, 47–51.

Ratcliffe, J. (2000). Aoristic analysis: The spatial interpretation of unspecific temporal events. *International Journal of Geographical Information Science, 14*(7), 669–679.

Ratcliffe, J. (2002). Aoristic signatures and the temporal analysis of high volume crime patterns. *Journal of Quantitative Criminology, 18*(1), 23–43.

Ratcliffe, J. (2004). The hotspot matrix: A framework for the spatio-temporal targeting of crime reduction. *Police Practice and Research, 5*(1), 5–23.

Ratcliffe, J. (2006). A temporal constraint theory to explain opportunity-based spatial offending patterns. *Journal of Research in Crime and Delinquency, 43*(3), 261–291.

Reaves, B. A. (2007). Census of state and local law enforcement agencies, 2004 (NCJ-212749). Washington, DC: BJS.

Reed, W. E. (1999). *The politics of community policing: The case of Seattle.* New York, NY: Garland.

Regoeczi, W. C. (2003). When context matters: A multilevel analysis of household and neighbourhood crowding on aggression and withdrawal. *Journal of Environmental Psychology, 23*(4)L, 457–470.

Reiman, J. (1998). *The rich get richer and the poor get prison: Ideology, class, and criminal justice* (5th ed.). Boston, MA: Allyn and Bacon.

Reisig, M. D., & Cancino, J. M. (2004). Incivilities in nonmetropolitan communities: The effects of structural constrains, social conditions, and crime. *Journal of Criminal Justice, 32*(1), 15–29.

Rengert, G. F., Piquero, A. R., & Jones, P. R. (1999). Distance decay reexamined. *Criminology, 37*(2), 427–446.

Reno, S. (1998). Using crime mapping to address residential burglary. In N. Lavigne & J. Wartell (Eds.) *Crime mapping case studies: Successes in the field* (pp. 15–22). Washington, DC: PERF.

Rich, T. (1995). *The use of computerized mapping in crime control and prevention programs.* Washington, DC: NIJ.

Rich, T. (1999). *Mapping the path to problem solving.* Washington, DC: NIJ.

Roehl, J., Huitt, R., Wycoff, M., Pate, A., Rebovich, D., & Coyle, K. (1996, October). *National process evaluation of Operation Weed and Seed.* Washington, DC: NIJ.

Roh, S., & Oliver, W.M. (2005). Effects of community policing upon fear of crime: Understanding the causal linkage. *Policing: An International Journal of Police Strategies & Management, 28*(4), 670–683.

Roncek, D. (1981). Dangerous places: Crime and residential environment. *Social Forces, 60,* 74–96.

Rosenfeld, R. (1986). Urban crime rates: Effects of inequality, welfare dependency, region, and race. In J. Byrne & R. Sampson (Eds.) *The social ecology of crime* (pp. 116–132). New York, NY: Springer-Verlag.

Rossmo, D. K. (1995). Place, space, and police investigations: Hunting serial violent criminals. In J. Eck & D. Weisburd (Eds.) *Crime and place* (pp. 217–236). Monsey, NY: Criminal Justice Press.

Rossmo, D. K. (1998). Geographic Profiling. Presented at the NCIS Conference, March 17–19, 1998. Available on-line at http://www.ecricana.com/geopro/krossmo.pdf.

Rossmo, D. K. (2000). *Geographic profiling.* Boca Raton, FL: CRC Press.

Rossmo, D. K. (2004). Geographic profiling. In Q. Thurman & J. Zhao (Eds.) *Contemporary policing: Controversies, challenges, and solutions* (pp. 274–284). Los Angeles, CA: Roxbury Publishing Co.

Roth, J. A., Roehl, J., & Johnson, C.C. (2004). Trends in community policing. In W. Skogan (Ed.) *Community Policing: Can it work?* (pp. 3–29). Belmont, CA: Wadsworth/Thomson Learning.

Rountree, P. W., & Warner, B. D. (1999). Social ties and crime: Is the relationship gendered? *Criminology 37*, 789–813.

Sacco, V., & Kennedy, L. (2002). *The criminal event: Perspectives in space and time* (2nd ed.). Belmont, CA: Wadsworth.

Sampson, R. (1985). Neighborhood and crime: The structural determinants of personal victimization. *Journal of Research in Crime and Delinquency 22*, 7–40.

Sampson, R. (1986). Neighborhood family structure and the risk of personal victimization. In J. Byrne & R. Sampson (Eds.) *The social ecology of crime* (pp. 25–46). New York, NY: Springer-Verlag.

Sampson, R. (1995). The community. In J. Wilson & J. Petersilia (Eds.) *Crime* (pp. 193–216). San Francisco, CA: Institute for Contemporary Studies Press.

Sampson, R., Eck, J., & Dunham, J. (2010). Super controllers and crime prevention: A Routine activity explanation of crime prevention success and failure. *Security Journal, 23*, 37–51.

Sampson, R., & Groves, W. (1989). Community structure and crime: Testing social-disorganization theory. *American Journal of Sociology, 94*, 774–802.

Sampson, R., Morenoff, J., & Gannon-Rowley, T. (2002). Assessing 'neighborhood effects': Social processes and new directions in research. *Annual Review of Sociology, 28*, 443–478.

Sampson, R., Morenoff, J., & Raudenbush, S. (2005). Social anatomy of racial and ethnic disparities in violence. *American Journal of Public Health, 95*(2), 224–232.

Sampson, R., & Raudenbush, S. (1999). Systematic social observation of public spaces. *American Journal of Sociology, 105*, 603–651.

Sampson, R., & Raudenbush, S. (2001). Disorder in urban neighborhoods— Does it lead to crime? *National Institute of Justice Research in Brief.* Washington, DC: USDOJ.

Sampson, R., & Raudenbush, S. (2004). The social structure of seeing disorder. *Social Psychology Quarterly, 67*(4), 319–342.

Sampson, R., Raudenbush, S., & Earls, F. (1997). Neighborhoods and violent crime: A multilevel study of collective efficacy. *Science, 277*, 918–924.

Schafer, J. (2002). Community policing and police corruption. In K. Lersch (Ed.), *Policing and misconduct*, (pp. 193–218). Upper Saddle River, NJ: Prentice Hall.

Schlossman, S., & Sedlak, M. (1983). The Chicago Area Project revisited. *Crime and Delinquency, 29*, 298–462.

Schlossman, S., Zellman, G., & Shavelson, R. (1984). *Delinquency prevention in south Chicago: A fifty-year assessment of the Chicago Area Project.* Santa Monica, CA: RAND.

Shaw, C., & McKay, H. (1969). *Juvenile delinquency and urban areas* (Rev. ed.). Chicago, IL: The University of Chicago Press.

Shearing, C. D., & Stenning, P. C. (1992). From the panopticon to Disney World: The development of discipline. In R. Clarke (Ed.) *Situational crime prevention: Successful case studies* (pp. 249–255). New York, NY: Harrow and Heston.

Sheldon, R. (2001). *Controlling the dangerous classes: A critical introduction to the history of criminal justice.* Boston, MA: Allyn and Bacon.

Sherman, L. (1995). Hot spots of crime and criminal careers of places. In J. Eck & D. Weisburd (Eds.) *Crime and place* (pp. 35–52). Monsey, NY: Willow Tree Press.

Sherman, L., Gartin, P., & Buerger, M. (1989). Routine activities and the criminology of place. *Criminology, 27*, 27–55.

Sherman, L., Gottfredson, D., MacKenzie, D., Eck, J., Reuter, P., & Bushway, S. (1997). *Preventing crime: What works, what doesn't, what's promising.* Washington DC: OJP.

Sherman, L., Schmidt, J., & Velke, R. (1992). *High crime taverns: A RECAP project in problem-oriented policing.* Washington, DC: Crime Control Institute.

Sherman, L., Shaw, J., & Rogan, D. (1995, January). *The Kansas City gun experiment.* Washington, DC: NIJ.

Sherman, L., & Weisburd, D. (1995). General deterrent effects of police patrol in crime 'hot spots': A randomized, controlled trial. *Justice Quarterly, 2*, 625–648.

Silverman, E. (1999). *NYPD battles crime: Innovative strategies in policing.* Boston, MA: Northeastern University Press.

Simons, C. (2002). The evolution of crime prevention. In D. Robinson (Ed.) *Policing and crime prevention* (pp. 1–18). Upper Saddle River, NJ: Prentice Hall.

Skogan, W. (1986). Fear of crime and neighborhood change. In A. Reiss, Jr. & M. Tonry (Eds.) *Communities and Crime*, (pp. 203–229). Chicago, IL: University of Chicago Press.

Skogan, W. (1988). Community organizations and crime. In M. Tonry & N. Morris (Eds.), *Crime and justice: A review of research*, (pp. 39–78). Chicago, IL: University of Chicago Press.

Skogan, W. (1990). *Disorder and decline: Crime and the spiral of decay in American neighborhoods*. New York, NY: Free Press.

Skogan, W. (2004). Representing the community in community policing. In W. Skogan (Ed.) *Community policing: Can it work?* (pp. 57–76). Belmont, CA: Wadsworth/Thomson Learning.

Snodgrass, J. (1976). Clifford R. Shaw and Henry D. McKay: Chicago criminologists. *British Journal of Criminology, 16,* 1–19.

Sorrentino, A., & Whittaker, D. (1994). Chicago Area Project: Addressing the gang problem. *FBI Law Enforcement Bulletin, 63,* 8–12.

Stiles, B., Liu, X., & Kaplan, H. (2000). Relative deprivation and deviant adaptations: The mediating effects of negative self-feelings. *Journal of Research in Crime and Delinquency 37,* 64–90.

Stretesky, P., & Lynch, M. (1999a). Corporate environmental violence and racism. *Crime, Law & Social Change, 30,* 163–184.

Stretesky, P., & Lynch, M (1999b). Environmental justice and the predictions of distance to accidental chemical releases in Hillsborough County, Florida. *Social Science Quarterly, 4,* 830–846.

Stretesky, P., & Lynch, M. (2001). The relationship between lead exposure and homicide. *Archives of Pediatrics and Adolescent Medicine, 155,* 579–582.

Stretesky, P., & Lynch, M. (2004). The relationship between lead and crime. *Journal of Health and Social Behavior, 45,* 214–229.

Stretesky, P. (2003). The distribution of air lead levels across U.S. counties: Implications for the production of racial inequality. *Sociological Spectrum, 23*(1), 91–118.

Swanson, C., Territo, L., & Taylor, R. (1998). *Police administration: Structures, processes, and behavior* (4th ed.). Upper Saddle River, NJ: Prentice-Hall.

Swartz, C. (2000). The spatial analysis of crime: What social scientists have learned. In V. Goldsmith, P. McGuire, J. Mollenkopf, & T. Ross (Eds.) *Analyzing crime patterns: Frontiers of practice* (pp. 33–46). Thousand Oaks, CA: Sage.

Tafoya, W. (1998). Foreward. In S. Gottlieb, S. Arenberg, & R. Singh *Crime analysis: From first report to final arrest* (2nd ed.). Montclair, NJ: Alpha Publishing.

Taylor, I., Walton, P., & Young, J. (1973). *The new criminology: For a social theory of deviance*. New York, NY: Harper Torchbooks.

Taylor, R., & Gottfredson, S. (1986). Environmental design, crime and prevention: An examination of community dynamics. In A. Reiss, Jr., & M. Tonry (Eds.) *Communities and crime* (pp. 387–416). Chicago, IL: University of Chicago Press.

Taylor, R., & Hale, M. (1986). Testing alternative models of fear of crime. *Journal of Criminal Law and Criminology, 77*(1), 151–189.

Taylor, R., & Harrell, A. (1996). *Physical environment and crime.* Washington, DC: NIJ.

Taylor, R., Gottfredson, S., & Brower, S. (1980). The defensibility of defensible space: A critical review and a synthetic framework for future research. In T. Hirschi & M. Gottfredson (Eds.) *Understanding crime* (pp. 64–75). Beverly Hills, CA: Sage.

Tien, J., & Rich, T. (1994). The Hartford COMPASS program: Experiences with a weed and seed-related program. In D. Rosenbaum (Ed.) *The challenge of community policing: Testing the promises.* Beverly Hills, CA: Sage.

Tittle, C., Villemez, W., & Smith, D. (1978). The myth of social class and criminality: An empirical assessment of the empirical evidence. *American Sociological Review, 43,* 643–656.

Tompson, L., Patridge, H., & Shepherd, N. (2009). Hot routes: Developing a new technique for spatial analysis of crime. *Crime Mapping: A Journal of Research and Practice, 1*(1), 77–96.

Trojanowicz, R., & Bucqueroux, B. (1990). *Community policing: A contemporary perspective.* Cincinnati, OH: Anderson Publishing Co.

Tunnell, K. (1992). *Choosing crime.* Chicago, IL: Nelson-Hall Publishers.

United Church of Christ Commission for Racial Justice (1987). *Toxic wastes and race in the United States: A national report on the racial and socio-economic characteristics of communities with hazardous waste sites.* New York, NY: United Church of Christ.

U.S. Department of Justice, Office of Justice Programs, Bureau of Justice Statistics (n.d.). The Nation's Two Crime Measures. Retrieved on August 20, 2010 from http://bjs.ojp.usdoj.gov/content/pub/html/ntcm.cfm.

Van Patten, I. T. (2007). Robbery Hot Lanes: Southeast Roanoke. Retrieved on August 20, 2010 from http://www.radford.edu/~ivanpatt/crimemaps/Hot-Lanes.pdf.

Van Patten, I. T., McKeldin-Coner, J., & Cox, D. (2009). A microspatial analysis of robbery: Prospective hot-spotting in a small city. *Crime Mapping: A Journal of Research and Practice, 1*(1), 7–32

Velasco, M., & Boba, R. (2000, Spring). Tactical crime analysis and geographic information systems: Concepts and examples. *Crime mapping news, 2,* 1–4.

Vellani, K., & Nahoun, J. (2001). *Applied crime analysis.* Boston, MA: Butterworth-Heinemann.

Vold, G., Bernard, T., & Snipes, J. (2002). *Theoretical criminology* (5th ed). New York, NY: Oxford University Press.

Wagers, M. Sousa, W., & Kelling, G. (2008). Broken windows. In R. Wortley & L. Mazerolle (Eds.) *Environmental criminology and crime analysis.* Portland, OR: Willan Publishing.

Walker, S. (1998). *Sense and non-sense about crime,* (4th ed.). Belmont, CA: Wadsworth.

Walker, S. (1999). *The police in America* (3rd ed.). Boston, MA: McGraw Hill.

Walker, S., & Katz, C. (2002). *The police in America.* Boston, MA: McGraw-Hill.

Walton, J. (1982). Cities and jobs and politics. *Urban Affairs Review, 18*(1), 5–17.

Weisburd, D. (1997). *Reorienting crime prevention research and policy: From the causes of criminality to the context of crime.* Washington, DC: NIJ.

Weisburd, D., Mastrofski, S., McNalley, A., Greenspan, R., & Willis, J. (2003). Compstat and organizational change: Findings from a national survey. *Criminology & Public Policy, 2,* 421–456.

Weisburd, D., & Mazerolle, L. (2000). Crime and disorder in drug hot spots: Implications for theory and practice in policing. *Police Quarterly, 3,* 331–349.

Weisburd, D., & McEwen, T. (1998). Crime mapping and crime prevention. In D. Weisburd & T. McEwen (Eds.) *Crime mapping and crime prevention* (pp. 1–26). Monsey, NY: Willow Tree Press.

Weisel, D., & Eck, J. (1994). Toward a practical approach to organizational change: Community policing initiatives in six cities. In Rosenbaum, D.P. (Ed.), *The challenge of community policing: Testing the promises,* (pp. 110–126). Thousand Oaks, CA: Sage.

Wekerle, G., & Whitzman, C. (1995). *Safe cities: Guidelines for planning, design, and management.* New York, NY: Van Nostrand Reinhold.

Willis, J., Mastrofski, S., & Kochel, T. (2010). The co-implementation of Compstat and community policing. *Journal of Criminal Justice, 38,* 969–980.

Wilson, W. (1950). *Police administration.* New York, NY: McGraw-Hill.

Wilson, W. (1980). *The declining significance of race.* Chicago, IL: University of Chicago Press.

Wilson, W. (1987). *The truly disadvantaged* (2nd ed). Chicago, IL: University of Chicago Press.

Wilson, J., & Kelling, G. (1982). Broken windows: Police and neighborhood safety. *The Atlantic Monthly, 249,* 29–38.

Winton, R., & Blankstein, A. (2010, July 7). Lindsay Lohan sentenced to 90 days in jail and 90 in rehab. Los Angeles Times, http://articles.latimes.com/2010/jul/07/local/la-me-0707-lohan-20100707. Accessed on-line November 15th 2010.

Wortley, R. (1996). Guilt, shame, and situational crime prevention. In R. Homel (Ed.), *The politics and practice of situational crime prevention.* Crime prevention studies, Volume 5. Monsey, NY: Criminal Justice Press.

Wortley, R. (1997). Reconsidering the role of opportunity in situational crime prevention. In G. Newman, R. Clarke, and S. Shohan (Eds.) *Rational choice and situational crime prevention.* London, UK: Ashgate Publishing.

Wortley, R. (1998). A two-stage model of situational crime prevention. *Studies of crime and crime prevention, 7,* 173–188.

Wortley, R. (2001). A classification of techniques for controlling situational precipitators of crime. *Security Journal 14,* 63–82.

Wortley, R. (2002). *Situational prison control: Crime prevention in correctional institutions.* Cambridge, MA: Cambridge University Press.

Wortley, R. (2008). Situational precipitators of crime. In R. Wortley & L. Mazerolle (Eds.) *Environmental criminology and crime analysis.* Portland, OR: Willan Publishing.

Wright, R., & Decker, S. H. (1997) Creating the illusion of impending death— Armed robbers in action. *Harry Frank Guggenheim Review, 2*(1), 10–18.

Youstin, T. J., & Nobles, M. R. (2009). Residency restrictions: A geospatial analysis of sex offender movement over time. *Crime Mapping: A Journal of Research and Practice, 1*(1), 55–76.

Zandbergen, P., & Hart, T. C. (2009). Geocoding accuracy considerations in determining residency restrictions for sex offenders. *Criminal Justice Policy Review, 20*(1), 62–90.

Zahm, D. (2007). Using crime prevention through environmental design in problem-solving. Washington, DC: USDOJ.

Index